After Middle Age

After Middle Age

A Physician's Guide to Staying Healthy While Growing Older

Richard Jed Wyatt, M.D.

McGraw-Hill Book Company
New York   St. Louis   San Francisco   Auckland   Bogotá
Hamburg   Johannesburg   London   Madrid
Mexico   Montreal   New Delhi   Panama
Paris   São Paulo   Singapore
Sydney   Tokyo   Toronto

Library of Congress Cataloging in Publication Data

Wyatt, Richard Jed.
   After middle age.

   Includes index.
   1. Aged—Diseases. 2. Aged—Care and hygiene.
   3. Gerontology. I. Title. [DNLM: 1. Aging—Popular
   works. 2. Geriatrics—Popular works. WT 120 W976a]
   RC952.5.W9   1984   618.97   83-11274
   ISBN 0-07-072135-1

Copyright © 1985 by Richard Jed Wyatt, M.D. All rights reserved.
Printed in the United States of America. Except as permitted
under the United States Copyright Act of 1976, no part of this
publication may be reproduced or distributed in any form or by
any means, or stored in a data base or retrieval system, without
the prior written permission of the publisher.

1234567890 DOC/DOC 898765

ISBN 0-07-072135-1

The editors for this book were Thomas H. Quinn and Diane Krumrey,
the designer was Naomi Auerbach, and the production
supervisor was Teresa F. Leaden. It was set in Times Roman
by Achorn Graphic Services Inc.

Printed and bound by R. R. Donnelley & Sons, Inc.

Medicine is an ever-changing art. As new research and clinical experience broaden our knowledge, changes in diagnosis and treatment are required. The author and the publisher of this work have made every effort to ensure that the drug treatment and dosage schedules as well as general diagnostic and treatment recommendations are accurate and in accord with accepted standards. Readers are advised, however, that it is always desirable to check with the professional help available to them.

This book was written by Richard Jed Wyatt in his private capacity;
the views expressed herein do not necessarily reflect those of the
National Institute of Mental Health.

Contents

Preface ix

1. Introduction: The Experience of Aging 1
   A Basic Philosophy 1

2. Living Independently 6
   Financial Planning 6
   Preventive Medicine 7
   Preventing Accidents 11
   Community Resources 16

3. Nutrition and Diet 19
   Requirements for an Adequate Diet 20
   Vitamins 21
   Minerals 25
   Other Factors in the Diet 27
   Diet and Weight 33
   Losing Weight 36

4. Foreign Travel 42
   Air Travel 43
   International Immunizations 45
   Traveler's Diarrhea in Foreign Lands 47
   Securing Medical Assistance While Traveling 49
   What to Take with You 50

5. Psychological and Psychiatric Problems 51
   Mental Reserve 51
   Compensation Strategies 52
   Nervousness and Anxiety 53

Contents

    Depression   55
    Suicide   56
    Insomnia   60
    Alcoholism   70
    Psychotherapy   73

6. **The Aging Mind**   81

    Senility   81
    Decisions Regarding Care   83

7. **The Nervous System**   86

    Headaches and Other Kinds of Pain   87
    Drugs Used to Decrease Pain   91
    Pain Clinics   93
    Tremors and Movement Disorders   94
    Numbness and Tingling   98
    Loss of Muscle Power   98
    Injuries   99
    Infections of the Nervous System   101
    Brain Tumors   102
    Convulsive Disorders   103
    The Kinds of Physicians Treating the Nervous System   105

8. **Seeing, Hearing, and Smelling**   106

    The Eyes   106
    The Ears   116
    The Nose   119

9. **Alterations in the Skin, Nails, and Hair**   121

    Aging Skin   121
    Spots of Many Colors   123
    Vascular Problems   128
    Corns and Warts on the Feet   130
    Skin Cancer   130
    The Nails   132
    The Hair   133

10. **Disorders of the Bones, Muscles, and Tendons**   136

    Joint Diseases   136
    Tumors   142
    Paget's Disease   143
    Low Back Pain   144
    Osteoporosis   146
    Tennis Elbow, Bunion, and Bursitis   147
    The Kinds of Bone Doctors   148

Contents

11. **Colds, Flu, and More Serious Problems of the Lungs and Respiratory System**   149

    Colds, Allergic Rhinitis, and Sore Throats   150
    Hoarseness and Laryngitis   155
    Laryngeal Cancer   155
    The Flu (Influenza) and Its Prevention   156
    Bronchitis and Emphysema   157
    Pneumonias and Tuberculosis   159
    Occupational Lung Disorders   162
    Lung Embolis   162
    Lung Cancer and Smoking   164

12. **Disorders of the Heart and Circulatory System**   168

    Hypertension (High Blood Pressure)   169
    Angina (Angina Pectoris)   178
    Heart Attack   181
    Heart Failure   188
    Cerebral Vascular Accident (CVA, Hemorrhage, or Stroke)   190

13. **Disorders of the Digestive System**   195

    The Mouth   196
    Importance of Teeth   197
    The Esophagus and Stomach   200
    Duodenal Ulcer   202
    The Intestines and Rectum   205
    The Liver   209
    The Gallbladder   210
    The Pancreas   211

14. **Disorders of the Urinary System**   213

    Infections   214
    Stones   217
    Kidney Failure   218
    Other Conditions   219

15. **Disorders of Sex and the Genitals**   222

    The Climacteric   222
    Menopause   224
    Difficulties with Sex   226
    The Breasts   229
    The Ovaries   234
    Growths in the Uterus and Cervix   234
    The Prostate   237
    Hernias   240

16. **The Endocrine Glands**   241

    Thyroid   242
    Diabetes Mellitus (Sugar Diabetes)   245

Contents

17. Cancer — 252
Diagnosis and Treatment   253
The Theory behind the Treatment   258
Managing Treatment   259

18. What to Do in Emergencies — 265
What Goes in a First-Aid Kit   266
Breathing and Choking   267
Bleeding and Wounds   268
Burns   270
Poisons   272
Fainting and Heatstroke   274
Broken Bones, Back, and Neck   275
Still Other Emergencies   276

19. Hospitals — 278
Choosing a Hospital   278
Emergencies   279
Inpatient Care   279

20. Nursing Homes and Outside Care — 281
When Is a Nursing Home Necessary or Desirable?   281
Different Levels of Outside Care   282
How to Find the Kind of Facility Needed   284
Things to Look for during a Nursing Home Visit   284
Costs and Contracts   290
Psychological Issues   291

21. Paying for Physicians, Hospitals, and Nursing Homes — 293
Medicare   293
Medicaid   297
Private Insurance   298
Health Maintenance Organization (HMO)   299

22. Death — 302
Attitudes toward Death   302
Dying   303
Funerals   306

23. A Note to Children and Grandchildren — 308
Relations between the Generations: The Four-Generation Family   308
The Need for Closeness   309
Visiting   311
When You Cannot Be There   313

Preface

After Middle Age describes the most frequently encountered medical disorders and difficulties that occur from the fifties onward. It is addressed to people who might need help for themselves as well as to people who are trying to help someone else.

After Middle Age is best used when you need background information. It explains what to expect when a problem surfaces, it helps formulate the right questions to ask, and it suggests whom to ask. It also concentrates heavily on prevention. This book is not intended, however, to replace a family or primary care physician or a community resource. The advice your physician or other professional gives is geared to suit the nature and extent of your specific problem and includes many personal factors that cannot be taken into account in a book. Furthermore, progress in medicine and advancements in social services are rapid; answers unknown or unavailable today will soon be commonplace. Finally, educated patients can go a long way toward helping the physician. They can better describe their symptoms, know when there is an emergency, and recognize untoward effects of treatment.

It is unlikely that anyone will read through *After Middle Age* in its entirety. Some of the chapters will be of general interest, while others are best used only for reference. Thumb through the book and find chapters you wish to read. For the chapters you do not wish to read now, keep *After Middle Age* on your bedside table so you will have it when it is needed.

After Middle Age is arranged by topics; cross-referencing is done by topic, also, not page number. Each section has a reference number. Specific topics can be found by looking them up in the index in the back of the book.

Most people first become aware that they are aging during their middle years. Everyone is getting older, and those who are 35 or 40 today will be

Preface

60 or 70 in a cosmic blink. A great deal can be done to make aging easy, pleasant, and graceful. If you have not begun to think constructively about getting older, now is a good time to begin. Educating yourself and developing good habits takes time and effort. *After Middle Age* is especially written for those who wish to begin now to meet the challenge of aging.

This book was written not only to educate the reader; I hope to learn from the reader, also. I have a commitment to making aging easier and would appreciate hearing from readers who find errors or have advice that might be passed on to others in future editions of *After Middle Age*.

Richard Jed Wyatt, M.D.

Acknowledgments

It gives me great pleasure to thank the many people who offered their support and assistance while I worked on this book. My wife, Rollyn, encouraged me to begin the project, helped with the research and writing, and provided an environment where I could work in tranquility. My children, Elizabeth, Chris, and Justin, often wanted to trade the time I spent at the keyboard for time wiring a dollhouse, throwing a football, or going on weekend excursions, but they were very patient about waiting for "later." Many friends and colleagues read drafts, asked questions, made corrections, and helped the final result to be more understandable. Tom Quinn at McGraw-Hill has been supportive, enthusiastic, and provided countless useful suggestions. Elaine Connelly, Joan Harris, Mollie Strotkamp, and Evan DeRenzo faithfully contributed to many stages of the book's production. And last, I want to thank parents Wanda and Edward Blackman and Marge and Hilton Simon, and grandparents Sophie and Sam Urman, who were and are models for growing older with intelligence, strength, and beauty.

After Middle Age

1

Introduction: The Experience of Aging

A BASIC PHILOSOPHY

(1-1) To live is to age, and from the moment of conception our path to old age is preordained. Gradually and quietly, as we count the years since birth, we also project how many remain. Thoughts about illness, pain, loneliness, and meaninglessness that once occurred only occasionally become part of our daily reality. Our world simultaneously expands and contracts: Children marry, grandchildren and great-grandchildren are born, but relatives and friends suffer failing health, have accidents, and die. These intertwined gains and losses add richness and texture to our lives. As our knowledge of the world becomes more profound, we redefine our sense of self. We learn that some truths of aging are harsh, but also that there are compensations. Although our grip becomes weaker, and reaction time slower, we also learn life's shortcuts; how to pack our suitcases lighter, to better anticipate where the ball will be, and to use our experience to see connections often missed by the young. We can give worthy service, leave a legacy to our children and society, and appreciate our continuity with life that continues beyond us.

Given that there is no antidote to aging itself, the best way to cope is to age with good grace, as interestingly and enjoyably as possible. All of us must adapt in our own way to the process of aging, but there are some basic principles that all who age successfully seem to share.

(1-2) *Work is necessary.* The first principle of successful aging is never to stop working. There is no substitute for continuing to do what you know how to do and have done well during the most productive years of your life. If you have a job this may mean postponing official retirement as long as you are able. When working a full day becomes too much, work

After Middle Age

half a day. If you have become disinterested in, or have grown to dislike, your life's work, that's no problem if you have a well-developed hobby or secondary occupation. They count as work, too, and "retiring" to something you want to do can be a source of great joy and satisfaction. Do not quit work, however, only to find that you can complete forty years of undone chores in a week and then find yourself desperately casting about for some way to fill your time. Being productive and having something meaningful to do with your life is essential for mental and physical health.

(1-3) *Appearances count.* When you are active and look well, it is much easier to feel good about yourself. Be confident of yourself and your achievements, past and present. A self-confidence that might not be attractive in a 35-year-old is charisma itself at 70! Beauty is not necessarily a 17-year-old face. Acknowledge what artists and professional photographers have always known—an aging, animated face with the contours and furrows of time and experience is a wonderful thing to behold. Be proud and accepting of the way you look, and do not try to hide your age. A woman in her sixties is expected to have gray hair. A man past middle age is often balding. Camouflaging these natural changes in appearance, when tastefully done, may improve your own and other people's feelings about you. But when overdone, they decrease dignity. Makeup is most effective when used sparingly and skillfully; careful thought should be given to a hairstyle that is classic, attractive, and easy to manage. Understatement in all artifice is the goal.

How you look signals those around you how to relate to you. If you look like the stereotype of an incompetent, absentminded, unkempt old man or old woman, you will most likely be treated as one. Stand erect and firmly. Dress comfortably and simply, but be neat and clean. Do not be too proud to aid failing senses with hearing aids and glasses.

(1-4) *Be assertive.* This book deals primarily with relationships you will have with medical professionals, although the advice to be assertive should apply to many other interpersonal relationships. Remember, having a conviction (being assertive) is not the same as being aggressive, which means to attack or quarrel. In your dealings with a physician, a clear description of what your symptoms are—or a clear phrasing of your question—many times is all you need to get the information you need. At other times, you may have to insist that the physician recognize what you are saying or asking and inform you about your condition. Physicians are sometimes preoccupied or not very interested in educating their patients. If there is one chance in ten thousand of your having a rare and terrible disease, for example, it is not necessary for your physician to tell you about that risk. On the other hand, if it looks as if you have a serious problem, you should know about it. Inform your physician that you want to be treated like an adult.

One situation where being assertive may be very useful is when you are making an appointment. If you need to speak to or see a physician quickly, do not be put off by a nurse, secretary, or answering service. If you are in an emergency situation, immediately let the person answering the phone know it. On the other hand, do not abuse your physician's time. If the problem can wait, don't press it, provided you can be assured of getting an answer within a reasonable period. The information in this book should help you decide how important time is for the problem you are having.

As a patient, I have found myself particularly annoyed by physicians who schedule ten patients for the same time (yes, physicians even do this to other physicians), letting some of them wait for hours. This practice is particularly prevalent in public institutions. Although it certainly is understandable that a physician will fall behind schedule from time to time, for this to happen regularly is inconsiderate of patients. Wanting to believe the best of their physician, patients do not always perceive this as rudeness. I remember one patient's remark about how important her physician was because she always had to wait for several hours for her appointment, and his office was always lined with patients. If your physician practices in this manner, point it out and ask if a change is possible. If you do not get a satisfactory answer, and unless your physician is truly, *uniquely* able (there are such people), find someone else to treat you.

In addition to your being assertive, your representative (physician, politician, lawyer, social-service worker, banker, or accountant) should be assertive on your behalf. You want these representatives to get you information, make appointments for you, and, when appropriate, attack a disease you might have. Assertiveness is a quality to look for in such people.

(1-5) *All the shoulds and should nots.* In many places where health advice is given, there is a short list of shoulds and should nots. The reader is familiar with these and has probably already tried to change his or her lifestyle accordingly. If you have obeyed these commandments, you drink alcohol (5-35), if at all, in moderation, are slim, avoid animal fats (3-5), do not smoke (11-26), sleep seven or eight hours every night (5-17), and eat a good breakfast (3-1). You also may be ingesting large quantities of vitamins (3-6) or fiber (3-35). Each of these nostrums and many more are discussed in this book. I try to evaluate their merit and make a recommendation for you to consider.

One area that I have not covered in any detail is exercise. At one point

After Middle Age

in the preparation of this book I had written an extensive chapter on exercise—I then removed it. While I believe exercise is important to good health and feeling well, the more I looked for data to support this belief, the less comfortable I felt in recommending my belief to others. I became even more uncomfortable in recommending a specific kind of exercise.

An example of why I am confused may be useful, because it illustrates the difficulty that frequently arises in giving meaning to scientific data. A few years ago a study of a large number of individuals who filled out questionnaires about their health habits was published in an important medical journal. At the time the questionnaire was filled out, all the participants were middle-aged or older and presumably healthy. Five years after they filled out the questionnaire, some of them had died. Investigators looked up the death certificates to ascertain the cause of death. The answers on the questionnaires were then examined in relation to the causes of death. Among the things that seemed to predict early death was lack of exercise. A conclusion one could derive from such a finding is that exercise is good for you. One could, however, just as well suppose that something about the health of some individuals, such as an undetected disease that later ended in death, made exercise difficult or unpleasant. Perhaps if these individuals had been exercising, their deaths would have come even sooner.

You might well ask, are there not many other studies supporting the utility of exercise? Yes, there are a number of scientific studies suggesting that exercise slightly prolongs life and may make you healthier during life, but all of them are significantly flawed. It may well turn out that today's jogger who is trying to avoid seeing the cardiologist tomorrow will, because he has developed arthritis, support his favorite orthopedist instead. Thus, while I believe that exercise in moderation makes one look and feel better, and in fact get regular exercise myself, in this book I have taken a neutral stand; I neither recommend exercise nor recommend against it. In the next section (1-6), however, I make a few simple suggestions for those who want to exercise.

The point is that all those who write magazine articles or books such as this one have their own "should and should nots." Some of these are based on known or unknown realities, others on superstition. One hundred years ago most medicine was based on superstition. Even then, however, much of it worked. Today we say treatments that work, but are based on superstition, result from the placebo effect. A placebo is a sugar pill. During the next hundred years, we will probably find that much of what we now believe to be based on sound scientific knowledge is in fact a superstition or a placebo. The belief that something works (as opposed to knowing that it works) is very powerful and undoubtedly plays an impor-

The Experience of Aging

tant role in a great deal of medical success. It is therefore generally beneficial. It becomes unhealthy, however, when superstition deprives one of something that might be more successful or even save one's life.

(1-6) *Exercise.* As I mentioned in the previous section (1-5), because of many uncertainties I do not recommend exercise. I have seen too many worn-out joints and torn ligaments and muscles to feel comfortable in recommending a specific program to anyone after 55. In future years I hope to be able to come up with a program that will be safe, comfortable, and effective. If you are now getting regular exercise such as tennis or golf, and are suffering no ill effects from it, you should continue. If you like to garden (and are not inclined to lift heavy objects) or like long walks and do not suffer from them, again, continue.

On the other hand, if you do not now get regular exercise, but wish for reasons of your own to start, first see your physician. Discuss with him your plans and if he agrees, begin. But begin very slowly. If you decide to set substantial goals for yourself, plan on getting there the long way. If you haven't played tennis in twenty years, start by playing a few minutes at a time against a backboard where there is no competition and no urgency to play a little longer because you are with a partner. When you finally do go out on the court with someone, make sure you limit in advance the length of time you are to play. Do not stay longer because you feel all right. Stop and plan another play date. At 30, you might have wisely considered adding five minutes a day if you were playing tennis daily for the first time. After 55, I would seriously consider adding no more than five minutes a month. At this rate you will be able to play a full hour after a year, perhaps without ill effects.

Of equal importance to progressing slowly is warming up. Professional athletes and dancers may warm up an hour or more before trying to perform. They know that muscles and tendons that are not loose will not work properly and are likely to tear. Cold muscles, including your heart, are more likely to cramp and cause pain. Warming up properly should greatly increase the value of the exercise and decrease your visits to the cardiologist and orthopedist.

There are many books on physical fitness, but as with diet books, I have some concern that many of them will get you into more trouble than they prevent. This is particularly true for people who are over 55 that try to use them. One you might try, however, is *Adult Physical Fitness,* Consumer Information Catalog No. 033E, published by the Consumer Information Center, Pueblo, Colorado 81009.

2

Living Independently

(2-1) Most people want to remain independent or semi-independent for as long as they can. This section contains suggestions on how to maintain independent living and on what can be done when this is no longer either desirable or possible. The keys to remaining independent are using proper financial planning, practicing preventive medicine, and knowing available community resources and how to use them.

FINANCIAL PLANNING

(2-2) Many resources are available for planning your financial future. These include family services, the Social Security Administration (2-3), accountants, lawyers, bankers, and insurance specialists. Good financial sense, however, is something every individual needs to develop over a lifetime. Every time a bill is paid, money invested, or income tax audited, it is a chance to learn. For example, if you end up paying $100 after an Internal Revenue Service audit, do not just walk away mad because of the lost time and money—learn something from the experience. Why was your return selected? If you had kept better records, could you have taken more deductions? Could you decrease your taxable income by earning your money in a different manner? Could you arrange your work so that more could be done at home with a greater deduction? While an accountant can advise you regarding these things, understanding them yourself is invaluable. For couples, both the husband and wife should understand their finances since it cannot be predicted which spouse will eventually have the financial responsibility.

You spend twenty to twenty-five years learning how to make a living

Living Independently

and run a household. It makes sense to spend the time necessary for proper planning of your retirement. The major question to ask is: How do you want to live, and what will it cost? The question needs to be considered in as much detail as possible and discussed with knowledgeable people at every opportunity.

(2-3) *Free information.* The following organizations can provide useful pamphlets about retirement finances at no cost: the Social Security office (listed in the phone book under U.S. Government, Social Security Administration), *Estimating Your Social Security Retirement Check* and *Buyer's Guide to Individual Retirement Account/Annuity;* the Internal Revenue Service (in the phone book under U.S. Government, Internal Revenue Service), *Tax Information on Individual Retirement Savings Programs,* Publication 590, Office of Public Reference Branch, Room 130, Federal Trade Commission, Washington, D.C. 20580. "A Word to the Wise About Old Age Groups" is available from your local bank, savings associations, or insurance company if you send them a self-addressed stamped office-size envelope.

PREVENTIVE MEDICINE

(2-4) Considerable attention has been given in both the medical and the public press to the practice of preventive medicine, and for a good reason. A number of diseases can be prevented, and many that cannot be prevented can be treated successfully if caught early. Most of this book is directed toward preventive medicine. Thus people who do not smoke, drink in moderation, are careful about diet, keep working or busy, decrease stress, and take few physical risks are already doing a lot for themselves. Regular breast examinations for females (15-7), good dental care, and regular dental (13-8) and medical checkups (2-5) are extremely important. Eliminating potential sources of accidents (2-10) and using automobile seat belts (2-13) can prevent a great deal of discomfort and morbidity.

(2-5) *Annual physical examinations.* For many years physicians encouraged their patients to have a yearly physical examination. The physicians reasoned that finding a disorder before it produced symptoms usually made the condition easier to treat. Recently the use of routine annual examinations has been challenged because large studies have found that treatable disorders are not usually discovered during these routine examinations, and because the examinations themselves are expensive. In addition, everyone has heard of someone who received a "clean bill of health" from such an examination but soon thereafter had a heart attack.

After Middle Age

Despite these arguments, I still recommend regular medical examinations. Although statistically few problems may be picked up during an annual checkup, it takes the discovery of only one to make multiple examinations worthwhile. Also, alleviating the worry that "something might be brewing" can be a relief if the checkup reveals no problems. You are worth the cost and time. There is also a more subtle reason for seeing a physician regularly. Some day you are going to need your physician in an emergency. If he or she knows you well, both medically and psychologically, your treatment is more likely to be tailored to your needs, and this is important when complicated personalities or difficult medical problems are involved.

(**2-6**) *How to choose a physician.* Choosing any kind of professional is difficult, and choosing a physician is no exception. Despite the trend to be somewhat suspicious of any authority figure, most people are satisfied with the physician they have chosen for themselves. People find their physicians in different ways: the recommendation of friends, of relatives, of another physician, or of the local medical society and, occasionally, through the Yellow Pages. If you can, get a referral from another physician. Alternatively, if you know any nurses or other medical people who are exposed to a number of different physicians, ask them whom they recommend. Friends and relatives tend to be more impressed by bedside manner than competence, but several recommendations of the same physician by different people are more useful than anything that can be learned from the Yellow Pages. As mentioned, the annual physical examination is a good place to get to know a physician, and if you are not satisfied with the physician you go to one year, you are not legally or morally bound to return to the same physician the next year. But in the meantime, you can still call on that physician in an emergency.

Knowledge of how a person gets to be a physician is useful. The pattern is the same whether the individual is a medical doctor (M.D.) or a doctor of osteopathy (D.O.). The individual studies for four years in college, usually taking premedical courses like chemistry and biology. Medical school takes an additional four years, and the program is fairly general— thus, the future psychiatrist learns to deliver babies and listen to hearts; and the future surgeon also has experience in psychiatry, radiology, and the other specialties. After medical school, the physician has an internship with increased responsibility and specialization—generally a year of intensive work at a large hospital—before residency or practice. After internship, the young physician may get a license and begin to practice. In today's world, however, most physicians go on to take a residency in a specialty, such as orthopedics, for study and supervised work. This is a period lasting from three to seven years.

Living Independently

Most states license a physician after internship. To earn a license, the physician must pass an examination and submit letters of reference from other physicians who can attest to competence and character. A few years after their residency, many physicians take another examination in their specialty. If they pass this, they become board certified in their specialty. Some specialty boards require recertification at periodic intervals. Unlike the license, which is a function of the state, board certification is a function of private professional organizations. While this certification carries no legal advantage, it does confer the assurance that the physician is recognized as a specialist by his or her colleagues.

In addition to being licensed and board certified, many physicians belong to professional associations, such as the American Academy of Internal Medicine. Some of these associations require nothing more than that the physician join the organization and continue to pay its dues. But other organizations require proof of excellence. The alphabet soup of professional association names is too complicated to explain here. The lay person may be interested in knowing that a physician who has been elected a fellow of an organization has earned special recognition. Some of these physicians use an "F"—Dr. Smith, M.D., F.A.C.S.—to signify that they are organizational "fellows" (in this case, of the American College of Surgeons).

Medicine is both a science and an art. There is a clear body of knowledge that the physician can apply to a given situation, but there are also many situations where the answers are not clear. It is then that the physician's intuition and personal experience become important. The various examinations physicians have passed and the societies to which they belong attest to their scientific understanding. But mastery of the art of medicine is not as easily measured. The ability to deal with special circumstances is what sets an excellent physician apart from others.

Remember, your relationship to your physician is a cooperative effort between the two of you. You need to trust him sufficiently to be able to tell him, when necessary, the most intimate details of your life as well as to be relaxed enough about your body in his presence to permit a complete examination. Of course, in order to earn this trust, the physician must respect you. If you have a problem, tell the physician, and perhaps you both can solve it. If you can't, perhaps you should go to another doctor.

You should have enough trust in your physician not to cheat on him. When he tells you to do something, you should ask what the boundaries of acceptable error are. Is it really important that you take your medicine before meals? If you forget, can you take it another time? What are the boundaries of the special diet you are to use? Can you occasionally eat something not on the diet. How often?

(2-7) *Asking for a consultation.* Most general practitioners will advise you to see a specialist for any problem that is best handled by someone with specific training or experience. Because medical ethics prohibit the referring physician from receiving any favor from a specialist, patients can feel confident that any referral is in their best interests. The referral is likely to be made within the network of specialists personally known to your physician, since knowledge of other physicians is limited. For an extremely rare or very complicated problem you might feel that a referral outside your own physician's network would be more appropriate. You may want to see a specialist's specialist. This situation frequently arises and can be handled easily. First, let the recommended specialist examine you. If the problem is an immediate danger, the recommended treatment is not irreversible (such as major surgery or very toxic drugs), and the specialist has your confidence, go ahead with the treatment. If you have any questions about your diagnosis or treatment, the specialist can suggest the names of professionals from whom you can obtain a second opinion. Specialists will gladly give you the names of two or three physicians to whom they would go if they had the same problem, and they will provide information concerning your health to the consultant of your choice. (Let your physician know about your decision, so that he or she can send ahead x-rays and other pertinent data.) In an emergency, of course, you have no choice but to take what is immediately available.

(2-8) *Generic versus brand-name prescriptions.* In most states, unless your physician prescribes the brand name of a medication, the pharmacist may fill the prescription with a less expensive generic drug. This means that if several companies make the same medication, you get the least expensive and save money—maybe. Even though manufacturers are required to put the same ingredients, in the same amounts, into a medicine, they may get them there by different means. All manufacturers do not possess the same scientific expertise and certainly do not have the same artistic ability. The same medication from different manufacturers may not work equally well. This problem is confusing for the patient, physician, and pharmacist.

My advice, if your have a choice, is two-pronged: For short-term prescriptions, or ones that you will need only occasionally, use the brand name and pay the few dollars' difference. For prescriptions you will need over a long period of time, there are great savings in a generic, and so, when there is a choice, use the generic.

Under any circumstances, shop around (use the phone); there is often considerable difference in price of prescriptions from one pharmacy to another.

PREVENTING ACCIDENTS

(2-9) *Preventing accidents with medicine.* Throughout this book I describe many conditions, their treatments, and some of the hazards of treatment. Many common medicines and their side effects are described. When a physician writes a prescription for you, it is important that you know the name of the drug—it should always be written on the bottle—what it is supposed to do, and what are the most common side effects. You should not try to treat yourself, but you should be knowledgeable enough about yourself, your condition, and its treatment to be an active rather than a passive participant. To be a good, active participant, you should be able to describe concisely and accurately how you look or feel and also be able to recognize early on when something may be wrong.

The following will help prevent medicine accidents: Keep all drugs away from children. Remember, young children can climb onto a sink to get into the medicine cabinet. Children also do not share the same reservations about going into your purse as does an older person. Since 1972 nearly all prescription medications come in child-resistant containers. Unfortunately, some of these are also adult-resistant. If you have difficulty opening child-resistant containers and there are no children likely to get into your medicines, you can get regular containers simply by asking the pharmacist for them.

When you must take a number of medications, each with its own schedule, get a calendar and write out the schedule. Each morning count the correct number of pills into a pillbox. Keep your calendar with you. Later, if you have any confusion—or are in an emergency—you will have the information you need. When you see your physician, remind him or her of everything you are taking including medicines that might be prescribed by another physician. Be sure to ask if there are to be any changes in the schedule for medicines you are taking. Never use medicines prescribed for someone else. Keep medicines used externally in a different place from those taken internally. If you take pills at night, keep only one night's supply by the bed—it is easy to wake up confused and overmedicate yourself. Throw out medicine after you are finished with it. It's best to go through your medicine cabinet once a year and get rid of any collections you might have been making.

(2-10) *Preventing falls.* Falling is the most dangerous and most common home accident. Most falls occur on flat surfaces and involve people tripping over a fold in the carpet. To prevent this, all rugs must be made slip-proof either by tacking them to the floor, basing them on a slip-proof pad, or applying a slip-proof backing to them. A mixture of paint and sand can give you a simple, effective slip-proof coating to be brushed onto

After Middle Age

a smooth floor or steps. Small rugs should never be laid on steps or at the bottom of steps where they might slide.

People often trip over stairs, too. Steps should be made more visible by painting a white strip at each edge. Handrails should be set out far enough from the wall on both sides of the stairway so that both rails can be firmly gripped. They must also be slender enough so that a person can get a good grasp. The rails should be well supported, particularly at the top and bottom, and they should be shaped so that you can tell when you have reached the top or bottom of the stairs. Most stair falls occur when a person misses the last step. Stairs should be well lighted from fixtures that can be turned on and off from either the top or bottom of the steps. There are relatively inexpensive devices available that will turn lights on and off remotely from places where three-way switches are not already installed.

Closets should have lights so that you can see clearly into them. And lights in bedrooms, bathrooms, and hallways should have switches placed so that you can turn them on before you enter an area. You should always be able to see where you are going. Hallways should be kept free of all obstacles. Floors should not be so heavily waxed as to make them slippery. Food should always be wiped from a floor's surface after it is spilled.

Bathtubs should be low enough so that entrance is easy. They should have a flat bottom. A built-in seat at the end of the tub is also useful. There should be a nonslip rubber mat in the bath or nonslip strips applied to the bottom of the tub. Horizontal bars anchored to a wall about forty inches above the floor, or bars over the tub, will help in getting in and out of a tub. Naturally, any of these bars should be sturdy enough to hold your weight. A shower stall should have a seat in it, a nonskid floor, and a well-anchored grab bar about forty inches above the floor.

If windows are not easily cleaned from the inside where you can safely stand, do not clean them yourself. A window washer should be hired for such purposes, or perhaps a family member or friend can help. Changing light bulbs and other chores that require a ladder should only be done if you are steady on your feet. Use a sturdy ladder, and be sure there is someone present who can help balance you if you start to fall. Although ceiling lights are in many ways convenient, if you have a choice, place light fixtures low enough so you can change the bulbs without standing on a chair or ladder. Use long-lasting bulbs in ceiling fixtures. All chairs should stand firmly on the floor so that they will not slide when leaned against or sat in. Balconies and porches should have strong, well-anchored rails in good repair.

(2-11) *Fire prevention.* Cigarettes should be treated like matches. They're dangerous. You must not smoke in bed or while sitting in any

Living Independently

piece of upholstered furniture where you might fall asleep. Broad-rimmed ashtrays should always be available for smokers. Many fires occur in the kitchen and can be prevented by simply remembering to turn off burners and other appliances. Unless they turn themselves off, appliances that generate heat should be equipped with lights that go on and off with the power. Switches should always be at the front of the range rather than on a back panel. As markings on the knobs begin to come off on old appliances, mark them with tape at appropriate cooking positions. Use lightweight utensils with well-insulated handles. Remember, you can easily be burned by steam, so raise pan lids with the opening away from you to protect your hands and face. Big gloves are often preferable to small potholders in cooking. Always use gloves or potholders when taking something from the oven. Fats should never be overheated, as they tend to blaze. A large pan top should be kept available to smother any flaming grease. Remember, never use water on a grease fire because it splatters the fire. If there is a fire in the oven, turn the oven off, and leave the door closed until the fire burns itself out. All appliances should be installed away from curtains.

Gas from an unlit stove that is left on can build up and then explode. Even a small spark from a doorbell or light switch can set off fumes inside a home. Dry cleaning fluid is usually just as explosive as gasoline and should always be used outdoors. Always keep gasoline and dry cleaning fluids in the containers in which they come—outside the house. When starting a heater, the pilot light in an oven, or a natural gas fireplace, always light the match first before turning on the gas. Do not go near an open flame with clothes that are not flame retardant or when wearing loose garments that might burst into flame. Finally and most important, wherever you are, always make sure that you know the location of the nearest exits. In an emergency, it frequently is a mistake to try to get out of a house by the way that you normally come in. There should always be at least one alternative, either through a window or a back door. If a window happens to open out onto a porch or roof, this is an excellent escape route. If you live on a second or third story, it is advisable to have a rope or chain ladder that can be dropped easily out the window after being securely attached to the windowsill.

Periodically check all electric cords for frayed or worn wiring. Replace worn wires immediately. When a fuse or circuit breaker blows or trips, you have probably overloaded the system and should unplug all appliances on that circuit before resetting the circuit breaker or replacing the fuse. Turn each appliance or light off before plugging it back in—separately turning on the switch to determine if it shorted or overloaded the circuit. If there is a slight tingle to your hand when turning out a light,

After Middle Age

it usually means there is poor wiring or insulation in the fixture. When lamp lights blink on and off, there is usually a loose connection that needs to be fixed.

(2-12) *Smoke detectors.* A substantial number of persons are injured or die each year because they are asleep and unaware there is a fire in their home. Smoke incapacitates them before they can reach safety. A properly placed smoke detector will wake you before the smoke becomes thick. Choose a battery-operated ionization-type smoke detector that is approved by Underwriters Laboratory (UL). They have a mechanism that tells you when the battery needs to be replaced. The detectors that depend on house current fail when the electricity is off, which can happen in an electric fire or during a power failure. A smoke detector should be placed outside each sleeping area.

(2-13) *The automobile.* When in an automobile, always wear seat and shoulder belts. In an accident they will prevent you from being thrown into the windshield or out of the car. You are not a rubber ball but a bundle of brittle sticks. Remember, you are just as likely to get into an accident driving to the grocery store as you are on a long trip. If as you get older your night vision greatly diminishes, try not to drive after dark. When you are a pedestrian, let the car have the right of way. Walk with lights at intersections—the little burst of speed you could put on to get across an intersection when you were 25 will not always be there. Also, your timing, vision, and hearing are likely to become less acute with age.

(2-14) *Protect yourself from the cold.* In addition to taking such commonsense protective measures as bundling up with gloves or mittens, warm shoes, hats, and earmuffs, people should recognize that many of us have different susceptibilities to cold. Some people have a special sensitivity to cold that is first noticed as an adolescent and lasts throughout life. Frequently, this condition occurs in successive generations. For individuals who have this sensitivity, cold is greatest in the arms and legs. Special sensitivity to cold also occurs with age. As people get older, they have difficulty maintaining their body temperature. It is not just a matter of comfort. Older people exposed to the cold can become hypothermic (a lowering of body temperature—especially to below 96°F, or 35.6°C). Symptoms of hypothermia are a pale, waxy color to the skin, trembling, slow breathing, confusion, sleepiness, and an abdomen that is noticeably cold to the touch. (Clinical thermometers do not usually go below 94°F, 34.3°C, and therefore cannot be used if the body temperature is very low—a freshly voided urine temperature taken with an outdoor thermometer, however, provides a rough indication.) Hypothermia requires immediate attention in a hospital. If you are with someone who has hy-

Living Independently

pothermia, do not give alcohol, but remove wet clothing and prevent further heat loss with blankets while getting the victim to the hospital.

Maintaining body temperature in older people may require keeping room temperatures higher than usually recommended in an energy-conscious nation. If you are over 60 years of age, you should keep the rooms that you spend much time in over 70°F (21°C). If you keep your house below 65°F (18.3°C) at night, use an electric blanket in bed.

When in the cold, keep moving and keep dry. Wear windproof outer garments. These can be light, but should be of a close knit. Remove any clothes, especially socks, that get wet, and replace then with dry ones. Do not wear constricting clothing that will cut off circulation. Mittens will keep your fingers warmer than gloves.

(2-15) *Be ready for emergencies.* Emergencies can strike at any time. For the unprepared a minor mishap can become a disaster, while those who are well-prepared can frequently survive under the most difficult circumstances. Keep a gallon bottle or covered plastic container of water for each person who lives with you. If drinking water becomes unavailable, this should last for at least four days. You should also have enough boxed and canned food to last for about a week. All these should be part of your regular food supply and used periodically so that they don't go bad.

The most common home emergency comes from electric power failure. You should have waterproof, battery-powered flashlights as well as candles and matches to use in an emergency. Keep these where you can easily get to them in the dark—usually in a bedside table. You should also have a battery-powered radio. If you live in a high-rise apartment and the elevator isn't working, do not attempt to climb more flights of stairs at once than you are used to. Go slowly and calmly—you'll eventually get there. During cold periods you will need heat. You might use a gas oven or fireplace, but the easiest and safest thing to do is to put on warm clothes.

During heavy rains or a flood stay on high ground; if you are told to leave your home by a government official, leave it! Most deaths come to people who wait until the last minute. When driving in storm conditions stay away from back roads and side streets. If you are outdoors and there is lightning, do not stand under a tree, wires, or metal—you are safer in the middle of a field. If you are caught in the middle of a field, crouch, or lie down—you will be less of a lightning rod! If a car, bus, or train is nearby, go into it. These vehicles are safe from lightning.

In cold climates, be prepared for winter storms. Have enough food in the house so that you do not have to go out until the walks and driveway have been cleared. Falls on snow and ice are very common. If you must shovel snow, do it for a fixed period of time (have someone in the house keep track and call you when it is time to come in). If you get tired before that time, quit. Avoid the tendency to take "just one more shovelful." Inside, warm up and rest before going out again. When driving, use chains or tires with good traction and stay on the main roads. Keep a full tank of gas in your car. Before you start, make sure your windshield is clear and that your wipers are in good condition.

Keep a record of your belongings at home in a safe deposit box or at the office as proof of ownership for insurance purposes.

COMMUNITY RESOURCES

(2-16) A wide variety of services are available in many communities across the nation. They help to prevent isolation of older people and permit them to remain in their homes. In addition to the services described here, most communities have services provided by church groups, civic associations, and publicly funded agencies. These may be recreational centers, day-care centers for rehabilitation, sheltered workshops, night and day hospitals, as well as activities sponsored by the local welfare department. Speaking to friends, ministers, and social workers will help to identify these resources.

(2-17) *Transportation.* Getting from one place to another by public transportation can be very expensive. For this reason most communities have introduced special fares for senior citizens. Frequently these fares are good only during non-rush hours or on weekends and nights. Some airlines, interstate bus companies, and railroads also offer reduced fares for the elderly. Check before you buy tickets. Hospitals and clinics often have volunteers who provide transportation to and from medical appointments. Civic and church groups and some local governments provide buses and vans for special trips as well as to and from shopping centers. New buses designed for the physically handicapped will help greatly in overcoming the physical barriers that now exist for users of public transportation.

(2-18) *Service.* Many older individuals decide that they want the opportunity to continue to serve others. Your skills and experience are of value to the community. Sometimes there is compensation for these services, other times not. Babysitting, childcare, helping retarded or disturbed children, and working as homemakers or household repairers are just some of the many things you might do. If you have a special skill, its part-time use may be very valuable to someone.

Living Independently

(2-19) *Senior centers* are gathering places for older individuals, and they sponsor a range of activities from card playing to swimming. Some centers provide lunch at minimal or no cost. There are many advantages of eating in a group. Usually people eat more and have better-planned meals. This offers something to look forward to as well as an opportunity to make new friends.

(2-20) *Admission to theaters and recreational facilities.* Many movie theaters offer a "golden age pass" or similar identification card that allows admission at a reduced rate. Sometimes the pass can be used for only certain performances, so call ahead. Opera, ballets, and legitimate theaters also have similar arrangements. The National Park Service provides a golden age pass to those 62 years of age and older for free entrance to the national parks. Some states and communities offer discount admission to parks and campsites as well as for fishing and hunting licenses.

Many colleges offer free classes to the elderly. Often libraries post information about such programs.

(2-21) *Telephone reassurance* programs provide daily phone contact at a specific time every day. They give isolated individuals an opportunity to talk with someone. In addition, if there is no answer, help is summoned from a predesignated neighbor or a professional organization. Your telephone operator or telephone company relations supervisor can be of help in locating this service. The best people to provide this service are the elderly themselves. You can set up a program with a friend, neighbor, or relative.

(2-22) *Friendly visiting* is a service in which social workers or other professionally trained workers make regular home visits to isolated persons. These visits can be social as well as practical. The visitor can help with the shopping, letter writing, reading, or just chat about interesting news. Most services employ older persons as the visitors, but responsible high school students can also be of great help.

(2-23) *Meals-on-wheels* provides prepared hot meals usually at noon. A cold meal is left for supper. The meals are brought by a private car or special vehicle. The cost is usually based upon the ability of the person to pay. In addition to good nutrition, the meals provide some contact with the outside world.

(2-24) *Homemaker service* makes it possible for many people to live at home who otherwise would have to be institutionalized. Relatives who normally provide help may need temporary relief for a vacation or to attend to some other affairs. The service usually provides a skilled woman experienced in marketing, planning of meals and special diets, light cleaning, clothing care, managing funds, and paying bills. The homemaker, however, is neither a nurse nor a maid. Some services also provide home

After Middle Age

maintenance workers to mow lawns, replace light bulbs, and do other light jobs. While these services, provided by governmental or private agencies, may seem expensive, the monetary cost of institutional care is much greater. Homemaker service is usually sponsored by the Visiting Nurses Association or the local welfare department. Some private agencies that specialize in homemaker services may be listed in your telephone directory under "Nurses."

(2-25) *Writing for information.* There are many sources of free or inexpensive information. Unfortunately, much of what you receive is not very useful. I have listed in the appropriate sections resources I have found helpful. In addition, there are a number of organizations that you may join or write for information:

National Gray Panthers, 3700 Chestnut Street, Philadelphia, Pennsylvania 19104, has many publications and newsletters helping older people fight against age discrimination. There are many local chapters throughout the country.

Action Agency, 806 Connecticut Avenue NW, Washington, D.C. 20525. This is a government agency that runs a number of volunteer programs, a few that pay older workers. Write for qualifications.

National Council on the Aging, 600 Maryland Avenue SW, Washington, D.C. 20024, has chapters throughout the country. They offer programs, and lobby for the elderly.

American Association of Retired Persons, 1909 K Street NW, Washington, D.C. 20049, offers newsletters and magazines of interest to older people, and lobbies on many important issues.

Administration on Aging, Department of Health and Human Services, 330 Independence Avenue SW, Washington, D.C. 20201, has many free or inexpensive publications. Write for a list.

3

Nutrition and Diet

(3-1) Establishing and practicing good eating and drinking habits are probably the most important things that can be done to maintain health. This can be more difficult than it sounds if other problems are present. People with diminished incomes, with deteriorated teeth, with gall bladder or some other disease affecting nutrition, or without the energy to help themselves may fall into bad habits. Yet, whatever your circumstances, moderation should be a guide. Keeping lean with a low-fat, low-cholesterol diet; getting sufficient rest, yet not becoming sedentary; drinking alcoholic beverages moderately if at all; and not smoking—all are themes of common sense. Our living brains and livers were not meant to be preserved in alcohol; the use of poisonous gases such as those found in cigarette smoke has been outlawed, even in warfare; and finely tuned engines like the body and mind need proper fuel.

While it's obvious what heavy drinkers (5-35) and heavy smokers (11-29) must do if they are to stop the deterioration of their health, others find that determining what is best nutritionally is not always easy. Nutritional fads are both epidemic and endemic: They come in waves and are always with us. Nutritional scientists are making progress in understanding the body's needs for optimal functioning, but this understanding is far from complete. Consequently, the suggestions made here are based both on scientifically gathered data and on hunches (that I like to think are common sense).

There is no easy way to good nutrition. Those who have avoided butter for twenty-five years because it is high in cholesterol may find that the margarine they have been using is thought to produce cancer. (There is no evidence, however, for this.) In some localities, people who avoid the

After Middle Age

intake of table salt (which contains iodine) may find that they are becoming iodine-deficient. My suggestion is to avoid all fads, whether they are for losing weight or for more general health purposes, unless prescribed by a physician. Do not jump onto the latest low-carbohydrate, high-protein, grapefruit, or other fad diet. If you want to lose weight, do it slowly and sensibly—and keep it off by maintaining good, steady habits.

REQUIREMENTS FOR AN ADEQUATE DIET

(3-2) In addition to the enjoyment that eating often brings, people eat as a matter of health. Foods—which are either carbohydrates, proteins, or fats, but usually combinations—supply energy, which is measured in units called calories and can be converted either to heat, movement, or fat. Calories are present in all foods, with fats containing twice as many calories as proteins or carbohydrates when measured per unit of weight. Accessory substances—vitamins, minerals, and water—are also needed for nutrition but contain no calories or energy.

(3-3) *Proteins* are the basis of all life. They supply the amino acids that are the building blocks needed to produce the new proteins, used to make muscle and blood. The human body must obtain from the diet twenty different amino acids, which make thousands of different proteins. Because some foods contain protein low in one or more of the amino acids, they are called poor protein foods. Many cereals and vegetables are poor sources of protein, and a diet consisting strictly of cereals and vegetables is ill-advised for good health. Good-quality protein is found in meat, fish, poultry, milk, cheese, and eggs. However, a diet high in vegetables and vegetable protein, including small amounts of animal protein, may be the healthiest diet supplying the necessary amino acids but little fat. An ounce (28 grams) of good animal protein, such as might be found in dairy products including milk, cheese, and eggs, in combination with an ounce of protein from other sources, fills most daily needs. Protein has the same calorie count as starch or sugar.

(3-4) *Carbohydrates*. Much of our energy comes from carbohydrates, which are either starch, sugar, or fiber (cellulose). Starches are found in potatoes, grains, and root vegetables. About 3.5 ounces, or 100 grams (400 calories), of carbohydrates are required daily to maintain weight.

(3-5) *Fats* add to the flavor of food, carry vitamins, and are also a major energy source. Our brains are largely made of fats, as are many of our sex and steroid hormones. Fats account for the smooth curves in our bodies, particularly in females. Much of this fat is lost with age, which is one reason why the skin tends to become loose. While the dietary require-

Nutrition and Diet

ments for fats are unknown, most nutritionists believe about 30 percent of the total calories is optimal. In the United States about 40 percent of the average diet is made up of fat.

Animal fats, which solidify at room temperatures, are called saturated because they have a full complement of hydrogen atoms. Saturated fats can be converted to cholesterol (3-29), while unsaturated fats (usually liquid) cannot. Unsaturated fats, found in margarine and all vegetable oils except coconut oil, neither raise nor lower cholesterol. Polyunsaturated fats (which are less saturated than unsaturated) actually decrease blood cholesterol concentrations and are found in corn, soybean, cottonseed, and safflower oils.

VITAMINS

(3-6) Vitamins are the chemical grease or catalysts the body uses to run smoothly. Precisely, vitamins facilitate the thousands of enzyme reactions constantly taking place in the body. Because they are used over and over again, vitamins are needed only in very small amounts, but since the body is chemically unable to manufacture vitamins, they must come from the diet. (Strictly speaking, some vitamins such as A and D, which under certain circumstances the body can make, are not really vitamins. As a matter of convention, however, they are called vitamins.)

Like much of what we know about the body, we know about vitamins because of the diseases that occur when they are deficient. Scurvy, for example, killed many sailors on long sea voyages until the late 1700s. In 1747 the Scottish naval surgeon, John Lind, performed the first controlled study in modern medicine. He started with a group of twelve scorbutic sailors, all of whom had lost their teeth because of putrid gums. Their legs were so weak they could not stand. The sailors were divided into four groups of three each. Each group of three was given a different diet. The three sailors who were given oranges and limes became fit for duty within six days to a month. While limes (the origin of the name "limey") were subsequently used by sailors all over the world to prevent scurvy, it was only in 1932 that the antiscorbutic factor was chemically identified as ascorbic acid, vitamin C.

(3-7) *Megavitamins.* There are a number of people, some very prominent such as the Nobel prize-winner Linus Pauling, who advocate taking large amounts of vitamins on a routine basis. Most of the advocates of large vitamin dosages (megavitamins, or orthomolecular medicine) state that no one really knows the quantities of vitamins that are needed for optimum health. In other words, since it has been scientifically proven

After Middle Age

that small quantities are necessary for good health, why not take large doses for even better health? Besides, since vitamins are natural substances, they can do no harm.

While there are specific medical circumstances that require large doses of vitamins (3-17), I believe that taking large quantities of vitamins in general is a bad idea. The minimum daily requirement for vitamins is the amount needed to prevent specific vitamin deficiency diseases such as scurvy. The evidence that larger doses prevent disorders or make people feel better is anecdotal, and there is considerable data that large doses of vitamins, like large quantities of many things, are harmful. Since large vitamin doses have not been given to large numbers of people for long periods of time in a manner that can be scientifically evaluated, we do not know all the risks. The ability to synthesize vitamins in a factory in any significant quantity is a recent scientific development. For example, vitamin C has been available in large quantities only for the last thirty years. Previously it required 150 pounds of potatoes to extract the equivalent of 10 grams (a single day's dose for some megavitaminists) of ascorbic acid.

To understand the risks of taking large doses of substances that on the surface seem beneficial, we only have to look at the medical use of oxygen. Just before World War II, physicians noticed a form of blindness in babies that had never been seen before. It occurred only in babies born prematurely and was called retrolental fibroplasia. Years later, the number of cases was still increasing, yet no one knew the cause. In 1951, an Australian pediatrician, Dr. Kate Campbell, came to the conclusion that the blindness was caused by the high concentrations of oxygen used to help premature babies breathe more easily while they were in the hospital nursery. A year later, Dr. Arnall Patz at Johns Hopkins Medical School did a study in which half the premature infants were given a high level of oxygen and half a low level, on a random basis. The results were conclusive. None of the low-oxygen infants had retrolental fibroplasia, while seven of twenty-eight of the high-concentration infants did. But not until the 1960s did everyone agree that high oxygen levels should be used only in the most unusual of circumstances with premature infants. This was some thirty years after its introduction as a new nontoxic therapy.

If you are now taking large doses of vitamins (say, ten times more than the recommended daily allowances) and you wish to stop, do not do so all at once. Your body may have become used to metabolizing the vitamins, and stopping suddenly might leave you with a relative deficit. In the case of vitamin C, for example, there may be bleeding into gums and skin. To avoid this withdrawal effect taper off the vitamin doses by about 10 percent a day until you get to the recommended dosage.

(3-8) *Naming the vitamins.* At a time when scientists did not know

Nutrition and Diet

the chemical structure of the vitamins, they were given the names vitamin A, B, C, etc. for simplicity. Now vitamins that are found in the fatty part of the body or dissolved in fatty foods are called fat-soluble, while those found in the water parts of the body or that can be dissolved in water are called water-soluble. The water-soluble vitamins (vitamins B, C, and folic acid) are leached into the water when foods are boiled, but remain available in soups. The fat-soluble vitamins are A, D, E, and K. Vitamin B was originally thought to be a single compound, but subsequent research and observation proved that it is made up of many.

(3-9) *Vitamin A (cretinol).* Daily requirement: 2500 IU.* This vitamin prevents poor sight at night (night blindness), overgrowth of the skin (follicular keratosis), and dryness of the white of the eye, the first symptom of which is itching (xerophthalmia). Vitamin A occurs only in foods derived from animals. Carotene, the pigment that makes plants such as carrots yellow, is found in both plants and animals and is converted in humans to vitamin A. Unlike other vitamins, vitamin A and carotene are not lost in cooking, even in water. The inclusion in the diet of carrots or dark green vegetables, or liver once a week, will help maintain a good vitamin A level. In the last few years there has been some evidence in animals that maintaining a *normal* amount of vitamin A in the diet is useful in preventing cancer from becoming started. (It does not help, however, once cancer has started.) Because vitamin A has been found to be toxic in large amounts, do not take more than that which is in one multivitamin tablet a day plus a normal diet unless you are recommended to do so by a physician.

(3-10) *Vitamin D (calciferol).* Daily requirement: 400 IU. This vitamin aids the absorption of calcium from the intestines, and so deficiencies may result in weakening of the bones. Individuals exposed to sunlight synthesize vitamin D in their skin, so people who spend all their time indoors, who wear heavy clothing outside, or who work outside in an atmosphere with smoke, haze, or fog probably do not get enough sunlight to make vitamin D. For most people enriched milk is the principle source of vitamin D. Because oils bind fat-soluble vitamins (A, D, E, and K), chronic mineral oil users may not absorb vitamin D and may, therefore, become deficient.

---

*An international unit (IU) is a standard of activity that was developed before the vitamin could be made synthetically. Vitamin A used to come from fish liver (cod-liver oil), and in order to determine how much was present in the liver oil, the oil was fed to vitamin-depleted rats. The amounts of vitamin A required for measured growth of the rat was defined as a unit. (Other vitamins are also measured by IU, or by weight in micrograms [μg] or milligrams [mg].)

After Middle Age

(3-11) *Vitamin K.* Daily requirement: not known. This vitamin is important in the clotting of blood when anticoagulants are being used, but vitamin K deficiencies are not known in the adult.

(3-12) *Vitamin E (tocopherol).* Daily requirement: 12 IU. This vitamin has at various times been claimed to prevent heart disease, warts, baldness, and aging, as well as to increase sexual performance. Good studies have failed to demonstrate its usefulness in any of the above. There is no known adult disorder produced by a vitamin E deficiency. The taking of very large doses, over 800 IU, may produce adverse effects. Since vitamin E is needed in the development of infants, it is normally present in breast milk. Women who nurse their babies may be encouraged by their obstetricians to take vitamin E supplements.

(3-13) *Vitamin B_1 (thiamine).* Daily requirement: 1 mg. This vitamin prevents beriberi, a disorder consisting of heart failure, edema, and confusional states. Although thiamine is leached from food cooked in water, it is plentiful in most diets, and a deficiency is unusual in western societies.

(3-14) *Vitamin B_2 (riboflavin).* Daily requirement: 1.5 mg. Deficiency of this vitamin is associated with sores in the mouth, a sore tongue, red, dry lips with cracks radiating from their margins, and a flaking rash between the nose and lips (seborrhoea). High quantities of riboflavin are contained in milk, but they are lost when milk is exposed to sunlight for long periods of time. To prevent this loss dairies either package their home-delivered milk in an amber glass container, deposit it in a home storage box, or package it in a carton. Unless an individual eats considerable amounts of liver, drinks two cups of milk a day, and eats considerable amounts of leafy green vegetables, riboflavin deficiency is likely to result. To prevent this, take a daily multiple-vitamin supplement.

(3-15) *Vitamin B_3 (nicotinamide, niacin).* Daily requirement: 10 mg. Deficiency in vitamin B_3 can cause pellagra, a disease marked by gastrointestinal disturbances, diarrhea, red peeling skin, and confusion. Nicotinamide survives most food processing and is present in ample amounts in balanced diets, especially since wheat flour and flour products are enriched. The persons likely to be deficient in nicotinamide are either the truly malnourished or the food faddists who inadvertently eat foods lacking nicotinamide—for example, someone who continually avoids enriched cereals.

(3-16) *Vitamin B_6 (pyridoxine).* Daily requirement: 1 mg. This vitamin is not associated with any specific deficiency in the adult. Pyridoxine is found in many foods and is present in adequate quantities even in the poorest of diets.

(3-17) *Vitamin B_{12} (cyanocobalamin).* Daily requirement: 3 mg. This

Nutrition and Diet

vitamin is necessary for the normal production of red blood cells. Its absence, which results in pernicious anemia, is usually due to a hereditary lack of a substance known as an intrinsic factor, which promotes intestinal absorption of dietary B_{12}. The deficiency of this factor (which is made in the stomach) usually becomes apparent only after 35 years of age. If one parent has the deficiency, there is a 50 percent chance that the offspring will have it. Pernicious anemia also can occur among extreme vegetarians or persons having a tapeworm. The symptoms of vitamin B_{12} deficiency are shortness of breath, weakness, and the feeling of your heartbeat (palpitation). The tongue becomes smooth and red and sore. There is numbness and tingling in the hands and feet, along with weight loss, nausea, vomiting, and diarrhea. Pernicious anemia is treated by injecting vitamin B_{12} into the muscle because, with the intrinsic factor absent, it cannot be absorbed from the intestines.

(3-18) *Folic acid (pteroylglutamic acid).* Daily requirement: 0.1 mg. Deficiency of this vitamin, like that of vitamin B_{12}, produces an anemia (too few red blood cells). The symptoms are weakness and rapid breathing. Folic acid is ample in most adult diets. It is recommended that vitamin preparations containing more than 0.1 mg not be used because they mask, but will not treat, the symptoms of other vitamin deficiencies.

(3-19) *Vitamin C (ascorbic acid).* Daily requirements: 25 to 30 mg. Deficiency of this vitamin is known as bachelor's or widower's scurvy and occurs only among the undernourished or poorly fed. Its symptoms are swollen, bleeding gums and pinpoint hemorrhages in the skin. Vitamin C is also necessary to the proper healing of wounds. Cooking vegetables for long periods decreases their vitamin C content substantially. Packaging, such as freezing of orange juice, has little effect. Most individuals eating a well rounded diet should have an adequate vitamin C intake.

(3-20) *General vitamin recommendations.* To ensure that you get the daily vitamin requirements, I recommend that you take a daily multiple-vitamin capsule with trace minerals. Also, it might be a good idea to take slightly more calcium than is usually recommended. Furthermore, as discussed in the section on colds (11-6), you can take an additional 150-mg capsule of vitamin C. I advise against routinely taking the very large (megavitamins) vitamin does recommended by some people. I believe they present a real danger to health, especially in the elderly.

MINERALS

(3-21) As life sprang from the earth, it found ways of making use of the available elements, especially minerals. They are involved in all aspects

After Middle Age

of the body's function and, like calcium, form the literal backbone of the body's structure. See (3-1) for iodine.

(3-22) *Calcium* is important for forming the matrix, or body, of bones and teeth. Because the bones are constantly being built up and torn apart, the continued presence of calcium in the body is absolutely necessary. The established adult calcium requirement is 800 mg daily, although recent studies show that postmenopausal women may need up to 1500 mg calcium daily to preserve their bones. Dairy products are rich in calcium; a glass of milk contains about 300 mg, as does a cup of yogurt. If you prefer not to drink milk or eat yogurt, you can obtain calcium by eating green leafy vegetables. Most multivitamins, even those containing mineral supplements, will supply only a portion (10 to 20 percent) of the needed calcium. If your diet does not contain enough calcium—and the diet of most people past 50 does not—think about taking a daily calcium supplement. Ask your physician about this, since people who have kidney stones or are at risk for kidney stones may not be able to take supplemental amounts of calcium.

Calcium is present in some antacids such as Alka-Seltzer. Check the labels of all antacids for their contents and avoid taking too much calcium by using more than the recommended dosage of antacid.

(3-23) *Phosphorus* is closely related to calcium in the body, since it also makes up the matrix of the bone. In addition, the mechanism by which the body chemically transfers energy from food to the muscles utilizes phosphorus. Phosphorus comes from the same food as calcium, and the recommended minimum daily requirement is the same, 800 mg.

(3-24) *Magnesium* is also used to form bone, though in much smaller quantities than calcium or phosphorus. Animals given diets deficient in magnesium have increased cholesterol in their arteries, but there is no reason to believe magnesium in quantities greater than the minimum daily requirement will prevent cholesterol from depositing in the arteries. The requirement for magnesium per day is 300 mg in women and 350 mg in men, which is obtained from most American diets.

(3-25) *Iron* is needed to make red blood cells. The daily requirement is 10 mg. A person can become deficient in iron only through bleeding or breast feeding. It is true that women lose iron during menstruation, but unless bleeding is heavy, healthy women need only the iron that is present in a normal diet.

Despite what they say on the television commercials, you should not take supplemental iron (other than that contained in a multiple-vitamin mineral capsule) unless a physician advises you to do so. Excess iron can irritate the bowel, and in large amounts it will be deposited in organs such as the liver. One way people can get too much iron is if all their foods are cooked in iron pots. But before you throw away your iron cooking utensils, ask your physician if he or she thinks you are getting too much iron; you probably are not.

(3-26) *Trace metals,* such as copper and zinc, which are needed in very small amounts, are readily obtained in most diets. Taking a daily multiple-vitamin capsule with minerals will ensure that you get adequate amounts of trace minerals.

(3-27) *Salt or sodium.* Many people with high blood pressure are advised by their physicians to restrict their salt intake. Salt is contained in many foods but it is also added in cooking and at the table. The normal daily salt intake is from 7 to 10 g. In the usual low-salt diet the salt is kept below 2 g (2000 mg), or 1 teaspoon a day. Salt comes as sodium chloride and monosodium glutamate. You should be able to keep your daily salt intake under 2 g if you do not add salt at the table or in cooking and if you avoid the following foods: just about all cheeses; salted, smoked, and canned fish; smoked and prepared meats such as bacon, bologna, and frankfurters; snack foods such as potato chips, pretzels, and rolls with salted toppings; canned and dry soups; ketchup, mustard, soy sauce, etc.; and vegetables prepared in brine such as sauerkraut and pickles.

(3-28) *Potassium.* There is twice as much potassium in the body as there is sodium, most of it located inside the cells. Potassium is in a delicate chemical balance with sodium in the body. Together they regulate the work of nerves and muscles, and in the elderly they are of particular importance for the heart muscles (12-10).

OTHER FACTORS IN THE DIET

Almost every day someone claims that substance X or ingredient Y should be or should not be part of your diet. Because this information is often contradictory, it is confusing and difficult to act upon. I have evaluated a few of the more popular current topics.

(3-29) *Cholesterol.* Cholesterol (12-14) is a substance that is similar in structure to many hormones. It is deposited in the arteries (which supply blood from the heart to all parts of the body), causing narrowing of these tubes (atherosclerosis). Atherosclerosis is the major cause of the illness and the mortality of cardiovascular disease. To slow or even reverse the process of atherosclerosis, many physicians recommend that we eat minimal quantities of foods such as egg yolk, that are rich in cholesterol (3-30). Saturated fats, such as those in meat, are converted in the body to cholesterol. Lean meats—veal, flank and round steak, pot and rump roasts—are low in saturated fats. As much as possible of the visible fat on

After Middle Age

meats should be trimmed away. If the meat is broiled, the drippings should be discarded and not used in gravy. Very frequently the less expensive grades of meat—choice and lower—have less fat, particularly the marblized fat that imparts such excellent flavor to such American classics as prime ribs and steak. Chicken and turkey, especially the white meat, are low in fat. But the skin should be avoided. Ducks and geese are especially high in fat. The fat in fish is polyunsaturated and actually tends to lower cholesterol. Fruits and vegetables are low in fats, high in vitamins and minerals. It is a good idea to know what the relative amounts of cholesterol in some common foods are (3-31). Curb the use of fatty oils or rich salad dressings.

Your physician may measure your cholesterol from time to time. While the upper limit of normal varies depending on your age and on the laboratory making the determination, cholesterol levels above 240 to 270 per 100 mL of blood are considered high.

(3-30) **Foods High and Low in Cholesterol**

High in Cholesterol	Low in Cholesterol
Avocado	Fruit or fruit juice, fresh, frozen, canned, or cooked
Cream chicken or meat stock soups	
Pork, mutton, duck, fish roe, shrimp, oysters	Any cereal or rice with skim milk
	Vegetable soup with meat stocks
Brains, liver, eggs, butter, solid margarine	Lean baked or broiled beef, lamb, veal, chicken, turkey, fish, liquid shortening, soft margarine, egg substitutes, cottage cheese, mozzarella, synthetic cheeses
Sweet potatoes	
Bread containing egg yolk, cream, solid shortening	
	Fresh or frozen vegetables, including potatoes
Whole milk, cream or cream products	
	Bread not containing egg yolk, lard, or cream
Cakes, chocolates, pastries, ice cream	
	Tea, coffee, skim milk
Gravies, mayonnaise, egg noodles	Gelatin desserts, sherbets and ices
Macadamia and cashew nuts	Angel food cake
Cream substitutes made with coconut oil	French dressing
	Pasta
	Sugar and syrups

Nutrition and Diet

(3-31) Cholesterol Content of Certain Foods

Food	Amount	Cholesterol in mg
Milk, skim or reconstituted	1 c (8 oz)	5
Milk, whole	1 c	34
Light table cream	1 oz (2 tbsp)	20
Half and half	1/4 c (4 tbsp)	26
Cottage cheese, uncreamed	1/2 c	7
Cottage cheese, creamed	1/2 c	24
Cheddar cheese	1 oz	28
Butter	1 tbsp	35
Regular ice cream, 10% fat	1/2 c	27
Egg	1 yolk or 1 whole egg	250
Beef, pork, lobster	3 oz, cooked	75
Chicken or turkey—dark meat	3 oz, cooked	75
Chicken, turkey—light meat	3 oz, cooked	67
Lamb, veal, crab	3 oz, cooked	85
Oysters, salmon	3 oz, cooked	40
Clams, halibut, tuna	3 oz, cooked	55
Shrimp	3 oz, cooked	130
Liver—beef, calf	3 oz, cooked	370
Kidneys	3 oz, cooked	680
Brains	3 oz, raw	1700

(3-32) *LDL and HDL.* Most of the cholesterol accumulating in the artery walls comes from substances called low-density lipoproteins (LDL), which contain great quantities of cholesterol. Once the LDLs get into the artery walls, generally through some sort of break, they leave the cholesterol there. Eventually this accumulation closes off the artery. Whereas LDL is thought to contribute to atherosclerosis, high-density lipoprotein (HDL) is thought to decrease it. Because HDL also contains cholesterol, how it acts to prevent atherosclerosis is a mystery. One hypothesis is that HDL may help remove cholesterol from the artery wall. Your physician may want to monitor your LDL and HDL by taking venous blood. Ideally you should have low amounts of LDL and high amounts of HDL. LDL can be decreased by diet, and HDL elevated by exercise. Average HDL is about 55 mg per dL for women and 45 mg per dL for men, but may vary depending on age and laboratory standards. Average LDL for both women and men in their fifties is about 144 mg per dL.

(3-33) *Sugar.* Some nutritionists believe that refined sugar—white or brown, granular or liquid—is injurious. Though they acknowledge a need

After Middle Age

for carbohydrates, which include the simple sugars glucose and fructose, these experts point out that there is no physiological requirement for such refined sugars as sucrose and dextrose. Even so, there has been a large increase in the use of refined sugar in the diet during the last 200 years. While it has not been proved that refined sugar is harmful to people, and in spite of the enjoyment I and many others get from sweets, I recommend cutting back on sugar consumption.

(3-34) *Fiber* is the part of fruits, nuts, vegetables, and whole grains that is not digested as it passes through the gastrointestinal system. Some physicians and nutritionists believe that diet high in fiber, or roughage, will help prevent cancer of the bowel as well as other bowel diseases. Softer stools produced by the fiber in the diet may remedy constipation and relieve the pressure in the lower bowel that causes hemorrhoids. Fiber is usually lost in milled or refined foods. It can be found in breakfast cereals, especially bran cereals, as well as fruits, nuts, and fresh vegetables. But a word of caution: Too much fiber can produce stomach pain.

(3-35) *Vegetarian diets.* From the nutritional point of view, vegetarians can be divided into three groups. Complete vegetarians, or vegans, do not eat meat, fish, fowl, eggs, or dairy products. Lacto-vegetarians drink milk and eat milk products such as butter and cheese. Lacto-ovo-vegetarians also eat eggs. If lacto-vegetarians and lacto-ovo-vegetarians eat a variety of foods, they should get enough protein and vitamins, particularly from milk and milk products. Complete vegetarians should be careful to select a well-rounded vegetable diet and to take a protein supplement and 5 mg of vitamin B_{12} each day.

(3-36) *Coffee, tea, and cola.* Coffee, tea, and colas contain a group of chemicals called xanthines, the most potent of which is caffeine. Caffeine is a stimulant to the heart, making it beat faster and, at times, irregularly. It is also a stimulant to the brain, quickening reactions and decreasing drowsiness.

Beverage	*Mg Caffeine in 6 oz*
Coffee, brewed	80–120
Coffee, instant	60–80
Sanka	3–5
Tea	40–100
Cola	17–55

Tea and colas also contain other xanthines that are not as potent as caffeine. While many people become irritable after drinking coffee ("coffee nerves"), other people, particularly those who drink coffee before breakfast, cannot start the day without it—it gives them a feeling of well-being and alertness. Large amounts of caffeine, greater than 750 mg per day, may cause nausea, sleeplessness, jumpiness, and anxiety. Some people are especially sensitive to caffeine—for them a single cup of coffee can produce the above toxic effects.

People who drink large amounts of coffee and have symptoms must gradually reduce their intake. Those who are especially sensitive must abstain. Remember, caffeine is also in a number of medicines and is the C in APC (aspirin, phenacetin, and caffeine).

(3-37) *Synthetic sweeteners.* Saccharin and aspartame are the only synthetic sweeteners widely used in food in the United States. Because cyclamate has produced an increased rate of bladder cancer among rats, it has been banned. Xylitol is used in some chewing gums. While xylitol has the same caloric value as sugar, cavity-producing bacteria are unable to use it to grow. There is, however, no evidence that xylitol reduces cavities.

Saccharin's safety has not been proven, and in one recent Canadian study it was found that men who used artificial sweeteners (primarily saccharin) had 60 percent more bladder cancer than those who did not. Women who used artificial sweeteners, on the other hand, had fewer bladder cancers than those who did not. Saccharin should not be used by children and pregnant women. Adults should not use it unless they truly have a weight problem—and then not regularly.

In 1981, the Food and Drug Administration (FDA) approved the use of aspartame (NutraSweet, Equal), a nutritive sweetener made from two naturally occurring amino acids. For the same amount of sweetness, sugar has 180 times more calories than aspartame. Thus, we are gradually seeing aspartame substituting in many places where sugar or saccharin has been used. Despite the FDA's approval, some scientists still believe that high quantities of aspartame may produce brain abnormalities. Thus, I advise using aspartame in moderation.

(3-38) *Nitrates and nitrites.* Potassium and sodium nitrites have been used by food processors for many years in hot dogs, bacon, ham, luncheon meats, some imported cheeses, and smoked fish as preservatives against botulism. Nitrites also add flavor and color to food. When the U.S. Food and Drug Administration (FDA) scientists check these foods for the amount of nitrites, they frequently find they contain more than the law allows. Nitrites by themselves are not considered dangerous; but when they combine with the chemicals known as amines, they form nitrosamines, which have been shown to produce cancer in animals. Fortunately the nitrites in every food except dry-cured bacon (making up only 1 percent of all U.S. bacon) do not form nitrosamines.

Nitrates have the same preservative action as nitrites, and are found naturally in water and some vegetables. They are not thought to be harmful unless they become converted to nitrites and from them to nitrosamines. This conversion takes place when food spoils. My recommendation is not to worry about nitrites unless you are a baconoholic.

(3-39) *Cost of food.* Every shopper recognizes that the more often a product is handled (from farms to processing plants to grocery store), the more expensive it will be. The produce offered at a roadside stand next to a farm is less costly than that at your neighborhood market. Convenience or prepared foods are more expensive than those you prepare yourself. Buying at a farmer's market or co-op is usually cheaper than at a chain supermarket, but the supermarket is usually cheaper than the small neighborhood grocery store. Buying in bulk, perhaps as a member of a buying club, can save money if you get what you want and do not have to purchase wasteful quantities.

For most people, convenience rather than price dictates where they shop and what they buy. The travel money and time lost will usually outweigh the savings from food that is less expensive but bought at a distance.

Since the most important foods are those containing proteins, it makes sense to evaluate foods by their relative cost per gram of protein. Measuring cost in this way provides a good perspective on nutritional choices. In the following table, the cost of protein is based on early 1984 prices in suburban Maryland supermarkets. Where house brands were available, they were used. The leanest cuts of meats were also used, which in some cases may make prices more expensive since "lean" is not always synonymous with "cheap." The price of hamburger was indexed 100 and other items were compared with it and given a numerical rating for their relative prices. Chicken, which costs less per gram of protein than hamburger, came to 47, while porterhouse steak, which was about twice as expensive per gram of protein, came to 212. The higher the number (relative cost), the more expensive the item is as a protein source.

An excellent pamphlet on diet and food purchases for older people is *For Older People, Eating Right for Less* (1977), which can be purchased from Consumers Union, Mount Vernon, New York.

Relative Expenses of Protein Sources

Protein Source	Relative Cost per Gram of Protein
American cheese, processed	130
Bacon, sliced	101
Beans, green, frozen	457
Bologna	129
Chicken, whole	47
Eggs, grade A large	72
Ground beef (hamburger)	100
Ham, rump	74
Hotdog	125
Lamb chops	406
Liver, calf	968
Liverwurst	76
Peanut butter	45
Pork sausage	256
Porterhouse steak	212
Sardines, canned	210
Sirloin steak	143
Tuna, canned	74
Turkey	46
Veal cutlet	354

DIET AND WEIGHT

(3-40) There are few persons in our society today who are not weight conscious because of a concern for their appearance, health, or well-being. This is all to the good, for weight—overweight or underweight—has definite effects on health. The main problem is of course excess weight, which is a factor in high blood pressure, heart attacks, stroke, kidney disease, liver and gallbladder disease, cancer, diabetes, cirrhosis of the liver, hernia, and intestinal obstruction.

The overweight person has good reason to return to a normal weight. But what is normal? This problem has been solved in part by tables of "desirable weight." The tables in sections (3-41) and (3-42) give desirable weights that are lighter than will be found in most other sources. This is

After Middle Age

because they represent weights without clothing, and they are adjusted to take age into account. All desirable weights are based on gender, height, and skeletal structure, so that an individual can establish a range that is desirable. But by themselves, the tables do not tell you exactly what you should weigh. Your ideal weight also depends on such factors as your age, how you feel, and how you look. There may be other departures from the ideal, too. In some cases, because muscle is heavier than fat, exceptionally thin people can carry much more weight than the ideal if there is a preponderance of muscle on their frames. As you get older, muscle mass usually decreases. Since on a volume basis muscle is heavier than fat, you should weigh less at 60 than you did at 40. Certainly your clothing size should be no larger. I believe that, if possible, it is healthier to be on the slim side.

Once a desired weight is targeted, a decision must be made on how to achieve it. Essential to any weight-reduction program is this one fact: It takes 3500 calories to produce one pound of fat (although there may be small differences from person to person). Thus, if your weight is stable and your level of activity unchanged, and if you consume 100 fewer calories a day than before, you will lose one pound in 35 days. At this rate, you will lose 10 lb a year.

(3-41) Desirable Weight—Male*

Height (Barefoot)	Weight in Pounds		
	Small Frame	Medium Frame	Large Frame
5 ft 2 in	112–120	118–130	126–141
5 ft 3 in	115–123	121–133	129–145
5 ft 4 in	118–126	124–136	132–149
5 ft 5 in	121–130	127–140	135–153
5 ft 6 in	125–134	131–144	139–158
5 ft 7 in	129–138	135–149	144–163
5 ft 8 in	133–142	139–153	148–167
5 ft 9 in	137–147	143–157	152–171
5 ft 10 in	141–151	147–162	156–176
5 ft 11 in	149–159	151–167	161–181
6 ft 0 in	151–161	155–172	165–186
6 ft 1 in	153–164	159–177	170–191
6 ft 2 in	157–168	164–187	175–196
6 ft 3 in	161–172	169–197	179–201

*Suggested weights without clothing for 60-year-old males (as ages increases, the suggested weight should decrease slightly).

Nutrition and Diet

(3-42) Desirable Weight—Female*

Height (Barefoot)	Weight in Pounds		
	Small Frame	Medium Frame	Large Frame
4 ft 10 in	93–101	98–110	106–122
4 ft 11 in	96–104	101–113	109–125
5 ft 0 in	99–107	104–116	112–128
5 ft 1 in	102–110	107–119	115–131
5 ft 2 in	105–113	110–123	118–135
5 ft 3 in	108–116	113–127	122–139
5 ft 4 in	111–120	117–132	126–143
5 ft 5 in	115–124	121–136	130–147
5 ft 6 in	119–128	125–140	135–152
5 ft 7 in	123–132	129–144	138–155
5 ft 8 in	127–137	133–147	142–160
5 ft 9 in	131–141	137–152	146–165
5 ft 10 in	135–145	141–156	159–170

*Suggested weight without clothing for 60-year-old females (as age increases, the suggested weight should decrease slightly).

(3-43) Weight Conversion—Pounds to Kilograms*

Pounds	Kilograms	Pounds	Kilograms
50	22.7	165	75.0
75	34.1	170	77.3
80	36.3	175	79.5
90	40.8	180	81.8
95	43.2	185	84.1
100	45.4	190	86.4
105	47.7	195	88.6
110	50.0	200	90.1
115	52.3	205	93.2
120	54.5	210	95.4
125	56.8	215	97.7
130	59.1	220	100
135	61.4	230	104.5
140	63.6	240	109.1
145	65.9	250	113.6
150	68.2	260	118.2
155	70.4	270	122.7
160	72.7	280	127.3

*Number of pounds divided by 2.2 equals kilograms; number of kilograms multiplied by 2.2 equals pounds.

After Middle Age

(3-44)   Height Conversion—Feet and Inches to Centimeters*

Feet and Inches	Centimeters (cm)	Feet and Inches	Centimeters (cm)
4 ft	121.3 (1 m, 21.3 cm)	5 ft 7 in	170.2
4 ft 6 in	137.2	5 ft 8 in	172.7
4 ft 7 in	139.7	5 ft 9 in	175.3
4 ft 8 in	142.2	5 ft 10 in	177.8
4 ft 9 in	144.8	5 ft 11 in	180.3
4 ft 10 in	147.3	6 ft	182.9
4 ft 11 in	149.9	6 ft 1 in	185.4
5 ft	152.4	6 ft 2 in	188.0
5 ft 1 in	154.9	6 ft 3 in	190.5
5 ft 2 in	157.5	6 ft 4 in	193.0
5 ft 3 in	160.0	6 ft 5 in	195.6
5 ft 4 in	162.6	6 ft 6 in	198.1
5 ft 5 in	165.1	7 ft	213.4
5 ft 6 in	167.6		

*Number of inches times 2.54 equals centimeters; number of centimeters divided by 2.54 equals inches.

(3-45) *Diet and activity.* As a person grows older, nutritional requirements change little, although the caloric need may decrease. Nevertheless, people may develop special nutritional needs based on digestive or metabolic disturbances. Once a desirable weight has been established, maintaining that weight is probably the simplest method of measuring good nutrition. Caloric needs can vary enormously from person to person, depending on constitutional factors, as well as on activity and climate. Very active people living in a warm climate will need more calories to maintain their weight than less-active people living in a cool climate. The average-sized man at age 65 will need 2100 calories daily composed of 70 g (10.5 oz) of protein, 340 g (51 oz) of carbohydrate, and 70 g (10.5 oz) of fat. The average-sized woman will need 1400 calories to maintain weight composed of 58 g (9 oz) of protein, 230 g (35 oz) of carbohydrates, and 45 g (7 oz) of fat.

LOSING WEIGHT

(3-46) *Fad diets.* Every few years a new diet catches the fancy of the nation. Often the diet has been developed by a doctor and embodies an outrageous concept (for example, calories do not count). Every such diet will have its advocates and disciples. It will be ballyhooed on television

Nutrition and Diet

and radio talk shows and in the press, usually by the doctor-author who has "tested this revolutionary diet on hundreds of patients."

With few exceptions the concepts behind these diets are quite old—they are merely packaged in a new way—and the diets themselves have not been tested rigorously for either efficacy or safety. Though their proponents may earn large sums of money through the sale of books and, at times, special foods, in two or three years the diets will be forgotten.

If you want to lose more than ten or fifteen pounds in a limited period of time, your best course is to follow the instructions of your physician. This does not mean getting a physical examination and then going on a crash or fad diet. Some healthy people have even lost their lives in this manner. But you should make sure your physician understands the diet you are about to undertake, agrees to it, and will examine you at regular intervals. If your goal is a modest loss of ten to fifteen pounds, the calorie-counting diet explained later in this chapter (3-53) should be safe. It is slow, but it teaches good eating practices that you can continue to use after you have reached the desired weight.

(3-47) *Low-carbohydrate diets.* Most carbohydrates are "empty" calories that do not provide nutrients in the form of proteins for building muscle. So it makes sense to restrict your consumption of them. There are two basic kinds of low-carbohydrate diets. The first is proposed by Dr. John Yudkin in *The Complete Slimmer,* Dr. Donald S. Mart in *The Carbo-Calorie Diet,* and Drs. Sidney Petrie and Robert B. Stone in *Martinis and Whipped Cream.* It suggests that the dieter take in a constant but limited amount of carbohydrate each day, thus decreasing calorie intake. One version of the low-carbohydrate diet, *The Drinking Man's Diet,* by Gardner James and Elliot Williams, allows one to be sociable but still lose weight. There is nothing wrong with low-carbohydrate diets, although the implication of the title that one can drink with impunity is dangerous.

The second basic type of low-carbohydrate diet is typified by Dr. Robert Atkin's *Dr. Atkin's Diet Revolution: The High Calorie Way to Stay Thin Forever* and Dr. Herman Taller's *Calories Don't Count.* According to this type of diet, you produce a ketosis by eating foods high in fat—the part of fat the body cannot use—which shows up in the blood and urine and can be checked with a simple test. These diets make little sense to me, especially if you are trying to restrict saturated fats and cholesterol. After about two days into the diet many people suffer from tiredness and headaches. I believe there is potential for serious risks in these diets, including dehydration, nausea, and vomiting. Ketosis may be especially dangerous to an individual who is a prediabetic. These diets may also pose unknown risks.

(3-48) *High-protein diets and protein-sparing diets.* A number of books emphasize eating foods high in protein and drinking plenty of water or noncaloric fluids to prevent the formation of kidney stones. Among them are *The Last Chance Diet* by Robert Linn and Sandra Lee Stuart, *The Doctor's Quick Weight Loss Diet* by Irwin Maxwell Stillman, and *The Complete Scarsdale Medical Diet* by Dr. Herman Tarnower and Samm Sinclair Baker. These diets are monotonous and, at least in the beginning, make the dieter tired. They may produce headaches, nausea, vomiting, diarrhea, cramps, irregular heartbeat, and even death. Under no circumstances should these diets be undertaken if you have liver or kidney disease. See your physician immediately, if you feel faint. The Cambridge Diet (of Dr. Alan Howard) is a liquid diet sold in cans and contains 330 calories per day. After a law suit on the grounds of misleading claims, Cambridge now warns against the use of the diet for more than four consecutive weeks. It also advises consultation with your doctor even though the company provides a nonmedical counselor (the Cambridge counselor is in part a salesperson). If you use this diet, do so with your physician's supervision.

(3-49) *Diet clubs.* TOPS (Take Off Pounds Sensibly), Weight Watchers, and other group approaches to weight loss have helped many people. If you feel secure and are able to laugh at yourself, these clubs may be for you.

TOPS is a nonprofit corporation with nominal membership dues. Competition among the participants over weight loss (you may be a queen for losing the most weight), strong group pressure, confessionals, and weekly weigh-ins all emphasize accomplishments and help make TOPS work.

Weight Watchers is a for-profit corporation similar in many ways to TOPS. It asks for a greater commitment: You pay a weekly fee whether you attend your meeting or not. There are weekly lectures, and many commercial products are available. In general, TOPS is more homey, and Weight Watchers is more polished.

(3-50) *Drugs.* Until the early 1970s, physicians who specialized in weight reduction (sometimes called bariatricians) were very likely to hand patients a box of pills at each visit. The pills came in many colors and sizes and were taken several times a day. There is little reason to think that any of the drugs affected fat reduction, and many of them were hazardous.

Fortunately, this practice has decreased greatly in recent years, because of both unfavorable publicity and federal regulations on the use of these drugs. Nevertheless, from time to time a physician will prescribe a drug to be used as a reducing aid. These drugs include stimulants such as amphetamine, Plegine, Preludin, Pre-Sate Syndrox, Tenuate, and Tepanil. A new drug, fenfluramine, is marketed as Pondimin. These stim-

Nutrition and Diet

ulants can cause nervousness, restlessness, tremors, loss of sleep, and the feeling that the heart is racing. Some people will become dependent on or addicted to them. Fenfluramine may cause sleepiness, diarrhea, and a dry mouth. If stimulants have any effect at all on weight reduction, it is only for the first few weeks.

Until the early 1970s, other drugs were also widely used in weight-reduction programs. The heart stimulant digitalis produces a loss of appetite, but only when a person has taken a poisonous dose. Thyroid hormone also produces weight loss, but in doses that are intoxicating. Small doses of thyroid hormone may, however, be appropriate in those who are on very restricted diets, since these people stop making their own hormones during this time. Chorionic gonadotropin, which is derived from the urine of pregnant women, has never been shown to be effective or safe. Diuretics, or water pills, shed water but not fat. Laxatives evacuate the bowel but do nothing to fat.

There is little advantage in using drugs to bring about weight reduction, and a great deal of danger. If a person is really obese and consequently in poor health, the extra strain placed on the body by these drugs can only make matters worse. And some drugs, when mismanaged, kill.

(3-51) *Surgery.* A drastic approach to weight reduction is surgery. In an operation known as a jejuno-ileal bypass, the intestines are severed and then rejoined in such a manner that food is not absorbed into the body. The operation may work by actually suppressing the appetite for an as-yet unknown reason. It is usually reserved for persons whose massive overweight is a clear risk to life.

(3-52) *How to lose weight.* There are hundreds of weight-reduction diets. One plan may be easier for one person to follow than another, but for any diet to succeed, the body must use more calories than it takes in. For the average person who wants to lose 5 to 15 pounds, here are some simple rules:

1. Buy an accurate bathroom scale, and place it on a solid floor. Since most bathroom scales use springs and rarely give an accurate weight for very long, you should purchase a scale like those found in a physician's office. But these scales, which use a balance beam with weights, are expensive, and many people cannot afford them.

2. On a sheet of paper, rule off two months of days on the horizontal—about a quarter-inch for each day. Then, on the vertical, rule down the number of pounds you wish to lose from your present weight. Tack your chart to the wall over the scale along with a pencil on a string.

3. Every morning weigh yourself completely nude and put a check in the appropriate box.

After Middle Age

4. During the first week count your calories each day, and place the number in a box under the day.

5. Analyze the chart at the end of the week. If your weight has not varied more than 2 or 3 pounds during the week, you are probably burning as many calories as you take in. If your weight appears to go up during the week, decrease the number of calories ingested per day by 400 during the following week. For example, if you find you took in an average of 3000 calories per day during the first week and gained weight, eat only 2600 calories per day the next week. Follow this schedule of reducing calories by 400 per day each week until your weight is stabilized.

6. When your weight is stabilized, decide how fast you wish to lose weight. One to two pounds per week is ideal. To lose one pound you must take in 3500 calories fewer per week than you did when your weight was stable. For example, if you ate 2000 calories per day for a stable weight, you would be able to lose 1 pound per week on 1500 calories per day or 2 pounds a week on 1000 calories. Decide what caloric intake is possible, and stick to it until the desired amount of weight is lost.

(3-53) *Aids to losing weight*

1. Keep track of your weight on your weight chart every morning.

2. Plan your calories so that you can eat three small meals a day. Don't skip breakfast. If you have a martini every night, include it (200 calories).

3. Try to have all your food intake at the same place each day. (Eat out as little as possible.) Make sure the table is set the same way—never eat standing up or while watching television. When you eat, concentrate on eating.

4. Cut your food into small pieces. Put only one piece of food in your mouth at a time. Chew the food completely and swallow it before putting something else into your mouth. Put down your fork between mouthfuls.

5. Unless there are medical reasons for doing so, never eat between meals or before bedtime. (Remember: Always eat in the same place.)

6. Exercise sensibly. While exercising may not help you eliminate weight, it will decrease your appetite.

7. Once you are at the desired weight, find the caloric intake you need to maintain it, and then follow the above rules for six months.

8. Many people "splurge eat," consuming several hundred or more calories within a few minutes. Splurge eating may happen when you are bored or depressed, anxious or angry. Try to understand what causes your splurge eating and distract yourself at these times by getting out of the house, exercising, talking on the telephone—whatever will get your mind off food.

Nutrition and Diet

(3-54) Four excellent books on dieting and nutrition are:

Theodore Berland and the editors of Consumer Guide, *Rating the Diets,* Signet, New York, 1979.
Jane Brody, *Jane Brody's Nutrition Book,* W. W. Norton and Company, New York, 1981. (This book not only covers dieting and nutrition, but also presents excellent plans for meals and menus)
Jean Mayer, *A Diet for Living,* Pocket, New York, 1977.
Albert J. Stunkard, *The Pain of Obesity,* Bull Publishing Company, Palo Alto, California, 1976.

(3-55)

Weights and Measurement Equivalencies

60 drops	=	1 teaspoon
3 teaspoons	=	1 tablespoon
2 tablespoons	=	1 liquid ounce
4 tablespoons	=	¼ cup
16 tablespoons	=	1 cup
8 ounces	=	1 cup liquid
2 cups	=	1 pint
2 pints	=	1 quart
4 quarts	=	1 gallon
16 ounces	=	1 pound

(3-56)

Conversion Tables

From U.S. to Metric Measurements

U.S.	Metric
1 inch	= 2.54 centimeters
1 foot	− 30.48 centimeters
1 foot	= 0.30 meters
1 ounce	= 28.35 grams
1 pound	= 453.6 grams
1 pint	= 473.2 milliliters
1 quart	= 946.4 milliliters
1 quart	= 0.94 liters
1 gallon	= 3.78 liters

From Metric to U.S. Measurements

Metric	U.S.
1 centimeter	= 0.39 inches
1 meter	= 3.28 feet
1 gram	= 0.032 ounces
1 kilogram	= 2.2 pounds
1 liter	= 1.06 quarts

4

Foreign Travel

(4-1) Many people as they become older find they have more time and money for foreign travel. With age, however, travel becomes more and more difficult. The body and the psyche adapt less well to the changes and inconveniences encountered during travel—for instance, a person with arthritis or severe heart disease cannot run through airports. The trip must be planned accordingly.

For people who have not traveled much, an experienced travel agent can be of considerable help in making trips both more pleasurable and less stressful. Travel agents make their living from commissions, receiving a percentage of what they sell. Their services do not raise a traveler's cost, and many times a travel agent can find ways to decrease costs. Large travel agencies and agents who are themselves older frequently know how to provide arrangements for elderly people who must be on a special diet, use a wheelchair, or cannot walk up steps. Although group tours designed for the elderly are usually promoted by clubs, churches, or national organizations, occasionally a travel agent will know about one. The number of specific group tours planned for the elderly, the handicapped, or both is increasing. If a person is blind or in a wheelchair, these tours provide aids to overcome natural or artificial obstacles. TWA, for example, has a motorized lift for wheelchairs in a number of cities where a person would otherwise have to climb steps to get into a plane. Amtrak has just built a barrier-free station in Miami and is outfitting some of its trains with seats for the handicapped.

Foreign Travel

AIR TRAVEL

(4-2) *Swelling of ankles.* Though airplanes have made travel much easier, they have also produced some problems. Long flights often require passengers to sit in one place for many hours. Because movement of the legs helps the blood flow back to the heart, blood will pool in legs and feet that remain idle, causing them to become swollen. This is particularly likely to happen if you have poor circulation.

Many people, out of habit, cross their legs when they sit. The pressure of one leg on top of the other for any length of time tends to cut off blood circulation. This produces the feeling that your "foot is asleep," but also produces swelling of the foot and leg. Learn to sit with your legs uncrossed.

Tight-fitting clothes also can cut off circulation. Garters, girdles, tight belts, and stockings with elastic tops are particularly apt to decrease circulation. If you have not done so already, take a tip from the younger generation and, at least when you travel, dress less formally.

If you are steady on your feet, take an aisle seat and get up frequently for short walks. (Be sure to hold onto the seat backs while standing or walking.) If you are less steady, you can help yourself with frequent movement (shifting) of the legs while remaining in your seat. You can also perform isometric exercises, in which one muscle is pitted against another or against an immovable object, such as the floor or a wall. Aboard a plane you might try pressing your feet against the floor as hard as possible for a count of five, then release for a count of five. Repeat until you begin to tire. This exercise may be done every 15 minutes throughout a trip.

(4-3) *Ear pain.* Aero-otitis media (air in the middle ear) may accompany changes in air pressure that occur within the cabin of an aircraft as the plane ascends and descends. You can understand how this occurs if you think of the middle ear as a small balloon, the stem of which empties into the back of the throat. (The stem corresponds to the eustachian tube.) When the plane ascends and cabin pressure decreases, the high-pressure air in the middle ear easily passes to the throat, but when the plane descends and air pressure becomes higher in the cabin, passage of air into the middle ear is more difficult, and if there is any blockage of the eustachian tube, air cannot pass at all. The result is a partial vacuum in the middle ear with hearing loss, a sensation of fullness in the ear, and autophony (hearing one's own voice louder in the affected ear). The attack usually passes off within a few hours, but if it persists for any length of time, it can be treated in an emergency room.

Aerootitis can be prevented by either yawning or swallowing during the descent. Chewing gum may be helpful. A person who repeatedly has trouble can ask the physician to suggest a nasal decongestant spray that can be taken just before the plane begins to descend. The nasal decongestant dilates the eustachian tube, allowing air to pass through it more easily.

(4-4) *Motion sickness.* The sweating, the cold, clammy feeling, and the nausea and vomiting that may occur on bumpy airplane rides or on stormy seas can make travel extremely unpleasant. As a rule, the larger the airplane or ship, the less likely it is to produce motion sickness. There are a number of medications that can be taken to prevent motion sickness. All produce some drowsiness, but I have found that meclizine, an antihistamine that is sold without a prescription as Bonine, is good at preventing air sickness and has little sedative effects. Moreover, it does not have the disagreeable taste of Dramamine. One tablet (25 mg) of meclizine taken an hour before beginning a trip should be effective for about twelve hours. When travel lasts longer, a tablet can be taken once every twelve hours. One recent study indicates a teaspoon of ginger prevents motion sickness better than Dramamine.

(4-5) *Sleep and rhythms.* Many people who travel across several time zones in only a few hours find that they have difficulty adjusting their sleep habits for a few days after arrival. The internal clock, with its preset alarms, keeps ticking, and it is not easily reset. For example, when a businesswoman flies from the west coast to the east coast, she loses three hours of her day during the five hours spent on the airplane. When she left, it was morning; when she arrives, it is evening. By the time she gets to her hotel, it may be time to go to bed. She is not tired and so has difficulty falling asleep.

The problem of going from east to west is just the opposite. The businesswoman may leave later in the day and, after two meals on the airplane, arrive on the west coast only two hours later (by the clock). As a result, she might eat five meals in a single day and feel bloated. And, since people often eat in restaurants when they travel, there is a tendency to eat more than usual or to eat very rich or heavy food. The most difficult problem, however, is waking up two to three hours earlier than usual.

The reasons for these difficulties have been explored for over 100 years, but only now are they becoming understood. The organization of everyone's life is in part determined by the clock. It is expected that certain things will happen at certain times of the day, week, month, and year, and for the most part they do. We usually get upset when they do not.

But it is not just external clocks that determine when things will happen: We have internal clocks that control when we get hungry and when we get sleepy. Thus, when a person is used to going to sleep at a certain time and awakening at another, the internal clock locks into those times

Foreign Travel

preparing the body for sleep and waking. This clock is slow to recognize shifts in time zones.

Following a few simple rules will help the internal clock adjust to external time changes. Eat lightly on travel days. If you are inclined to eat in three-star restaurants in France, do not do so on your first night there. If you are going to be in one place for more than a few days, go to bed at the time you normally would go to bed: If you go to bed at 11:00 P.M. at home, go to bed at 11:00 P.M. in your host city. If you have trouble sleeping, this is an appropriate time to take a sleeping pill.

It helps to view falling asleep much as you view catching a train—you have to be at the right place at the right time in order to catch the train. Whether out at a party or in a chair reading a book, you may get a feeling of sleepiness around the usual bedtime. You can accept it by getting into bed and preparing for sleep, or you can reject it by continuing your activity. If you decide not to become a passenger on the sleep train, you may feel it pulling away without you, and again you are wide awake. In fact, you may now have trouble falling asleep for several hours—until the next train comes. For many people, the arrival of the sleep train is scheduled by the internal clock.

(4-6) *Ozone,* a colorless gas that is a form of oxygen, is present in significant amounts at 35,000 ft above the earth. In very cold climates such as the polar region, ozone is present at even lower altitudes. Exposure to ozone for long periods in aircraft can produce shortness of breath, coughing, chest pains and dizziness, especially in people with cardiac or respiratory diseases. Most commonly, people are only affected when going over the north pole or on nonstop flights between New York and Tokyo. Several airlines have placed filters on many of their planes to alleviate this problem. Nevertheless, if you are making a long overseas flight and have cardiac or respiratory problems, ask when you make your reservation if the airline has installed ozone filters.

INTERNATIONAL IMMUNIZATIONS

(4-7) The function of immunization is to enable the body to fight off an attack by a virus or bacterium that produces illness. To immunize, an inactivated form of the virus or bacterium is injected into the body. It produces a specific defense (antibody). When the active form (the real infection) invades the body, it is met full force by the antibody.

Immunizations are not required when you leave or reenter the United States. Currently, however, inoculation against yellow fever is encouraged when you return from countries where yellow fever exists.

After Middle Age

These include some countries in Asia, Africa, and South America. A yellow fever vaccination is good for ten years. A few countries, particularly in Africa, require evidence of immunization from all travelers. While the United States does not require it, a cholera vaccination may be required before entering some countries in the Middle East and Asia. When traveling to some countries it may be advisable to take an antimalarial agent (usually chloroquine) and immune globulin to prevent hepatitis. Chloroquine is taken once a week beginning one week before the trip, during the trip, and for a number of weeks after returning. Immune globulin is given by injection as close to departure as possible. Before traveling outside the United States, check with the nearest Public Health Service Office, listed in the telephone directory under U.S. Government, Public Health Service, or write to International Health Information and Visa Medical Activity, Division of Quarantine, Freeway Park (16TC) Room 207, Center for Disease Control, Atlanta, Georgia 30333.

(4-8) *Cholera* causes massive diarrhea and vomiting, and when not properly treated it can cause death. It has been eliminated in most developed nations. Unfortunately, it is not proven that cholera immunizations are successful in preventing it, and they are usually painful. Two injections are given four to six weeks apart.

(4-9) *Typhus* begins with generalized tiredness and headache. This is followed by abrupt chills and fever, and by the fourth to seventh day a rash appears over all the body but the face, palms, and soles. The mortality rate from typhus used to be as high as 40 percent, but with today's antibiotic treatments, there are usually no deaths. Immunizations are recommended by health authorities in areas of epidemic typhus, such as southeastern Europe and parts of Africa and South America. Two injections are given four to six weeks apart.

(4-10) *Smallpox* was once a major cause of disfigurement and death, but it has been entirely eliminated from the planet. Routine vaccination is no longer recommended.

(4-11) *Polio.* Because the number of children getting polio immunizations has unfortunately decreased, the disease, which should have been eliminated fifteen years ago, is still with us. Although it remains primarily a disease of the young, it can occur at any age. If somehow you have missed getting the polio vaccination (either oral or injected) with a followup booster a year later for the injected vaccine, ask your physician whether you should get it now. Most physicians will only recommend vaccination for adults who are going to foreign countries where the incidence of polio is high. There is small risk (about five cases per year in the United States) of getting polio from the live oral vaccine, and this possibility must be weighed against getting polio when you are traveling. The

Foreign Travel

injected vaccine has few risks to it, but must be given in three injections one to two months apart, with a fourth dose one year later.

(4-12) *Tetanus.* Tetanus is caused by a bacterium that enters the body through wounds. Wounds open to the air are safe from tetanus, but deep, closed wounds, such as punctures from nails or knives, which the air cannot penetrate, may produce a fatal illness. Have any puncture wound cleaned by a physician, who should also give you a tetanus booster if you haven't had one within five years. This assumes that you have already been vaccinated once against tetanus (it is the "T" in "DPT" shot—diphtheria, pertussis, tetanus). If you have not, then you should get the vaccination on the next regular visit to your physician. After the initial shot, you should get a booster every ten years.

(4-13) *Typhoid,* which comes from contaminated food or water, starts with a chilly sensation, tiredness, and a headache. Within a week the temperature rises and rounded, rose-colored spots may develop on the abdomen and chest. They disappear within two to five days, but the temperature may remain elevated for a total of two weeks. Toward the end of this period there may be considerable diarrhea. Only in severe cases is it necessary to administer antibiotics. The mortality is very low. If you are going to be in an area where typhoid is present or where water is untreated, you should be immunized against typhoid. Two injections just under the skin are given one month apart.

TRAVELER'S DIARRHEA IN FOREIGN LANDS

(4-14) *Traveler's diarrhea,* commonly called "tourista," is an illness of sudden onset that consists primarily of frequent and watery stools. It may also be accompanied by nausea, vomiting, abdominal cramps, chills, and a slight fever. This annoying ailment is most likely to occur within a week of your arrival in a developing country. It is a consequence of exposure to bacteria to which your body is unaccustomed. The new bacteria—some varieties of *Escherichia coli*—are only slightly different from those already in your gastrointestinal system, but they may make you sick. If you are in a country for any length of time, you will adjust to the new bacteria, but the odds are in favor of your getting sick first. If you are going to be in a country for only a short time, it is best to avoid exposure to the bacteria. Drink only bottled water and other bottled drinks—do not even use tap water to brush your teeth, and do not eat uncooked foods. Water that is used to clean foods, particularly fruits and salad vegetables, will also contain bacteria. If fruits and vegetables are uncooked, eat them only if you peel them yourself. Otherwise, make sure all food you eat is cooked.

After Middle Age

One product that seems to be successful in treating traveler's diarrhea is Pepto-Bismol. Two tablespoons should be taken at the onset of diarrhea, continuing with 1 tablespoon every half hour until the diarrhea stops, but not more than 8 tablespoons. If the diarrhea persists for more than 48 hours, see a physician. A physician also should be seen if the stool has blood in it. Some travelers take Pepto-Bismol routinely to prevent traveler's diarrhea. They take 4 tablespoons before each meal for the first 7 days after arriving in a country where "tourista" is common. This adds up to a number of bottles, though, and is inconvenient to carry. Pepto-Bismol should not be taken by persons taking other medicines unless it is prescribed by a physician, because it decreases the absorption of many drugs by the intestine.

In a 1978 study of Peace Corps volunteers in Kenya a tetracycline antibiotic, doxycycline, was shown to provide excellent prophylaxis against traveler's diarrhea. While 9 of 21 volunteers taking a placebo (sugar pill) got traveler's diarrhea within 5 weeks of their arrival in Kenya, only 1 of 18 taking doxycycline did. The volunteers took a 100-mg capsule daily for 5 weeks, and even when they discontinued the drug they seemed to be protected. If you are going to a country known to have a high incidence of traveler's diarrhea, such as Mexico, you should ask a physician if it is advisable for you to take doxycycline.

Doxycycline, in 100-mg capsules, comes as Doxy-II in blue capsules marked "USV" and as Vibramycin in blue capsules marked "Pfizer 095." Because doxycycline stains the teeth of young children, pregnant women and young children should avoid taking it. If you develop diarrhea while taking doxycycline, you should see a physician since it may be due to bacteria that are not killed by doxycycline. Some people who take doxycycline become especially prone to severe sunburn, and because of this possibility you should stay out of sustained direct sunlight when taking it; alternatively, use a sunscreen with a high number (9-31). If you develop a rash while taking doxycycline, talk to your physician. If you cannot reach a physician, discontinue taking doxycycline for prophylaxis against traveler's diarrhea.

(**4-15**) *Iodochlorhydroxyquin (Entero-Vioform, Mexaform, Clioquinol)*, an antidiarrhea drug, was taken off the market in the United States because it can produce severe neurological side effects. Nevertheless, it can still be purchased both with and without a prescription in many countries. It or any compound containing it should not be used. If you are given an antidiarrhea medication, ask your doctor or druggist specifically if it contains iodochlorhydroxyquin.

(**4-16**) *Diphenoxylate,* available in tablet form as Lomotil, is a combination of a narcoticlike agent and atropine or belladonna. Therefore, it must be prescribed by a physician. In the recommended dosage Lomotil is not addictive, but take care not to use more than the prescribed amount. The larger doses will not produce a "high," but the atropine will make you sick.

The initial dosage is one tablet, followed by a second tablet if the diarrhea continues beyond 6 hours. If necessary, you can take 2 tablets every 6 hours thereafter for a period of 24 hours. If the diarrhea has not subsided after 24 hours, see a physician. Lomotil is a white tablet with "SEARLE" written on one side and "61" on the other. It should be used with caution by people who have liver disease or who are taking any form of tranquilizer at the same time.

SECURING MEDICAL ASSISTANCE WHILE TRAVELING

(4-17) Getting sick anywhere can produce many anxieties. In a foreign country, where you do not know anyone and cannot speak the language, it can be frightening. Finding a good physician abroad may be difficult, not because they do not exist—good physicians abound in large cities throughout the world even in the most underdeveloped countries—but because language and customs are so different.

If you are going to be staying in one place for any time, identify a physician before you start your journey. Several organizations can be of help. For $3, American Express cardholders can get a list of physicians around the world. Call or write the closest international office. Intermedic provides the names of English-speaking physicians in foreign countries. For a single person to join costs $6 a year, for a family $10 a year. To get a membership card and directory, write Intermedic Inc., 777 Third Avenue, New York, N. Y. 10017. Diabetes Travel Services, Inc., 39 E. 52nd Street, New York, N.Y. 10022 provides information on diabetes treatment and specialists around the world.

In a real emergency abroad have your hotel call a taxi or ambulance to take you to a medical school hospital or, if that is not possible, to the largest convenient community hospital. English has become the language of the medical world, and you should be able to communicate with some of the hospital staff. If you have more time, call the American embassy or consulate. They will have a list of physicians they have used.

(4-18) *Other tips.* Unless you are really ill and have no choice, do not accept an injection unless the needle is disposable. Reused needles often spread hepatitis from person to person. Disposable needles usually come packaged in plastic or paper. Avoid over-the-counter drugs that contain dipyrone. Dipyrone is used in some pain killers, but can cause serious

After Middle Age

blood disease. Buy aspirin, not aspirinlike compounds, since you cannot be sure what other ingredients are included.

WHAT TO TAKE WITH YOU

(4-19) Travelers going abroad should pack the following.

1. Certificates of vaccination or immunization (if you are going to a country where these are needed).

2. If you are taking prescription medication, a typewritten copy of prescription, with trade and generic names, and dosage. If you run out of your medicine or it becomes damaged, you can have the prescription refilled. For similar reasons carry along a prescription for your eyeglasses.

3. If you use digitalis and anticoagulants, take along an extra supply. They vary considerably in quality from country to country. Carry some in your purse or pocket and some in your suitcase, or have someone else carry the extra supply.

4. Aspirin or other pain relievers.

5. Sleeping pills if prescribed by your physician.

6. Pepto-Bismol, doxycyline, or Lomotil.

7. Medication for motion sickness.

8. If you use a heating pad, electric shaver, or other electrical appliances, you will find that many countries have different voltages and shapes for their plugs. Hardware and variety stores sell universal electric adapters that will allow you to use your appliance. The adapters should include both a transformer to reduce the voltage from 220 to the 110 U.S. appliances use and a plug that will fit into foreign sockets.

5

Psychological and Psychiatric Problems

(5-1) While getting older decreases the risk of developing devastating psychiatric disorders such as schizophrenia, the development of other psychiatric problems becomes more likely. Fortunately, most of the psychiatric problems associated with advancing age can be prevented, treated, or greatly ameliorated. Because of health impediments, retirement, deaths of close friends or relatives, children leaving home, and loss of income and consequent loss of financial flexibility, there is a tendency for older people to become isolated and to be without the psychological support they had when they were younger. It is more difficult to have meaningful social interactions and to find people in whom one can confide. Many people face not only these social realities but also the negative attitudes of the young toward the old. Just as pervasive is older people's rejection of their contemporaries. For the unprepared person, isolation—if it occurs—can lead to loneliness, anxiety, and depression. Others who remain active, have a high self-regard, or are comfortable with solitude remain psychologically well.

MENTAL RESERVE

(5-2) The body is built to manage physical activities easily and to use its reserve capacity when stressed. For example, a healthy heart can pump much more blood than is usually needed. Its reserve capacities are used only when strenuous physical activity is undertaken. The mind, too, has an enormous reserve capacity that goes unused most of the time. But as people grow older, the reserves of physical and mental energy dimin-

After Middle Age

ish. It becomes harder to rise to the demands of stress and change. It is necessary to learn compensation strategies and how best to use one's valuable store of previous experience to meet stressful situations.

COMPENSATION STRATEGIES

(5-3) Chapter 2, on living independently, provides many suggestions for maintaining psychological health. There are a number of other strategies that can also be used. One problem is that some people become firmer in their opinions as they get older, less able to adapt to change and less tolerant of others. While it is unfair to say that all rigidity or resistance to change is unhealthy, at times such attitudes bring confrontation and stress.

For some, change requires learning something new. If you have made learning a lifelong process, you will want to continue it as you become older. But if you stopped learning new things after high school or college, it is difficult to begin again at 65. For those who are interested in learning, the opportunities are abundant. Public television and radio have many fine programs. Most public school systems teach courses both during the day and at night. These courses cover everything from cooking to car repair to literature. Of course, the programs that get you out of the house also provide an opportunity to interact with other people.

It is natural for people to become more conservative with age. Their views of the world might have been formed two or three generations ago. Since many things have changed in that time, their present-day behavior may seem cautious. When people feel they have a great deal to lose and relatively little to gain, they are unlikely to change. By the same token, some people find that giving no answers or taking no action is preferable to the risk of being wrong—and thus become nonparticipants. Certainly their actions will be slowed by these concerns. Thus it is important that as people become older they maintain risk-taking behavior. The risks should be affordable risks, however; there is no point in risking a broken bone or one's savings. But experimentation with new kinds of seed in the garden, new foods, and new places for vacations are affordable risks for most people.

Probably the most important factor in maintaining mental health for most people of advancing age is generativity—that is, being creative, productive, useful. During younger years, generativity often means bearing and guiding the next generation. Others may create through their work. Where relations across generations remain good, and geographical distances are not great, generativity can be continued by guiding

Psychological and Psychiatric Problems

grandchildren or great-grandchildren. Others can continue to generate through working in gardens, handling their own investments, or contributing time to charitable activities with a great deal of satisfaction.

When people fail to be generative, they turn inward, and while turning inward works for a few people, most stagnate. If mental reserve is diminished and compensation strategies fail, psychological problems develop. They must be recognized and treated.

NERVOUSNESS AND ANXIETY

(5-4) *Nervousness* is a general term that refers to restlessness, tension, irritability, or excitability. For most people nervousness is basically a mild form of anxiety—a feeling of fear or apprehension about things to come. Strictly speaking, fear is apprehension about a specific object, situation, or action, while anxiety is more diffuse, taking the form of a nameless dread, a vague sense of threat, or an exaggerated response to a real problem.

(5-5) *Causes of anxiety.* As we grow older, we must find new ways to adapt to the changes in our bodies, in our social lives, and in the society around us. From middle age on, the effort required in each adaptation to change becomes greater. There are usually fewer choices open to us, and our mental reserves may be drained.

Learning to adjust to and accept changes in our bodies and in our social affairs is often difficult and stressful. Anxiety may develop, particularly when there is loss of capability or failure in some endeavor. Some elderly people handle this anxiety, without their being aware of it, by becoming rigid and inflexible in their thinking. This response has obvious disadvantages, but it does provide a framework in which to function—permitting the illusion of maintaining a measure of control over oneself and others. This may be very important for the person battling loneliness, illness, or the fear of impending death. Along with this "stubborn thinking" may come suspiciousness and apparent forgetfulness. It is possible for an outsider to mistake these efforts at managing anxiety for the beginnings of senility.

(5-6) *The symptoms of anxiety.* Anxiety takes many physical forms. There may be rapid breathing and rapid pulse, breathlessness, awareness of one's heartbeat (palpitation), choking sensations, restlessness, trembling, sweating, and flushing. In distress over such symptoms, people may constrict their activity. They may develop a fear of travel, or of being left alone, or of being helpless. The anxious person may also experience a variety of sleep problems, most often insomnia.

After Middle Age

Anxiety may be experienced for a few minutes or hours, or it may last for weeks or months. It may simply cause an uncomfortable state of mind, or it may be severe enough to render a person incapable of performing routine tasks at work or at home. From time to time almost everyone has an episode of anxiety that lasts up to a few days and is clearly connected with a specific event. That is a part of normal living. Nevertheless, continued or severe anxiety should always be brought to the attention of a physician, for it can be produced not only by psychological factors, but by medical factors as well. Prolonged anxiety that has no medical cause is usually accompanied by depression.

(5-7) *Treatment of anxiety.* Before prescribing any treatment for anxiety, your physician will try to determine its source. Generally, by this time, you will have considered the obvious possible causes. If the source is evident, a treatment plan can usually be developed. If you cannot determine the underlying cause and deal with the problem by self-analysis, however, exploration with a psychiatrist or another highly trained professional in the field of mental health usually is necessary. Such a specialist may prescribe some medication; in fact, drugs used to treat anxiety are the most frequently prescribed drugs in the country. In the opinion of many professionals the use of antianxiety drugs, which people tend to lump together under the general heading "tranquilizers," has gotten out of hand. Most people who are taking these drugs should not be doing so. Except in special circumstances, to temporarily control anxiety's symptoms, these drugs can do more harm than good.

(5-8) *Drugs for anxiety.* Phenobarbital (average dosage 45 to 90 mg per day) comes in 15-, 30-, 60-, and 100-mg white tablets and is mildly effective against anxiety. It produces sedation, although paradoxically it may at times also produce excitement. It may also produce depression, and it can be addictive, so it must be used with caution. Because phenobarbital overdosage can be lethal, it must be kept away from children.

Meprobamate (Equanil, Miltown, average dosage 800 to 1600 mg per day) comes in 200- and 400-mg scored white tablets. Tybamate (Tabatran, average dosage 750 to 1000 mg per day) comes in 125-, 150-, and 350-mg green tablets. Meprobamate and Tybamate have the same addictive properties as phenobarbital. Overdosages can be lethal.

The following drugs are effective against anxiety and are relatively safe. They produce some daytime drowsiness and can also be used for nighttime sedation, but long-term use can lead to dependence (5-22). Their side effects include unsteady walking, confusion (not knowing where you are, what time it is, or even who you are), and at times, paradoxically, excitation, increased anxiety, and aggressiveness. Overdoses are rarely lethal.

Psychological and Psychiatric Problems

Chlordiazepoxide (Librium, average dosage 15 to 30 mg per day) comes in 5-mg green and yellow, 10-mg green and black, and 25-mg green-and white capsules.

Diazepam (Valium, average dosage 6 to 40 mg per day) comes in scored tablets: 2-mg white, 5-mg yellow, and 10-mg blue with a "V" punched out.

Oxazepam (Serax, average dosage 45 to 90 mg per day) comes in 10-mg pink and white, 15-mg red and white, and 30-mg maroon and white capsules.

Clorazepate (Tranxene, average dosage 30 mg per day) comes in 3.75-mg gray and white, 7.5-mg gray and maroon, and 15-mg gray capsules.

Prazepam (Centrax, average dose 30 mg per day) comes in 5-mg yellow, 10-mg green, and 20-mg yellow capsules labeled "Centrax."

Lorazepam (Ativan, average dosage 2 to 6 mg per day) comes in 0.5-mg five-sided tablets with a raised "A" on one side and "WYETH 81" on the other, 1-mg five-sided tablets with a raised "A" on one side and "WYETH 64" on the other, and 2-mg white oval tablets with "WYETH" on one side and "65" on the other.

Alprazolam (Xanax, average dosage 1.5 to 3 mg per day) comes in 0.25-mg white, 0.5-mg peach, and 1-mg lavender ovoid tablets labeled "Xanax." Alprazolam also may be used to treat depression and panic disorder.

Halazepam (Paxipam, average maintenance dose 20 to 40 mg three or four times per day) comes in 20-mg orange tablets labeled "Schering 251" and 40-mg white tablets labeled "Schering 538."

DEPRESSION

(5-9) *Causes of depression.* The hallmark of depression is a sense of hopelessness. Other typical feelings of someone afflicted with depression are worthlessness, helplessness, sadness, guilt, and boredom. Physical symptoms include insomnia, morning tiredness, loss of appetite, body pains and discomforts, and loss of sexual interest. Depression can be as insignificant as the transient "blues" that everyone experiences from time to time, or it can be so severe as to shatter all self-esteem, any sense of reality, and the ability to maintain normal relationships with others. Severe depression can lead to suicide. Depressed people frequently become withdrawn and refuse help, producing considerable difficulties for all concerned. At times, depression is precipitated by an obvious cause, such as the death of someone close, the loss of a job, or some other marked change in life. If this lasts less than two months, it is called grief reaction. When it lasts longer, it is called a reactive depression, meaning a depres-

After Middle Age

sion that is a reaction to an event. On the other hand, a depression may not be associated with any specific life alteration. Some depressed people feel so bad about themselves that they feel responsible for their condition. This is referred to as an endogenous depression, implying that there is a biochemical cause within the person for the illness.

(5-10) *Treatment of depression.* Almost all depressions will go away by themselves, given enough time. The time, however, can be lengthy—sometimes several years—during which there may be the danger of suicide. Fortunately, treatment usually can greatly shorten the period of depression, relieving much suffering as well as preventing suicide. A mild depression can usually be helped by a program of planned activity, understanding the issues involved, and regular contact with concerned relatives and friends. A moderate depression can usually be treated by psychotherapy or an antidepressant drug, or both. A severe depression usually requires a brief stay in the hospital, where an antidepressant drug (5-15) and/or electroconvulsive therapy (ECT) (5-16) may be used.

(5-11) *The criteria for deciding* when to see a physician about depression are: (1) when your personal discomfort goes beyond the regular ups and downs of normal life; (2) when there is any earnest thought of suicide; or (3) when the depression causes your performance at work, at home, or in social settings to fall below its usual level for a month or longer. You may be in a position to help someone whom you think is depressed but who is not getting professional help. Apply the same criteria to that person's situation. Since many people are much more resistant to getting psychiatric treatment than they are to getting medical treatment, it is frequently difficult to help. My advice is to be honest. Tell such relatives or friends that you are concerned about them, that they are eating and sleeping poorly, crying all the time, or exhibiting whatever other symptoms have become apparent to you. Since the problem has not resolved itself, it is necessary to seek professional help. Accompany them to the physician to ensure that appointments are kept.

SUICIDE

(5-12) People most frequently have suicidal thoughts during periods of depression, great mental or emotional stress, or considerable pain. Psychotic individuals may kill themselves because a voice tells them to do so or because suicide is the only way they can rid themselves of psychological torment. The most common cause of suicide, however, is a strong personal conviction that life is simply not worth living, or that the person wants to control his or her destiny, including the time and circumstances of death, leaving it neither to nature nor to accident. If a friend or relative speaks of suicide, do not dismiss it as a bid for attention. It is unusual for a person to commit suicide successfully without having talked about it to a relative or friend several times in the preceding few months.

(5-13) *What to do when you think you might kill yourself.* Be sure to seek help. Do one of the following: (1) Call your physician and ask for psychiatric help or go to a hospital emergency room. (2) Call a suicide prevention center. If one exists in your area, the number can be obtained from the directory or by dialing information (5-14). (3) Call your clergyman; many are well trained in psychological counseling. (4) Call a relative or a friend—but this is something to consider carefully. A good friend will always want to help you within the limits of her or his ability. But friends or relatives might be so afraid of making an error in judgment while trying to help out in such a critical situation that they might very well withdraw from the relationship with you out of fear. (5) If none of the above are available to you, call the police. This may sound strange to those who think a police officer's only function is law enforcement. Actually, the police are regularly involved in people's most serious personal problems and can be very calm and supportive in distressing situations. Remember, the police often have the unhappy task of investigating a suicide. They would rather prevent it.

(5-14) *What to do when you think someone else intends to commit suicide.* What you do when you believe someone may commit suicide depends on a number of factors, but the mere fact that you try to help someone can have an important positive effect. If you have a strong belief, religious or otherwise, that suicide is wrong, you must act on that belief. On the other hand, if you have a fierce conviction that every person has a right to complete self-determination, you will do nothing. Most of us fall between these extremes. Our attitude toward the suicide of a person who is in severe terminal psychological or physical pain or is extremely and permanently debilitated is different from our attitude toward someone who has a possibly transient difficulty and good chances of recovery. In the latter situation, most of us will make every effort to prevent suicide.

A person who fully intends to commit suicide must first choose a method. What is chosen depends in large part on what is available. Thus, men commonly choose guns and women sleeping pills. Any close friends or relatives who intervene will try to take away control of these items from anyone contemplating suicide, and acknowledge frankly that they are worried about the situation. Once this has been done, professional help should be sought. Many communities have suicide prevention centers where a trained, sympathetic counselor is available by phone 24

After Middle Age

hours a day. If, however, you discover a person already in the act of attempting suicide, call the police.

(5-15) *Drugs for depression.* It usually takes about three weeks before the benefit of drug treatment for depression appears. Maximal effects may take longer. There are two general kinds of antidepressants. The most commonly used are the tricyclics (named for their chemical structure), which include the following.

Imipramine (Tofranil, average dosage 75 to 150 mg per day) comes in 10-, 25-, and 50-mg coral-colored sugar-coated tablets.

Amitriptyline (Elavil, average dosage 75 to 150 mg per day) comes in 10-mg blue, 25-mg yellow, 50-mg beige, 75-mg orange, and 100-mg blue round tablets.

Desipramine (average dosage 75 to 200 mg per day) as Norpramine, comes in 10-mg blue, 25-mg yellow, 50-mg green, 75-mg orange, and 100-mg peach coated tablets. As Pertofrane it comes in 25-mg pink and 50-mg maroon and pink capsules.

Nortriptyline (average dosage 50 to 100 mg per day), as Aventyl, comes in white-and-yellow 10- and 25-mg capsules with "Lilly H 17" and "Lilly H19," respectively, printed on them. As Pamelor it comes in 10- and 25-mg orange and white capsules with "Pamelor" written on them. It also comes in 75-mg orange capsules.

Amoxapine (Asendin, average maintenance dosage 300 mg per day) comes in 25-mg white seven-sided tablets with "LL" above "25" on one side and "A13" on the other, 50-mg orange seven-sided tablets with "LL" above "50" on one side and "A15" on the other, 100-mg blue seven-sided tablets with "LL" above "100" on one side and "A17" on the other, and 150-mg peach seven-sided tablets with "LL" above "150" on one side and "A18" on the other.

These tricyclic drugs have few serious side effects, though they can produce daytime drowsiness. Dry mouth, blurred vision, and constipation are frequent nuisances and should be brought to the attention of your physician. If very bothersome, these side effects may require altering the dosage. Temporary confusion is common in the elderly; this requires decreasing the drug dosage. The drugs are rarely given to patients with glaucoma or urinary retention (usually associated with prostatic enlargement), since they can make these conditions much worse.

There are a number of new nontricyclic antidepressants which seem to act the same way as the older tricyclics and usually have the same side effects, although they vary in degree. These agents include:

Maprotiline (Ludiomil, average maintenance dose 75 to 150 mg per day) comes in 25-mg oval dark orange tablets labeled "CIBA 110," 50-mg

Psychological and Psychiatric Problems

round dark orange tablets labeled "CIBA 26," and 75-mg oval white tablets labeled "CIBA 135."

Doxepin (average maintenance dose 75 to 150 mg per day), as Adapin, comes in 10-, 25-, and 50-mg yellow capsules labeled "18–356," "18–357," and "18–358" respectively, and in 75- and 100-mg capsules labeled "18–361" and "18–359" respectively. As Sinequan it comes in 10-mg red and pink, 25-mg blue and pink, 50-mg white and pink, 75-mg white, 100-mg white and blue, and 150-mg blue capsules.

Trazadone (Desyrel, average maintenance dose 150 to 400 mg per day) comes in 50-mg round orange tablets labeled "Desyrel" and in 100-mg round white tablets labeled "Desyrel." Unlike the tricyclics, trazadone rarely produces dry mouth, constipation, or retention of urine.

Less commonly used in the treatment of depression are the monoamine oxidase inhibitors (named because they block an important enzyme with this name). These include:

Phenelzine (Nardil, average dosage 45 to 90 mg per day) comes in 15-mg orange-coated tablets with "PD 270" written on them.

Isocarboxazid (Marplan, average dosage 10 to 20 mg per day) comes in 10-mg peach-colored scored tablets.

Tranylcypromine (Parnate, average dosage 20 to 30 mg per day) comes in 10-mg red-coated tablets.

Monoamine oxidase inhibitors work very well against depression, but they must be used with great caution. Other drugs should not be taken at the same time as a monoamine oxidase inhibitor unless prescribed by a physician. This is particularly true of cold, hay fever, sinus, or diet medication. In addition, amphetamine, methyldopa (Aldomet), dopamine, ephedrine, epinephrine, and norepinephrine should be avoided, along with foods containing the substance tyramine, which is a small molecule present in some foods that can raise blood pressure. Normally tyramine is destroyed by the enzyme monoamine oxidase in the intestine and liver before it can raise blood pressure, but when monoamine oxidase is inhibited by drugs, tyramine's presence in the body can suddenly produce a hypertensive crisis, that is, a sharp blood pressure increase that can be fatal. Ripened cheeses such as cheddar, Swiss, gruyere, stilton, brie, and camembert have a high concentration of tyramine. Unripened cheese, such as cottage cheese, cream cheese, and yogurt, contain little tyramine. Other foods with significant tyramine content are pickled herring, bologna, salami, pepperoni, summer sausage, chicken liver, beer, chianti wine, sherry, bananas, avocados, canned figs, chocolate, fava beans, and yeast extracts or preparations (but bread is acceptable). The symptoms of a hypertensive crisis are severe headaches, stiffness of the neck, nausea, and vomiting occurring several hours after ingestion of the food or drug. If any of these should occur, call your physician immediately; if you cannot reach anyone within a few minutes, go to a hospital emergency room.

(5-16) *Electroconvulsive treatment (ECT).* ECT, or "shock treatment," is as safe as, or safer than, drug treatment for depression. It may be much safer than drugs in older people who have serious medical problems. In many cases, it also gives the fastest results, and therefore may be the preferred form of treatment. ECT is given when suicide is a likely possibility; when excitement, agitation, or hostility threaten to cause injury to the patient or someone else; or when severe depression prevents the patient from caring for even the most basic needs, such as food, clothing, and shelter. There are natural negative feelings associated with the use of ECT. ECT used to cause rapid thrashing (similar to epileptic convulsion) which was frightening to see. Modern psychiatry, however, has diminished these concerns by developing ECT into a safe and painless procedure.

While it is not known how electrically produced convulsions can decrease depression, it has been established that in well-selected patients ECT is very effective. The ECT procedure requires that the depressed patient avoid eating anything during the 12 hours before treatment. In the treatment room the patient lies quietly on a table, and a belt is placed around him or her for safety. The patient is given a fast-acting barbiturate through a vein, which causes loss of consciousness. A muscle relaxant is then injected to prevent forceful muscle contractions. Two metal electrodes are pressed to the head and a current briefly passes through the head to produce a small convulsion. Usually six to twelve treatments are given over several weeks.

The principal aftereffects of ECT are confusion and partial memory loss. The confusion disappears within hours. It may take days or weeks to recall events of the period immediately before and after the shock, but memory of events that happened several months earlier is not lost. ECT does not subsequently interfere with ability to remember newly learned things.

INSOMNIA

(5-17) There are many ways of defining insomnia; I define it as a patient's subjective feeling that he or she is not getting enough sleep. It is how you feel that determines whether you are suffering from insomnia. The immediate physical reactions of loss of sleep are red and burning eyes with drooping lids and feelings of fatigue and irritability. Prolonged in-

Psychological and Psychiatric Problems

somnia may result in anxiety. It is therefore important to know how much sleep you require in order to feel good—and then to obtain it.

With advancing age most people require less sleep. Whereas the average young adult sleeps six to eight hours each night, people in their fifties, sixties, or seventies usually require fewer hours. Nevertheless, there are people who normally sleep as little as three or four hours a night, and others as much as nine or ten hours. What may be normal for one person may not be normal for another.

There are a great many causes of insomnia and many can be easily rectified.

(5-18) *Inadequate sleeping conditions.* While a few people want to sleep in a warm room, most prefer the room to be cool. If you're having trouble sleeping, check the room temperature to make sure it is in your comfort range. Try to provide adequate ventilation as well. If you live in a dry climate, or if the heat dries the air in your bedroom, use a room humidifier, particularly if your throat or nostrils become dry while you sleep. Have a glass of water by the bed for sips during the night, but since you do not want to get up often to urinate, drink fluids sparingly in the hours before bedtime. Do something routine in the hour before bed. Read an unstimulating book, watch an unexciting television program, or listen to the radio. For poor sleepers, all this activity should take place outside the bedroom—the bedroom being reserved for sleep only.

Consult your physician and, provided you have approval, get exercise. While a lack of exercise does not necessarily produce insomnia, many people with insomnia find they sleep better if they get regular exercise. The best time to exercise is in the afternoon or early evening. (Exercise late at night tends to keep people from sleeping.) Try to exercise every day. If you must have a large meal, eat several hours before going to bed, since most people become uncomfortable after large meals.

Sleep as little as possible during the day. If you nap, do not nap in the evening. Daytime naps should be kept under 30 minutes unless you have been advised to rest longer for health reasons. The problem with taking naps is that they are the start of a vicious cycle. The evening nap takes the edge off of being sleepy, which makes it more difficult to fall asleep and stay asleep at the regular bedtime. This nighttime insomnia often causes daytime sleepiness, which in turn encourages more nap-taking. The cycle of nap-induced insomnia has begun.

(5-19) *Rumination.* If you are attempting to solve a problem that is continuously on your mind but about which you do not have intense feelings, your ruminative insomnia can be treated in the same manner as insomnia associated with anxiety (5-7).

(5-20) *Sexual arousal.* Sexual arousal usually subsides after minutes or hours, but at times a person can be aroused for long periods unless he or she has an orgasm. If you cannot sleep because you are aroused and interpersonal sex is not available, self-stimulation, or masturbation, should decrease the sexual pressure. But relaxation after orgasm is highly variable; although it will relax most people, it will not relax everyone.

(5-21) *Fear of sleep.* Are you afraid of some phenomenon associated with sleep or concerned about loss of consciousness? For most of history, sleep was thought of as being a state just a little ahead of death. Today we know that sleep is an extremely active process. You do not in fact "fall" asleep—the body pushes you to sleep. For unknown reasons, some parts of the brain actually become more active during sleep than during waking. You may be concerned that you might die in your sleep. This is a realistic concern for the seriously ill, since death might come at any time. There is, however, no reason to believe death is more likely to occur during sleep.

(5-22) *Bad dreams.* If you had a bad dream recently, you may be afraid you will have it again. While nightmares (with terror) become rarer as people grow older, unpleasant dreams occur throughout life. Most dreams are made up of things that happened within the last 24 hours, disguised and connected in bizarre ways to older memories. Bad dreams usually run in short cycles lasting not more than a few nights.

Sometimes a person's bad dreams are produced by the drugs prescribed by a physician. This is most likely to be true of sleep-producing and antianxiety drugs. This situation is often made worse when the patient reports these bad dreams to the physician, who in turn prescribes more rather than less of the drug. If bad dreams develop while you are taking sleeping (5-34) or antianxiety agents (5-8), discuss the possibility of discontinuing them with your physician.

(5-23) *Worry about not sleeping.* Are you concerned that not getting enough sleep will make you sick? While we do not know the function of sleep, people who have remained awake for prolonged periods do not seem to have any serious effects other than feeling tired. Concern about not sleeping is one of the biggest contributors to not sleeping.

(5-24) *Depression.* One frequent symptom of depression (5-9) is not being able to fall asleep and/or waking in the middle of the night or early morning. If depression lasts more than a few days, you should seek help from your physician.

(5-25) *Discomfort.* Ben Franklin required fresh cool sheets to go to sleep. You may also have specific needs. Is your insomnia caused by an unusual or uncomfortable situation? Is there noise where you are sleeping? Is there a light, or does the sun come through the window at an early hour? Is your mattress lumpy? Are the sheets or blankets too short? Does

Psychological and Psychiatric Problems

your bed partner crowd you or become restless? As you get older, you will probably find you are less adaptable to new sleeping arrangements than when you were young. Some married couples may want separate beds or even separate rooms.

(5-26) *Change of activities.* Your sleep may have been unavoidably disrupted by your activities. Alterations of your normal sleep and activity routines by travel, work, illness, or social life can be very disruptive of sleep patterns. If some change in your life alters the time you normally go to sleep, you may expect to have trouble sleeping. If the disruption is to last only one night, you can certainly live with it; but if the disruption will last many nights, which might happen when traveling through different time zones, you have a problem. Some aids in dealing with this can be found in the section on travel (4-5).

(5-27) *Overstimulation.* At one time or another almost everyone has become overstimulated by some food or drink, or by some combination of medications. Drug-related insomnia can come from stimulants such as the caffeine found in coffee and in over-the-counter remedies like No-Doz and APC. Although colas and tea also contain caffeine, they rarely prevent sleep. Drugs normally thought of as sedatives, such as alcohol or sleeping pills (hypnotics), can paradoxically act as stimulants and keep you awake. Use of hypnotics or alcohol over long periods of time is one of the major causes of insomnia. While these agents promote sleep initially, long-term use usually makes insomnia much worse. The reasons for this are not understood. Do not discontinue drugs on your own, however; seek the advice of your physician. Sudden withdrawal can produce extreme anxiety (5-7), sleeplessness, suicidal thoughts (5-12), or even epileptic-type seizures.

(5-28) *Middle-of-the-night or early-morning awakening.* Many people find they have no difficulty falling asleep but after a few hours of sleep they awaken. Then they cannot get back to sleep, or they stay awake for many hours before finally dropping off. By the age of 50, many men find that they have to urinate one or more times per night because of an enlarged prostate (15-31). This awakening and going to the bathroom may so fracture their sleep that they feel tired the next morning. The treatment is surgical removal of the enlarged prostate.

Women, too, may awaken with the need to urinate as they get older. Surgery may also help with this problem.

Nocturnal leg cramps are very common after 60, and like pain from any source, can greatly alter the ability to sleep. Similarly, shortness of breath from congestive heart failure—in which insufficient blood is pumped to maintain normal circulation—can prevent a person from sleeping (12-42).

After Middle Age

People who awaken night after night, cannot go back to sleep, and are tired the next day, should consider the possibility that they are depressed (5-9).

(5-29) *General remedies.* If you are in bed thirty minutes or longer and can't fall asleep, or if you awaken in the middle of the night and have trouble falling back asleep, get out of bed and sit in a chair. Then consider why you cannot get to sleep—and what you can do about it. (If you find yourself getting sleepy in the process, go back to bed!) If you are anxious (5-4) about something that happened during the day or that you expect to happen, your first goal is to ask yourself whether there is anything constructive you can do about it at that hour of the night rather than in the morning. Decide what will be the first or most important thing you will do about the problem the next day, and then do not allow yourself to think anymore about it. You need to distract yourself by thinking about something relaxing. (This is the rationale behind the traditional task of "counting sheep.") You might go back to reading your book or watching a nighttime talk show on television (5-18). If you get excited about football, however, do not expect to watch *Monday Night Football* until 1 A.M. and then immediately fall asleep. Sometimes it helps to do some effortless little chore you have been putting off; or try eating a small amount of a bland food—ice cream, milk, or cottage cheese. It is not certain how these work, but they seem to help. The use of alcohol or sleeping pills as aids to induce sleep is controversial. Based on my experience, I think that—in conjunction with the diverting techniques mentioned here—alcohol or sleeping pills can be useful. It is reasonable to take a sleeping pill that has given good results for you in the past. But if you have never taken a sleeping pill before (5-34), it is better not to be alone the first time you try one. Sleeping pills may produce excitement rather than sleep; in older people, they can also produce confusion. If you have a new medical problem and are now taking new drugs that might interact with sleeping pills, consult your physician. Also, you should not try a new sleeping pill if you have something important to do the next morning. Sleeping pills can leave you with a hangover, causing your mind to be sluggish the next day. Sleeping pills can also cause you to sleep longer than you wish in the morning, so set an alarm clock.

Alcohol is the oldest known drug used for insomnia. If used *sparingly,* it can be taken as a medication. Such use should be rare, however, because alcohol is highly habit-forming. One to two ounces for people who know their reaction to alcohol (5-35) is not unreasonable if used no more than two or three times a month.

(5-30) *Sleep disorder clinics.* During the last few years a new subspe-

Psychological and Psychiatric Problems

cialty in medicine has developed. The practitioners, usually psychiatrists, neurologists, or psychologists, are sometimes called polysomnographers (to take several measurements of sleep). They examine the sleep of persons with insomnia (or other kinds of sleep disorders) using a battery of psychological and physiological tests. These tests frequently include an all-night electroencephalogram (EEG). The latter measures brain waves, the occurrence of eye movements, and changes in muscle tone and respiration. For the majority of patients with insomnia, these tests do not offer much except reassurance. Occasionally, however, sleep disorder clinics pick up an unusual disorder that may be treatable.

(5-31)   A partial list of sleep disorder clinics is given below.

Sleep-Wake Disorders Center
Montefiore Medical Center
111 E. 210th St.
Bronx, N.Y. 10467
Director: Michael Thorpy, M.D.

Sleep Evaluation Center
University of Pittsburgh
Western Psychiatric Institute and
   Clinic
3811 O'Hare St.
Pittsburgh, Pa. 15213
Director: David J. Kupfer, M.D.

Sleep Disorders Evaluation Center
Ohio State University College of
   Medicine
Upham Hall
Room N144
473 W. 12th Ave.
Columbus, Ohio 43210
Director: Helmut Schmidt, M.D.

Sleep Disorders Center
515 Melish Ave.
Cincinnati, Ohio 45229
Director: Martin Scharf, M.D.

Sleep Disorders Center
Baylor College of Medicine
Texas Medical Center
1200 Moursund Ave.
Houston, Tex. 77030
Director: Ismet Karacan, M.D.

Sleep Disorders Center
Stanford University Medical Center
Stanford, Calif. 94305
Director: William C. Dement, M.D.

Sleep Research and Treatment
   Center
Hershey Medical Center
P.O. Box 850
Hershey, Pa. 17033
Director: Anthony Kales, M.D.

(5-32) *Sleep apnea.* One treatable condition that produces daytime sleepiness is sleep apnea. The daytime sleepiness usually begins in the teens, but it can come on at any age. Since it is a newly recognzed disorder, it has not been diagnosed in many people who have it. In addition to daytime sleepiness, people with sleep apnea usually snore.

The word "apnea" means "suspension of breathing," and people with sleep apnea stop breathing soon after they fall asleep. In order to begin breathing again they must briefly wake up, and since this process of stopping breathing and waking up may occur several hundred times a night, they are tired the next day. The person is usually totally unaware of what is happening, although the bed partner may recognize it. The cause of most cases of sleep apnea is a collapse of the throat during sleep due to loss of muscle tone in the tongue, throat, and larynx.

In addition to sleepiness, some people with sleep apnea may be forgetful or confused for a few minutes on waking, and may have visual hallucinations. The latter occur when the person is awake but sleepy, and the person usually recognizes that the hallucinations are not real. Occasionally, however, some sufferers might act on these hallucinations—when a phantom person suddenly walks in front of the car, for example, the driver might slam on the brakes.

Diagnosis is made by polysomnography, which shows whether the person stops breathing while asleep. There is no cure for sleep apnea, but when it is considered life-threatening (some people develop severe hypertension and respiratory problems) it frequently can be relieved by medications or the surgical procedure of tracheostomy. A tracheostomy is an opening made through the skin to the windpipe, or trachea, into which a T-shaped hollow tube is placed. At night the patient breathes through this neck hole rather than through the nose. This bypasses the collapsing muscles of the throat, and respiration becomes normal. During the day the external hole is covered so that the person can talk and breath normally.

If you think you might have sleep apnea, avoid all sleeping medications until you have been reassured by your physician that you do not have it. Many sleeping medications depress breathing, and that quality of the drugs combined with the breathing stoppage associated with sleep apnea can be fatal.

(5-33) *Narcolepsy.* While narcolepsy is a disorder that usually begins in young adulthood, many people who have it are undiagnosed. People with narcolepsy may find it very difficult or even impossible to prevent themselves from falling asleep during the day. Sometimes the sleepiness occurs in an awkward situation, such as when driving a car, during excitement, or when laughing. People with narcolepsy may fall to the ground or drop things they are carrying. While they are fully aware of what is happening and usually have enough control over themselves to prevent injury, for brief periods of time they are unable to move. This inability to move is caused by a temporary paralysis of the muscles that is called "cataplexy."

Other symptoms include hypnagogic hallucinations, sleep paralysis, automatic behavior, and disrupted nocturnal sleep. Hypnagogic halluci-

Psychological and Psychiatric Problems

nations occur when a person in a darkened room sees things that are not real before going to sleep or on awakening. These hallucinations can be frightening, but usually the person realizes they are not real. Hypnagogic hallucinations can occur in people who do not have narcolepsy, but this is rare.

Sleep paralysis is a frightening symptom that many people have had a few times during their life. Narcoleptics may have it often. The person, on awakening, is fully alert to his surrounding but cannot move for several minutes unless someone touches him.

Automatic behaviors are behaviors that occur without the person's being aware of them. For example, I once saw a patient with narcolepsy who was driving home from work in downtown Washington, D.C., to his home in suburban Maryland. About an hour after he left work, he suddenly found himself driving in Baltimore without any knowledge of how he had gotten there. He had safely navigated his car for over 30 miles without being aware of it.

Finally, many people with narcolepsy have disrupted nighttime sleep, usually awakening early in the morning and being unable to fall asleep again.

Narcolepsy appears to be a dysfunction related to rapid eye movement (REM) sleep. REM sleep is sleep associated with dreaming; it occurs about every ninety minutes throughout the night. During dreaming, the eyes move rapidly under the closed eyelids and there is a loss of tone of many of the muscles of the body. The cataplectic attack looks very much like REM sleep, except that the person is not asleep, and the problem comes on suddenly, during the day.

Narcolepsy is treated first by recognition that one has the problem. This is important, for example, if you are in a job that requires constant vigilance, or if you drive a car. Do not fight the attack; it will likely overwhelm you. If you are driving, pull off the road; if you are a crane operator, you had better find another job. Try to sleep regular hours each night and take ten-minute naps frequently during the day. A number of drugs can be used. Stimulants, such as methylphenidate (Ritalin), dextroamphetamine (Dexadrine), and pemoline (Cylert), are used to treat the problem of daytime sleeping. In fact, this is one of the few legitimate uses for these drugs. Cataplexy can be treated with the tricyclic antidepressants (5-15).

For further information about narcolepsy, write the American Narcolepsy Association, Information Distribution Center, P.O. Box 5846, Stanford, California 94305.

A book that explains sleep and some of the problems associated with it

After Middle Age

is Mendelson, W. B., Gillian, J. C. and Wyatt, R. J., *Human Sleep and Its Disorders,* Plenum Press, New York, 1977.

(5-34) *Drugs for insomnia.* Sleep drugs (hypnotics) that are sold without a physician's prescription (over the counter) are generally not recommended. Most of these drugs have not been shown to be effective. In addition, they contain scopolamine, an agent that can produce confusion, particularly in the elderly. It is also a respiratory depressant (that is, it decreases breathing) and tends to produce urinary retention. Furthermore, with drugs that affect as many systems as sleeping medications do, it is important that a physician prescribe them, using his or her knowledge of any medical condition present and other drugs being used.

There are many prescription drugs available that effectively induce and sustain sleep. But almost all the drugs used to produce or enhance sleep can have a paradoxical effect; instead of producing sedation, they produce excitement. This is particularly true with respect to people over 50. The first time any hypnotic is used, the lowest possible dosage should be taken until your reaction is determined. This is also true if the drug is used only on rare occasions. Most of the hypnotics can produce nausea and vomiting, confusion, unsteady walking, dizziness, and falling. All drugs used to induce sleep can produce morning hangovers: You will have trouble waking up; or once you are awake, you may feel that your head is cloudy (this can last for several hours); or you may even be totally confused. Because the probability of having a hangover as well as being excessively stimulated is so high, never take a sleeping pill for the first time when you have an important task the following morning or when you are alone. Even if you do not feel hung over, your reaction time in performing tasks such as driving will be altered the morning after a sleeping pill. Thus, try your first sleeping pill when you are with someone else and when you have an easy morning planned—even if this means taking the pill at a time when you do not actually need it.

Sleeping pills should be used with caution if you have a disease of the liver, kidney, or lung. Since chemical constituents of the drugs are broken down in these organs, the malfunction of these organs will enhance and prolong the drug's effect. An overdose may be lethal. Most hypnotics are habit-forming and should not be used more than one or two nights a week unless a physician specifically recommends greater frequency. If you have taken sleeping pills steadily for a long time, you should not discontinue them without first consulting your physician. Usually a gradual, rather than an abrupt, reduction in dosage is recommended. Like any drug, sleeping pills can produce rashes and other symptoms of allergies. Some hypnotics are:

Psychological and Psychiatric Problems

Glutethimide (Doriden, average dosage 250 to 500 mg per night) comes in 250- and 500-mg white scored tablets.

Methyprylon (Noludar, average dosage 200 to 400 mg per night) comes in 50- and 200-mg white scored tablets (imprinted with "Roche 16" and "Roche 17") and 300-mg amethyst and white capsules.

Flurazepam (Dalmane, average dosage 15 to 30 mg per might) comes in 15-mg orange and ivory and 30-mg red and ivory capsules.

Diazepam (Valium, average dosage 2 to 10 mg per night), comes in 2-mg white, 5-mg yellow, and 10-mg blue scored tablets. Diazepam, while usually considered an antianxiety agent (5-8), is one of the best drugs for inducing sleep. This is because it is very rapidly absorbed from the intestines. It should not be used by people with narrow-angle glaucoma.

Triazolam (Halcion, average dose 0.125 to 0.25 mg 30 minutes before bedtime) comes in 0.25-mg powder blue and 0.5-mg white tablets.

Ethchlorvynol (Placidyl, average dosage 100 to 750 mg per night) comes in 100- and 200-mg red pills, 500-mg red capsules, and 750-mg green capsules. If you become giddy or if your walk is unstable shortly after taking the drug, take subsequent doses with a glass of milk to slow absorption.

Diphenhydramine (Benadryl, average dosage 25 to 50 mg per night) comes in 25- and 50-mg pink and white capsules (7-25). Diphenhydramine is a relatively safe hypnotic for young people, but considerable care must be taken by older people who use it. Also, the drug should probably not be given to patients with asthma, narrow-angle glaucoma, prostatic disease, peptic ulcer, or other gastrointestinal disease.

Chloral hydrate (average dosage 500 to 1000 mg per night) comes as Noctec in 250- and 500-mg brown capsules; as Kessodrate, in 250-mg green and white capsules; and as Felsules, in 500-mg blue capsules as well as a variety of liquid-filled red and green capsules. Chloral hydrate also comes in syrups and suppositories. This is an especially good hypnotic for the elderly. It must be used with caution, however, if taken with blood-thinning medications (anticoagulants). There is some concern that the diuretic furosemide (Lasix) and chloral hydrate interact to produce vascular shock in some older people. Ask your physician about this before you take both drugs at the same time.

Secobarbital (Seconal, average dosage 100 mg or 1 1/2 g per night) comes in 50-mg (3/4 g), and 100-mg (1 1/2-g) orange capsules.

Pentobarbital (average dosage 100 mg per night), as Nembutal, comes in 30-mg yellow, 50-mg white and orange, and 100-mg yellow capsules. The 30-, 50-, and 100-mg capsules are inscribed with "CE," "CF," and "CH," respectively.

ALCOHOLISM

(5-35) *What are drinking problems and alcoholism?* We choose to drink alcoholic beverages for a variety of reasons—to be holding something at a social occasion, because of the taste, because of religious or social traditions, for the relaxation alcohol produces, for its sedative qualities, for the courage to cope, for escape, and to forget worries. Many alcoholics do not want to be intoxicated (that is, to experience temporary loss of mental and physical control) any more than anyone else; in fact, they abhor intoxicated behavior. An alcoholic would like to be able to drink without getting intoxicated, and most do. A drinking problem (difficulties of living related to alcohol) exists only when there is irresponsible drinking—drinking that involves harming oneself or others. This occurs when you must drink steadily to cope with life, when there is frequent intoxication, when you go to work intoxicated or miss work because of intoxication, when you drive a car while intoxicated, when the drinking becomes a destructive element in interpersonal relationships, or when you do something detrimental while drinking that you would not do otherwise. Alcoholism refers to the physical addiction to alcohol, which involves tolerance (the ability to handle more alcohol over time), alcohol withdrawal symptoms, shakiness, and delirium tremens (5-37) on discontinuation of drinking.

(5-36) *How to minimize the effects of alcohol.* The best ways to prevent intoxication are, first, to get some food in your stomach before drinking and, second, to sip the drink slowly while paying attention to your internal response to the alcohol. This way, when the alcohol "hits your head," you can slow down or stop drinking.

(5-37) *The effects of alcohol on the body.* Occasionally elderly people will have a paradoxical effect from even small amounts of alcohol. Whereas alcohol once had a sedating or tranquilizing effect, it now can cause extreme excitement. In this state, people may make inappropriate sexual overtures, become overtalkative, or speak of depressing things. When this happens, they should abstain from drinking. If these symptoms develop in an elderly person who in the past has been able to handle a drink or two, a family member or friend should tactfully but firmly point out what is happening and encourage the cessation of alcohol use. It may actually be reassuring to the person that alcohol and not senility has triggered such behavior. Unfortunately, though, this kind of advice is usually met with anger or the denial that a problem exists, sometimes leading to further drinking.

A hangover is the unpleasant morning-after discomfort of fatigue, nausea, and headache. The best treatment is two aspirins, bed rest, and

Psychological and Psychiatric Problems

solid food as soon as possible. A single hangover is not dangerous, but the cumulative effects on the body of heavy drinking can be extremely grave.

The most important alcohol-related medical problems are gastritis (inflammation of the stomach characterized by indigestion or by the vomiting of blood), ulcers, pancreatitis (inflammation of the pancreas), and liver damage (cirrhosis). The symptoms of liver damage are jaundice (yellowing of the skin and whites of the eyes), swelling of the abdomen, fever and chills, tiredness, and spiderlike red spots on the skin. Alcoholic cirrhosis is serious, and if drinking continues, it may bring on death. The treatment of cirrhosis depends on its severity. It will require the attention of an internist, frequently with long-term hospitalization. The patient will have to abstain from drinking.

Another serious effect of alcohol is the blackout spell (suffered by people who, after drinking but not necessarily becoming intoxicated, have periods of which they have no memory). While a brief loss of memory can be unfortunate, it has no other health implications and can be prevented by not drinking.

Delirium tremens (DTs) occur during withdrawal from chronic use of alcohol. Anxiety mounts to terror, occasionally mixed with euphoria, vivid hallucinations (seeing or feeling objects that are not there), and sleeplessness. Seizures can occur. The drinker's mind is confused; he may not know who or where he is, the day of the week, the month, or the year. Delirium tremens is a medical emergency and should be treated immediately in a hospital by a physician. The treatment includes the use of tranquilizers such as diazepam (Valium) and intravenous fluids. In an emergency, where no medical treatment is available, delirium can also be treated by the continuous administration of alcohol, which prevents withdrawal.

Alcoholic hallucinosis, which is uncommon, consists of persecutory auditory hallucinations. The drinker hears tormenting voices that seem to come from specific directions. Treatment requires hospitalization. It usually takes many weeks for the hallucinations to disappear. The patient must discontinue all future drinking.

Korsakoff syndrome may follow long-term alcohol use. It consists of gaps in memory which are filled in by active fantasy (confabulation). The condition is thought to be brought about by failure to ingest enough vitamins while drinking. The only treatment is rigid imposition of an alcohol-free environment.

(5-38) *Alcohol and drug interactions.* Whether you are an occasional drinker or an alcoholic, you should know that of the 100 most commonly prescribed drugs at least one-half interact adversely with alcohol. To some extent, these interactions are dependent on the dose of both drug

After Middle Age

and alcohol, but the interactions are more likely to occur with advanced age. Among the drugs that should not be combined with alcohol are the barbiturates (generally used as hypnotics) (5-34), the minor tranquilizers (5-8), including meprobamate (Equanil, Meprospan, Miltown), and the benzodiazepines (Librium, Valium, Dalmane), which in addition to tranquilization (5-8) are used as hypnotics (5-34). Combined use of barbiturates and alcohol can cause death, as can combined use of minor tranquilizers and alcohol, although there is less risk involved. Of equal or greater concern is that the combined use of the minor tranquilizers and alcohol can impair driving and other sensorimotor skills. If you are taking medication for any purpose, ask your physician if it is permissible to have an occasional drink.

(5-39) *Correcting misconceptions about alcohol and the alcoholic.* (1) Alcohol is not a stimulant; it is a sedative that suppresses judgment, discrimination, discretion, and normal inhibition. It is the loss of normal inhibition that makes alcohol appear to be a stimulant. (2) The ability to stop drinking for periods of time does not mean there is no drinking problem. An alcoholic only stops being an alcoholic as long as he or she never drinks. (3) Alcoholics are usually not skid-row types; they may have responsible jobs or be managing a home. (4) Alcoholics drink beer and wine, not just hard liquor.

(5-40) *Treatment of alcoholism.* Whenever alcoholism produces any of the serious syndromes described earlier, medical attention is necessary. Of course it is best to seek and find successful intervention before the development of serious medical or social disruption. The preeminent organization in this field is Alcoholics Anonymous (AA), a loosely knit, voluntary fellowship of alcoholics who meet to get sober and stay sober. To become a member of AA, you must admit your inability to control alcohol. Much of the program is spiritual—asking for God's help—but AA is nonsectarian. AA is a cross section of society—physicians, lawyers, businesspeople, housewives, laborers—all with a common problem, who have decided to depend on each other instead of alcohol. In some communities there are even physicians' groups and clergymen's groups. AA is as close as the phone. The address of the national headquarters is: Alcoholics Anonymous, 175 Fifth Avenue, Room 219, New York, New York, 10010. Because physical disease may be present, it is imperative that while going to AA you also see a physician for a physical examination.

One effective method of treating alcoholism is with physician-prescribed disulfiram (Antabuse), which comes in white tablets with "250" and "500" imprinted on them. The average daily dosage is 125 to 500 mg taken each morning. Disulfiram with even a small amount of

Psychological and Psychiatric Problems

alcohol produces a very unpleasant reaction consisting of flushing, feeling the heart beat (palpitation), rapid breathing, nausea, vomiting, a severe pounding headache, and drowsiness. The individual will fall asleep and awaken recovered. If disulfiram is taken regularly and this reaction is experienced once, it is so miserable that it will discourage drinking. If you have such a reaction, call your physician for advice. Disulfiram itself has some side effects. It can produce fatigue, slight loss of potency in men, and stomach irritation. On occasion, it can produce bizarre thinking. An advantage of disulfiram is that it keeps a person from having to make a decision many times a day about whether to have a drink. The decision is made just once—in the morning when the pill is taken. Alcoholics continue taking disulfiram until they are in complete control—when they know they will not drink. To avoid a reaction, do not drink seventy-two hours before taking disulfiram or seventy-two hours after.

Al-Anon is an organization for the families of alcoholics that gives support to the spouse and children and tells where help for the drinker can be obtained. It also provides day-to-day advice. The national address for Al-Anon is: Al-Anon Family Groups, 1 Park Avenue, New York, New York 10016. In the home, alcoholism must be dealt with openly: it is far better to talk about the problem than to let it destroy someone. Alcoholism should be explained to children as you would explain any other illness. It should be emphasized that there will be many setbacks before there is a cure. Many alcoholics will sincerely promise on repeated occasions to stop drinking, but will fail. It must be recognized in advance that these setbacks will be disappointing. Emotional appeals should be avoided. Screaming on either side only worsens the situation. Let the alcoholic face the problem he or she has created—do not shield them. Do not drink with an alcoholic. Do not ride in a car when the driver is intoxicated.

PSYCHOTHERAPY

(5-41) *What psychotherapy is.* Technically, psychotherapy is the use of any method, including drugs, that aims at lessening emotional discomfort or improving effectiveness in a social setting. In practice, however, psychotherapy usually refers to a process that helps develop an understanding of, or insight into, factors contributing to a difficulty which is unrecognized by you or which you cannot control.

Unrecognized thoughts or feelings can compel you to behave in a way that injures yourself or others. Almost everyone has had the experience of being angry about something and then, instead of directing the anger at its proper target, directing it elsewhere. How many times have you come home from work angered by something that happened there and snapped at your spouse? We are generally aware of why we act this way, but we do it anyway; we are not in control. At times, however, we are not aware that we are angry, or we do not understand what it is that we are angry about. This happens particularly in situations that are more complex than those that produce simple anger, that transpire over a longer period of time, or that have been forgotten, perhaps because of the passage of time or our not wanting to remember. Psychotherapy can help you understand your behavior and prevent behavior you wish to eliminate.

(5-42) *Psychotherapy's aims.* Psychotherapy tries to achieve one or more of three goals. The first goal, one you may have already achieved by the time you decide to see a mental health worker, is to define carefully what might seem like vague symptoms so that you can see them as concrete problems. What are your feelings? Are you angry, happy, despondent? More likely your feelings are a complex combination of such emotions. In what part of your body do you experience these feelings? When are they present, and how intense are they? Are there specific issues that need to be faced, such as a coming marriage, divorce, loss of a job, or death? Or do you feel that you understand the issues but are unsuccessful in trying to resolve them?

The second goal of psychotherapy is to understand (gain insight into) why you behave or feel the way you do. Many disturbed thoughts and feelings are buried in the labyrinth of our brains—they are in us but not really known to us—and they bring inner discomfort that may cause us to feel or behave in a detrimental manner. Psychotherapy helps us understand these thoughts and feelings. Some persons will already know the connection between these disturbed thoughts and their feelings and their symptoms but simply be unable to break the connection.

The third goal of psychotherapy is to learn to control—or, better yet, to break—the driving force connecting the inner thoughts or feelings and the symptoms. How far you proceed with any of these goals will very much depend on the nature of the problem, its severity, the limitations of any program of mental healing, and your time and resources.

(5-43) *Types of psychotherapy.* Most symptoms needing psychotherapy require only careful definition (goal 1) and can be dealt with satisfactorily in a few weeks, using short-term psychotherapy. This treatment is comparatively quick—usually requiring about ten once-a-week fifty-minute visits. Problems that fall into this category are the issues involved in making an important decision (marriage, divorce, change of job), grief over a loss (loss of a job or loved one), and the sudden appearance of a fear (concerns about driving in a car or plane).

Psychological and Psychiatric Problems

Many symptoms that cannot be treated successfully by definition alone do not require insight (goal 2) but can be dealt with by breaking or diverting the connection between the symptom and its disturbance (goal 3). This is the purpose behind the behavior modification method, which is often successful in solving a single problem with a very clear demarcation. For example, the fear of snakes or of driving in automobiles can often be treated with behavior modification. A method frequently used by behavioral therapists is called desensitization. For example, if you are afraid to travel in planes, the therapist will first try to bring you to a positive state, perhaps by inducing relaxation. When you are comfortable, the treatment may begin by having you simulate phoning for a plane reservation. When you are comfortable with this, you simulate buying the ticket. When you again are comfortable, you work your way up to the simulation of flying in the plane. Eventually you "fly" in rough conditions or are forced to land at a secondary airfield. This process may take half a dozen once- or twice-a-week visits for a simple problem, with longer times being required in more complex situations.

Where the connections between a symptom and its underlying cause are complicated and do not respond to short-term therapy or behavior modification, long-term psychotherapy is advised. There are fundamentally three types of long-term psychotherapy, although all three also can be used for short-term treatment. Group psychotherapy involves a weekly (or more frequent) meeting, usually lasting ninety minutes, of several people with a therapist, where each group member talks about his or her problem. (At times—for instance, when male-female balance is needed—two therapists may be present, in which case they are called co-therapists.) You may at first be hesitant to talk about your problems in a group, but as you get to know other members and learn to trust them, you will find yourself opening up. The other group members can be particularly helpful since, once they get to know you and care about you, they will tell you things about yourself that your family and friends will not. Group members often develop a feeling of being "in the same boat," which brings a helping hand and a sense of belongingness. Couples psychotherapy involves a husband and wife, and family psychotherapy involves other family members talking with each other and a therapist. This latter type of therapy is particularly useful when there is difficulty communicating within the family and across generations. Each session usually lasts fifty minutes, once or twice a week. In individual psychotherapy, you talk directly with the therapist; long-term individual psychotherapy is usually directed at goals 2 and 3. That is, you try to understand why you have your symptoms and how you can deal with them. Most long-term individual psychotherapists use some of the techniques first described by

After Middle Age

Freud and practice psychoanalysis or psychoanalytically oriented psychotherapy. Psychoanalysis usually requires a commitment of at least three years during which your feelings and memories are intensively explored. By exploring both your past and the ways you handle present situations, psychoanalysis leaves you with a detailed map telling you how you got to be the way you are. A psychotherapy session usually lasts fifty minutes, and there may be as many as four or five sessions a week. Psychoanalytically oriented psychotherapy is less intense than psychoanalysis and takes less time. You explore your feelings and their origins only to the point needed for the resolution of what is bothering you.

One of the most important aspects of psychotherapy is transference. This involves transferring an attitude toward one person (or thing) onto another. Older people almost always live in the past as well as the present; thus the therapist may be seen as a familiar relative from the past. For example, an older woman might see a certain resemblance between a therapist and her son or daughter. Whether the feelings surrounding these apparent similarities are positive or negative, they are an important element in psychotherapy. Both the patient and the therapist can make use of them to better understand the patient's relationship with a son or daughter. Unless a person is in psychoanalysis, however, this transference will not be analyzed in detail.

There are many issues that psychoanalytically oriented psychotherapy can deal with in older people. One example is ambivalence. It is not unusual for people to have ambivalent feelings about other people. In fact, it is probably more common to be ambivalent than to have just positive or negative feelings. One can love, like, and admire a spouse and at the same time be extremely angry with him or her. Thus, despite outwardly positive feelings, inward or unconscious feelings might be mixed (positive and negative). If a spouse dies, inner negative feelings can produce guilt with a sense of some responsibility for wishing the death or for not doing everything possible for the spouse during the spouse's lifetime.

Psychotherapy can help a person to explore the cause of the ambivalence and ways to deal with them. For mature people who are otherwise in control of themselves, moving a bothersome feeling from the unconscious to the conscious is extremely important. In a real sense, knowledge becomes power.

(5-44) *When to go to a psychotherapist.*

1. When you have symptoms that are disabling (being afraid to drive, too depressed to eat or sleep, etc.)

2. When you have significant mental discomfort or pain that is not

Psychological and Psychiatric Problems

transient—certainly any such discomfort lasting a month or longer should be brought to the attention of your physician or psychotherapist

3. When your work or relationships with others are impaired

4. When you are facing a crisis about a loss or disappointment or cannot make an important decision

5. When you find your ability to communicate with others (to be understood by them) is breaking down

6. When you feel like killing yourself or someone else

7. When you hear or see things that are not real

8. When you feel continuous anger, resentment, or despair

9. If you are curious about yourself and have a desire to understand why you are the way you are

Health insurance will not pay if your purpose is to satisfy your curiosity, but many persons find their understanding so rewarding that this is not a consideration.

(5-45) *Practitioners of psychotherapy.* Psychiatrists (from the Greek for "healing of the mind") are physicians who have taken special training in psychiatry beyond their medical training. Some psychiatrists are very directive (giving specific instructions) and deal quickly with a specific problem area. Others will lead you by asking questions; still others will only listen. All can prescribe drugs and are aware of medical complications. Psychoanalysts are psychiatrists who have taken very specialized training in order to practice psychoanalysis, the therapeutic method originated by Freud. In a certain sense, analysis attempts to restructure your life—not something many older people will want to do. A psychoanalyst is generally nondirective; that is, does a lot of listening and does not give specific advice about a problem. You gradually understand yourself by exploring your deepest feelings about your parents, yourself, your dreams, and even your relationship to your analyst.

Psychologists have either an M.A. or Ph.D. degree, and while they are not able to deal directly with medical problems or to prescribe drugs, they are trained in the theory and practice of therapy. They are also trained to do psychological testing, which can be helpful in diagnosis and treatment. Social workers who are psychotherapists have an M.A. or Ph.D. degree in social work and, like psychologists, are trained in the theory and practice of psychotherapy. They do not do psychological testing, but are very knowledgeable about community resources. Other social workers, without advanced degrees, frequently work in social agencies handling welfare, Medicare, and Medicaid problems. They are not trained to treat

After Middle Age

psychological problems with psychotherapy. Psychiatric nurses specialize in psychiatry and are capable of doing psychotherapy, and under a physician's orders they can administer drugs and monitor their effects. Members of the clergy are using psychotherapeutic techniques more and more. Frequently they have had special training in both the recognition of psychiatric problems and their treatment. They are not trained to recognize or treat medical disorders or to use drugs.

(5-46) *Choosing a therapist.* Fortunately, as you get older, you usually know what works best with you better than you did when you were young. Thus, undertaking psychoanalysis will make less sense to older people than to the young. Before getting into any form of psychotherapy, you should be sure that your problem is not caused by a treatable physical ailment. This means that you need to talk about your problem with your physician. Many medical disorders are disguised—they present themselves as psychological disturbances. On the other hand, many psychological disturbances initially produce physical signs. Although social workers, psychologists, and members of the clergy may recognize such medical diseases masquerading as psychological problems, they are not trained to do so. Your physician can help you decide if therapy is necessary and what kind of therapist to see. Some physicians may not want to make this decision and may suggest that you see a psychiatrist or psychologist for a psychiatric diagnostic evaluation. This usually involves tracing the history of your problem. Knowledge of your psychological background and that of your family helps in defining your problem (goal 1). You may also be asked to take tests such as the inkblot (Rorschach) test or parts of an intelligence test to help the psychologist determine aspects of your problem that might not otherwise be apparent. Ultimately, after all the preliminary testing, you will have to decide for yourself what kind of, and which, therapist to see. If drugs are to be involved in your treatment, you will have to see a psychiatrist or an internist for their administration.

If you are going to be seeing the therapist regularly, you will want to find someone whose office is convenient and whose hours are compatible with the ones you are willing to schedule—do not forget to count travel time. Finally, on the dollar-per-hour basis psychotherapy is relatively inexpensive compared with most medical treatments, but if it is to last any length of time, it will add up to a considerable amount of money. In many metropolitan areas, a psychotherapy hour with a psychiatrist now costs about seventy-five dollars or more. Thus, a forty-eight-week course of treatment will cost about $3600. As a rule, psychiatrists are more expensive than psychologists, who, in turn, are more expensive than social

Psychological and Psychiatric Problems

workers. If you have health insurance, Medicare, or Medicaid, you will want to determine what it will cover, and for how long. Unfortunately, few health insurance policies cover long-term treatment. Most communities have public clinics that charge according to what you can afford.

Some general rules: (1) Make sure the form of therapy you choose is generally recognized. Avoid fads and outlandish-sounding programs. While most psychotherapy is "iffy," the major forms have at least stood the test of time and have not depended on the charisma of a single leader. (2) Select the therapist who is likely to be attuned to you and your problems. Because psychotherapy is much more of an art than are most kinds of medicine, the quality of the therapist is usually more important than the kind of treatment he or she practices. (3) Find out the licensing requirements in your state. Whereas all states license physicians, only some license psychologists and social workers. If your state does license psychologists and social workers, be sure that the person who is going to treat you is licensed, unless he or she is in training or works in a recognized clinic.

(5-47) *Choosing your individual therapist.* There is no one perfect therapist, although some will be better for you than others. You must choose a therapist with whom you are comfortable. This comfort may take some time to develop, but if it does not come, this fact should be brought out into the open and discussed with the therapist. If you remain uncomfortable and you think you might do better with someone else, make a change. A mature therapist will not take this as a personal affront.

There are important aspects to look for when choosing a therapist. (1) Is the therapist a good listener? (2) Does the therapist have respect for you, for what you are? (3) Is the therapist unshakable, so that you can drop your social facade and defenses? (4) Does the therapist evoke a feeling of trust? (5) Is the therapist's behavior a good model for yours—or at least inoffensive to you? (6) Is the therapist someone to whom you can relate? (7) Does the therapist have warmth, understanding, and empathy? (Remember, however, you are not looking for someone to hold your hand; some supportiveness is good, but you want to develop new, and keep old, independence.) (8) Is the therapist nonjudgmental, respecting your feelings and decisions?

(5-48) *Myths and facts about psychiatrists and other psychotherapists.*

1. *Myth:* Psychotherapists are so strange (neurotic), they could not possibly help anyone else. *Fact:* While it is true that some mental health professionals have peculiar habits or have sometimes been unsuccessful in handling their own personal problems, it does not necessarily follow that they cannot help you. Many psychiatrists, in attempting to deal with

their own problems, have learned a great deal about human nature, allowing them to be more empathetic with other people's problems and also to understand them better.

2. *Myth:* You will have to spend a lot of time talking about your childhood. *Fact:* Depending on the nature of your problem and to whom you go, you may or may not spend time talking about your childhood. An analyst very likely will want to know a great deal about it. Childhood is one of the most important times. It is when your self-image is established. It is when you learn how to relate to others, particularly to your parents and to brothers and sisters. If harmful patterns have been formed, they may need to be recognized and broken. But a therapist who predominantly uses behavior modification or offers short-term therapy will not explore this kind of history in depth.

3. *Myth:* You will be on a couch while the therapist silently listens. *Fact:* The couch is used only in psychoanalysis. It provides a relaxed setting designed to encourage you to talk about your most intimate feelings and thoughts. You do not see the analyst, so that there is no facial or other expression to influence you. Those therapists who need to be doing something with their hands will knit or play with a pipe. Most therapy is face to face, however, with you in one chair and the therapist in another.

4. *Myth:* You will lose whatever creativity or spontaneity you have. *Fact:* Psychotherapy will not cause you to lose your creativity or spontaneity. What it can do, however, is cause you to use these attributes more effectively.

The Aging Mind

SENILITY

(6-1) *Senility* is a term generally used to describe a progressive decline in brain function that is occasionally seen in those over 65. Actually, relatively few elderly people have any appreciable loss of brain function. Dementia is a medical term that has the same meaning as senility but is applied to people of any age. Senility is more pejorative than dementia and is misused, at times, to mean a pathological consequence of normal aging. Usually, the first symptom is a change in mood or personality, including depression (5-9), euphoria, irritability, and paranoia (a high degree of suspiciousness). Rapid mood changes are common. For example, a person's behavior might quickly change from tearfulness to excitement to despair in the space of a few minutes, rather like a baby's mood swings. Friends and relatives may note faulty judgment, perhaps in business decisions resulting in financial losses. Frequently there is a loss of inhibition with a decrease in neatness and personal care.

Although a memory impairment almost always occurs in senility, it may go unnoticed for some time. Initially, one cannot remember something just learned, such as a person's name or phone number. Later there is failure to recall more remote events such as birthdates or anniversaries. It is important to remember, however, that an occasional forgotten phone number or name is not senility.

Disorientation begins about the same time as memory loss. The sense of time becomes shaky, and at first a person may hide this by avoiding any allusion to days of the week or dates. Next the ability to find the way from one place to another is lost. This is particularly likely to occur at night,

After Middle Age

when a person may wander away from home. Finally, knowledge of names and recognition of familiar people are lost.

Senility is produced by alteration in brain cells, a process that usually occurs over a number of years. The medical name for these changes is Alzheimer's disease—also called primary neuronal degeneration of the Alzheimer's type—and its cause and cure are not known.

Less often, senility is produced by a narrowing of the arteries (arteriosclerosis) that leads to the brain. This type of senility (also called multi-infarct or vascular dementia) has an uneven course compared with the slow but steady decline of Alzheimer's disease. Thus, there may be long periods (days or months) between the most severe confusional episodes. Loss of function and its restoration can occur from moment to moment or hour to hour. Dizziness and headaches usually occur. Multi-infarct dementia is often associated with other symptoms of cardiovascular disease such as high blood pressure. Treatment is the same as that for arteriosclerosis involving the heart.

(6-2) *Senility before age 65.* The presenile dementias (irreversible brain damage resulting in decreased intelligence) are disorders that seem very much like senility except that they occur between the ages of 45 and 65. Marked alterations in personality associated with intellectual deterioration are the usual symptoms, together with a general downhill course. Most people are able to keep up a social facade during the early course of the illness, but after a time this breaks down. The best known of the presenile dementias are Alzheimer's and Pick's disease, named after the people who first described them. Alzheimer's disease occurring before 65 is probably the same as that which occurs after age 65 (6-1). Both forms involve loss of brain cells. While Alzheimer's and Pick's disease are not curable, some unusual forms of presenile dementia can be cured. Therefore, it is very important for anyone with the symptoms described to be examined carefully by a neurologist (a physician who specializes in diseases of the nervous system).

The neurologist will ask what medications you are taking, since many drugs have side effects resembling the symptoms of senility. In fact, medications are the most common cause of senility, and when they are discontinued, the disturbance is "cured." The neurologist will evaluate your ability to see and hear, your memory for things past and present, your attention span, your ability to solve problems, and your judgment. The neurologist will want to know about your home situation—whom you live with and how you feel about them—your work, and your state of mind. Depression (5-9) in older people may misrepresent itself as senility, and when the depression is treated, the signs of senility disappear. The neurologist will take a number of blood tests and may have a computed tomography (CT) scan of your brain done. The CT scan can tell the neurologist if there is a tumor or if the brain has become smaller (atrophy), a normal accompaniment of aging that is exaggerated with Alzheimer's disease.

DECISIONS REGARDING CARE

(6-3) Loss in intellectual or emotional function due to progressive destruction of the brain is tragic. It is painful to watch able, contributing members of the community regress to a point where they cannot take responsibility for themselves. This is a time of tension and sadness for everyone involved—including the doctors and nurses, even though they have seen the phenomenon many times. One husband of a patient recently described taking care of his wife: "like living a thirty-six hour day."

Sometimes relatives are so upset by the course of events that they cannot make wise decisions. They may have to be told about the realities of the situation many times and in many ways before they grasp the implications of what is being said and what it means. Some people just cannot tolerate the discomfort and turn away from the situation. Most people, however, grow from the experience of coping with tragedy. The experience can be used to explore one's fears and feelings of disability and death and to come to terms with them.

To help deal with the experience and provide information, family groups have developed in many places in the country. These groups have recently joined together, forming the Alzheimer's Disease and Related Disorders Association (360 North Michigan Avenue, Chicago, Illinois 60601), to encourage research, education, and family services.

A book by Nancy L. Mace and Peter V. Robins, *The 36-Hour Day: A Family Guide to Caring for Persons with Alzheimer's Disease, Related Dementing Illnesses, and Memory Loss in Later Life* is very helpful. It was published by The Johns Hopkins University Press in 1982.

(6.4) *Home care.* In the early stages of the disease supportive psychotherapy can help the patient and family to deal with the many problems arising from senility. Psychiatric symptoms such as depression and anxiety may precede the more disabling defects in judgment, memory, and orientation. When this happens, appropriate drugs (5-15), (5-8) may improve functioning for months or even years. It is always important to encourage as much self-care and responsibility as is realistic. This encouragement not only increases feelings of self-worth, but minimizes the burden on friends and relatives. The additional demands and gradual loss of a loved one can evoke in the family numerous feelings, including anger. These feelings are to be expected and should be accepted, although professional help frequently is necessary to achieve acceptance.

Senile people may neglect good nutrition, particularly if they eat alone. This neglect can result in vitamin deficiencies, which make the mental impairment seem worse, and a decreased fluid intake, which increases debilitation. Although vitamin supplements are simple enough to give, if a person fails to eat and to drink properly, specialized care is usually required. Depending upon the problem, it may be helpful to use flexible straws and avoid dry foods that are difficult to swallow.

Some patients become fearful, particularly at night. A nightlight near the bed may prevent the quiet dark from being frightening or even terrifying and cut down on nighttime wandering. A good lock on the door can keep the nighttime wanderer off the streets. Skin sores can develop in people who must be immobilized in bed for long periods of time. If the person loses bowel or bladder control, diapers can prevent soiling. While the use of diapers may be disturbing at first, they are effective and allow people to remain at home who otherwise might have to be in an institution.

Rehabilitation and physical therapy can help in making the best use of the functions that are retained. Exercise, particularly walking, should be encouraged even if assistance is required. While large gains cannot be expected, every effort to maximize and to adjust to the decreased level of functioning should be pursued. Eventually, custodial care may become necessary. Depending upon the nature of the problem, Medicare may pay a portion of the initial cost. It will never assume the major cost, however, particularly if long periods of care are needed. A family needs to discuss the financial aspects of this problem with its physicians and other professionals, carefully considering family needs and the available facilities. Social workers (5-45) are usually the professionals most knowledgeable about the various possibilities.

(6-5) *Institutional care.* Senility increases the likelihood that eventually a patient will require some form of institutional care. For people living with others who just need someone around for reassurance and gentle restraint, institutionalization is unnecessary. But, when greater vigilance is necessary—for example, to keep the person from wandering the streets—even the most devoted family and friends may not be able to provide adequate care. The care of an aging parent most often falls to one child in the family, with the other children contributing some assistance. The child who takes on this kind of responsibility easily can become resentful. So it is important for the other family members to let the caretaker know how much he or she is appreciated and to share the burden in every way possible. When a decision has been made to opt for some form of institutional care, both the patient and all family members must have a clear understanding of exactly what to expect and whether the admission is for treatment or for short- or long-term care.

(6-6) *Compulsory admission.* Every state has some provision to help people who refuse needed care. Programs, however, vary considerably from state to state. The usual requirements for compulsory admission are that there is a likelihood of danger to the patient or to someone else and that the refusal to be admitted to a facility is a product of the illness—a result of poor judgment or a delusion. Terminally ill people who say they want to die at home should be allowed to do so if possible. People who say they are taking good care of themselves at home—but are not—constitute another problem. If there is not sufficient help at home to care adequately for someone, that person must be placed in an institution. Ideally, the act of commitment is a joint endeavor in which the family, physician, and court work together toward the same goal and share the responsibility. The loss of civil rights is a grave procedure for anyone and should not be entered into lightly, for where there are dissident forces, everyone's discomfort is increased. A person who has been committed to an institution does not necessarily lose other rights. For example, depending on the nature of the legal procedures, the person may retain the right to make monetary decisions or to vote.

(6-7) *Financial affairs.* The senile individual will always need someone's help with financial affairs. If a patient needs help only in signing and depositing checks and getting bills paid, a bank can help obtain a power-of-attorney form and have it signed so that the person's relative or friend may take over these activities. If the assets are substantial and the patient's understanding is insufficient to sign over the power of attorney, a court procedure may be necessary, and the family will need to seek the advice of an attorney.

(6-8) *Use of drugs.* Drugs can make life a little easier. Overriding illnesses such as infections must be treated with antibiotics, while tranquilizers or sleeping pills (5-34) can ensure a night's sleep and decrease nighttime restlessness and wandering.

7

The Nervous System

(7-1) The nervous system provides the means of communication among the various parts of the body and between the body and the outside world. For the most part, we are unaware of the nervous system until a problem develops within it. We normally pay little attention to placement of our feet when we walk, the control of our hands when we write, or the sensation of pressure that causes our bodies to shift from one position to another while we sleep. It is only when our finger touches a hot stove that we become aware of the pain receptors in that finger. Even then, we feel the pain only after we have reflexively pulled the finger off the stove.

The nervous system consists of the peripheral sensors such as the pain receptors. Other receptors sense temperature, touch, and the position of the joints. From these receptors, signals are sent along nerves into the spinal cord. If the response to the signal is to be automatic, such as withdrawing one's finger, the message is sent directly out of the spinal cord to the muscles which pull the finger back. At the same time, the signal is sent up the spinal cord to the brain where the kind of stimulus present (hot) registers on our consciousness. The brain may instruct the arm to pull back only a few inches, because if the arm went any farther it might knock over a tea kettle. This is now conscious recognition of the situation (hot stove as well as the position of things around it), and the instruction to restrict the pulling back is done by the cerebral cortex, the two large hemispheres just under the skull. The cerebral cortex is also responsible for complex functions such as speech. The movement is made smooth by the extrapyramidal system (which goes astray in Parkinson's disease) and by the cerebellum, located in the back of the skull. Disordered nervous system function may cause pain, tremor, and weakness.

The Nervous System

HEADACHES AND OTHER KINDS OF PAIN

(7-2) People have different sensitivities to pain. Some people experience extreme discomfort from a wound or internal disorder, whereas others may shrug off the same problem, giving it little attention. A person and his or her relatives and close friends should know about that person's tolerance to pain. This is important because a complaint of discomfort from someone who never complains should be taken very seriously and quickly brought to the attention of a physician. Similarly, someone who finds that life brings a great deal of physical discomfort should seek evaluation of new pain or of exacerbations of old discomforts. Depending on the nature and severity of the complaint, a quick call to a physician may bring reassurance if that is all that is indicated, or a thorough evaluation if the physician decides that might be prudent. Frequently seeking consultation is better than failing to get an evaluation. Such an evaluation can lead to a determination of the cause of pain and to a lessening of fear. Bear in mind, however, the fable of the boy who cried "Wolf!" once too often. Physicians are human, and if they are called a great deal about complaints that turn out to be meaningless, there is a chance they may begin to regard all of your problems with the same jaundiced eye.

Anxiety plays an important role in a person's perception of pain. An experience may feel more painful when you are tense or anxious (5-4) than when you are calm and relaxed. Different kinds of pain are felt in individual ways. A person who may become very frightened by a headache may be able to cope easily with a severe leg fracture. Finally, most people deal with pain that is isolated to a single area, such as a knee joint, far better than pain that is more generalized.

(7-3) *Headache.* Everyone experiences headaches. There are several different kinds of headaches, each with specific patterns and causes. Most headaches are mild and can be controlled easily, though some can cause great pain and even incapacity. Since their causes range from the medically insignificant to the very serious and pressing, persistent headaches should be brought to a physician's attention.

Headaches can occur as a reaction to eating certain foods. These commonly are associated with foods containing additives such as monosodium glutamate (often used as a seasoning in Chinese food) or food containing antibiotics. Penicillin, for instance, may be found in meat because that antibiotic is sometimes used in animal feed. Headaches can be caused by hunger, by poor eating habits, by habitually drinking too much coffee (coffee-withdrawal headaches), or after excessive consumption of alcohol (5-35).

A dental abcess or a dying root can cause severe pain, frequently extending into the jaw or cheek. (Surprisingly, sudden pain in the jaw can

After Middle Age

also be the only sign of heart attack.) The eyes, ears, and nose have their ways of telling us something is wrong. Some people are sensitive to bright or flickering lights and can get headaches from reading in bright sunlight or driving in a fast-moving vehicle. A flickering light, often a fluorescent bulb, can have the same effect. It is unusual, however, for visual problems that have been present for some time suddenly to cause headaches in the elderly.

Ear pain frequently signifies an infection in the middle ear or possibly a boil in the external ear, both of which are treated easily by a physician. Pain in the middle ear can occur when you are in an airplane that is descending rapidly or when you are driving up and down steep grades. It can be relieved by chewing gum, swallowing, yawning, or (if necessary) using nasal decongestants. The latter are designed to open the eustachian tube connecting the back of the throat to the middle ear. Colds and allergies that affect the nasal mucosal membrane inside the nose can also affect the sinuses and produce pain above the eyebrows, behind the cheekbones, or deeper within the skull. Nasal decongestants usually are helpful here, along with cold mist (cold, not hot, shrinks the membrane) from a vaporizer. But if the pain persists for more than two or three days, especially when there is also a fever, a physician should be contacted.

Headaches also can signal physical difficulties in other parts of the body requiring medical attention. Occasionally, high blood pressure, diabetes, and other metabolic problems produce headaches. Trauma, tumors, and serious cardiovascular problems also can produce headaches, which are usually persistent and severe.

The most common headache, called "tension headache," is often set off by an emotional trigger. The pain is produced by muscle contractions around the head and neck. Such headaches frequently are described as causing a pressing or squeezing pain. The distinction sometimes made between a tension headache and a migraine is that the tension headache feels as if a belt were being tightened around the head, while the migraine feels as if somebody were hitting the head with a hammer. You may remember a well-made Anacin advertisement showing this a few years ago. Symptomatic relief from the tension headache can often be achieved by kneading the muscles of the back of the neck, the temples, and jaws for ten to twenty minutes. Simply concentrating on these muscles in a quiet room and trying to relax them is often effective. Common aspirin is the most effective nonprescription drug for headache or any other mild pain. It is also the major active ingredient in the combination drugs, such as Anacin, that can be purchased without a prescription. (But remember, what you are paying for when you buy aspirin by these trade names is expensive advertising.)

The Nervous System

(7-4) *Migraine headache* occurs periodically, and visual disturbances and vomiting are often associated with it. These headaches usually start after puberty and continue into late middle age, becoming less severe as life advances. They may occur for the first time, however, during menopause in women and in the fifth or sixth decades in men. Migraines are symptoms of a hereditary disorder that is in part related to societal factors, such as the pressures of contemporary living that force some persons—especially women (migraine is much more common in women than men)—to become tense and anxious as they try to achieve.

These headaches often occur during relaxation following a period of stress. There may be intervals of days or months between headaches. A migraine attack is believed to be caused by changes in the walls of vessels supplying blood to the brain. Changes in vision commonly occur before an attack starts. Vision may become blurred, or brilliant colors may be seen around lights. This symptom may last up to half an hour, followed by a headache affecting one or both sides of the head. Headaches that occur only on one side do not necessarily recur on the same side each time. The pain is usually severe, throbbing, and is associated with nausea, vomiting, aversion to light, and sweating. Usually an attack does not last longer than a day, and commonly it ends after a night's sleep. Because coffee contains caffeine, mild attacks sometimes can be aborted by drinking several cups of black coffee at the very beginning.

If the attack is not severe, aspirin or codeine can be helpful along with rest in a quiet, darkened room until the attack passes. Aspirin should be taken at the first sign of an attack. If the migraines are severe, a physician can prescribe relief through several drugs, including ergotamine (Ergomar and Gynergen) or an ergotamine and caffeine mixture (Cafergot).

(7-5) *Treating the acute migraine attack.* Ergomar, which is dispensed in green 2-mg tablets, should be placed under the tongue at the beginning of an attack and at half-hour intervals thereafter. No more than three tablets should be taken in any twenty-four-hour period.

Gynergen comes in 1-mg ivory-gray, sugar-coated tablets labeled "Sandoz" on one side and "78–48" on the other. Two tablets are swallowed at the beginning of an attack and one every half hour thereafter as needed, up to a total of six in twenty-four hours. Ergotamines are most effective, however, when injected by syringe under the skin or into a muscle during an early stage of an attack. If nausea accompanies an attack, ergotamines may be used in rectal suppository form. Inhalers are effective, but since it is hard to regulate the dosage and the side effects are serious, expert supervision is needed. Ergotamines are not advised for persons who are pregnant or who have had stroke, angina, or other vascular diseases.

Cafergot comes in pink sugar-coated tablets imprinted "Cafergot" and

After Middle Age

contains ergotamine and caffeine. Caffeine increases intestinal absorption of ergotamine, but it may also prevent sleep, and sleep seems to be helpful in relieving migraine. Compounds containing ergotamine cannot be taken for extended periods of time because they produce various undesirable side effects ranging from nausea, vomiting, stomach cramps, and tingling of the fingers and toes to gangrene of the fingers and toes.

(7-6) *Prevention of migraine* can be achieved with methysergide (Sansert). Methysergide comes in 2-mg yellow sugar-coated tablets with "Sandoz" imprinted on one side and "78–58" on the other. It is taken with meals in the dosage of 4 to 8 mg daily. It has been found to be very useful in migraine prevention, but since it can produce severe side effects, it should be used only when the migraine is disabling and then only for several months at a time. Side effects include insomnia, personality changes, difficulty in concentrating, restlessness, and a loss of hair. A more serious side effect, however, is overgrowth of fibrous tissue inside the body (retroperitoneal fibrosis). The overgrowths, like weeds in a garden, begin to choke vital organs, such as the ureters coming from the kidney. Fortunately, these overgrowths usually are reversible when the drug is discontinued. Clonidine (Catapres) (12-11), a drug that lowers blood pressure, is used in small doses for migraine. It does not have to be taken constantly since it continues to effectively stop migraine attacks for about three months after the patient has ceased to take it. Clonidine can be taken for three months and stopped and started again when needed. It does have side effects, though—depression, drowsiness, and dry mouth in particular. Propranolol (Inderal) (12-20), a blood pressure-lowering drug that is also used to treat angina, has been found to be useful in treating migraine.

(7-7) *Cluster headaches, also called histamine headaches,* are extremely painful headaches that occur on one side of the head. They frequently awaken a person from sleep and last thirty to ninety minutes. They occur in clusters within a period of a month or several weeks, disappear, and then return. The eye on the affected side becomes red and tearful. The nostril becomes congested, and the eyelid may droop. Unlike migraine, which causes a retreat to bed, cluster headaches usually cause a person to get up and pace the room. While migraine declines in incidence with age and usually occurs in females, cluster headaches do not begin until middle age and usually occur in males.

(7-8) *Facial pain (tic douloureux)* that occurs over the lower half of one side of the face may be due to trigeminal neuralgia. (The trigeminal nerve is the sensory nerve of the face.) This tic usually affects women and consists of sudden short bouts of excruciating pain that may be sharp, searing, or burning, and can be set off by a trigger zone (a small specific area). The pain can be triggered by washing the face, by speaking or

The Nervous System

eating, or even by a slight breeze. The attacks, lasting from one to fifteen minutes, can occur many times a day or a few times a month. To prevent the attacks, a person may speak without facial movement or eat food by cutting and swallowing small pieces rather than chewing larger pieces. After a few weeks of this, there may be no attacks for months; but eventually they will return. Relapses occur more frequently with time. The cause is unknown.

At the beginning of treatment, a physician will try a number of medications. The drugs most likely to be used, however, are carbamazepine (Tegretol, average dosage 600 to 800 mg once a day) or phenytoin (Dilantin, average dosage 300 mg once a day). They are normally used as anticonvulsant drugs. Tegretol comes in 100- and 200-mg round white tablets imprinted with "Geigy 47" and "67," respectively. Dilantin comes in a 30-mg white capsule with a pink band labled "P-D 365" and in a 100-mg white capsule with a brown band labeled "P-D 362." These drugs may provide complete or partial recovery at first, but the pain eventually may return. For greater effectiveness, the two drugs may be used together.

Side effects of phenytoin are slurred speech, tremors, drowsiness, and gum enlargement (this can be minimized by brushing the teeth vigorously). It also may cause nausea, indigestion, anemia, confusion, and rashes. Carbamazepine may cause dizziness, sleepiness, nausea, vomiting, dry mouth, rashes, and anemia. To prevent nausea, take these drugs with meals.

An injection of phenol into the trigeminal nerve can relieve pain for years, but it may have to be repeated. The nerve should be cut surgically only as a last resort.

(7-9) *Throat pain (glossopharyngeal neuralgia)* resembles trigeminal neuralgia in some respects. A nerve is involved, in this case the glossopharyngeal nerve, or the sensory nerve of the back of the throat. There is a trigger to the bouts of intense stabbing pain in the throat, sometimes extending to the ear. The trigger zone is located in the throat near the tonsils, and swallowing can set off the pain. Therapy consists of phenytoin or carbamazepine, the same drugs used to treat trigeminal neuralgia (7-8). If the drugs are ineffective, an operation to cut the glossopharyngeal nerve gives permanent relief.

DRUGS USED TO DECREASE PAIN

(7-10) *Nonhabit-forming drugs (nonaddicting, nonnarcotic)* can be used many times at a constant dosage without losing their effectiveness, unless the pain becomes greater. In addition, discontinuing the drug after using it for a long time does not require the body to undergo the adjust-

After Middle Age

ments associated with habit-forming drugs, such as temporarily increased anxiety, insomnia, nightmares, depression, thoughts of suicide, and the feeling that you need to go back on the drug.

(7-11) *Aspirin* is the best and the least expensive of the pain relievers that can be obtained without a prescription. The usual dose is two tablets (0.3 g each) every four hours. If it causes gastrointestinal irritation, it should be taken after a meal or with an antacid. Buffered aspirin (such as Bufferin) has only a small amount of antacid and offers little advantage over regular aspirin. Enteric-coated aspirin can also be tried when there is gastric irritation. Aspirin with an enteric coat passes through the stomach without causing irritation. It dissolves in the intestine and is absorbed into the body. Buy a brand name such as Ecotrin, since some of the generics sold under house names may never be absorbed into the bloodstream.

(7-12) *Aspirin compound (APC)* contains aspirin, phenacetin, and caffeine. It may be marketed as APC, Empirin, Fiorinal, or under a house name. Phenacetin is a weak pain reliever, and there is some question about whether it causes cancer. It has no advantage over aspirin by itself and is more expensive. If you like the stimulant qualities of caffeine, drink coffee, tea, or cola.

(7-13) *Acetaminophen* is an aspirinlike compound sold under such proprietary names as Tylenol, Tempra, Valadol, and Febrolin. Acetaminophen is about as potent as aspirin but is more expensive. Physicians may recommend its use when gastric irritation is a problem with aspirin. It may also be used when there is an allergy to aspirin or when the blood-thinning aspects of aspirin are a concern. As a rule, though, aspirin is preferred. Sustained use of acetaminophen occasionally produces kidney damage.

(7-14) *Propoxyphene (Darvon)* is a prescription drug that in most clinical trials has been less effective than aspirin and just a little better than placebo (sugar pill). It is much more expensive than aspirin and comes in 32- and 65-mg pink capsules labeled "Lilly HO2" and "Lilly HO3," respectively. Occasional side effects are dizziness, sleepiness, and nausea. It should be used only by people who cannot take aspirin or codeine. In early 1979, there was a good bit of controversy as to the safety of propoxyphene. Its chemical structure is that of an opiatelike narcotic, and there was concern that some people might become addicted to it and that it may even be causing some deaths. My own view is that, taken in the prescribed dosages, propoxyphene is a relatively safe, although not a very effective, drug. Do not take more than the prescribed dosage, however, and do not drink alcohol when you are taking propoxyphene (5-38).

(7-15) *Pentazocine (Talwin),* a prescription drug, is more potent than aspirin or codeine when given by subcutaneous injection. It is also avail-

The Nervous System

able in 50-mg peach-colored scored tablets. An oral dose of 50 mg is about the equivalent of 60 mg (1 grain) of codeine, but more expensive. Side effects include dizziness, nausea, vomiting, constipation, urine retention, and impaired thinking. Repeated use of pentazocine can be habit-forming, but this is less likely with pentazocine than it is with the narcotic pain relievers described below. Therefore, the use of pentazocine may be the better long-term practice.

(7-16) *Narcotic, habit-forming, and addicting drugs* are potentially dangerous if misused, yet they can be beneficial in many cases. In persons treated by physicians for acute pain for brief periods, addiction is very unlikely. When a person is terminally ill and the pain is chronic, concern about addiction ceases. The physician should prescribe the drugs in quantities large enough to alleviate the pain.

(7-17) *Morphine sulfate* is the best pain reliever generally available. A habit-forming drug, it can be given only by injection on a physician's order. It produces sleepiness, euphoria, constipation, and, occasionally, nausea and vomiting.

(7-18) *Meperidine (Demerol)* can be given either orally (50- and 100-mg white tablets with "W" stamped on them) or injected intramuscularly. It is somewhat less effective than morphine and has the same side effects, but these occur less often. Care must be taken to prevent addiction.

(7-19) *Codeine*, in a dosage of 8 to 65 mg taken orally every four hours, produces more effective pain relief than aspirin, although a combination of the two is more effective than when either drug is taken alone. Codeine is mildly habit-forming. It produces dry mouth, constipation, decreased cough reflex, and, occasionally, nausea and vomiting. In doses exceeding 65 mg, the side effects outweigh the benefits.

(7-20) *Heroin versus morphine.* Heroin in the United States can be used only for research purposes; this is because of its high potential for abuse. Yet there are impressionistic and anecdotal claims that it is a better analgesic for severe pain than morphine—particularly in helping terminally ill patients to live their last days without pain. The few carefully controlled studies that have been carried out, however, do not substantiate the impression that heroin is more useful than morphine for severe pain. If future studies also fail to demonstrate that heroin is more efficacious than morphine, it is unlikely that it will be released for clinical use in this country.

PAIN CLINICS

(7-21) When physicians have exhausted all reasonable resources in an effort to find the cause of pain, or when they know the cause of pain but are unable to relieve it, they may refer you to a pain clinic. Since persistent pain often causes people to shop around for a physician—which is both expensive and frequently discouraging—clinics dealing exclusively with pain can be enormously helpful. Pain clinics usually have teams of professionals (neurologists, neurosurgeons, psychiatrists, psychologists, and anaesthesiologists) trained to consider all the possible causes of pain. The team realizes that there is a problem (it is not simply "all in your head") and frequently can find a way to decrease the pain or cure it.

A note of caution: There are both medical and nonmedical pain programs that offer little help to the person with pain. Such "pain mills" should be avoided. Be sure to get your physician's advice about where to go, or ask the advice of someone in a university medical center. If you do not know someone at a medical school, you can often get the advice you seek by calling the secretary to the chairman of a neurology department, stating what you want, and asking to be put in touch with somebody in the department who can answer your questions.

TREMORS AND MOVEMENT DISORDERS

(7-22) *Tremors* are involuntary rhythmical movements, usually of the hands, feet, head, tongue, or jaws, occurring at a rate of three to eight per second. Though there are many different kinds of tremor, only a few are related to diseases of the nervous system. The parkinsonian tremor, occurring at an average rate of four to five per second, usually affects one or both hands. Characteristically, it occurs at rest. Movement suppresses it. For instance, a person with a severe tremor at rest is usually able to drink a glass of water without spilling a drop. The tremor resembles those of parkinsonism (7-24), but when it occurs in elderly people having no other symptoms, it will not progressively worsen in a manner like Parkinson's disease (7-24).

Action tremor (senile tremor) is the tremor typical of the aged. It occurs when a limb is held in a certain position (characteristic for each person) and during movements, such as writing. It is most pronounced when a person is being watched, and the embarrassment of the tremor aggravates the tremor. Others sometimes interpret it as a sign of nervousness. Similar tremors occur when alcoholics abstain, when a person is tired or very anxious, and in hyperthyroidism (overactive thyroid gland). Action tremor can be suppressed with the drug propranolol (12-20).

Intention tremor is a jerky interruption of forward movement that occurs when a person is performing a precise movement. It can seriously interfere with skilled acts and can be severe enough to put someone off

The Nervous System

balance. This type of tremor indicates a disease of the cerebellum (the rear, lower part of the brain that is concerned with the coordination of movements).

Tremors also can occur in association with states of agitation and confusion in a person who is taking a variety of medications. If you notice the sudden onset of a tremor, or if a tremor quickly becomes much worse, ask your physician whether it could be related to a medication you are taking.

(7-23) *Abnormal involuntary movements,* or dyskinesias, are inappropriate or excessive movements of limbs, face, or trunk. They frequently accompany getting older. Their origins are not known. Although they are a nuisance, most of these movements are medically insignificant. Some, however, are extremely important.

Common, but harmless, movements occur in other parts of the face in some people while they are blinking to avoid a bug or object moving toward their eyes. Twitching around the eye or in the cheek area (known as "live flesh") is common in fatigued persons. Various kinds of movement around the mouth are also common with age.

(7-24) *Parkinson's disease* is caused by degeneration of nerve cells in an area of the brain that contains dopamine, a chemical that is important because it allows brain cells to communicate with one another. The cause of Parkinson's disease is as yet unknown. Its symptoms, called parkinsonism, can also occur as a complication of other diseases such as viral encephalitis (inflammation of the brain) and arterial disease, and of some drug therapies and metal poisoning.

Parkinson's disease usually begins among persons in the 50- to 60-year-old age group. Often the first sign is a tremor of one hand and coarse, rhythmical movements likened to rolling a pill between the thumb and the index finger. Later, after months or years, the tremor appears in the other hand and even in the legs. The tremor of this disease is most obvious when the hands are at rest—it disappears during purposeful movements. Positions cannot be sustained for more than a few seconds before the tremor begins again (7-22). The tremor is made worse by emotional disturbances and fatigue. Soon after the hand tremor appears, movement of all parts of the body becomes slow, rigidity throughout the body becomes noticeable, and the face loses its expressive movements (a vacant or immobile expression appears). Until a person falls asleep at night, the tremor may shake the bed. Automatic movements, such as swinging of the arms when walking, decrease. The walk is characterized by short, shuffling steps that are more like a run than a walk. The hands are held rigidly. There may be cramps and muscle pain. Speech becomes rapid and monotonous, with slurring and repetition of syllables. Writing becomes cramped and progressively smaller. By making a concentrated effort, the

After Middle Age

patient can achieve normal movement, speech, and writing, but only for a short time until the concentration is lost.

The tendency for a patient with Parkinson's disease is to become immobile, and that eventually may lead to difficulties. Therefore, it is important that the help of a physical therapist be sought. Muscles of the hands and feet are most severely affected. The patient may have to be retaught how to stand up and sit down.

It is important both for victims of the disease and their close relations to understand that the symptoms of Parkinson's disease can be relieved and that the natural course of the disease is slow. The mental faculties are usually not affected, and life will continue for many more years. Some of the treatments for Parkinson's disease produce remarkable improvement and are compatible with near-normal life.

An excellent book describing Parkinson's disease is Roger C. Duvoisin's *Parkinson's Disease: A Guide for Patient and Family,* Raven Press, New York, 1978.

(7-25) *Drug treatment of Parkinson's disease.* There is no cure for Parkinson's disease, but many drugs do give relief. The belladonna, atropinelike anticholinergic drugs have been used for more than 100 years to treat Parkinson's disease, and they produce modest improvement by allowing more movement and sometimes decreased tremor. These drugs and the antihistamines, together with amantadine and bromocriptine (both drugs originally designed for treating other diseases), are usually the first medications used.

Trihexyphenidyl (Artane, average dosage 3 to 6 mg per day) comes in 2- and 5-mg scored tablets.

Benztropine (Cogentin, average dosage 1 mg twice daily to 2 mg three times a day) comes in 0.5-mg and 2-mg round white tablets and 1-mg white oval tablets labeled "MSD 21," "MSD 60," and "MSD 635," respectively.

Procyclidine hydrochloride (Kemadrin, average dosage 2 to 5 mg three times per day) comes in 2- and 5-mg scored tablets. The 2-mg tablet is labeled "F4B."

Biperiden (Akineton), average dosage 2 mg three to four times per day, comes in 2-mg white tablets stamped with a rounded triangle.

Anticholinergic drugs block the ability of certain nerves to transmit their signal. This blockade causes both beneficial results and unwanted side effects. The undesirable side effects are blurred vision, dry mouth, constipation, urinary retention, drowsiness, and mental confusion. Although the benefits of using these drugs usually outweigh the problems caused by them, your physician should always be told of these side effects since it may be advisable to change the dosage.

The Nervous System

Antihistamines have been used in combination with the anticholinergics and have fewer side effects, but the combination may cause sedation.

Diphenhydramine (Benadryl, average dosage 50 mg three or four times per day) comes in 25-mg pink and white capsules labeled "P-D 471."

Orphenadrine (Disipal, average dosage 50 mg three times a day) comes in 50-mg light green tablets labeled "Riker."

Amantadine (Symmetrel), a medicine developed to treat the flu virus, is also used for parkinsonism. The average dose is 100 to 200 mg per day. It comes in 100-mg red gelatin capsules (11-13).

Bromocriptine (Parlodel), comes in 2.5-mg tablets (labeled "Parlodel 2½") and 5-mg tablets (labeled "Parlodel 5"). The effective dosage varies considerably. Side effects include nausea, headache, and in some patients low blood pressure leading to light-headedness and blacking out when rising from a sitting position.

Another drug that may be prescribed for parkinsonism is L-dopa—by itself or in addition to other drugs. In the body, this compound is converted to dopamine, the brain chemical that is missing in patients with Parkinson's disease.

L-dopa or levodopa (average dosage 1 to 8 g per day) is available under different names: Bendopa comes in 250- and 500-mg capsules. Dopar comes in green 100-mg capsules, green-and-white 250-mg capsules, and green 500-mg capsules labeled "Eaton 13," "Eaton 14," and "Eaton 15," respectively. Larodopa comes in pink 100-, 250-, and 500-mg tablets labeled "Larodopa 100," "Larodopa 250," and "Larodopa 500," respectively, as well as pink and scarlet 100-mg, pink and beige 250-mg, and pink 500-mg capsules labeled "Larodopa 100," "Larodopa 250," and "Larodopa 500," respectively.

L-dopa can greatly diminish tremor and rigidity. Unfortunately, there are a number of side effects and other problems. One is abrupt loss of the drug's effectiveness, which may return just as suddenly, or daily fluctuation of the drug's effectiveness. Frequent small doses may avoid some of these problems. Pyridoxine (Vitamin B_6, which is found in most multivitamins) should be avoided because it may inhibit L-dopa's effectiveness. Nausea, vomiting, and loss of appetite also can occur. L-dopa may induce new kinds of movements, occasional depression (5-9), insomnia (5-17), irritability, or marked confusion. Blood pressure may fall. "Start hesitation" (trying to walk and failing), which may occur after taking L-dopa for a long time, can be relieved by decreasing the dosage. This drug may produce abnormal movements on its own, particularly around the face and hands. Because the effectiveness of L-dopa often diminishes with time, many neurologists reserve its use until late in the course of Parkinson's disease.

After Middle Age

Sinemet (dosage highly variable) comes in dark dapple-blue oval scored tablets labeled "MSD 647" and light dapple-blue oval tablets labeled "MSD 654." It is a combination of L-dopa and another drug (carbidopa) that enhances L-dopa's effect and therefore reduces the amount of L-dopa that is needed. Consequently, there is less nausea and vomiting associated with the drug. Occasionally, because of side effects such as nausea or cardiac arrhythmias, a patient will need more carbidopa than is in Sinemet. Your physician can prescribe carbidopa for you or get it by writing to Merck, Sharp & Dohme.

NUMBNESS AND TINGLING

(7-26) *Numbness* in the legs, toes, or fingers can occur from a number of causes. There is the transient numbness and tingling sensation ("my foot is asleep") that comes from crossing the legs or from sitting too long in one position. This numbness responds within a few minutes to moving the leg or to walking, both of which restore blood circulation.

Prolonged numbness and tingling can be a side effect of drugs, anemia (pernicious anemia), diabetes, and (rarely) syphilis. Often, however, it can be caused by arthritic changes in the neck affecting the nerves. If you have these symptoms, you should be seen by your family physician initially. Eventually, however, it may be necessary for you to see a neurologist.

LOSS OF MUSCLE POWER

(7-27) *Paralysis* is the loss of muscle power produced by damage to the brain, spinal cord, or nerves that go to the muscles. The most common kinds of paralysis follow strokes and trauma. When there is an inability to use the bladder or an arm or a leg, rehabilitation specialists are needed to help prevent further damage and to restore maximum function.

(7-28) *Facial palsy (Bell's seventh nerve palsy)* is a transient paralysis of one side of the face. The cause is unknown, but it is possible that an inflammation produces swelling and pressure on the facial nerve. There may be an initial pain behind the ear on the affected side lasting one to two days, then paralysis develops. The mouth hangs down, and saliva may run out at the angle. The eyelid may not close, and when an effort is made to close it, the eyeball rolls upward. Lines and facial expression disappear. The ability to raise the eyebrows and to whistle is lost. Food collects between the teeth and the paralyzed cheek, and there is a feeling of numbness similar to that brought on by a local anesthetic. There is no actual loss of sensation, however.

The Nervous System

Usually facial palsy improves spontaneously after four to six weeks, but it may take one to two years to mend completely. Treatment consists of taking aspirin (7-11) for any pain that occurs and steroids during the first week to lessen inflammation. The affected side should be protected from the cold, and an eye patch should be used to prevent particles from getting into the eye, since the normal blink reflex is absent. Electric stimulation of the muscles and gentle upward massage for five to ten minutes, two or three times per day, also helps maintain muscle tone. When recovery begins, special facial exercises prescribed by a physical therapist quicken recovery.

(7-29) *Ulnar nerve palsy* is a weakness of the arms and hands; it produces an inability to move the hand forward at the wrist. The fingers may take the form of a claw, and the small finger may lose its sensation. Since the ulnar nerve runs across the elbow, it is likely to be injured with trauma to that region.

(7-30) *Radial nerve palsy* produces an inability to straighten the elbow. The wrist and fingers cannot be moved backward, and sensation is lost over the back of the forearm. The palsy can develop from an injury in the armpit, from using a crutch, or from resting on the back of the arm. Recovery from pressure palsies of this type usually is rapid.

(7-31) *Carpal-tunnel syndrome* produces an inability to bend forward the index finger and end of the thumb. This results when the median nerve becomes compressed as it enters the palm of the hand. Surgery may be required to relieve the compression.

INJURIES

(7-32) *Head injuries* in the elderly are commonly caused by falls, although obviously they also can be caused by car accidents and other forms of trauma. Anyone sustaining a significant head injury shuld be examined by a physician to find out if damage to the skull and brain has occurred and whether there is bleeding within the skull. This is especially so if the injury is followed by unconsciousness, dizziness, blurring of vision, ringing in the ears, or nausea. Recovery from a head injury depends on the amount of damage, not to the skull, but to the brain itself.

There are two types of injury. Closed head injuries are those in which there is little or no injury to the skull. In the mild form, there is a brief loss of consciousness, lasting seconds or even minutes, after which there may be a loss of memory of the incident and of the events occurring immediately before it. In the more severe form, the person may lose consciousness for hours or days. In open head injuries, the complications are serious because there is a bone fracture, hence a potential route of infection from the outside. With this type of injury, the individual may not lose consciousness at once, but the brain may swell or hemorrhage, and that leads progressively to loss of consciousness. Damage to the brain usually is located either beneath the point of impact or directly opposite it.

There is an increased likelihood that a head injury will cause bleeding within the skull of an elderly person, even if the injury is slight. The danger is increased even more because the most typical hemorrhage in the elderly is subdural—that is, the bleeding occurs in the space between two of the layers covering the brain (the dura and the arachnoid). This bleeding is usually very slow, producing symptoms only after weeks have passed. The blood clot gradually becomes large enough to compress the brain, and this causes increased pressure within the skull. Symptoms are headaches followed by drowsiness, changes of mood, and changes of behavior. As the symptoms worsen, the neck becomes stiff. The treatment is surgical—it is necessary to open the skull and remove the clot.

All injuries to the head should be treated with care and watched for several weeks after the incident. Even when there are no symptoms, trouble may be silently spreading beneath the surface. If you sustain a head injury, don't hesitate to call on your physician for a thorough examination.

(7-33) *Spinal cord injury.* The common causes of spinal cord injury are falling down a flight of stairs or being in an automobile accident. Injuries from the latter have been greatly reduced by the use of headrests and seat belts. Neck injuries (whiplash) from rear-end collisions are sustained during the sudden stretching of the neck as the head snaps backward and then forward.

The spinal cord lies in the center of a canal formed by the bony vertebrae, which sit one on top of the other like a set of hollow blocks. When one of these vertebrae becomes displaced, the cord is stretched. The narrow bony canal in which the spinal cord lies thus becomes even narrower, compressing the cord and damaging it. As a result of this squeezing and stretching, small areas of the cord become injured.

The effects on the nervous system depend on which level of the cord is damaged. If the damage occurs in the neck, all of the body below the neck will be temporarily paralyzed, but if the damage is below the waist, the paralysis may be only of the muscles below the knee. At first all function is lost, and there is no sensation, no sweating, no movement. There is also loss of bowel and bladder function. This is called spinal shock. What happens next depends on how severely the cord is damaged. If the problem is minor, normal function may return within a few hours. Paralysis may last a few weeks in more severe cases. Very rarely, the cord is cut in two, and no recovery can be expected; the paralysis will persist.

The Nervous System

INFECTIONS OF THE NERVOUS SYSTEM

(7-34) *Meningitis.* Inflammation of the membranes covering the brain (meninges) is called meningitis. It is caused by bacteria, viruses, or fungi that find their way into the fluid surrounding the brain. Bacteria enter the brain through the bloodstream from infections in the ear or through a fracture of the skull. The most common type of meningitis in adults is caused by bacteria called the pneumococcus. The symptoms are a severe headache that spreads to the neck, fever, nausea, vomiting, stiffness of the back (pain on moving the head forward), an aversion to light, and sometimes convulsions (7-39). The patient may be irritable and lie curled up on one side. Subsequently the individual will become confused and drowsy and go into a coma. If meningitis is caused by a virus, the symptoms are less severe, and although no specific treatment is available, it usually clears up on its own.

It is important that the organism causing the meningitis be recognized early. If it is bacterial, it can be treated with a specific antibiotic such as penicillin. The organism is identified by taking some fluid from the spinal canal by a spinal tap. Although a spinal tap is occasionally painful and, to most people, frightening, it is usually only a mildly uncomfortable procedure; complications are rare. The needle is inserted in an anesthetized area, and fluid is withdrawn from around the spinal cord. The fluid is then examined under a microscope for the bacteria and cells that will establish a diagnosis. Attempts to grow (culture) the bacteria are also made.

To prevent a headache after a spinal tap, lie flat on your abdomen with your feet higher than your body for at least six hours. This eliminates leakage of spinal fluid out of the small hole left by the needle. Drinking glasses of fluid during this period also helps prevent headaches.

(7-35) *Brain abscesses* are cavities in the brain containing bacteria and pus. Infections can spread to the brain from the ear, from an open fracture of the skull, or from a distant infection by way of the bloodstream. Abscesses can be single or multiple.

If the abscess develops suddenly, such as might happen after a head injury, there will be headache, fever, vomiting, and drowsiness. The patient may lose consciousness. If treatment is delayed, with abscesses that develop slowly, the symptoms are similar to those of a brain tumor: headache, personality change, or unexplained ill health.

The treatment consists of antibiotics and drugs to reduce the pressure within the skull. When these measures do not help, the abscess is drained surgically. Because abscess can recur, it is important for the physician and the patient to be on the lookout for symptoms similar to the original ones after treatment is completed.

After Middle Age

(7-36) *Encephalitis* is an inflammation of the brain. Viruses that invade the brain and kill nerve cells usually cause encephalitis, but this disorder also can be caused by complications of a vaccination and by drugs, poisons, or bacterial toxins. The symptoms are fever, which may be as high as 103°F (39.4°C), sore throat, nausea, vomiting, drowsiness, convulsions, and coma. Other signs are stiff neck (pain on moving the head forward), tremor, paralysis, and headaches (caused by increasing pressure in the skull). Later, especially in the elderly, there may be complications such as pneumonia, retention of urine, and bedsores, as well as mental deterioration, parkinsonism (7-22) and seizures. Encephalitis usually lasts two to three weeks and is followed by a gradual recovery. There is no specific treatment for most causes of this disorder, but many of the symptoms can be greatly reduced and complications prevented. The pressure in the skull can be lowered with drugs, seizures can be controlled with anticonvulsants, and infections can be prevented with antibiotics.

BRAIN TUMORS

(7-37) *Brain tumors* are rare. When a tumor does occur, it can be benign, in which case surgical removal usually leads to the patient's recovery, or it can be malignant (cancerous), in which case successful treatment is less common. The symptoms of a tumor are caused by destruction of brain substance and increased pressure within the skull. The symptoms of both benign and malignant tumors resulting from brain destruction are changes in mood, personality, and eyesight and the development of paralysis. Not all these changes occur in any one individual—they depend on the position of the tumor within the brain. The symptoms resulting from a change in pressure are headaches, vomiting, and convulsions. The headaches, throbbing and bursting, are worse in the morning and become less severe as the day goes on, but they last progressively longer each day. They are made worse by exertion, lying down, coughing, and sneezing. As the tumor enlarges, drowsiness and even coma follow if the pressure is not relieved.

Brain tumors do not spread from the nervous system to other body systems. Most are secondary, arising from tumors of other systems such as the lungs, breasts, or gastrointestinal tract. About half the tumors originating in the brain are gliomas, tumors of the glial cells, which give structural support to nerve cells, and can be relatively benign or malignant. Another group of tumors comprises those of the meninges, the membranes covering the brain. These tumors, called meningiomas, are very slow growing and do not invade the brain. They are usually removed

The Nervous System

surgically. When they cannot be removed, the individual still enjoys many years of good health because of their slow growth. The last group comprises tumors of the pituitary gland, which is in the lower part of the brain behind the eyes. These tumors are usually benign.

The treatment of meningiomas, some pituitary tumors, and some gliomas involve surgery. Other types of brain tumors are treated by radiotherapy or drugs which give varying degrees of improvement. The symptoms of the tumors can be lessened. The pressure in the skull is lowered with drugs that remove some of the fluid around the brain. The headaches are treated with aspirin (7-11) or codeine (7-19). If the individual has seizures, anticonvulsant drugs can be given.

(7-38) *Computed tomography (CAT or CT) scan* is a relatively new x-ray method that allows radiologists to get a three-dimensional picture of the structures inside the head or other part of the body. The amount of radiation from the x-ray is small. Unlike most procedures used to diagnose serious brain disorders (which also may be used), the CT scan does not require the injection of dyes (although the radiologist may give an intravenous dye to give better contrast on the film), a spinal tap, or other invasive techniques. For a CT scan, the patient is placed on a movable table. The head or part of the body to be studied is held firmly, and the table is moved into a cylindrical x-ray device. The x-ray beam rotates around the head or body. The x-ray is scanned frequently by a sensing device, and information is fed into a computer, where a picture is made.

CONVULSIVE DISORDERS

(7-39) *Epilepsy.* An epileptic seizure or convulsion is a disorder involving extreme hyperactivity of the brain, usually associated with a change or loss of consciousness. The disorder has no relationship to intelligence. Epilepsy beginning in adulthood occurs in two forms: grand mal epilepsy, affecting the whole body, and partial, or focal, epilepsy, affecting only a part of the body. Usually there is an underlying disease of the brain, such as hardening of the arteries, a tumor, or a disorder primarily affecting another system of the body. After the first convulsion, investigations need to be carried out to find the cause.

A grand mal attack develops through several phases. The first phase, usually a change of mood lasting hours or even days, warns the experienced epileptic that an attack will occur. The second phase, which occurs only in some patients, is an aura lasting one or two seconds. Often the aura is a sensation starting in the stomach and moving to the neck and head. The third, or tonic, phase lasts 20 to 30 seconds as the individual loses consciousness and falls to the ground. All the muscles contract, including those controlling breathing. Air is forced out of the lungs, and the individual makes a crying sound. Breathing stops, and the epileptic becomes pale or even blue. The fourth, or clonic, phase also lasts about half a minute. During this time the individual makes powerful jerking movements, and saliva froths in the mouth. Then there is a period of relaxation, in which the individual lies quietly and is unresponsive to stimuli such as saying his name. There is then a change to normal sleep. This final phase may last only a few minutes. During the third and fourth phases, patients may injure themselves, bite their tongues, and be incontinent (lose control of the bladder).

Partial epilepsy is caused by a change in one region of the brain. There are many variations in its symptoms. The usual symptom is the involuntary movement of one limb. This type of seizure may include hallucinations (5-32) and déjà vu, a feeling of familiarity with a situation as if it had happened before, or movements that affect part of one limb. The movements may even spread to involve the whole body, and the individual may become unconscious.

A physician cannot be absolutely certain that a patient has epilepsy without witnessing an actual attack, and often this is not possible. The next best thing is to have a good description of what happened from an eyewitness, as well as the individual's own account of what happened. The next stage is an investigation to find a cause for the convulsions.

(7-40) *Emergency treatment of a seizure.* During a grand mal seizure, an object such as a handkerchief should be put between the teeth to prevent biting of the tongue. If possible, dentures should be removed, restrictive clothing (ties, belts) loosened, and hard objects and furniture on which the person could be injured kept out of the way. A convulsion is frightening but usually lasts only a few minutes. If it lasts longer, get the patient to an emergency room quickly. In any event, when the convulsion is over, a physician should be seen.

When possible, the cause of the convulsion should be treated. In many cases, anticonvulsant drugs such as phenobarbital (5-8) or phenytoin (Dilantin) (7-8) are needed. These drugs should never be discontinued suddenly by the patient, as this can trigger status epilepticus, a continuous succession of convulsions that occur without any period of recovery. These convulsions can be fatal if not controlled quickly. Those who are interested can join the Epilepsy Foundation of America to receive information about research on, and treatment of, the disorder. The address is Suite 528, 815 15th Street NW, Washington, D.C. 20005.

THE KINDS OF PHYSICIANS TREATING THE NERVOUS SYSTEM

(7-41) Many problems relating to the nervous system can be treated by an internist or physician in family practice. Specialists are sometimes needed, however. The neurologist specializes in the diagnosis and treatment of nervous system disorders and will have graduated from medical school, taken an internship, and then spent at least three years in a neurology residency program. Most neurologists are certified in neurology by the American Board of Psychiatry and Neurology. This certification is recognition of the physician's training and ability as seen by peers.

The neurosurgeon specializes in surgery of the nervous system and will have graduated from medical school, taken a surgical internship, and then spent six more years training as a neurosurgical resident. Most neurosurgeons are certified in neurosurgery by the American Board of Neurological Surgery.

Even among physicians as specialized as neurologists and neurosurgeons, there are subspecialists. Some may be experts, for example, in epilepsy or muscle disease. These highly specialized physicians can usually be found at medical schools or in large group practices.

Seeing, Hearing, and Smelling

(8-1) There is often a decrease in the ability of sensory organs with age. Because our eyes and ears are so important in providing constant contact with the world outside ourselves, both sensing danger and providing pleasure, their loss is of great concern. This chapter describes the problems that sometimes develop in these organs and what can be done about them.

THE EYES

(8-2) Age often brings impaired eyesight, and activities once taken for granted may no longer be possible. Reading and participating in certain hobbies may become more difficult. It is easy for a person with failing vision to become less interested and sometimes even fearful of the world. If your vision is still strong, protect it by seeing your eye doctor regularly (once every two years). If your vision has begun to weaken, there is even greater reason to be sure your eyes are getting the proper medical attention.

A number of changes occur in the eyes with increasing age, but many of them are quite harmless. For example, the arcus senilis, which is the grayish-yellow ring that partially or totally encircles the colored part (iris) of the eye, grows larger with age. The condition seems to be normal and does not alter vision. When it occurs in a young person, however, it is sometimes associated with an increase in blood lipids (12-16).

(8-3) *Types of eye doctors.* Ophthalmologists (oculists) are medical doctors (MDs) specializing in eye diseases. They treat any kind of eye emergency, prescribe drugs, perform surgery, and test for and prescribe glasses.

Seeing, Hearing, and Smelling

Optometrists specialize in detecting visual defects and in treating them with glasses. They also will detect other medical problems, but must refer them to an ophthalmologist for further diagnosis and proper treatment.

Opticians fit, adjust, and dispense various forms of eyeglasses from the written prescriptions of ophthalmologists and optometrists. Optometrists and opticians are not medical doctors.

(8-4) *Senile macular degeneration* is one of the most common eye problems of aging. But its cause, prevention, and cure are not known. The first symptom usually is increased difficulty in reading. The ophthalmologist looking into the eye of a patient with this problem sees an unusual dark coloration at the macula (center) of the retina (the part of the eye that transforms light into nervous impulses). The dark coloration means that the retina is degenerating. While much of the fine vision is lost, peripheral vision usually remains, and so the individual does not become totally blind. Reading can be aided by using strong reading glasses and a magnifying glass.

(8-5) *Myopia (nearsightedness).* The nearsighted person sees well those objects that are close by, but has difficulty seeing things at a distance. In fact, the near vision may be even better than normal. Myopic eyes focus the light rays at a point in front of the retina (8-4). Like a picture out of focus, the image is blurred. Nearsightedness is almost always caused by lengthening of the eyeball and develops in childhood or young adulthood. The young can accommodate for the defect by screwing up their eyes, but this leads to headaches. Eventually, glasses are needed for seeing objects at a distance. There is no difficulty with near vision unless there are different degrees of nearsightedness in each eye or unless an astigmatism is present. Astigmatism is an uneven curvature of the lens that also causes blurring of vision and discomfort when the eyes are used. Reading and fine motor activities should be done in a good light.

(8-6) *What is a good reading light?* To some degree this depends upon the person, the size of the type being read, and how the light reflects from the paper being read. While occasionally someone will actually read better in a dim light, most people as they get older need a stronger light. First, determine if you hold your reading material to one side. If so, that side is the side the light should come from—if the material is held to the right, the light should come over the right shoulder. If it is held directly in front of the eyes, the light should shine from behind, just over the forehead. Once you position the light, try out several bulbs of different wattages to see what works best for you. A 200-watt bulb may be needed.

(8-7) *Hyperopia (farsightedness).* When the eyeball is shortened, light rays are focused behind the retina (8-4), and objects close at hand are seen poorly. When there is only minimal shortening of the eyeball, there are no symptoms because the eye muscles can accommodate and refocus the image. But accommodation requires an effort by the eye muscles, and so the eyes may become strained while doing near work in dull or artificial light. The symptoms of eye strain are frequent blinking, pain and watering of the eyes, blurred vision, and headaches. Except when hyperopia is severe, vision remains normal for seeing objects more than twenty feet away, but glasses are needed for reading. Glasses carry out the same work as accommodation in reducing eye strain.

(8-8) *Presbyopia (loss of accommodation).* With age, the elasticity of the lens of the eye decreases. It is then impossible to focus on (accommodate) close objects. Reading matter, for example, has to be held farther away. Eventually normal print has to be held so far away to focus it that it is too small to read. The normal reading distance is usually 9 to 13 inches (23 to 33 centimeters), but it gradually increases to 18 inches (46 centimeters) by age 45.

Reading, sewing, and other types of close work have to be held farther away, and print becomes pale and indistinct. Headaches, watering of the eyes, and dimness of vision are symptoms, all of which become worse in low or artificial light. Yet there is no change in the ability to see things at a distance. When presbyopia occurs with farsightedness in persons over 45, two pairs of glasses should be used; a weaker pair for far vision and a stronger pair for near vision. Bifocals accomplish the same purpose, since the upper part of the bifocal is used for seeing things at a distance, while the lower, stronger part is used for seeing things close by.

The strength of the lenses needed for close work depends upon age, on the preferred reading distance, on occupational requirements, and on whether glasses are used to correct any other condition. If a person is farsighted and has presbyopia as well, the lenses must be stronger. A person with presbyopia who originally was nearsighted may be able to read without using glasses. Again, eyes should be checked every two years, since presbyopia progresses with age and may require stronger glasses from time to time. If you find you have your glasses changed very often, make sure you have your eyes examined for glaucoma (8-19).

(8-9) *Contact lenses* were invented in 1887, but they became popular only when the small corneal plastic lens was developed in the 1950s. There are two types of contact lenses: the larger scleral contact lens, which fits over both the sclera (the white of the eye) and the cornea (the clear part over the pupil), and the more popular corneal contact lens, which measures a centimeter (half an inch) or less in diameter. The inner surface of the contact lens fits the shape of the eyeball exactly, and the outer surface of the lens changes the power of the eye. The lens does not actually touch the eyeball but floats on the fluid of the eye's surface, and is held in place by the pull of, the fluid. Since the outer edge of the contact lens is thin, it slides easily under the eyelid when the eye blinks, and so it is not an irritant.

Contact lenses most often are used by the nearsighted and by those who have had their natural lenses removed because of cataracts (8-15). The advantages of wearing contact lenses are many: They make the image a more normal size than do glasses; they provide less distortion by moving with the eye so that vision is always through the center of the lens, and they are more attractive than thick-lensed glasses. There are also disadvantages: they need much more care than glasses, having always to be kept clean; they cause irritation at first, especially if they are poorly fitted; and they should not be used by people who are prone to conjunctivitis (8-12) or corneal ulceration, people who have glaucoma (8-19) or diseases of the tear glands, and people who are unable to look after the lenses properly.

The eyes have to adapt to wearing contact lenses. At first, then, the lenses cannot be worn for long periods of time. Initially, there is an awareness that something is in the eye, and there may be increased sensitivity to light and some tearing. When regular glasses are used again, vision will be temporarily blurred. All these symptoms disappear in time. If they don't, or if they become worse, the lenses should not be worn until a doctor has checked them. Lenses that are ill-fitting will either cause a burning sensation or tend to fall out. If the power of the lens is inaccurate or inadequate, or if the lens is warped, or if one has been inserted into the wrong eye, vision will be blurred. Foggy vision occurs immediately after the lens is inserted if the lens is dirty, and will last up to two to three hours if the cornea is irritated and swollen. The overwearing of contact lenses, either through overenthusiasm during the period of adaptation or by falling asleep with the lenses in the eyes, causes pain, swelling, watering of the eyes, and increased sensitivity to light for two to three hours after the lenses have been taken out. If the pain is intense, the most affected eye can be covered (physicians do not want to put a patch on both eyes at the same time), and it will recover in a day.

Contact lenses come in soft and hard varieties. Soft lenses are larger and more expensive than hard lenses, but they are less easily displaced and less likely to fall out (a major problem for some people). Wearers of hard lenses have found that it may take a week or more to adapt back to eyeglasses, something that usually can be done in an hour with soft lenses. Hard lenses must be worn every day for at least a few hours in order to maintain tolerance, whereas soft lenses can be tolerated if worn only occasionally. Soft lenses tend to keep foreign bodies away from the cornea because they are larger. Soft lenses may not, however, correct for

After Middle Age

astigmatism (8-5). Extended wear soft lenses that may be worn continuously for weeks are also available.

(8-10) *Problems of the eyelid.* In entropion the edge of the eyelid turns inward with resulting irritation of the cornea. Because continued scratching ultimately can lead to ulceration of the cornea, the irritation must be treated by an ophthalmologist who may suggest massage or application of adhesive tape to the inward-turned lid to pull the lid outward. Eventually, most people require simple outpatient surgery to rectify the problem. Ectropion is a turning out of the eyelid, resulting initially in tearing but later in itching and redness of the white of the eye. Surgical repair is necessary.

Drooping of the lids, or *ptosis,* often occurs as age advances and usually is of no consequence. In rare instances it is the first sign of generalized muscle weakness (myasthenia gravis). Treatment, if necessary, consists of using 10 percent phenylephrine (Neo-Synephrine) drops or applying adhesive tape. If all else fails, surgery may be necessary.

(8-11) *Tearing* that lasts for several days is caused either by excessive formation of tears or by poor functioning of the passages (lacrimal ducts) that remove tears. Conjunctivitis (8-12) is the most common cause of tear overproduction; crying, cold weather, and bright lights are other causes. Simple probing by an ophthalmologist usually suffices to clear stopped ducts.

(8-12) *Conjunctivitis (pink eye)* is an irritation of the white membrane covering the outer eye or the red inner part of the eyelids (conjunctiva). Conjunctivitis causes itching, burning, tearing, and redness. If it does not improve within forty-eight hours, a physician should be consulted. Conjunctivitis can occur during periods of heavy pollution, or even from spending many hours in a smoke-filled room. If it occurs immediately after swimming in a pool, the chlorinated water may be the cause, or the cause may be an infection requiring treatment by a physician. Conjunctivitis may result during spring or summer from an allergy to pollen. One very common source of conjunctivitis is an allergy developed from one of the many drugs used in the eyes. With age, there is often more need to use drops and ointments in the eyes, and this increased exposure to a larger number of drugs produces an increased likelihood of developing a drug-related allergy. Commonly used drugs that may produce allergy are antibiotic ointments, atropine, local anesthetics, and idoxuridine. But, because many of these medications contain preservatives or drugs that decrease redness, it is not always easy to identify the specific cause of the allergy. Treatment consists of stopping the use of the offending drug, but if it was originally a prescription, discontinuation should be discussed with a physician.

Seeing, Hearing, and Smelling

(8-13) *Eye washes* sold at the drug store without a prescription, such as Visine or Murine, are advertised as being able to clear up redness (8-12) or tired eyes. This they may do, but their use should be strictly limited. Irritations of the eyes will either go away by themselves in forty-eight hours or should be treated by a physician. I feel that eyewashes are useful primarily for people with known allergies who are seeking temporary relief from itching. Anyone who uses drops cosmetically to have whiter eyes will find they may work at first, but with continued use the redness may actually become worse.

(8-14) *Cinders, bugs, and other foreign bodies* that get into the eye produce itching, pain, redness, and tearing. Do not rub the eye, but allow the tears time (ten or fifteen minutes) to wash out the object. If this is not successful, and if your hands are steady, try to remove it yourself. Sit in front of a mirror and a strong light. (Have the light come from the side—do not look directly into it.) Then moisten an edge of a soft tissue, and gently wipe away the object. Do not use fiber materials like cotton because you are likely to leave a bit of fiber in the eye. If you cannot wipe off the object, or if you cannot see it, let a doctor take it out. CAUTION: Never dig into the eye or lid. It may take several hours after the object is out for the irritation to dissipate. Any time there has been an injury or a foreign body in the eye and there is discomfort after twenty-four hours, an ophthalmologist should be seen.

Do not put pain-relieving drops in the eyes. This should be done only by a physician.

(8-15) *A cataract* is an opacity of the normally clear lens of the eye. It can vary in density and size according to its cause and its age. The cataract can accompany diseases such as diabetes, but usually it is a result of aging, and commonly occurs after the age of 50. It is almost always present in both eyes, though in differing degrees. At first, the cataract is only slightly opaque and blurs distant vision. Later, it becomes completely opaque and swollen from increased water content. Finally, the cataract becomes dense and dehydrated as the water escapes, and blindness results. Cataracts are not visible to the casual observer until this final stage. After the pupil has become white, vision decreases—paradoxically, most in bright light. Therefore, it may be easier for people with a cataract to read in dim light or with sunglasses. Objects may look blurred or double.

Individuals who stop using their glasses because near vision has improved probably have a phenomenon called second sight. Often, when this happens, vision of objects ten or more feet away is usually poor. The discovery of cataracts frequently follows. While this can be corrected for a period of time with glasses, eventually the cataracts have to be re-

After Middle Age

moved. There is no treatment for cataracts except surgery. If you have cataracts, the ophthalmologist will want to examine you frequently to determine the optimal time for surgery. Generally, the following criteria are used to determine when it is time to operate on a cataract.

1. If there are signs of progressive cataract in the good eye, it is time for surgery in the bad eye. This is so because it may take some time for a patient to fully recuperate from the operation, and the good eye itself will eventually need surgery. By this criterion the affected person will never be without serviceable sight.

2. When a cataract is fully mature, it should be removed, because leaving it will produce difficulties.

3. When a cataract coexists with glaucoma (8-19), it should be removed.

4. When a cataract interferes with the individual's occupation or important avocation, it should be removed.

The operation, which is painless and takes less than one hour, involves removal of the whole lens of the eye, usually under local anesthesia. Most surgeons allow their patients to get up as soon as they recover from the anesthesia and permit them to go home by about the third day. At first temporary glasses take over the job of the removed lens. Then contact lenses (8-9) often are prescribed. They make for easier adjustment to regaining sight and cause less visual distortion than do glasses. If contact lenses are chosen, reading glasses also are needed. Following the operation, the corrected vision usually is very good. Things may have a pink hue, which is normal. A partially drooping lid (8-10) after surgery is common and eventually will return to normal. In the last few years most cataracts have been replaced with artificial lenses implanted directly into the eye at the time of surgery. Serious complications are uncommon.

(8-16) *Corneal transplantation.* The cornea (8-9) is the transparent layer than covers the pupil (the black area opening into the back of the eye) and the iris (the colored muscle around the pupil). In some corneal diseases, such as inflammation, ulcerations, or injury, the cornea becomes opaque. When this happens to the part of the cornea overlying the pupil, a visual disturbance results. Superficial opacities of the cornea generally can be taken care of by removal of its outer layers. If this is unsuccessful, a corneal transplantation may be necessary, involving replacement of the damaged cornea with one donated by someone who has died. Corneal transplantation requires hospitalization for about two weeks. After the operation, bandages are kept over the eye and changed every second day, at which time antibiotics are applied to the eye to prevent infection. Steroids sometimes are used to stop graft rejection, especially if there are signs that the graft is becoming opaque. Stitches are removed about a month after the operation, and the dressings a week or two later. There is rarely any pain associated with the operation except for some discomfort on the first day.

Corneas can be donated at death through a nonprofit organization, The Living Bank International, P.O. Box 6725, Houston, Texas 77265. Hospitals and individuals involved in the program are supplied with permission forms. The donor signs one form, and has two witnesses. Many states now mark donor volunteers on drivers' licenses.

(8-17) *Retinal detachment* is the falling away of the retina, the part of the eye that senses light from its attachment. Early diagnosis is important, for the problem is usually treatable. There is no pain. The symptoms include the sudden appearance in one eye of floating spots, which may clear up in a few days or months. If there is no treatment at this stage, the next symptom is a loss of vision in one part of the eye. (To test for this close the good eye. What you see will appear as if a curtain were pulled over a part of the open eye.) Vision usually improves when the patient is in a reclining position because gravity tends to pull the retina back into place. If these symptoms appear, the patient must see an ophthalmologist as soon as possible and always within 24 hours. Until then it is advisable to wear a patch over both eyes except when they must be used for moving about.

Surgery to repair the damage is usually performed after several days of bed rest. In effect, the surgeon glues the retina back onto its attachment. Sometimes this is done with a laser (a highly focused, intense beam of light) under general anesthesia. The procedure causes little pain, but the eyes may remain covered for a few days after surgery, which frequently causes the patient to feel disoriented, and may sometimes cause anxiety. The physician may prescribe a drug to relieve the anxiety. Hospitalization lasts less than a week, and there is a full return to normal activity within three to six weeks. The possibility of future detachment, however, is high, so the person who has had one detachment should remain aware of the symptoms and have both eyes examined every six to twelve months.

(8-18) *Vitrectomy.* The vitreous is a clear, jellylike material that fills most of the back of the eye. Usually as the result of diabetes (16-7), but from other causes as well, the vitreous may become clouded and vision may be lost. The remedy is an operation—developed in the 1970s—which involves removing the clouded vitreous and inserting an artificial one. The entire operation takes about ninety minutes and is performed through fine instruments inserted into the side of the eye (away from the cornea). There is a very small risk of bleeding from the back of the eye, which makes vision worse.

(8-19) *Glaucoma* is a disorder of the eyes caused by increased fluid pressure within the eyeball. Pressure rises when the fluid made in the anterior part of the eye is produced faster than it is discharged. Tragically, the disease leads all too often to blindness. People over 40 should have their eyes tested for glaucoma (tonometry) every one to two years; with early treatment, blindness can be avoided. Glaucoma is rarely suspected unless a person is over 40. The suspicion intensifies in people who have a history of visual loss in the family, whose glasses are unsatisfactory, or who have aching around the eyes. To make a diagnosis, the doctor—either an ophthalmologist or an optometrist—painlessly measures the pressure within the eye. After numbing the eye with a drop of local anesthetic, the doctor holds an instrument called a tonometer against the eyeball and reads the pressure. A high pressure on one occasion does not necessarily mean glaucoma is present. It must be measured again. Newer methods for determining pressure include a measured puff of air that makes a slight dent in the eye. The size of the dent indicates the internal pressure. Careful examination of the inside of the eye with an ophthalmoscope also tells a great deal about the range of the disorder.

Glaucoma is sometimes hereditary—passed on from one generation to the next. It may be either acute (suddenly arising) or chronic (persisting). Most common is the latter. Vision is slowly and irreversibly lost, though most people remain unaware of the loss at first. There is usually no pain, but the eyes may have a dull ache. An increased brightness may appear around objects (a halo) and there may be a loss of vision to the sides. For treatment, eye drops are used to reduce the amount of fluid. These drops do not cure the glaucoma, but they control it. They must be used throughout life or the disease will proceed to blindness. In some people, the drops do not reduce the pressure, and an operation is then necessary.

Attacks of acute glaucoma, on the other hand, occur in persons whose eye structure allows the fluid outlet to be suddenly shut off, causing a rapid buildup in pressure. This pressure is very destructive and leads to blindness unless it is treated immediately. The first symptoms are severe pain in and around the eye, which can extend to any part of the head. It is often associated with nausea, vomiting, and blurring of vision. Glaucoma attacks are usually triggered by dilation of the pupil. This happens normally when a person goes from bright light into darkness, but it also may be caused by emotional stress, heavy fluid ingestion, or the use of such drugs as atropine. An acute glaucoma attack is a medical emergency, treated with drugs to reduce the pressure in the eye and relieve symp-

Seeing, Hearing, and Smelling

toms. The physician may give pilocarpine 2-percent drops in each eye every five minutes for thirty minutes, then every ten minutes for one hour, and finally once every hour. Glycerol given by mouth or urea or mannitol given by an intravenous drip also are used. For those who cannot reach emergency treatment in three to four hours, six to seven ounces of whiskey should be taken to alleviate the symptoms temporarily. Medical treatment must still be sought as quickly as possible. When the eye has recovered after emergency treatment, usually within a few days, surgery (iridectomy) is performed on both eyes to prevent a recurrence. Conditions that predispose to glaucoma are trauma, diabetes, tumors of the eye, dislocation of the lens, and complications of eye operations.

(8-20) *Drugs used for chronic glaucoma.* These drugs keep down pressure in the eye. One of the major drugs used, pilocarpine, increases the fluid outflow from the eye. The usual dosage for pilocarpine is one drop of 1- to 4-percent solution administered three or four times per day. In the presence of a cataract (8-15), drug-induced constriction of the pupil can make vision difficult. Night driving can also be hazardous. Initially, there may be a slight ache around the brow or eyes, but this disappears with time. Redness of the white of the eye (conjunctiva) is a sign of an allergy to pilocarpine. When pilocarpine fails, various other drugs may be prescribed, but their use is more complicated.

Ocusert Pilo-20 and Pilo-40 are recently developed lens-sized objects, made of clear flexible plastic that can be placed under the eyelid for slow release of pilocarpine. When properly inserted, they are not visible. If a person gets used to them, and most persons do, they can be used for seven days at a time, so that the patient does not have to put in drops four times a day. Older individuals with loose lids, however, may lose the Ocuserts. A decrease in vision, extreme nearsightedness, and headache indicate that the device has failed or has been lost. Ocuserts are much more convenient to use than drops, but they are also much more expensive.

Systemic drugs taken by mouth, such as the carbonic anhydrase inhibitors, are very effective. These include acetazolamide (Diamox, average dosage 125 to 250 mg two to four times per day), which comes in 125- and 250-mg scored, white tablets labeled "DIAMOX 125" and "Diamox 250," respectively. Other drugs in this family include ethoxzolamine (Cardase, Ethamide), dichlorphenamide (Daranide, Oratrol), and methazolamide (Neptazane).

Possible side effects include tingling and numbness in the hands and feet, loss of appetite, nausea, vomiting, and diarrhea. Headaches, depression, and confusion can occur. If so, they should be brought to the attention of a physician immediately.

After Middle Age

(8-21) *Transient loss of vision in one eye* is almost always caused by a vascular (blood vessel) disorder. A migraine (7-4) occasionally will produce a loss of vision, but before doing so it will cause blank areas or darkening of vision. The distortions persist for a period of ten minutes or longer before dissipating. The headache may or may not follow these episodes. Until proved otherwise, however, loss of vision in one eye is best considered caused by an occlusion of the artery to the eye and treated as a serious matter. Therefore, a physician should be seen immediately.

THE EARS

(8-22) *Hearing loss.* Presbycusis, a loss of the ability to hear high-pitched tones, is present in everyone over the age of 15, but it only becomes noticeable in the seventh or eighth decade of life. Those who have been exposed to loud noises in the armed forces, at work, or at rock concerts, usually become deaf earlier. If you are affected by presbycusis, you may find yourself sitting forward in a chair, frequently asking for words to be repeated, or smiling at everything because you cannot hear what is being said. You may play the radio too loud, causing others to complain.

Presbycusis is nerve deafness; that is, it is a progressive loss of the cells that pick up high-pitched sounds. Persons with presbycusis may have trouble hearing birds singing, clocks ticking, telephones ringing. For some reason not yet understood the impairment in hearing of spoken sound is greater than would be expected simply from measurable loss of hearing. Consonants are more difficult to hear than vowels, and this distorts words. Low-pitched sounds can be heard distinctly, but if they are loud or shouted, the noise can become intolerable. The changes in volume produce auditory fatigue. For the unaided hard-of-hearing, listening to a long conversation is tiring. Some people lose their self-confidence, feeling that others are excluding them by not speaking clearly or by speaking in a low voice.

Often presbycusis becomes noticeable when another cause of hearing loss occurs simultaneously, such as wax in the ear, fluid in the middle ear, or ostosclerosis, the immobility of certain important earbones (8-25). This condition usually can be treated effectively. Wax usually comes out of the ear naturally, but as people grow older, it tends to solidify and lodge in the ear. A physician removes wax by syringing the ear with warm water, thus softening and dislodging it.

(8-23) *Hearing aid.* If a hearing loss cannot be medically or surgically corrected, your physician may prescribe a hearing aid. Many people ex-

Seeing, Hearing, and Smelling

press an initial concern about the embarrassment of wearing a hearing aid. Although the devices are now very small, they cannot be completely hidden. Most patients get over this concern because hearing again brings them a great deal of happiness and self-assurance.

Hearing aids are of two types: one worn at ear level for people with a slight hearing loss; the other with the receiver carried in the pocket of those with greater deafness. Because a hearing aid amplifies all sounds, problems may develop from background noise and the noise from clothes rubbing against the body. And, because low-pitched sounds usually are heard quite well by the hard-of-hearing, they appear to be overamplified when the high-pitched sounds are just right. This is why most modern hearing aids have a mechanism that allows them to amplify only the high-pitched sounds. The average cost of an aid is $350. Noncommercial hearing aid centers, usually attached to hospitals, have personnel trained to help people select the best aid for a particular problem. For information about hearing loss or other hearing problems, or any problems related to communication disorders, contact the National Association for Hearing and Speech Action, 10801 Rockville Pike, Rockville, Maryland 20852.

The professional who determines the type of hearing aid to be used, instructs in its use, and makes sure it is functioning properly is called an audiologist. There should be regular reevaluations by the audiologist to ensure that the hearing aid is functioning properly.

The wearer has to take proper care of a hearing aid. The earmold should be kept clean, and wax should be removed from the canal tip daily. The outside of the ear should be cleaned with soap and water occasionally.

(8-24) *Instructions for family and friends* or anyone, when talking with someone who is deaf or hard-of-hearing:

1. Talk in a voice that can be heard across the room, but not so loud as to be heard outside the room.

2. Talk face to face in a clear light so your lips can be read.

3. Be sure your hands do not get in front of your lips.

3. Speak more slowly than usual.

4. Leave intervals between thoughts, and give the person a chance to reply.

A good gift for someone who has a hearing difficulty is a vibrating alarm watch or clock.

(8-25) *Otosclerosis* is a common disorder of the middle ear. The middle ear consists of three very small bones—malleus, uncus, and stapes—whose function is to transmit sound vibrations from the outer ear to the nerve in the inner ear. With age, these bones become less mobile, causing

After Middle Age

gradual hearing loss. There also may be some ringing in the ears. The physician will use a common tuning fork to make the initial diagnosis. When the tuning fork is held on the top of the head, the side on which the sound is best heard is the more affected ear. This is so because the sound is conducted to the nerve through the bones of the head rather than through the bones of the middle ear. Similarly, with otosclerosis, the tuning fork is heard better when it is touched to the bony area behind the ear than when it is held a short distance from the ear.

Fortunately, otosclerosis can be helped with either a hearing aid (8-23) or surgery. As a rule, most patients prefer to have the surgical procedure—called a stapedectomy—which is performed under local anesthesia in an operating room and causes a minimum of discomfort. Using a microscope the surgeon can see the fine bones and remove the diseased stapes. A plastic or wire prosthesis is inserted. The procedure usually restores hearing to normal, and the risk of complications is small.

Complete sudden hearing loss can occur within hours or a few days in one ear. It may happen while you are quietly resting, with nothing more significant than a "pop" preceding total silence. When hearing loss is sudden, it usually returns by itself. This loss of hearing, however, must be brought to the attention of a physician immediately (within eight hours). While many times the cause will be unimportant, it may be a sign of important pathology, such as a stroke or hemorrhage due to anticoagulants.

(8-26) *Ear infections.* Infections may occur either in the external part of the ear (otitis) or in the middle ear (otitis media). When the external ear is inflamed, the symptoms are itching, redness, tenderness, and a feeling of fullness in the ear that is followed by a discharge. The inflammation usually is caused by bacteria and generally can be cured by antibiotics. Depending on the patient's discomfort, the physician should be seen within twenty-four to forty-eight hours.

Otitis media occurs when an infection, usually from a cold, reaches the middle ear along the eustachian tube (a connection between the throat and middle ear). Such an infection is potentially dangerous because, on rare occasions, it can spread to the brain. The symptoms are pain, hearing loss, and fever. A physician should be seen within twenty-four hours after symptoms begin so that antibiotics and decongestants can be used immediately as treatment. If pus collects in the middle ear, the eardrum can be pierced and the pus removed. The procedure hurts intensely for a moment, but relief follows instantaneously. Prevention of otitis media can be accomplished by using decongestants and a vaporizer (you can simply stand in the shower with the water running; use cold water, this shrinks the swelling) when you have a cold.

Many persons whose ears are damaged and not treated when they were

Seeing, Hearing, and Smelling

young may now regain hearing by having their ears reconstructed. This surgical correction was not available until 1965. Hence, anyone whose ears were damaged before that date should now visit an otolaryngologist to determine whether the problem can be corrected.

(8-27) *The sense of balance* is controlled by three fluid-filled semicircular canals located in the inner ear. Because of this, generally it is the same physician who treats hearing problems who also treats balance problems. Surprisingly, evolutionary evidence suggests that hearing was an afterthought, and the primary function of the ears is for balance.

(8-28) *Sudden dizziness (vertigo)* can produce extreme anxiety and nausea, and affected persons often attempt to compensate for the apparent motion by tilting the head. There are many causes of dizziness (8-29). Any occurrence of sudden dizziness needs to be evaluated by an otolaryngologist.

(8-29) *Ménière's syndrome,* which usually begins between the ages of 40 and 60, produces dizziness, ringing in the ears, loss of balance, and increasing deafness on one side. At first, these symptoms are slight, but they become progressively worse. Sometimes the onset of dizziness is marked by a sudden pain in the ear. Sooner or later there is a sudden bout of dizziness, headache, and sweating, which may last from a few minutes to a few hours. An attack may be preceded by a fall. Usually there is nausea and some vomiting too. The deafness and ringing become worse during the attack, then subside, but may never fully disappear.

During an attack a person must lie absolutely still. An antiemetic drug such as promethazine (Phenergan) may be prescribed to stop the vomiting. A vitamin, nicotinic acid (niacin) (3-15), which dilates blood vessels, is of value in preventing attacks, as are antihistamines such as diphenhydramine (Benadryl) (5-34). Diuretics are sometimes used, and sedatives such as phenobarbital or diazepam (Valium) (5-8) can be tried. If drugs do not successfully prevent attacks, surgery, ultrasonics, or the drug streptomycin can be used to destroy the semicircular canals (balancing system), and stop the attacks. Unfortunately, in many patients the surgery destroys both the balance system and hearing.

This disease may last for many years, but, at least, as the deafness increases, the attacks of dizziness diminish.

THE NOSE

(8-30) *Smell and taste.* With age, there is frequently a loss of smell. A significant decrease of the sense of smell and the closely related sense of taste can cause a loss of interest in food. Food may all "taste the same." To put some taste in the food, it may have to be loaded with salt and spices, too much of which is ill-advised. Although little can be done about this problem directly, it is good to recognize when senses have diminished, so that compensations can be made. Food that no longer has taste can be made interesting by altering its appearance and texture. If for health reasons heavy use of salt or condiments is not advised, food might be made sweeter with sugar or sugar substitutes.

Not only does loss of smell and taste produce problems for proper nutrition, but loss of smell can cause serious accidents. Gas that is piped into our houses has a small amount of a very distinctive odor mixed into it so that it can be easily detected. This acts as a warning that gas has been left on or that there is a leak in the pipes. An inability to smell escaping gas obviously can lead to tragic accidents. Thus, if the sense of smell is lost, it might be wise to consider the use of electric appliances. During the last few years, certain physicians have developed a subspecialization in taste and smell problems. However, they can be found in only a few medical centers.

(8-31) *Nosebleeds* are common, and almost everyone has a remedy. Profuse bleeding or a moderate condition that cannot be stopped within an hour must be attended to by a physician. Similarly, if you have many nosebleeds in the same day or over a few days, you must also see a physician. A major concern is to determine the total amount of blood lost, which is difficult because much of the blood may go down your throat. To stop the bleeding, sit straight up, find a watch or clock, and for ten minutes (no less) press the sides of the nose together between the thumb and forefinger. Press the soft cartilage just below the bony ridge of the nose. It is most important during the ten-minute interval not to stop or loosen the pressure to see if there is still bleeding. The pressure causes a clot to form, and lessening the pressure even for a moment may break the clot. If you have many nosebleeds, or if they are becoming more frequent, see a physician several days after the last nosebleed. During this interval the nose becomes clear of blood so that the physician can see where the bleeding was coming from.

Most nosebleeds occur in winter, when the air is dry and when the house may become overheated. The nasal mucosa becomes dry and tends to crack. To prevent dryness where there is forced-air heat, invest in a central humidifier. If this is not feasible, use cold mist room humidifiers in the areas where you spend the most time—particularly in the bedroom at night.

(8-32) *Types of doctors who treat the ear, nose, and throat.* Because the ear, nose, and throat have much in common, including anatomical connections to each other through the throat, they are treated by the same physician, a specialist called an otolaryngologist, whose training is mostly in surgery.

Alterations in the Skin, Nails, and Hair

AGING SKIN

(9-1) The skin ages faster than most other parts of the body because of its virtually continuous exposure to the sun, cold, and wind, and to frequent abuse (trauma) in the form of abrasions, cuts, and scratches. With age, skin becomes thinner, losing its elasticity and the supporting fat beneath it. Gradually skin folds form in areas of substantial fat loss. Wrinkles develop around the eyes and neck, and lines frequently form around the lips. Other changes that may occur in the aging skin are dryness, increased pigmentation, and loss of body hair.

(9-2) *Dry skin (xerosis).* As the body ages, skin becomes dryer and tends to flake, crack, and become more sensitive to injury. This both is uncomfortable and increases vulnerability to injury and infection. Good skin care cannot begin too early in life. Those who frequently get sunburned will find that skin has a memory. For each glorious tan of the past forty years, the skin ages more rapidly. Although sunburn is certainly bad for the skin, even slow deep tanning seems to be ultimately harmful.

Exposure to the wind and to dry-heated rooms robs the skin of its moisture. Very hot towels and scalding water should be avoided, too. Strong soaps and hot water remove the fatty substances from the skin and increase dryness. Mild soap or a skin cleaner such as Neutrogena should be used. Moisturizers, which keep water close to the skin, can be useful but are expensive. Moisturization can be accomplished inexpensively, although less aesthetically, by first wetting the skin with water (this is best done in a bath), then applying a petroleum jelly (Vaseline) or mineral oil. Light oil can be used during the day, with the excess tissued off, and the petroleum jelly can be used at night. Even vegetable cooking oil such as

After Middle Age

Crisco can be used effectively. When the skin becomes markedly dry, tiny cracks (fissures) develop in its lines and folds. When these fissures become irritated, they look like irregular railroad tracks and begin to itch. A physician should be asked to look at these, since they can become badly infected.

Itching or pruritus of the skin commonly develops with age. It usually occurs as the skin dries and thins—and sometimes is called senile pruritus. This kind of itching covers a large area, and when severe it may be hard to control. Wearing light clothing and applying calamine lotion to the affected areas sometimes helps. Cold cream also may be useful. Steroid (hydrocortisone acetate) ointments which now can be purchased without a prescription will temporarily help, but may make the problem worse if used for a long period. Ask your physician before using them for more than a week. For dry itching skin use the ointment (not cream or lotion), 0.5 percent. A physician may prescribe an antihistamine (11-7) such as promethazine (Phenergan) which comes in 12.5-mg gray and 25-mg white tablets. The average dosage is 25 mg before bedtime. Its major side effect is sedation, which is why the drug is best taken before going to sleep. Promethazine will enhance sedation produced by narcotic analgesics and sleeping medications. Tell your physician if you are taking such drugs, so that their dosage can be adjusted. Other side effects include dryness of the mouth and blurred vision.

Any itching that lasts for more than a few days and is severe should be brought to the attention of your physician. It could be an easily treatable condition, or it might be an early and important sign of a generalized disease such as diabetes.

(9-3) *Pruritis ani, or rectal itching,* that lasts more than a week should be treated by a physician. It is not that rectal itching usually represents something serious, but it is important to find out which of many causes is involved. Hemorrhoids and anal fissures can cause itching (both are also accompanied by bleeding and a sharp pain when a bowel movement is passed). With hemorrhoids you can often feel a lump just outside or within the rectum. An allergic or hypersensitive reaction (to deodorants and cosmetics) or to creams used around the rectum may cause itching. These include hemorrhoid treatment preparations. A contact dermatitis (rash) might develop if the skin comes in contact with the element nickel, which is incorporated into many metals used to make pins, snaps, and clasps (that may be used in this area to hold sanitary napkins). Other causes of itching are medicines, particularly antibiotics and laxatives, and spicy foods. When the itching is due to an allergy, the offending agent must be removed and the area soothed with petroleum jelly (Vaseline) or a steroid ointment (9-2).

Alterations in the Skin, Nails, and Hair

Fungal infections, particularly moniliasis or candidiasis, often called yeast infections, are a frequent cause of rectal itching. They are likely to occur in people who cannot keep themselves as clean as they would like, but they can also occur in people who are not debilitated. Your physician will probably give you a prescription for nystatin (Mycostatin) cream, to be used three or four times a day until the itching disappears.

Rubbing or chafing from tight clothing or nylon underwear (which may cut the skin) is a frequent cause of rectal area itching. If heavy sweating is a problem, make sure to shower or bathe daily and use a light powder (baby powder) afterward.

(9-4) *Night sweats* become increasingly common with advancing age. Usually the person wakes out of a deep sleep, often shivering in soaked nightclothes. These night sweats may be caused by being too warm, by menopause, or perhaps by nothing identifiable. On the other hand, night sweats may be a symptom of illness and should be reported to a physician.

SPOTS OF MANY COLORS

(9-5) *Drug rashes.* The sudden appearance of bright red spots or patches very often signifies a drug reaction that should be brought to the attention of a physician. These reactions also can produce hives (raised lesions with a clear white center and a red border). They itch. Hives can come from allergies to food, insect bites and stings, sprays, and nervous tension. If the source of the hives is unknown, or if they do not go away within an hour, a physician should be called. Since hives from allergies sometimes are associated with obstruction of the airway, any trouble breathing should be reported to a physician immediately. If this is not posible, go to a hospital emergency room.

(9-6) *Allergic contact rashes* usually begin with multiple small, raised, fluid-filled vesicles surrounded by reddened areas that itch. The blister walls release their fluid when broken. Crusting (scabs) then covers the area. Scratching can produce an infection, as indicated by yellow pus. As a rule, with age there are fewer contact rashes, but when they do occur, they are more difficult to cure. The items one can become sensitive to are numerous. There are obvious hazards such as poison ivy, but many not so obvious. Local irritation can develop from contact with almost any plant, including chrysanthemums, ivy, and philodendrons; from insecticides and weed killers; from dyes such as paraphenylenediamine (found in dark clothing, shoes, and hair coloring); from rubber in shoes; elastic in girdles or bandages; and nickel that may be in jewelry, keys, zippers, or garters. Local irritation also can arise from medicines that are put on the skin, and

After Middle Age

from Formalin in some permanent-pressed clothes, laundry, and dry-cleaning agents. A person who develops an allergy should try to identify the allergen (what causes the problem). Until the affected area has healed, sunlight, astringent soaps, and detergents should be avoided. Crusted lesions can be covered with cool wet cloths, and a physician may prescribe a steroid cream (9-2), a little of which goes a long way. Use a lotion or cream for a wet lesion. In otherwise healthy individuals experiencing serious reactions, oral steroids or antihistamine drugs (9-2) may be prescribed.

(**9-7**) *Poison ivy,* poison oak, and poison sumac all have similar appearance, and the adage "leaflets three, let it be" is a useful one. Poison ivy is usually a vine or an erect shrub found in central and eastern portions of the United States. Poison oak, found mostly on the west coast, is a shrub with oaklike leaves. Poison sumac is found in swampy locations and grows to be a 5- to 6-foot tree with green berries.

Contact with the leaves and vines or with clothes or shoes that have been in contact with the plant can produce the rash. Burning poison ivy (and oak) can produce a severe reaction in the lungs of sensitive individuals breathing the smoke.

Eruptions usually occur on exposed surfaces such as the hands, forearms, legs, or feet within forty-eight hours of contact with the allergen. The skin itches, then bumps form. Vesicles occur, later to break, causing oozing and eventual crusting.

If you know or think you have been exposed, wash the area (clothing included) immediately with a strong soap and copious amounts of water. If blisters erupt, cover them with a bandage or light gauze. Do not scratch the area; this might lead to infection and scarring. Once the urushiol (the allergen of poison ivy) is removed from the surface of the skin and clothing, poison ivy will not spread and is not contagious to another person.

For local eruptions, calamine lotion or steroid cream (9-2) and (9-6) works as well as or better than other preparations. For severe poison ivy, steroids taken by mouth may be necessary; they must be prescribed by a physician. The poison ivy rash disappears within a few days. Desensitization by injection (or orally) of poison ivy extract has only mild benefit. Sensitivity to poison ivy frequently, but not always, decreases with age.

(**9-8**) *Flat, shiny, ruby-red lesions (cherry angiomas),* occasionally slightly elevated, occur in increasing numbers over the body with age. They are harmless but can be removed if desired.

(**9-9**) *Small, blue dilated veins (venous stars)* in the skin of the feet and legs occur increasingly with age. They occasionally occur with liver disease, but they are usually not related to disease.

(**9-10**) *Soft, purple raised lesions (venous lakes)* occurring over the

Alterations in the Skin, Nails, and Hair

face, neck, lower lip, and ear occasionally may bleed. These are rare in women, are not dangerous, and can be removed.

(9-11) *Enlarged, red, superficial blood vessels (telangiectasis)* in fair-skinned persons give the appearance of solid redness from a distance. They are painless, harmless, and can be hidden by face powder; but they are not easily removed.

(9-12) *Reddish-purple lesions (senile purpura)* on the backside of the forearm are fairly common. These are caused by breaking of blood vessels, which subsequently bleed into the skin. The discoloration usually disappears within three weeks unless more vessels break. There is no treatment. Occasionally, small, white patchy spots that are slightly depressed develop in the area of the original lesion. These pseudo-scars are painless but do not go away. If they break open, they need to be covered with a bandage to prevent further trauma.

(9-13) *Redness of the palms of the hands (palmar erythema or liver palms)* occurs frequently with a variety of liver diseases as well as during pregnancy, but when it occurs with age, it frequently is due to poor nutrition. To some degree this condition will abate with the return to a good diet.

(9-14) *Small freckles and large brown spots (solar lentigines)* are flat and usually appear after age 50. They are found on the back of the hand, arms, back, and face. Once present, the lesions do not go away, but their darkening can be prevented by shielding the affected areas from the sun through the use of clothing or sunscreen (9-32). These lesions can become cancerous. They are usually larger than an inch (2 cm) in diameter and are irregularly pigmented (brown) with a rough outline. They are slow growing and, unlike melanomas, are easily treated. A physician should look at these during the annual physical exam.

(9-15) *Small, grayish-white, round elevations* found over the shins and back of the forearms increase in number with age. Called stucco keratosis, they are harmless and can be removed with simple outpatient surgical procedures.

(9-16) *Thickening of the skin* on the back of the neck occurs typically in men who spend a lot of time outdoors and comes from repeated exposure to the sun. The lines of the neck become thickened and deep, eventually leathery and dark. There is no treatment.

(9-17) *Small, yellow, transparent elevations* on the upper part of the face and back of the hand, called colloid milium, develop with age. While there is no treatment, they are harmless.

(9-18) *Fissures in the skin at the angles of the mouth* which are red and wet are called perleche or cheilitis. Typically, as the skin on the cheeks loses its support, the folds of the mouth overlap. Then saliva collects and becomes an irritant. Properly fitting dentures frequently can correct this. Other causes are vitamin deficiencies and diseases, such as diabetes. Steroid ointments (9-2) can be used to decrease the inflation and soreness until the cause is corrected.

(9-19) *Sudden loss of coloring (vitiligo)* can occur almost anywhere on the skin. It is more obvious in blacks and others with dark skin and may become noticeable in whites only when they have a suntan. When it occurs in the older person, it should be brought to the attention of a physician, since it frequently occurs in association with other disorders.

(9-20) *Blackheads (comedones)* around the eyes and nose develop with age. They are round, flat, and dark. The pore opening fills with a waxy substance, and then dirt attaches to the wax. While it is difficult to prevent this development entirely, the tendency for them to widen can be decreased. The waxy substance can be softened by placing a face cloth soaked in warm (not hot) water over the face for two minutes (this opens the pores). After the pores are open, wash with a light soap. Rinse your face of soap, hold the cloth in cold water and then on your face for another two minutes (this closes the pores). The procedure will keep your pores clean and help to prevent their widening. Your physician may prescribe a cream containing vitamin A.

(9-21) *Cold sores,* or fever blisters, usually begin with an itching or tingling sensation followed a few hours later by bumps that form on the skin at the edge of the nostril or lip. The bumps turn into small blisters, which coalesce to form larger ones. The skin around the blisters becomes swollen and red. Within two to three days, the blisters break open, ooze out a clear fluid, and finally become crusted. The scab usually gets knocked off or cracked several times before the skin clears, which happens in about two weeks. Cold sores generally recur in the same place at intervals of once every month to once every few years.

Cold sores are caused by a virus (herpes simplex) that a person was exposed to, usually early in life. After exposure, the virus lives quietly in the nerve until it travels down the nerve to the skin. Because the virus, for the most part, lives deep inside the nerve, devising a treatment has been difficult. (The best treatment is probably no treatment.) To get some relief, allow the blister to dry in the air. Witch hazel or spirits of camphor can diminish the itching by quickening the process of crust formation. These remedies should be used twice a day at the earliest sign of the sores. Some people believe that taking 1000 mg per day of lysine (an amino acid) when the lesions first begin and continuing until they disappear greatly decreases the length of time the lesions will last. Good scientific studies on this are just being completed but lysine taken for brief

Alterations in the Skin, Nails, and Hair

periods of time should be safe. It can be purchased without a prescription from natural food stores. The treatment that was popular a few years ago, involving a dye with subsequent exposure to fluorescent light, is thought by many experts to be unsafe because it may activate the herpes virus to produce a tumor.

Cold sores are highly contagious when they are in the oozing stage. Infection is caused by direct contact, such as kissing or through an intermediate object such as an unwashed eating utensil. The times when people are undergoing stress, have some other infection, are debilitated, or have been sunburned or windburned are the most likely times for cold sores to develop.

(9-22) *Warts (verruca),* which are probably caused by a virus, take a year or more to fully develop. They are elevated, usually flesh-colored, and rarely larger than a quarter inch (0.5 cm) in diameter. They may occur singularly or in bunches. Treatment can be attempted at home with Vergo (a combination of calcium, ascorbic acid [vitamin C] and starch), which may be purchased without a prescription. After cleaning the area with soap and water and rinsing, apply Vergo to the wart. Do not try to rub it in as you would most creams. Cover with a bandage. Repeat each morning and evening before bed for one month, unless the wart disappears earlier. If there is no progress, see your physician, who may remove the wart surgically after giving you a local anesthetic. Even surgical removal cannot guarantee the elimination of the wart virus, since some of it can be easily missed.

(9-23) *Shingles (herpes zoster)* is a viral eruption that produces considerable pain along the course of a nerve, usually involving one side of the face or trunk. It is, in fact, the chickenpox virus returning in a new form. The lesions it produces are linear and roughly parallel to the ribs. Pain may precede the appearance of a vesicular lesion (blister) by up to forty-eight hours and persist after the vesicles have disappeared. The clear vesicles become cloudy and finally develop into a scab. The disease lasts ten days to three weeks. Since the pain can be severe, a physician should be seen promptly. The physician will prescribe something for the pain, usually containing codeine (7-19). Calamine lotion can be used locally to relieve some of the itching. If the lesions are in the eye, the drug idoxuridine (Stoxil) will probably be administered as an eye drop or ointment. In the elderly, pain following the disappearance of the lesions can be persistent and may take many months to dissipate. Even years later the pain may recur with certain positions or with sudden temperature changes.

(9-24) *Athlete's foot (ringworm of the feet)* is a fungus infection that

After Middle Age

begins between the toes and spreads toward the bottom of the feet. The infection is red and rough; it itches and burns. It is contracted when the foot touches an area where other people who have had the infection have placed their feet. This is most likely to occur in a shower or on the apron of a swimming pool. Most people can readily treat athlete's foot themselves. If there is pain or swelling, however, see a physician, since the area may also be infected by bacteria and need special treatment. Make sure to shower (not bathe) daily, washing the infected area and then thoroughly drying the area by patting with tissue or a clean dry towel. Apply an antifungal ointment. I have found tolnaftate (Tinactin) to be the most useful. It comes as a liquid, cream, or powder. The latter is packaged in an aerosol spray that I think is easiest to use. Use two or three times daily for three weeks. You will need only very small amounts. If after two or three weeks the soggy lesions have not been replaced by new skin, see a physician.

VASCULAR PROBLEMS

(9-25) *Varicose veins* are enlarged, winding, superficial veins in the leg (*varix* is Latin for swollen vein). Because they are immediately under the skin, varicose veins do not get the support from surrounding muscles that veins deeper in the leg receive. A person can have very prominent varicose veins without any symptoms and therefore be only concerned about their appearance. Another person may have mild varicosities with or without severe symptoms. (The symptom is an aching discomfort in the lower leg.) Varicose veins are usually most noticeable after a period of relative inactivity or after a lengthy period of sitting or standing. Movement of legs normally helps pump blood through the veins back to the heart. When the legs are not moving, the blood pools in the veins, which causes the aching of the legs as well as swelling (edema) of the foot or leg. At first, the swelling is soft, but after several years it acquires a woody feeling. The skin may be dry, itchy, and scaly. On the lower third of the leg and ankles ulcers may occur—usually shallow and red, with blue discoloration around the rim.

Treatment is based on decreasing the amount of blood retained in the leg and thus decreasing the pressure in the veins. Elevation of the legs when possible is the simplest and most effective procedure to follow if you suffer from varicose veins. Sleep with the foot of the bed elevated to chest level. When possible, instead of sitting, lie down with the legs elevated (sitting does not elevate the legs high enough). Active exercise such as walking and isometric contraction of the leg muscles while stand-

Alterations in the Skin, Nails, and Hair

ing will help. Compression of the veins with elastic support is very helpful, but the elastic must not be so tight as to cut off circulation. If the elastic support is working well, there will be no swelling of the ankles at the end of the day. Since elastic bandages can be molded to the individual's leg, they are preferable to elastic stockings. When elastic stockings are used, they should be purchased with a full heel so support is given under the ankle. Similarly, elastic bandages (Ace bandages) should be wrapped to give support below the ankle. If there is an ulcer, local medications should be avoided unless there is an infection. Pressure over the affected area with a rubber sponge pad and elastic bandage can usually heal the ulcer. Surgical treatment for varicose veins is used sparingly, but in individuals who are otherwise in good health, surgical removal (stripping) of the vein usually offers relief. Alternatively, just the ends of the vein may be tied to prevent it from swelling.

(9-26) *Leg ulcers* heal slowly, and once healed, tend to recur. There is a tendency to keep off the feet with ulcers, but activity is important to maintain good circulation. Long periods of standing still should be avoided, as should crossing the legs and exposure to extreme heat. Leg ulcers must be treated by a physician, but usually on an outpatient basis.

(9-27) *Pressure (bed) sores (decubitus ulcers).* When an individual fails to move about normally and pressure is placed for long periods of time on one spot, the blood supply to the spot becomes decreased and the overlying skin may die. This is especially likely to occur when a person is confined to bed for long periods and when the blood supply is already compromised by conditions such as diabetes (16-7). The presence of urine and feces on the skin also contribute to its breakdown. Bony areas, such as the heel, sacrum, and hip, that press on hard mattresses are especially prone to pressure sores. In the beginning, the area becomes red, progressively swollen, and hard. At this point, before the skin breaks down, all weight must be removed from the area.

Bed sores can be prevented by increased movement, both passive and active, and by ensuring that vulnerable areas are kept dry, clean, and warm, and that the individual rests on soft materials. The weight of the covers can be taken off the feet of a person who must remain in bed for a long time by constructing a tent at the bottom of the bed to hold the covers. A trapeze can be built over the upper part of the bed to use in lifting oneself about. Pressure sores frequently develop on heels of paralyzed legs or on the remaining heel after one leg has been amputated. Any sore in a pressure area is serious and needs to be watched carefully lest it be a seed for further tissue breakdown. The attention of a physician is urgently needed here.

CORNS AND WARTS ON THE FEET

(9-28) *Corns* are raised, well-localized overgrowths that occur where there is pressure or rubbing on the toes and feet. They can make walking painful. Corns differ from plantar warts (9-29) in that there is a glassy core revealed when the surface is scraped away. (Plantar warts on the soles of the feet have multiple bleeding points when they are scraped.) Treatment consists of correcting poorly fitting shoes or orthopedic deformities that cause friction or pressure. Tight-fitting shoes must be avoided. At home, one can try to remove a corn by soaking in warm (not hot) water and peeling it off—never tear it off. A physician or a podiatrist may prescribe a preparation such as Keralyt to be used each night. After placing the gel on the corn, cover the area with a piece of plastic food wrap. Remove the wrap in the morning. Diabetics (16-7) should never attempt to treat themselves.

(9-29) *Plantar warts* are warts on the bottom of the feet. Like other warts (9-22), they are caused by a virus. They usually take up to a year to fully develop, and are elevated. They vary greatly in shape and appearance, but usually grow only to a quarter inch (0.5 cm) in diameter. They are tender to pressure. Unless they are scraped (9-28), they are difficult to distinguish from corns. Plantar warts can be removed surgically, using a local anesthetic, or with a formalin-salicylic acid plaster cut to size and applied at home under a doctor's supervision. One good product, Duofilm, consisting of salicylic acid and inctic acid in flexible collodion, can be put on with a plastic applicator. These warts can also be treated by shaving them with a safety razor after soaking the feet. This treatment sometimes takes a year or longer to work. Diabetics (16-7) should never attempt treatment themselves.

SKIN CANCER

(9-30) The skin cancer called basal cell epithelioma (also called rodent ulcer, because it burrows into normal tissues) usually forms discrete, pale, waxy nodules. Most commonly found on the head and neck areas exposed to the external environment, these nodules may vary greatly in appearance. They tend to enlarge and ulcerate rather than heal, and thus should be seen by a physician. Although they are destructive in the sense that they grow directly into adjoining tissue, these tumors rarely metastasize (spread) like other forms of cancer. They can be treated by surgical excision.

Another skin cancer that fortunately is rarer than basal cell epithelioma, is squamous cell carcinoma, which occurs in areas that are

Alterations in the Skin, Nails, and Hair

exposed to the elements or are at a site of chronic irritation. These growths are small, elevated, and scaly or horny. When attempts are made to scrape them off, they bleed, These lesions should be brought to the attention of a physician. Treatment includes excision of the tumor cells along with removal of any lymph nodes where extensions are suspected.

(9-31) *Moles and melanoma (malignant melanoma).* Colored (pigmented) moles (beauty marks, nevi) are among the most difficult skin alterations to evaluate. The vast majority will never undergo cancerous changes, and unless they are irritated by clothing or are cosmetically unattractive, most people do not think about them. Occasionally a mole will undergo a cancerous change, but it is unjustifiable to undertake wholesale excision of all pigmented moles. There are several useful considerations for assessment of pigmented moles. First and foremost is any sudden change of color in which the mole becomes darker (usually from brown to black), although lightening also may be serious. Other problems are enlargement, increase in height of the mole, and a previously smooth surface that becomes rough or bleeds. Moles that itch or tingle also should be considered with suspicion. Moles become darker during puberty, pregnancy, and after exposure to sunlight, and these factors should be taken into consideration. Somewhat surprisingly, the growth of stiff hairs from a mole is generally a reassuring sign that the mole is not malignant. Moles may grow at the junctions of the external and internal skin of the mouth and the anus, but there is no particular site where melanomas are most likely to occur. These are the worst of the skin cancers, and if you suspect you might have one, see your physician immediately. Melanomas usually are excised with fairly large areas of the skin surrounding them. Frequently, the lymph nodes that drain the area of the melanoma will also be removed.

(9-32) *Sunburn* is damage to the skin. Repeated sunburns cause premature aging of the skin with wartlike growths, wrinkling, and thickening. (Skin cancer also may be a result of too much sun.) Occasional sunburn causes discomfort. To prevent sunburn, limit your exposure at first, increasing suntime by fifteen minutes each day. Remember, the sun burns brightest between 10 A.M. and 2 P.M. Haze and fog screen some of the sun's rays, but not enough to forget about burning. When out at noon in fog or haze, consider it to be the same as being out at 2 P.M. Snow, but not water, increases the power of the sun to burn. Even if you do not burn, the suns rays are damaging to the skin. This damage, however, is not visible for many years. The sun destroys the skin's elastic fibers, which keep it taut.

Sunscreens contain light-absorbing substances such as para-aminobenzoic acid (PABA) that partially or totally screen out the sun's burning rays or allow some of the tanning rays through. Many sunscreen manufacturers rate their products by a ratio—the sun protection factor, or SPF. The SPF is the time it takes to produce redness of the skin (erythema) through a sunscreen divided by the time it takes without the sunscreen. SPF range is from 2 (little protection) to 15 (almost complete protection).

Start off each sun season with the higher numbers and as you tan use the lower numbers. Sunscreens should be applied, when convenient, two hours before going into the sun and then repeated after swimming or sweating. Since some people may be sensitive to a sunscreen, before spreading it over your entire body, use the one you purchased on a small area at least 24 hours before you expect to need it. If there is no itching or redness, you probably are not allergic to it.

Sunshades are opaque substances that physically block the sun from reaching the skin. They are usually used on the nose and lips for prolonged sun exposure.

Tanning lotions and pills are to be avoided. There appears to be a significant risk in using chemicals to change the color of the skin, and the color change probably does not protect against burning. Also "instant-tan" centers are even riskier than the real sun because the ultraviolet (UV) rays from the electric light are very strong.

THE NAILS

(9-33) *Care of the nails* takes little work—as a rule, the less the better. Keep nails short, and leave the cuticle alone. It protects the nail bed against infection, and pushing it back frequently may lessen this normal protective function. Nail polish use is a matter of taste, unless you are allergic to it. If a fingernail is injured, it takes about three months for it to be replaced entirely. With advancing age or serious illness nail growth is slowed. Brittle nails result from exposure to strong chemicals, particularly acids, alkalis, Formalin, and detergents. Fingernail splitting is not uncommon. Those who use chemicals should try to protect their hands and nails with gloves. Some people have nail problems without exposure to chemicals. In these cases there probably is no useful treatment to strengthen nails. Calcium or vitamin preparations have not been proven effective. Some persons believe that they are helped by taking gelatin. This is safe and can be tried for a three-month period—the time it takes the nail to grow out. Use one envelope of gelatin mixed in juice daily.

(9-34) *Infection of the nail (paronychia)* produces a warm, red, swollen, painful area under the cuticle. Treatment at home in healthy individ-

Alterations in the Skin, Nails, and Hair

uals may be tried, but if the infection gets worse after twenty-four hours, it should be brought to the attention of a physician. Treatment consists of soaking the area in warm (not hot) water every two hours while awake. This should bring the pus to the surface, where light pressure will extract it. A physician can prescribe antibiotics to be used locally and perhaps orally. If there are infections in more than one place, you should not try to treat them yourself. The nail fold can also be infected with a fungus, in which case there is usually no pus.

(9-35) *Ingrown nails* occur when the outside edge of the toenail grows into the surrounding skin. The side of the nail curves downward, and the skin becomes tender to the touch, swollen, and red. There also may be yellow pus. Healthy people can try treating ingrown nails themselves, but those who have poor circulation, diabetes (16-7), or a red swollen area that spreads or will not subside, must see a physician. For self-treatment, let the nail grow out beyond the outer edge of the toe. Then cut the nail squarely rather than rounding it off. While waiting for the growth to take place, soak the foot three to four times a day in warm (not hot) water. This allows the pus to work its way out. If the red or painful area enlarges, see a physician.

(9-36) *Fungus infections (onychomycosis)* of the nails are usually painless. The nails are thickened and discolored, and there may be some redness at the nail bed. The infections cannot be treated with locally applied creams, but require at least a six-month trial of a physician-prescribed oral antifungal drug such as griseofulvin (Grifulvin V or Fulvicin-U/F). Both brands come in white, scored tablets. The former have "Ortho" imprinted on them; the latter, "Schering" on one side and "AUG" or "496" on the other. The usual dosage for nail infection is one 500-mg tablet twice a day. Adverse reactions are usually various forms of rashes or hives. If you are allergic to penicillin, you might be allergic to griseofulvin (they both come from similar sources—the fungus penicillium). If you are taking an anticoagulant or barbiturates, remind your physician, who may want to adjust your dosage.

THE HAIR

(9-37) It is somewhat of a cultural curiosity that scalp and body hair, which has little physical function, probably receives more attention than any other body part. Some myths about hair can be dispensed with easily: Graying of the hair cannot occur overnight, although it can occur within a few months—the time it takes for the roots to grow out. For most persons, hair growth and loss cannot be altered by cosmetics. If the scalp is

After Middle Age

healthy, frequent shampooing will not hurt it. Hair growth is not affected by plucking, cutting, or shaving.

(9-38) *Hair loss or baldness (alopecia).* For the most part, balding is a natural process, although any sudden loss of hair should be called to a physician's attention because it may be associated with a hidden medical illness. A small amount of hair is lost every day. Hair loss becomes apparent only when fairly large amounts are lost rapidly. Balding is common in males, who can form expectations as to their future hairline by observing their fathers'. Hereditary hair loss begins simultaneously on both sides of the forehead. These areas of hair loss enlarge slowly, eventually coalescing with an enlarging area of hair loss on the back of the head. There is no treatment and no way to prevent it. Hair is an inert substance, and it is unlikely that any lotion directly applied to the hair will restore it. Currently there are no medications that will restore hereditary hair loss. Some men, however, decide to use a toupee or hair implants.

Many women find they begin to lose their hair slowly after age fifty. This form of hair loss begins at the back of the head and is incomplete. While the cause is not yet fully understood, it is thought to be a hormonal imbalance. Effective treatments currently are unknown. The most common form of hair loss in women is more temporary in nature. Hair may fall out in handfuls from almost every part of the head, although there are no patches of baldness. This temporary form of hair loss follows a psychological disturbance, crash diet, operation, or pregnancy. Hair grows more rapidly than usual during pregnancy, and when this sudden growth stops, there is a period when more than the usual amount of hair is lost.

(9-39) *Sudden, patchy hair loss (alopecia areata)* on scalp and/or face can occur at any time of life. It can be produced by use of drugs such as heparin, excessive vitamin A, as well as many drugs used to treat cancer. The area of hair loss enlarges slowly for a six to twelve-month period, after which the hair usually begins to grow back with no treatment. The new growth is frequently white, but normal color eventually returns.

(9-40) *Excessive hair growth* distributed over the body occasionally occurs in women. Coarse, dark hairs grow on the upper lip, chin, and side of the face. Other areas such as around the nipples, over the bony part (sternum) of the chest, and the shins can also be involved. This usually occurs after menopause, when there are multiple hormonal changes, and it should be brought to the attention of a physician. The simplest remedy is bleaching. Shaving with an electric razor may be desirable, but leaves stubble. Depilatory creams will do the job, but many women find them irritating. Electrosurgery (electrolysis, electrodiathermy), which involves an electric current being passed into the skin to destroy the hair follicle, can produce a permanent result. This must be done by a skilled techni-

Alterations in the Skin, Nails, and Hair

cian—get the name of one from a dermatologist (a physician who specializes in skin diseases).

(9-41) *Graying of hair* is a normal part of aging as the amount of pigment in the hair gradually decreases. Fully pigmented hairs are replaced by hairs with less pigment. There is, therefore, always a mixture of colors on the way to white. Graying of the hair is in part inherited. There is little scientific reason to think it can be changed by nutrition, stress, or trauma. Most of us, however, have had the experience of watching someone under stress graying much more rapidly than we would have expected.

(9-42) *Dandruff (seborrhea)* is the overproduction by the scalp of oily secretions that dry and flake. Although dandruff is primarily a problem for adolescents with dark complexions, it may continue well beyond middle age. It cannot be cured, but it can be suppressed by removing the oils of the scalp. Many physicians prescribe a diet low in oils and fats. While this may be wise for a number of reasons, using one of the many dandruff shampoos is the most effective treatment. The selenium-containing Selsun Blue shampoo is one of the most effective over-the-counter preparation. Dandruff shampoo should be used about twice a week.

10

Disorders of the Bones, Muscles, and Tendons

(10-1) The bones are the foundation of the musculoskeletal system. Ligaments connect the bones to each other, and tendons connect them to the muscles, which are the motors that move the bones. Like the parts of any machine, body parts are vulnerable to wear and tear. Unlike other machines, whose parts can be exchanged for new ones periodically, the body is continuously rebuilding and repairing itself, With time, however, the stresses and strains take their toll, and the natural repair processes become less adequate. The joints where movement, weight, and friction are greatest are likely to fail first.

It is the unusual person who goes through life without some difficulties of the musculoskeletal system. This chapter describes ways of preventing the development of these difficulties and what can be done about them when they do develop.

JOINT DISEASES

(10-2) *Arthritis* is an inflammation of a joint or joints. The principal symptom is pain, which can come when the joint is either at rest or in motion. The afflicted joint may be warm to the touch and enlarged. The causes of arthritis are many. It may follow an infection or drug reaction. When arthritis has such a specific origin, treatment can be directed accordingly. The causes of the more common forms of arthritis, however, such as rheumatoid arthritis (10-3) and osteoarthritis (10-4) are not known, and treatments are directed primarily at decreasing the symptoms.

Disorders of the Bones, Muscles, and Tendons

(10-3) *Rheumatoid arthritis* is a chronic disease, principally of the joints, but it also involves other body systems. Women are more often affected than men. It is not inherited. It usually begins between the ages 25 and 45, continues with remissions (relatively symptom-free periods), and relapses (return of active symptoms) for varying lengths of time, until it burns itself out, at times leaving permanent damage. The onset, usually slow, is marked by symptoms of a slight fever, fatigue, weight loss, a poor appetite, and pain and stiffness of a joint or joints. The joints become swollen, red, and warm. Joint pain and stiffness are worst in the morning, at times taking several hours to diminish, and they tend to be relieved by moderate exercise. Fatigue comes easily. Any movable joint can be affected, but rheumatoid arthritis usually involves the limbs symmetrically. Thus, if a joint on one side of the body is involved, the same joint on the opposite side of the body is likely to become involved. Rheumatoid nodules may be present. These are painless lumps lying under the skin at bony points such as the wrist, elbow, finger, or heel.

During the attack, the membranes of the joint become inflamed and swollen, and the cartilage covering the joint surface is eroded. In periods of remission, the joint begins to heal, but after repeated attacks the joint becomes progressively more deformed—even fused and immobilized. The muscles above and below the joint will waste away if not used. Thus, muscle mass will decrease, and there will be an ensuing weakness.

The cause and cure of rheumatoid arthritis are still unknown, but it is thought that the disease is probably traceable to an abnormality in the body's defense mechanisms, part of which is the immune system. In rheumatoid arthritis the body's immune system reacts improperly to substances normally occurring within the body. To diagnose this condition (known as autoimmunity) the physician will take simple blood tests to measure the body's immune system and will x-ray the involved bones. In some cases the physician may need samples of the fluid from the involved joints or tissue samples from linings of the joint.

There are no specific cures for rheumatoid arthritis, but there are many treatments to relieve the symptoms. Most treatments are applied more vigorously during flare-ups of the illness. The chance of improvement is very good. Rheumatoid arthritis is often managed successfully with regular naps, bed rest for twelve to fourteen hours a day when the disease is very active, and complete bed rest when it is severe. In bed the body should be as flat as possible, without pillows under the head or knees. Prolonged bending can produce flexion contractures (the body becomes locked in a bent position) that prevent future bending or straightening. Rest is combined with heat from warm baths to relax the muscles. Exercises and physical therapy are necessary to preserve the optimum range of joint movement. The physician may remove fluid from a swollen joint or inject a steroid hormone (such as hydrocortisone, prednisone, or prednisolone) into it. Cortisone cannot be injected often, however, because it may cause the joint to further disintegrate. Usually patients do not need to change their diet.

Pain-relieving drugs are used in the treatment of rheumatoid arthritis, especially aspirin (7-11), which also reduces inflammation. Aspirin is administered in the highest doses that can be given without causing side effects of ringing in the ears, dizzinesss, blurred vision, nausea, vomiting, or indigestion. The average adult can take twelve to eighteen tablets a day; the elderly usually must take less. Doses should be spaced four to six hours apart. In high dosages, aspirin should always be taken after a meal, and at bedtime with milk or an antacid. Indigestion, the most common side effect of aspirin, can be alleviated with buffered or coated aspirin and concomitant ingestion of milk. Also, when problems arise, the dose should be reduced. Do not take large aspirin doses on your own. Consult your physician. If you have asthma or ulcers, remind your physician, since these may be contraindications to aspirin use.

If aspirin is not sufficient to control the pain, other drugs may be prescribed such as indomethacin (Indocin) (10-7), ibuprofen (Motrin), fenoprofen (Nalfon), naproxen (Naprosyn), sulindac (Clinoril), tolmetin (Tolectin), phenylbutazone (Butazolidin) (10-7), or oxyphenbutazone (Tandearil). Sometimes corticosteroids (cortisonelike drugs) such as prednisone and prednisolone are used to supplement aspirin. All these drugs are taken by mouth to reduce inflammation, but they do not cure the disease, and they have significant side effects. Consequently, phenylbutazone, oxyphenbutazone, and steroids, which have the strongest side effects, are used only when there is no response to other drugs, and then only for short periods.

Ibuprofen (Motrin, average dose 300 mg four times per day) comes in 300-mg white and 400-mg orange round tablets, and 600-mg football-shaped tablets labeled "Upjohn Motrin." Allow ibuprofen up to two weeks to work. If possible, take ibuprofen with meals. Common side effects include abdominal pain or cramps, indigestion, heartburn, nausea, vomiting, and bleeding from the stomach as well as blurred vision, skin rashes, ankle swelling, and dizziness. These symptoms should be brought to the attention of your physician immediately.

Fenoprofen (Nalfon, average dose 200 to 600 mg every six to eight hours) comes in 200-mg white and ocher capsules and 300-mg yellow and ocher capsules, both imprinted with "Nalfon." Common side effects are similar to those produced by ibuprofen.

Naproxen (Naprosyn, average dose 250 to 375 mg twice daily) comes in

Disorders of the Bones, Muscles, and Tendons

250-mg yellow scored round and 375-mg peach oblong tablets with "Syntex" imprinted on them. Common side effects are similar to those produced by ibuprofen.

Sulindac (Clinoril, average dose 150 mg twice a day) comes in 150 mg yellow hexagonal tablets with "MSD 941" and 200 mg yellow hexagonal tablets stamped with "MSD 942." Common side effects are similar to those produced by ibuprofen.

Tolmetin (Tolectin, average dose 400 to 600 mg three times per day), comes in 200-mg white tablets imprinted "Tolectin," and 400-mg orange capsules imprinted "Tolectin DS" (double strength). Common side effects are similar to those produced by ibuprofen.

Diflunisal (Dolobid, average maintenance dose 500 mg two to three times per day) comes in 250-mg peach capsule-shaped tablets labeled "MSD 676" and 500-mg orange capsule-shaped tablets labeled "MSD 697." Diflunisal produces the same gastric irritation as aspirin but not as often.

Piroxicam (Feldene, average maintenance dose 20 mg once a day) comes in 10-mg maroon and blue capsules labeled "Pfizer 322" and 20-mg maroon capsules labeled "Pfizer 323." Common side effects include gastric irritation similar to aspirin and decreased blood count.

Oxyphenbutazone (Tandearil, average dose 100 mg three to four times per day) comes in 100-mg round, tan tablets labeled "Geigy 24." Call your physician immediately if your temperature rises or if a sore throat or a sore in your mouth develops. Stomach pain, shortness of breath, bloody or dark stools, and skin rashes also should be brought to a physician's attention immediately.

Gold salts (chrysotherapy) are sometimes given by injection. The gold accumulates in the body and improvement is gradual. Itching and rash are side effects of gold therapy. If these treatments do not help the pain, or if there is severe disability, orthopedic operations can be done to replace the affected joints (10-5), or to fuse painful joints together so that motion does not cause pain (10-5).

There are several simple measures that can greatly help arthritis sufferers to accomplish common daily activities. To make it easier to get in and out of bed, the bed should be raised on six-inch blocks. For support, a one-inch plywood bedboard running the full length of the bed should be placed between the mattress and box spring. Chairs should be straight-backed and raised on blocks so that the bottoms of the thighs are flat on the chair while the feet are flat on the floor.

Because rheumatoid arthritis is a distressing disease for which there is no cure and because chronic pain will cause some people to try anything, Americans with arthritis spend more than $250 millions on "quack drugs" every year. Many of these overpriced products contain only aspirin (if the patient is lucky) in one form or another. Others contain drugs that can have serious side effects without affecting the disease. To obtain reliable information about these "miracle cures," ask your physician or contact the Arthritis Foundation, which has chapters in most large communities and whose main office is at 3400 Peachtree Road, N.E., Room 1101, Atlanta, Georgia 30326. The American Medical Association puts out a pamphlet, "Medicine's Back to Work Plan," listing rehabilitation services. It can be obtained by writing to AMA, 535 North Dearborn Street, Chicago, Illinois. The Independence Factory, P.O. Box C, Middleton, Ohio 45042, sells practical aids such as zipper pulls and large-handle toothbrushes for those with decreased hand or limb function.

(10-4) *Osteoarthritis, or degenerative joint disease,* affects everyone over the age of 50. Fortunately, not everyone has symptoms. Osteoarthritis affects the weight-bearing joints, such as the knee, hip, and neck, as well as the non-weight-bearing joints, such as fingers. The symptoms, which are worse in the morning, include mild pain, stiffness, and changes in the shape and the tenderness of the joints. There is no general illness or fever, as there sometimes is with rheumatoid arthritis, and the disease as a rule is annoying rather than severe. Structures surrounding the joint, such as membranes and ligaments, become thickened, so that the joint looks swollen, but there are no signs of the redness and heat that accompany rheumatoid arthritis. In fact there usually is no inflammation, which is the reason for the alternative name, degenerative joint disease.

The physician directs treatment toward relieving the pain, restoring the function of the joint, and preventing disability. The condition usually affects only a few joints. These joints should be rested for some time during the day but not so long that they become stiff—perhaps for one hour each morning and evening. Exercise prescribed by the physician should be done to maintain the range of joint movement.

(10-5) *Total joint replacement.* During the last few years there has been dramatic improvement in the surgical treatment of degenerating, unstable, and painful joints. As an alternative to reconstructive surgery, there is total replacement of some joints. Replacement of a damaged hip joint can have an extremely good result. Using metal to replace the upper part of the thigh bone (femur) and plastic to replace the cup (acetabulum) it fits into, surgeons have good results at least 80 percent of the time. Patients who experience constant pain, need a cane or crutches in order to walk, and are unable to work or function normally at home are candidates for the operation. If previous reconstruction of the hip has failed, hip replacement may work. The operation usually takes two to five hours, and hospitalization generally lasts less than three weeks. As a rule, mild

Disorders of the Bones, Muscles, and Tendons

pain is experienced for only a few days after the operation. The patient begins to walk with crutches within a week, then uses a cane, and finally is able to walk comfortably without external support.

Pain is the major indicator for total knee replacement. Although most orthopedic surgeons prefer reconstructive surgery on the knee, many today are moving toward total knee replacement, particularly for badly damaged knees in the elderly. Both hip and knee replacement surgery require surgeons who have had extensive experience. This means that they should have participated in 50 to 100 supervised operations before undertaking one on their own.

Total ankle replacement, as well as the replacement of the joints of the upper extremity and hand, are relatively new procedures and are being done only in a few medical centers.

(10-6) *Gout.* Although gout may attack any joint at any time, the common situation is the development of a swollen, red, painful big toe, usually around 2 A.M. Bedclothes covering the toe cannot be tolerated, and there may be chills and shivering. Pain increases over time.

Gout is caused by elevated levels of uric acid, which does not dissolve in blood, but crystallizes in the joints, kidneys, and even in the margins of the ears. These crystals, the size of gun shot and known as tophi, cause pain in the joints and damage the kidneys. The tendency for gout is inherited, and is rare in women. Not everyone who has high uric acid levels gets gout.

Uric acid is formed from substances known as purines, which some foods contain in quantity. Thus, it may be helpful to limit or avoid alcoholic beverages, liver, sweetbreads, brains, and kidneys. People undertaking a crash diet are advised to undergo a test for uric acid, since such a diet may precipitate an attack of gout in those who have borderline high uric acid levels.

(10-7) *Drugs in the treatment of gout.* Colchicine, one of the oldest drugs, is used to relieve pain and inflammation during a gout attack. Many patients carry it with them at all times. Its principal side effects are diarrhea (this can be controlled with paregoric, which requires a prescription), nausea, and vomiting. It comes in 0.6-mg tablets that are taken every hour or two beginning at the first warning of an acute attack, and continuing until the pain subsides. Maximum dose is 10 mg (20 tablets).

Phenylbutazone (Butazolidin, average dosage 100 mg every eight hours) comes in 100-mg red tablets labeled "Geigy 14" and is helpful in cases of acute gout. It can be used only for a short time and should not be given to individuals with a history of stomach ulcer or duodenal ulcer. Side effects include edema (collection of fluid) in the legs, nausea, and vomiting. The vomiting of blood or the presence of blood in the stool is a

After Middle Age

serious side effect that should be brought to your physician's attention immediately.

Indomethacin (Indocin) is also used for acute attacks in doses of 25 mg every six hours, with a maximum of four such doses. The dosage is then tapered off over a week. It comes in 25- and 50-mg opaque blue and white capsules labeled "MSD 25" and "MSD 50," respectively. Indomethacin should not be taken by persons with ulcers, high blood pressure, or heart problems.

Most long-term drug treatments attempt to reduce uric acid in the blood by increasing its excretion in the urine. Probenecid (Benemid, average maintenance dosage 1 to 1.5 g per day) comes in 0.5-g yellow-coated, scored tablets labeled "MSD 501." Possible side effects include nausea and vomiting, loss of appetite, and headache. Since probenecid can cause kidney stones, it should be taken with food, and the fluid intake should be increased. Blood in the urine or pain in the lower back should be brought to a physician's attention immediately.

Sulfinpyrazone (Anturane, average maintenance dose 400 to 800 mg per day) comes in 100-mg white, scored tablets and 200-mg green capsules stamped "Ciba 41" and "Anturane 200 Ciba 168," respectively. Since side effects may include nausea and vomiting, it is best to take sulfinpyrazone with meals. If vomiting or gastrointestinal disturbances persist, or if blood is vomited or seen in the stool, notify your physician immediately.

Long-term treatment also can be achieved by inhibiting uric acid synthesis with allopurinol (Zyloprim, average dosage 200 to 600 mg per day). Allopurinol comes in 100-mg white and 300-mg peach scored tablets bearing the letters "ZYLOPRIM U4A" and "ZYLOPRIM C9B," respectively. The most common side effect of this drug is a rash. Notify your physician immediately if a rash occurs.

TUMORS

(10-8) *Tumors of the bones.* Most common tumors of the bones are cancers that have spread from other parts of the body. Thus, cancer of the breast (15-16), prostate (15-36), stomach (13-19), and lung (11-25) may first show as a tumor of the bone. For this reason, bone pain in the absence of injury, especially if it wakes you or keeps you awake at night, should be brought to the attention of a physician. This holds true for back pain and sciatica (10-10), too, since they are sometimes caused by tumors.

Tumors originating in bones can be benign or malignant. The symptoms are enlargement of the bone, which can be felt through the skin; the

Disorders of the Bones, Muscles, and Tendons

limitation of movement of a joint; pain in a bone; or the breaking of a bone under nonstressful circumstances. Benign tumors are removed surgically; malignant tumors are usually treated by x-rays and drugs and by surgery.

The most common cancer of the bone itself is plasma cell myeloma (multiple myeloma). It begins with the same symptoms as other bone tumors. As it progresses, it produces an abnormal protein, called Bence-Jones protein, in the blood and urine. Precise diagnosis is usually made by a biopsy (17-4) of an affected area, and the growth of the tumor is followed by measuring the amount of Bence-Jones protein excreted. Treatment involves the use of a combination of drugs and radiation (17-11).

A useful technique in the diagnosis of bone tumors is the bone scan, which is done in a medical center as an outpatient procedure. A radioisotope is injected into a vein. Within four hours the isotope is incorporated into the structure of the bone, and can be seen on x-ray. A few minutes before the scan is started, the patient is asked to urinate because the isotopes also collect in the urine and will obscure the pelvic area. The patient is then asked to lie on a table while a counter—sensitive to the radiation emitted—is passed over or under the patient. The counter, in turn, forms a picture of the source of the radiation on a small television screen, and finally an instant camera takes a picture of it. The picture is of the bony skeleton, and any abnormalities in the skeleton can be picked out by the radiologist. The radiologist can determine not only where the abnormality is but what kind of abnormality is present. The radioisotope itself is harmlessly excreted from the body within a few hours.

PAGET'S DISEASE

(10-9) *Paget's disease* is a bone disorder occurring in about 3 percent of those over the age of 40. Its cause is not known. It may affect only one bone or many, beginning with a destructive phase in which the bone is melted away (reabsorbed), followed by a phase of formation of new "pagetic" bone. This new bone, although thicker, is structurally less well-organized than normal bone and therefore weaker.

Paget's disease involves the pelvic bones, femur (thigh bone), skull, tibia (shin bone), and spine. Symptoms vary, depending upon the location and extent of the disease. In most cases, the disease is not widespread, and there are no symptoms. It may show up only on an x-ray. When the disease is more extensive, there is swelling and deformity of the bones, which are more liable to bend. The skull becomes larger, there are headaches, bones tend to fracture easily, and there is dull bone pain. There also may be a loss of hearing and sight from pressure of the enlarged bone

After Middle Age

on the nerves that run through them to the ears and eyes. Blood flow to the involved bones increases, and blood pressure may be raised. Blood calcium is raised as it is leached from the bone. Kidney stones develop. Some formation is more likely to occur if the individual is immobilized for some time. Infrequently, benign or malignant tumors occur. They can be recognized by increased pain and swelling of the bone involved.

Most cases of Paget's disease exhibit no symptoms and do not need to be treated medically. If pain and complications develop, or if the disease progresses rapidly, aspirin in large doses (10-3) suppresses the symptoms. If the patient cannot tolerate aspirin, indomethacin (Indocin) (10-7) can be used. A hormone that regulates bone reabsorption, calcitonin (Calcimar), is helpful in moderate to severe cases. Pain diminishes within two to six weeks of starting calcitonin treatment. Calcitonin is given by subcutaneous (under the skin) injections, which patients can learn to give themselves, like insulin (16-13). Nausea and vomiting are occasional side effects. This treatment is, unfortunately, very expensive. Occasionally, damage to a hip joint is so bad that the joint must be replaced.

LOW BACK PAIN

(10-10) *Low back pain* is experienced at one time or another by most people. It has many causes, from disease of the spine to referred pain (originating in another part of the body). In this case, pain in the abdomen and pelvis may feel like it is coming from the lower back. Low back pain should be brought to the attention of a physician if it lasts more than a few days. The most common cause of acute backache, which starts abruptly and generally lasts only a few days, is straining of the back muscles and ligaments by a sudden effort or a fall. An overworked muscle goes into sustained contraction, or spasm, with the muscle becoming hard. Chronic backache lasting more than two to three weeks can be caused by obesity, weak muscles, osteoarthritis (10-4), osteoporosis (10-12), or a degenerated or injured vertebral disc. Less frequently, the cause is a tumor within the bones of the spine, kidney disease (14-7), or psychiatric states such as depression (5-9).

The pain may be confined to the local area, or it may be generalized to a large area of the back. The pain is usually increased when the patient stands for long periods or moves the spine. The pain is decreased by bed rest and sometimes by moderate exercise. When the backache is caused by osteoarthritis, the pain is worse in the morning, after sitting in soft chairs, and when poor posture is maintained. A common symptom associated with backache is sciatica—pain running down the back of the leg.

Disorders of the Bones, Muscles, and Tendons

Stretching the leg aggravates the pain. Sciatica is caused by irritation of the sciatic nerve roots where they emerge from the spinal cord. This is commonly caused by a protruding disc. The disc is the gelatinous material lying in the spaces between the bony vertebrae that make up the scaffolding for the spine. Normally the disc cushions forces traveling through the spine. If the force exceeds that which the disc can safely absorb, the disc may tear, or herniate (push) through the surrounding ligaments, and irritate a nerve. The discs that tend to rupture are in the lower back, or lumbar area; and the nerve they press on is the sciatic.

For many years physicians have used a myelogram for diagnosis of disc problems. This complex x-ray procedure uses a dye injected into the spinal canal to outline the area where a disc is protruding. Now the myelogram can often be avoided and a painless CT scan (7-38) is done, which gives much more detail.

Treatment of backache aims at curing the cause and relieving the pain. General measures for relief of pain are bed rest on a firm mattress, lying on one side with the knees drawn up, or on the back with a pillow under the knees. Aspirin (7-11) and a heating pad applied to the painful area help ease the pain. Muscle-relaxant drugs such as diazepam (Valium) (5-8) are frequently prescribed by physicians. Much of the chronic pain is caused by muscle spasms (cramps) produced by nerve irritation. Supports—corsets for women and belts for men—keep the spine fixed during walking and are helpful when used along with back-strengthening exercises. They should not be worn without exercising, because when used alone, they may weaken back-support muscles. Individuals suffering from back pain should not lift heavy weights or bend and twist their bodies. When lifting an object, bend at the knees, not at the waist. Sit on chairs that are hard and straight-backed, undertake regular exercise, and maintain normal body weight. (Obesity aggravates the condition, placing great stress on the back.)

Treatment by a physical therapist (under the supervision of a physician) can be useful for the relief of backache. Skillful application of heat and massage can greatly relax the muscle spasms that produce pain. Operations are occasionally indicated for disc problems.

In late 1982, chymopapain (Chymodiactin) became available for patients not responding to conservative treatment. An enzyme that a specially trained orthopedic surgeon can inject into a herniated disc and dissolve it, chymopapain allows the patient to avoid surgery, but is usually given with a general anesthesia. The patient is required to stay in the hospital after the injection for one or two days. Unfortunately, because some people are allergic to chymopapain, the risk of death is about the same as for surgery. Also, there often is post-injection back pain or spasm

After Middle Age

of the back for several days after the injection. As with surgery, there is a small risk of paralysis of the legs.

(10-11) *How not to strain the back.* When prolonged standing is necessary, keep the hips and knees bent, and shift your weight from one foot to another. If possible, raise one foot onto a stair, chair rung, curb, or other slightly elevated object. When lifting an object, stoop with the knees bent and the back straight—never lean forward—and keep the load close to the body. When carrying suitcases or briefcases try to balance the weight between both arms; if you cannot, switch arms often. Do not lift heavy loads higher than your chest. Make every effort not to fall. Do not walk or carry things on slippery surfaces. When you are carrying a load and need to turn, do not twist your body. Instead, turn your feet. The best way to sleep is on your side with the hip and knees bent. If your lower back is sore, place pillows or blankets under your knees when lying on your back.

OSTEOPOROSIS

(10-12) *Osteoporosis* is the process in which the amount of bone decreases with age. All people lose bone as they age. This is known as age-related bone loss, but when the loss occurs to excess and is accompanied by back pain, fractures, and a specific x-ray appearance, it is called osteoporosis. This condition is far more common in women than men. Osteoporosis is responsible for the decreased height that occurs with age. There is an increased risk of fracture of the bones, especially the femur (thigh bone), which often breaks near the hip and has to be pinned together or replaced so that it is strong enough to bear weight.

The bone loss of osteoporosis is caused by bone reabsorption by the body, but the cause of the reabsorption is not known. There are suggestions that it may be due to a dietary deficiency of calcium, hormonal disturbance, or decreased physical activity. It is also known to be more common in people with such chronic diseases as rheumatoid arthritis (10-3) and diabetes (16-7).

Symptoms of the disorder are back pain and manifestations of compression of the vertebrae (spine), such as forward bending of the spine, hunched back, and buffalo hump (fat on the back of the neck). Many people with x-ray evidence of osteoporosis have no symptoms.

The most important prevention and treatment of osteoporosis is keeping physically active and maintaining a diet adequate in protein, vitamins (especially vitamin D), and calcium (1 to 1.5 g a day)—which can be provided by nonfat milk as a beverage or used in cooking, or cheese as a

Disorders of the Bones, Muscles, and Tendons

diet supplement (3-3). Drugs, such as female sex hormones for women and male sex hormones for men, are used as treatment, but their effectiveness has not been proven. For back pain from osteoporosis, use a corset during the day, a hard mattress over a bed board at night, and aspirin (7-11).

TENNIS ELBOW, BUNION, AND BURSITIS

(10-13) *Tennis elbow* is an inflammation of the area of the bone attaching to the muscle that causes the forearm to straighten. The pain usually is felt just below the elbow on the outside of the forearm. The pain is felt especially when making backhand strokes, but may also be felt when shaking hands, opening a door, or turning a faucet or a screwdriver. Tennis elbow can also be on the inside and back of the elbow. Both excellent and poor tennis players get tennis elbow—it may come from repeated use of the forearm in other activities, such as raking leaves.

Using a heating pad or warm water soaks before play may offer considerable relief. An armband or elastic bandage placed just below the elbow may be of some help. A light racket, rather loosely strung, will absorb some of the ball's impact. Playing for shorter periods of time each day may prevent aggravation of the condition. Putting the elbow in ice immediately after playing can abort the inflammatory reaction. Stretching exercises with light weights, supervised by an orthopedist, may condition the elbow and prevent symptoms. There are drugs that may be of help, but the amateur player has no reason to take any medication stronger than two aspirins. Tennis elbow will improve with rest.

(10-14) *A bunion* is a dislocated joint at the base of the large toe. Swollen and painful enough to make walking difficult, it usually occurs after many years of being on the feet and wearing cramped shoes. It is most apt to occur in women who wear high heels—the weight of the body impacts on the toes. Treatment is directed at finding properly fitting shoes, which are usually larger than those previously worn; no longer wearing high heels; and staying off one's feet when they are painful. The pain can be alleviated by soaking the feet in warm (not hot) water for ten minutes four times a day. Most patients eventually want to see an orthopedist or podiatrist (foot doctor). Surgery is usually performed to restore the joint. If a local anesthetic is used, you may be in the hospital for only a few hours, but you will have to walk with a crutch for as long as six weeks.

(10-15) *Bursitis* is a term usually reserved for inflammation of the sac, or bursa, that covers the bony prominence of the shoulder, although there also can be inflammation of the protective bursa of the elbow or knee. The most common symptom is sudden shoulder pain when there has been obvious injury. The pain prevents patients from lifting their arms to the side above shoulder height. On an x-ray of the shoulder, a calcium deposit can often be seen. Most often, resting the arm is sufficient to relieve pain although anti-inflammatory and pain-relieving drugs (7-10) usually are of help. Occasionally, local injections of corticosteroids are necessary, and in some cases the calcium deposits must be removed surgically.

THE KINDS OF BONE DOCTORS

(10-16) *Orthopedists* (from the Greek words meaning "straight" and "child") are medical doctors (M.D.s) with at least five years of graduate training who specialize in diagnosis and medical and surgical treatment of bone, joint, and muscle problems.

(10-17) *Osteopaths.* Osteopathy started off differing from traditional medicine by using manipulative therapy. A modern osteopath (D.O.) still uses this type of treatment but is otherwise trained along essentially the same lines as traditional medical doctors, and specializes as they do. A person having a bone disease can go to an osteopath specializing in orthopedics.

(10-18) *Chiropractors,* or doctors of chiropractic (D.C.s), base their theories and practices on three principles: (1) conditions outside the body can irritate the nervous system and change the manner in which it operates; (2) the back and pelvic bones, which are subjected to considerable strain, can trigger irritation of nerves that come from the spinal cord; and (3) those persons who are predisposed (prone) to disease may have that predisposition augmented by (1) or (2). Chiropractors make a diagnosis by taking a history, making a physical examination (with special attention to posture and the spine), and performing standard laboratory tests. Treatment, when appropriate, is usually aimed at adjusting the back or pelvic bones. Generally chiropractors have attended one and a half years of college and have graduated from a chiropractic college. They then must pass an examination given by the state where they practice. Chiropractic manual manipulations of the spine to correct an x-ray-demonstrated defect are covered by Medicare and some private health plans. Chiropractors cannot prescribe drugs or perform surgery.

11

Colds, Flu, and More Serious Problems of the Lungs and Respiratory System

(11-1) The respiratory system is made up of the lungs and the windpipes (larynx, trachea, and bronchi) which bring air to and from the lungs. The larynx seen from outside is the Adam's apple and contains the vocal cords. The trachea extends downward from the larynx and divides into two main bronchi before entering the lungs.

With age, the chest wall and lungs become less elastic than they once were, and there is more difficulty inhaling and exhaling air. When there is less filling and emptying of the lungs, some of the respiratory reserve is lost. With loss of respiratory reserve, exertion produces shortness of breath, and lung infections are more severe. With age, too, the body's immune system against infections diminishes, and people are more likely to get bronchitis and pneumonia.

Coughing is the most common symptom of respiratory disease. A cough usually means the person has a cold but a person who has a frequent cough should see a physician. Under no circumstances should any cough that lasts longer than two weeks go unreported. Bringing up phlegm (sputum) for over three days is another symptom that needs a physician's attention. Most commonly yellow or green sputum suggests a bacterial infection. Other colors of sputum may be associated with a specific disease and should be reported. Coughing up blood is a medical emergency—you must seek attention immediately.

Shortness of breath (dyspnea) can be produced by a variety of conditions—some very serious, some less serious. While anxiety (5-6), anemia, and diabetes (16-7) can all produce sudden severe shortness of breath, the most common causes are related to problems of the heart and lungs. Anyone with chronic shortness of breath must have its cause determined.

COLDS, ALLERGIC RHINITIS, AND SORE THROATS

(11-2) *The common cold,* also called an upper respiratory infection (URI), is an infection of the inside linings of the nose, throat, and sinuses (hollow spaces in the bone of the forehead above the nose and in the cheeks). Swelling of these linings leads to nasal stuffiness, made worse by the mucus and fluid that form inside the nose. When this mucus leaks from the back of the nasal passages (postnasal drip), it catches in the throat and produces a cough. Headaches, usually under the eyes or in the forehead, may result from fluid building up in the sinuses. There is a dry, but not really sore, throat. Colds normally last ten days to two weeks. Colds are caused by a number of different viruses and there is no cure; medicines only treat symptoms. Temperature can rise to 102°F (38.9°C) orally. An oral temperature higher than 102°F or one of 101°F (38.3°C) that lasts more than forty-eight hours should be brought to the attention of your physician.

People react differently to colds. Muscle aches and weakness keep many people home or in bed for the first few days of a cold. Others have constitutions that allow colds to make them miserable for several days—almost totally incapacitated. Still others seem to have very little difficulty. Following the two weeks of the cold, the postnasal drip may last another week or two, producing a cough. Many people will have two or three colds a year no matter what they do to prevent them.

When you have an elevated temperature, you lose fluids more quickly than usual through your skin and lungs. This loss causes accentuation of the aches and pains of a cold and makes the mucus in your nose and throat thicker. The loss of salt with the fluids may produce dizziness. Drinking liquids in greater than normal amounts, particularly salty ones like bouillon and chicken soup, helps to decrease these symptoms.

(11-3) *Antibiotics for colds* are sometimes prescribed even though these drugs are useful only against bacteria, not the viruses that cause colds. There is some controversy about this, but many physicians argue that the infection from a virus lowers resistance to a secondary bacterial infection. Antibiotics prevent this secondary infection. On the other hand, there is a risk in taking antibiotics for colds. If a bacterial infection occurs even though you are taking an antibiotic, it will be more difficult to treat than it would be otherwise. Also, the more often you use an antibi-

Problems of the Lungs and Respiratory System

otic, the more likely you are to become allergic to it and to be unable to use it when you need it for a more serious infection.

One way to get relief from the symptoms of a cold involves inhaling cool mist from a room vaporizer. This helps in clearing the nose and decreasing the cough. Cool mist is preferable to steam because when you have a cold your nasal passages are already engorged with blood and steam will swell them further, making it even more difficult to breathe. Cool mist, on the other hand, will shrink the passages, and break up mucus. Cool mist vaporizers that can be put by a bed are inexpensive. Do not put medication in the vaporizer unless told to do so by your physician. Washing out the nasal passages with warm, slightly salty water (one-eighth teaspoon per cup of water) three to four times a day using an infant ear syringe is frequently helpful, too.

(11-4) *Cough medicines.* Preparations that contain small amounts of codeine (7-19) are very useful for decreasing the cough of a cold; they require a prescription. Many patients find little use for cough medicines obtainable without a prescription unless a cough is keeping the patient up at night. In this case there are two kinds of cough syrups that can be purchased without a prescription: one contains glycergyl guaiacolate, which breaks up the mucus and allows it to be coughed up; the other contains dextromethorphan, a true cough suppressant. Read the labels—syrups containing glyceryl guaiacolate also often contain considerable sugar or alcohol, which would present a problem if you are either a diabetic or an alcoholic. Dextromethorphan may produce drowsiness. Many pharmacies put up preparations that contain one or the other of these compounds. The housebrand will be less expensive than the brand names.

(11-5) *Oral nonprescription cold remedies.* There are over 100 nonprescription oral cold remedies available. Most contain an antihistamine, a decongestant, and an analgesic. The antihistamines (chlorpheniramine, pyrilamine, phenyltoloxamine, pheniramine, as well as others) dry the nasal secretions and, as a side effect, produce drowsiness. The decongestants (phenylephrine, phenylpropanolamine, pseudoephedrine) constrict blood vessels in the nose and in large enough doses constrict other blood vessels, and this in turn may raise the blood pressure. The analgesics (aspirin, acetaminophen, salicylamide, phenacetin, carbaspirin) relieve some of the headache and general discomfort of a cold. Since none of the analgesic compounds is better than aspirin, it is probably wise to purchase one without aspirin and take it as needed and tolerated. In addition, take two aspirins every four hours to bring down a temperature. This is important in the afternoon and evening since the evening is when the symptoms of a cold are worse. The cold remedies contain a variety of other substances including caffeine, dextromethorphan, aluminum hydroxide, magnesium hydroxide, and ascorbic acid. These other substances are usually present in low dosages and do not add to the effectiveness of the cold remedy. Most individuals have a favorite cold remedy, but it would be a good idea to ask your physician at your next regular visit if the one you like has side effects that make it inadvisable for you to take.

(11-6) *Vitamin C.* Despite the loud claims of advocates of vitamin C that it can prevent colds, I can find no reliable evidence from the reported research that this is true. The most impressive data in favor of vitamin C comes from a series of studies done at the University of Toronto. Researchers found that while large doses of vitamin C did not prevent colds, they did decrease the cold's severity—as did relatively small doses of vitamin C. The reasons for this are not clear. It has long been known, however, that during stress, vitamin C is handled differently by the body than at other times—in fact, at these times the body may require more vitamin C. To meet this requirement, I suggest the following: take a multiple vitamin capsule (3-6) that contains 100 to 150 mg of vitamin C each day. This will ensure that your tissues are saturated with vitamin C. More vitamin C than this is probably wasted—in some individuals it may even prove harmful. At the first sign of a cold, take an additional 1.5 g of vitamin C (not the multiple vitamin) each day for four days. Take the least expensive tablet you can purchase since vitamin C, no matter what its source, is still vitamin C. Until it has been demonstrated scientifically that vitamin C is absolutely safe, even these relatively small doses should not be taken by pregnant women or children.

(11-7) *Allergic rhinitis* causes sneezing, watery and itching eyes, mucus-filled throat, and nasal congestion. It is brought on by exposure to substances in the air to which a person is allergic (sensitive). The common allergens (substances to which one is allergic) are pollens, molds, and dust. In the allergic process, the blood makes antibodies that help fight off the allergens but that also produce the allergic symptoms. The word "allergy" comes from Greek words for "other work," implying an inappropriate or unusual reaction to a stimulus.

Pollen is made up of the male germ cells of plants that float in the air in search of a female partner to fertilize. When they come in contact with the inside of the nose or upper respiratory passages of an allergic person, a reaction is set off. Trees, weeds, and grasses produce the most important of the allergen pollens. Ragweed, which causes hayfever, is the best known. Pollen is produced seasonally—trees pollinate in the early spring, grasses in late spring and early summer, and weeds in the late summer.

Molds are fungi such as that found on old bread in the form of mildew,

Problems of the Lungs and Respiratory System

or that which produces penicillin. The seeds of fungi are called spores; when inhaled, they can cause seasonal allergies. In most climates seasonal allergies occur in the summer. Winter allergies may come from furnaces and humidifiers contaminated with molds.

Dust is not one substance but the sum of many kinds of fine particles, including natural fibers such as cotton, feathers, bacteria, mold, bits of plants, and dander from pets. Dust is everywhere and, unlike pollens and molds, is not seasonal. Allergic rhinitis from dust is also not seasonal.

If you suffer from an allergy, the first task of your physician or allergist may be to perform simple skin tests to determine what you are allergic to. The suspected offending agent is scratched or injected into the skin. If you are allergic to the substance, the skin around the affected area will become red for a short period of time.

Treating allergic rhinitis may require any or all of four measures: avoiding the offending substances, using medications as your physician prescribes, using nasal washes, and taking hyposensitization injections.

If you are allergic to dust, an antidust program at home should be of some help. The bedroom, the room in which you spend most of your time, needs the most attention. Use plastic coverings on mattresses, box springs, and pillows. Even if they are "nonallergenic," they still hold dust and release it when you put pressure on them by lying down. Vacuum the room; do not sweep it with a broom or a carpet sweeper, which can stir up dust. Dust furniture with a damp cloth so the dust will stick to the cloth. Wear a mask that covers your nose and mouth when cleaning or dusting. If you have forced hot air heat, the system will spread dust from one part of the house to another. If possible, keep hot air registers closed in the bedroom. If this cannot be done, put a fiberglass filter over the register. Do not purchase an electrostatic air filter for your furnace unless specifically told to do so by a physician. These filters are expensive and unless they are good they won't help.

In general, stay away from smoke-filled rooms, fumes, sprays, and, if possible, air pollution. If convenient, take a vacation at the time of the year when your allergy is the worst so you can avoid local pollens and molds.

There are a number of antihistamine-type drugs that can be used for allergic rhinitis. Chlorpheniramine (Chlor-Trimeton and other brands) can be purchased without a prescription, comes in 4-mg yellow tablets with "TW" imprinted on them, and is best taken just before the time of day the allergy is at its worst. Do not take more than four tablets a day without consulting your physician. The value of chlorpheniramine over many other antihistamines is that, while it produces some drowsiness, only a little real sedation is involved. If you become drowsy, do not drive or

After Middle Age

perform other functions that require alertness. Other less common side effects include restlessness, dry mouth, and dizziness.

The prescription nasal spray cromolyn (Nasalcrom) can prevent allergic rhinitis from occurring, but is less effective once allergic rhinitis does occur. Treatment should begin before exposure to the allergen and continue throughout exposure. One metered spray to each nostril is given three to six times a day. If the nose is congested it should be cleared before giving the spray with blowing or with a decongestant. Sneezing, stinging, and burning are common side effects. Occasionally headache and bad taste may occur.

Nasal irrigation can greatly help when antihistamines do not bring sufficient relief. Irrigation is especially useful to break up mucus that collects in the nasal passages and throat and produces difficult breathing, hoarseness, and cough. A Grossan Nasal Irrigator Tip, which can be attached to a Water Pik handle, is sold by Hydro Med Inc., P.O. Box 91273, World Way Postal Center, Los Angeles, California 90009. The tip sprays salt water into the nose and breaks up the mucus. Dissolve one-eighth teaspoon of table salt in a cup of water and pour into the reservoir of the Water Pik. Turn it on at the lowest possible setting and test the pressure against your arm to determine if it is too great. Then spray the salt solution into each nostril for thirty seconds three to four times each day. Cheaper and equally effective is the use of an infant ear syringe to irrigate the nose.

Your physician can hyposensitize you with once- or even twice-weekly allergy shots to increase your tolerance to the allergen. The doses begin small and build up. Unfortunately, symptom reduction may take six to eight months. In addition, because of the need for frequent visits, the procedure is both time-consuming and expensive.

(11-8) *Sore throats.* The most common cause of a sore throat is sleeping in a dry, warm bedroom. A room humidifier or a humidifier attached to a central heating system is the best prevention. Nasal irrigation (11-7) and warm salt water gargles also can help. Having a glass of water on the bedstand that can be sipped during the night is very useful.

Viral infections produce sore throats much more often than do bacterial infections, but it is hard to tell them apart. Fever may accompany either. The best way to determine the cause of the infection is to have a physician take a throat culture by brushing an applicator stick with a cotton tip against the back of the throat. The cotton picks up bacteria, which are then grown in an incubator and become numerous enough for identification. If the throat culture is beta-streptococcus (the cause of "strep throat"), the physician will probably treat the infection with penicillin or another antibiotic. As explained earlier (11-3), if you do not

Problems of the Lungs and Respiratory System

have a bacterial infection, no antibiotics are indicated. If the sore throat persists, however, it is possible that what started off as a viral infection has become bacterial—and will require a second visit to your physician.

Gargles, including mouthwashes, are of little use for most sore throats. Chewing gum containing aspirin may help relieve the pain, but two aspirin in an eight-ounce warm-water gargle is more effective. Throat lozenges containing benzocaine relieve some of the pain for a few minutes, but they can also produce allergies. Two aspirins taken by mouth every four hours do as much to relieve the discomfort as anything.

HOARSENESS AND LARYNGITIS

(11-9) Some hoarseness (ranging from slight huskiness to complete loss of voice) is usually associated with colds and heavy smoking. If the hoarseness is due to a cold, it will disappear as the cold improves. If you are a smoker and have chronic hoarseness, you should be examined by your physician.

Other common causes of hoarseness are viral or occasionally bacterial infections of the vocal cords in the larynx (laryngitis). Hoarseness may occur together with cough, pain, running nose, or a tickling sensation, but it may also be the only symptom present. A person with laryngitis that lasts more than forty-eight hours without improvement or that makes it difficult to breathe should see a physician. There may be a treatable cause such as an infection or a benign or malignant tumor.

LARYNGEAL CANCER

(11-10) Laryngeal (voice box) cancer usually begins as hoarseness lasting more than three weeks. A "frog in the throat," sudden changes in the pitch of the voice, narrowed voice range, fatigue on talking, continued throat clearing, the presence of a lump in the throat, or chronic cough may also be signs of laryngeal cancer. A physician can usually make a preliminary diagnosis by placing a dentist's mirror in the back of the mouth and then using a fiberoptic laryngoscope, if necessary, to see a suspicious area more clearly. A biopsy (17-4), the microscopic examination of a tissue sample, will tell the complete story.

Radiation treatment is generally used to treat early cancer, is highly successful, and leaves few, if any, lasting side effects. For more advanced cancers surgery is used along with radiation, but since the larynx contains the vocal cords, every effort is made not to cut them. In most cases, the vocal cords can be saved, but early detection and treatment are essential.

After Middle Age

Even when it is necessary to remove the larynx, and natural speech is no longer possible, individuals can learn esophageal speech, which is produced by expelling air through the esophagus. Learning to speak in this way must begin as soon as surgery is completed. The International Association of Laryngectomees sponsors Post Card Clubs and New Voice Clubs which help individuals with speech problems.

THE FLU (INFLUENZA) AND ITS PREVENTION

(11-11) *The flu* is a virus infection that produces a sudden onset of headache, fever, and aching all over the body. Treatment of the flu is two aspirins every four hours and a lot of fluid. The most serious complication of the flu is a secondary bacterial infection—usually pneumonia. While antibiotics are of no use against the viruses that produce the flu, they are useful in preventing or treating secondary bacterial infections. As mentioned earlier (11-3), this is an extremely controversial subject. Most physicians will not use an antibiotic for the flu unless they are particularly concerned about a secondary infection.

Since older individuals often have difficulty fighting off the flu, most physicians recommend a flu shot when an epidemic is expected. Annual vaccination is recommended for individuals with heart disease, lung or kidney disease, diabetes, or cancer. Most vaccines should not be given to individuals allergic to eggs, egg products, chickens, or chicken feathers, since the virus for the vaccine is usually grown in eggs. If you have any question about your being allergic to the vaccine, ask your physician to give you a scratch test before giving you the shot. Fever, chills, muscle pain, and headaches occur in about 20 percent of those given the vaccine, but this side effect is less severe than the flu itself and much less dangerous for high-risk individuals. Since the viruses that cause the flu constantly change, the vaccine must be adjusted. For this reason, flu shots have to be repeated every year or so.

(11-12) *Guillain-Barré syndrome* is a disease that has been recognized for over 100 years but only recently became known to the general public. A few months after people began to be inoculated with the swine flu vaccine in 1976, there was an increase in the incidence of Guillain-Barré among people who had been inoculated. Since then there has been evidence that Guillain-Barré might, on rare occasions, follow other inoculations. Generally, the disease begins by a loss of ability to move first the feet, then the legs. There may be numbness and tingling in the toes and legs. Occasionally, the arms become paralyzed, and breathing becomes difficult. The disease may require hospitalization, but most people fully

Problems of the Lungs and Respiratory System

recover. Improvement may occur very rapidly or take a year or more. Only a few patients fail to respond. Steroids or the steroid-stimulating hormone ACTH can be given. Problems with breathing are the most serious, but modern care can help most people through the disease.

(11-13) *Alternatives to flu immunizations.* Most people who get flu live through it, although viral pneumonia or secondary bacterial pneumonia (or both) will kill a small percentage of people. If you decide not to take the vaccine and you become ill with the flu, be aware that pneumonia is a possibility; and if you find yourself feeling worse, see your physician. Be alert for epidemics. If an epidemic is breaking out in a different part of the country, there may be time to get the vaccine and develop immunity. Ask your physician about taking amantadine (Symmetrel), which comes in 100-mg red capsules with "Symmetrel 56-105" imprinted on them. The usual dose is one capsule twice a day. Amantadine is an oral antiviral drug that is moderately effective in preventing type A (Asian) flu. It has to be taken at the first sign of an epidemic and continued daily until the epidemic is over (four to six weeks). Taken at the first symptoms of flu, amantadine will shorten the duration of the illness from an average of four days to one and a half days. Side effects may include psychological depression, increased seizures in people with epilepsy, worsening of heart failure in susceptible persons, swelling of the ankles, light-headedness when getting up quickly from a sitting or a lying position, inability to empty the bladder completely, and blurred vision. These side effects should be brought immediately to your physician's attention (7-25).

BRONCHITIS AND EMPHYSEMA

(11-14) *Chronic bronchitis (smoker's cough).* The symptoms of chronic bronchitis are a cough with sputum (occasionally blood-streaked) lasting more than a month, and recurrent lung infections. Bronchitis is frequently found in heavy smokers. Atmospheric pollution also is thought to play an important part, and chronic bronchitis is aggravated in those individuals living in or near large urban areas. The symptoms are worse during the winter and in very humid, warm weather when the air is likely to be polluted. Severe, uncontrollable bouts of coughing may be present. People may for a time maintain their vigor even with chronic bronchitis, but it is as severe a breath-robbing disease as emphysema and should not be taken lightly.

(11-15) *Diagnosis of chronic bronchitis.* Any cough lasting more than two weeks should be brought to the attention of a physician. In addition to x-rays of the lungs and culture of the sputum, the physician may want to

After Middle Age

perform a bronchoscopic examination to be sure that there is no tumor or piece of food lodged in the throat. Modern bronchoscopy starts with the application to the nasal membranes of a local anesthetic, usually xylocaine spray. Then a thin fiberoptic tube is passed through the nose to the lung. The physician can then see into the lung because of the unique properties of the glass, which reflects light around bends. With this procedure, a biopsy (17-4) can be taken. Only a few years ago this was an uncomfortable procedure, but modern techniques have made the discomfort minimal.

(11-16) *Treatment of chronic bronchitis.* An important advance in recent years has been the finding that when chronic bronchitis is identified early, the damage can be partially reversed. First, individuals who smoke must give it up (11-29). Other irritants, such as fumes and allergic agents, must be avoided, too. The physician may prescribe a cough suppressant such as codeine (15 to 30 mg every four hours). Thick sputum can be liquefied with both the ingestion of fluids (drinking more than usual amount of water) and cool mist inhalation (11-3). Wheezing can be treated by inhaling from a nebulizer containing isoetharine (Bronkometer) no more than four times a day. Also, aminophylline (Somophyllin) can be taken by mouth. If there is an infection, the physician will prescribe an antibiotic. When nothing else helps, a physician may prescribe the steroid prednisone to reduce inflammation (10-3). The average dose is 5 to 10 mg every six hours for three to four days. In special cases, the physician may start by prescribing up to 60 mg per day in either one or divided doses. This dosage will then be tapered down over the next three to four days.

(11-17) *Emphysema* is a disease in which the smallest bags of air (alveoli) in the lung become overextended and destroyed. After taking air in, the alveoli are unable to return to their normal shape, and the air is not expelled. The chest eventually becomes enlarged and may look like a barrel. An abnormal backward curvature may also develop in the spinal column (kyphosis). At first, breathlessness is present only upon exertion, but with time the breathlessness occurs even at rest. Chronic bronchitis (11-14) with its symptoms of cough, discolored sputum, and frequent sudden infections usually accompanies emphysema. Aggressive treatment is required to prevent irreversible damage. Intermittent bouts or continued wheezing may also occur and require medication. Minor lung infections to which most people would pay little attention may become debilitating.

A physician examining a patient with these symptoms will x-ray the chest, in addition to performing a routine physical examination. It is possible to determine the degree of impairment and whether it is reversible by having the individual breathe into a respirometer, a machine de-

Problems of the Lungs and Respiratory System

signed to measure lung function. You can perform a simple test on yourself with a stopwatch. After taking as deep a breath as possible, start the watch and expel as much air as you can. If completely expelling the air takes longer than three to five seconds, you may have significant disease. A blood test may be taken to determine if emphysema is due to a hereditary deficiency of a substance known as alpha-one-antitrypsin.

The treatment for emphysema is similar to that for chronic bronchitis (11-16). Since emphysema is thought by most physicians to be greatly aggravated and, in many cases, caused by smoking, smoking must be stopped.

Recently steroids in aerosol form have been found to be very helpful for the wheezing that may be associated with bronchitis and occasionally with emphysema. These steroids in the recommended doses avoid the complications of steroids given by mouth because they stay in the lungs and do not affect the rest of the body. Beclomethasone (Vanceril) is the first of several such agents to become available in this country. The Vanceril inhaler gives a measured dose with each squeeze. The number and frequency of inhalations must be carefully regulated. The usual dosage is two inhalations three to four times a day, but more may be recommended by your physician.

PNEUMONIAS AND TUBERCULOSIS

(11-18) *Bacterial pneumonia* is usually due to an infection by the pneumococcal bacteria. It begins with a shaking chill, fever, and chest pain. If there is pain from pleurisy (inflammation of the membranes surrounding the lung), it will be made worse by deep breathing. The diagnosis and treatment of this type of pneumonia are usually easy. Blood and expectorated sputum are examined, and a chest x-ray is taken. Penicillin or another antibiotic is given, occasionally by injection, and subsequently by mouth. Depending upon the severity of the pneumonia and the person's general health, the physician may recommend hospitalization for a few days. With good treatment the prognosis is excellent.

There are a number of bacteria that cause pneumonia other than pneumococcus. Proper treatment demands that the bacteria be identified. This is done by culturing the blood and examining the sputum. Once the bacteria is identified, the most efficacious antibiotic can be chosen.

In 1980 a vaccine (Pneumovax, Pnu-Imune 23) against pneumococcal pneumonia became widely available. Like all vaccines, the pneumococcal vaccine forces the body to manufacture an antibody to the pneumococcal bacteria, and that antibody will thus destroy the bacteria if they invade the body. After vaccination, there is frequently local swelling and redness at the injection site lasting forty-eight hours. Temperatures up to 101°F (38.3°C) are common; if temperatures go higher, alert a physician. There are eighty-three different forms of pneumococci. But since twenty-three of them cause 90 percent of the pneumonias, the immunization only affects that prevalent group. Older persons with any form of chronic disease (lung disease, heart disease, diabetes) that makes them more susceptible to infection should consider getting the vaccination. This is especially true of people who have had their spleen removed, because their chances of getting pneumococcal pneumonia are high. You should not receive Pneumovax or Pnu-Imune 23 if you have previously received a pneumococcal vaccine.

(11-19) *Legionnaires' disease* first came to national and international attention after an outbreak of pneumonia with many deaths associated following an American Legion convention in Philadelphia in the summer of 1976. It now appears there had been a number of previous outbreaks that had just passed as particularly severe pneumonia.

The disease begins two to ten days after exposure with tiredness, muscle aches, and a slight headache. A cough that does not produce sputum is another early symptom. Body temperature reaches 102° to 105°F (39° to 40.5°C) within twenty-four to forty-eight hours, and there may be pain in the abdomen. Later, the cough produces sputum. Usually patients become so ill within two to three days that they require hospitalization. Diagnosis of pneumonia is made by x-rays of the chest. The bacteria-like organism can now be isolated, but often the individual must be treated before a positive identification can be made. Erythromycin (Erythrocin), an antibiotic, appears to produce a fairly quick response most of the time.

(11-20) *Viral pneumonia* involves a cough that usually produces sputum that is sometimes tinged with blood. Fever, loss of appetite, muscle aches, and headaches may be present, too. The pneumonia can be diagnosed by x-ray. There is no specific treatment: antibiotics that are used for bacteria are ineffective against these organisms (11-3). Occasionally, physicians will decide to treat with antibiotics (usually a tetracycline) to prevent a bacterial infection from also infecting the lung (secondary infection). Otherwise, treatment is aimed at keeping temperature down with two aspirins every four hours as needed. Patients should try to sit up in a chair or in bed because an upright position prevents fluids from collecting in the lungs. It's important to drink plenty of liquids, too, and to eat food as it can be tolerated. Fever and cough may persist for three to five days. After recovery, there is usually a long period (up to several months) of unexplained tiredness.

(11-21) *Mycoplasma (primary atypical pneumonia)* is very similar to

Problems of the Lungs and Respiratory System

viral pneumonia but usually is less serious and is felt to respond to antibiotics, including tetracyclines and erythromycin. Fluid that gathers between the lungs and rib cage (called pleural effusion) may have to be removed (tapped) with a needle. Before the tap, the area is anesthetized with xylocaine. This procedure is relatively painless.

(11-22) *Tuberculosis* is still in existence, although it is much less common than it once was. The reasons for the decline in tuberculosis are better nutrition and the success of screening procedures that were used heavily after World War II. X-rays and skin tests identified tuberculosis carriers early, before they spread the bacteria by droplet infection to other people. The carriers were and are treated with drugs. Tuberculosis is now predominantly a disease associated with the aged who suffer poor nutrition, or people with alcoholism, diabetes, or cancer.

The symptoms of tuberculosis develop gradually—an elevated afternoon or evening temperature, tiredness, weight loss, sweating at night, and a persistent, sputum-producing cough that is worse upon rising. Most people with tuberculosis, however, never have symptoms. They are usually diagnosed by chest x-ray or a skin test. The latter involves injecting a standard-strength purified protein derivative of tuberculin (PPD) or introducing PPD by making multiple punctures (Tine or Heaf Test) into the skin of the forearm. The test is read at the end of seventy-two hours. A doubtful to positive result is indicated by the presence of a firm, slightly raised area, 0.5 cm or more in diameter (the width of an eraser at the end of a pencil). Anything smaller is definitely negative. X-rays of the chest are used to look for active infection, and sputum is examined. Frequently, the bacteria can be seen with a microscope, but when there are few, it may take several weeks for them to grow in a culture.

Treatment for tuberculosis has changed drastically in the last twenty-five years. Patients used to be sent off to open-air sanitoriums and some had their chest surgically collapsed. Today's highly effective drugs have made surgery unnecessary. Only a brief stay in a general hospital may be required until the drugs have had a chance to work, and in many cases there is no hospitalization. Once the drugs take effect and there is no longer a possibility of contagion (that is, when the sputum does not contain tuberculosis bacteria), a patient can leave the hospital. Patients are usually discharged within two weeks, though drug treatment continues for at least nine months and longer when necessary. The majority of persons infected may successfully defeat the infection even without medications, though they remain at high risk for reactivation of the dormant infection.

Other members of the patient's family should also be treated. Many physicians will want to treat young children who are known to have been exposed to tuberculosis, even if the children have negative tuberculin tests. Persons who test positive but have no other signs of the disease may be treated preventively. This depends on a number of factors, including other illnesses and results of their past examinations for tuberculosis.

Isoniazid (INH), average dosage 300 mg per day, in combination with rifampin (Rifadin), average dosage 600 mg per day, is the usual treatment. Both medicines have few side effects but should be used with caution in people with diseases other than tuberculosis. Side effects include jaundice (liver impairment manifest by yellowing of the skin) and occasional numbness and tingling in the hands or feet. These side effects should be brought to your physician's attention immediately. It is rare today when even the most serious cases of tuberculosis cannot be brought under control within a year, although continued drug treatment may be necessary for considerably longer.

OCCUPATIONAL LUNG DISORDERS

(11-23) *Occupational lung disorders* (allergic alveolitis and pneumoconioses) are increasingly being recognized as major health problems. Hypersensitivity to inhaled fine particles in their early stages can produce asthma (wheezing, shortness of breath, cough with sticky sputum). Later chills, fever, muscle aches, and tiredness occur within a few hours of exposure and last for two to three hours. Associated with the latter or chronic form are a frequent cough, difficulty breathing, tiredness, and weight loss.

Workers are vulnerable when exposed to the following: cotton dust, cheese, sugar cane, moldy cork dust, moldy hay, moldy bark, mushroom compost, pigeons or other birds, paprika beans, and wood-processing facilities. Persons with jobs that place them in heavy contact with silica, asbestos, beryllium, bauxite, coal, and iron ore that might be inhaled are also vulnerable. All workers should know the hazards of their jobs, wear the proper protection (in some cases a mask or a respirator), and remove dust with vacuums.

Recognition of the disorder, once it has begun, is extremely important so that further exposure to the offending agent can be eliminated. Individuals with the above symptoms should ask their physicians to refer them to a specialist in chest diseases (pulmonary medicine).

LUNG EMBOLISM

(11-24) The symptoms of embolism (a blood clot moving from one part of the body to another through the blood vessels) to the lung are very

Problems of the Lungs and Respiratory System

similar to those that occur with many heart attacks. There may be sudden pain in the midchest region and a feeling of tightness, like a band, around the chest. The individual becomes short of breath and breathes rapidly. There may be pain or pressure that comes on suddenly and occurs with each breath. Apprehension and cough are frequent symptoms, and the cough may bring up blood. A pulmonary embolism, like a myocardial infarction (heart attack), is a medical emergency that may produce death—the patient must be taken immediately to the hospital. X-rays, including a radioisotope study (lung scan), and EKGs are done for diagnosis.

Treatment of the embolism is aimed at decreasing its effects as well as preventing its recurrence. Oxygen, an intravenous (IV) anticoagulant (heparin), and something to reduce the pain are given initially. Those who are taking heparin should know that subsequent intramuscular injections of other drugs may result in bleeding into the muscle. But heparin causes no difficulty when blood is drawn or injections are made into veins. Aspirin, which is also an anticoagulant, may have to be discontinued. Tests of how fast the patient's blood clots (partial thromboplastin time) will be performed often. An enzyme, streptokinase or urokinase, that dissolves the clot will be given. If there is loss of blood pressure, an intravenous drip of dopamine (Intropin) is given. Rarely, surgery to remove the embolus (embolectomy) is performed on individuals for whom medical treatment has not been successful.

Once the patient's condition has been stabilized, treatment is directed at the source of the embolism—usually the lower leg. To prevent recurrences, elevate the leg onto a pillow, apply heat, and prevent heavy bedclothes from resting on it. After the anticoagulant is working (usually within four days), exercise of all extremities is recommended. An elastic bandage—wrapped from the foot up to the knee—is used to prevent swelling when walking.

Once the period of immediate danger is over, efforts are made to prevent future emboli. Blood is kept from clotting in the veins through use of anticoagulants like warfarin or dicumarol for periods usually under six months. It is important that the right amount of anticoagulant drug be used. To monitor the dosage the patient's blood will be tested frequently by a procedure called prothrombin time (PT). Aspirin alters the results of these tests.

If drug treatment is unsuccessful as evidenced by repeated emboli, surgery is recommended. The operation is called a vena caval interruption which, in essence, puts a sieve in the vein that returns blood from the legs to the heart. If a clot does break loose from the leg, the sieve catches it

After Middle Age

and prevents it from traveling to the heart and from there to the lung. An alternative operation occludes (stops up) the vein entirely.

LUNG CANCER AND SMOKING

(11-25) *Lung cancer.* The first symptoms of lung cancer are a gradual increase in coughing (cigarette cough), chest pain, wheezing, blood-streaked sputum, and hoarseness. The disease may also show up by chance on x-rays or from symptoms of metastases (spread) to other organs. When a patient reports one or more of these symptoms, the physician will want to hear more as well as do a thorough physical examination. If there is a suspicious shadow on a chest x-ray, in many cases the physician will not be sure of the diagnosis until a biopsy (17-4) is performed. A lung biopsy is done with a bronchoscope—an instrument for inspecting the interior of the lung. If the growth is found to be benign but is pressing on an important area, it may have to be removed surgically. If it is malignant and it can be removed surgically, the surgeon will remove the tumor and any lymph nodes to which the malignancy may have traveled. X-ray treatment and drugs may also be used.

While the current chances of living a normal life with the most common forms of lung cancer are not good, in the last several years there has been considerable progress in treating cancer of other organs with several drugs given in combination. Whether this success will carry over to treatment of lung cancer is not yet known. Also, several small studies have reported success in treating lung cancer with surgery and a vaccine.

Lung cancer is, however, usually preventable. Only one out of ten persons who get lung cancer is a nonsmoker. It is believed that other factors that contribute to this 10 percent are air pollution and long-term exposure to some industrial compounds. The federal government and employers are becoming increasingly concerned over such environmental factors; as these factors become better understood, ways to more fully protect the worker will be devised.

(11-26) *Does smoking really cause lung cancer?* Nine of every ten individuals with lung cancer are smokers. In the average smoker, lung cancer is ten times more likely to develop than in the nonsmoker. In the heavy smoker it is thirty times more frequent. These figures have been known since 1936, but most people do not understand such odds. I have often heard the following rationalization: If something happens only one time in a million, an increase of 10, equivalent to one in a hundred thousand on an individual basis, does not pose much of a threat. Many smokers use this rationalization or something like it to continue smoking.

Problems of the Lungs and Respiratory System

The problem is that lung cancer is much more common than one in a million. A helpful way to consider these odds is to think about a high school softball team. Each of the ten members of the team has smoked a total of two packs of cigarettes since age 16. It is now their fortieth team reunion and they are 56 years old. One of them will not show up because he or she is dead or dying of lung cancer. The same can be said of any group of ten people who has smoked long and hard. One will get lung cancer. Only one out of one hundred nonsmokers will develop lung cancer. Heavy smoking will shorten the life span of a middle-aged man by an average of eight years. When smoking is discontinued, the cancer risk diminishes very rapidly so that no matter how old you are, stopping makes sense.

(11-27) *Do you want to stop smoking?* The first step in stopping smoking is to decide that you want to stop. Why do you want to stop smoking? The major reason people want to stop smoking is for their health. Have you convinced yourself smoking is dangerous? On a scale of zero to 10, with zero being "I don't believe at all" and 10 "I firmly believe smoking is harmful," how do you rate yourself? If you do not give yourself greater than a 5 rating, your reason for stopping is not good enough, and you should learn more about smoking and health.

Do you want to stop smoking to set an example for others? It is very hard to expect children or grandchildren not to smoke if they see someone who is influential in their lives smoking. For example, it is known that twice as many high school students smoke if both their parents are smokers. Again, if you do not feel strongly about it, this reason will not be useful in motivating you to stop.

Do you want to stop smoking because you find that smoking is unaesthetic and messy, causes bad breath, occasionally burns holes in your clothes, stains your teeth and fingers, or diminishes your sense of taste and smell? Unless these reasons are very important, they will not be sufficient for you to stop.

Do you want to stop smoking because smoking has controlled you rather than you it? Do you place cigarettes in your mouth and not remember putting them there? When you haven't smoked for some time, do you have a craving for one?

A Smoker's Self Test is available from the Office on Smoking and Health, 5600 Fishers Lane, Park Building, Room 110, Rockville, Maryland 20857.

(11-28) *Things to think about before stopping smoking.* Why do people smoke? People are different and smoke for a variety of reasons. Some people smoke because it brings stimulation or relaxation. It may be a stimulant, waking them up or giving them energy, or it may release tension, making them feel more at ease and less nervous; and it may clear their minds. They may smoke because they need to be doing something with their hands—a cigarette in one hand and a drink in the other. People smoke because they like the feeling of smoking; it is one of pleasure. Some smoke because they are physiologically addicted—the minute they put down one cigarette, there is a buildup of urgency until they begin smoking again. Finally, they may smoke simply because it is a habit—unknowingly their hands reach for a cigarette that their mouth cheerfully accepts.

(11-29) *How to stop smoking.* There are two ways to stop smoking—gradually or abruptly (cold turkey). If you are one of those who smoke out of habit, it is probably easier to stop gradually. A ten-week schedule for a one-pack-a-day smoker or twenty-week schedule for a two-packs-a-day smoker in which each week two less cigarettes are smoked each day makes sense. (If you are a pipe or cigar smoker you can arrange a similar schedule.) At the beginning of each week the proper number of cigarettes is counted out into seven packages for that week—for the first week, eighteen cigarettes are placed into each of seven packs (actually two removed from each), sixteen for the second week, and so on. Wear a watch at all times, and prespace each cigarette over time. If you normally smoke twenty cigarettes over a sixteen-hour period, you smoke a little over one per hour—actually, one every forty-eight minutes. When you cut yourself down to fourteen, you may want to select two hours when you will omit smoking. The point of this kind of regimen is to make you more aware of your habit. Since heavy smokers are also addicted to nicotine in the tobacco, the gradual and timed reduction of nicotine will make stopping easier.

When you smoke for one of the other reasons, it usually is easier to stop "cold turkey." If you are sick and don't feel like smoking, or if you are going on a trip where cigarettes are impossible to get, this provides an automatic opportunity to stop. In this case, stopping is relatively easy—the major effort is not to begin again. But if such opportunities do not occur, a decision must be made and a firm quitting date set. This may be made easier by saturating yourself, perhaps tripling the number of packs smoked during the three days before quitting.

Some smokers benefit from Smokenders, a commercial company that offers a course for people who wish to stop smoking. The One-Step-At-A-Time filter system (Water-Pik), which reduces nicotine ingestion gradually and separates the physiological addiction from the fidget factor, has been found useful by some smokers.

More rational substitutions are toying with pencils or jewelry for those

Problems of the Lungs and Respiratory System

who smoke because they need to finger something; physical and social activity for those who smoke for stimulation, for pleasant relaxation, or because of psychological addiction. Many individuals find they eat or drink more during the withdrawal days. Thus, it is not surprising to put on twenty pounds in the months after discontinuing smoking. Once you stop smoking, you must behave like an alcoholic and never smoke even one cigarette again. You cannot experiment.

12

Disorders of the Heart and Circulatory System

(12-1) *The circulatory system* consists of arteries, which carry oxygenated blood from the heart to the brain, the kidneys, and all other organs; capillaries, very small vessels through which the blood actually enters and leaves the body tissues; veins, which return the blood to the heart; and the heart itself, which is located in the middle of the chest and consists of two pumps. One pump, the right ventricle, pushes blood into the lungs where it rids itself of built-up carbon dioxide and obtains oxygen before being returned to the heart. Then the second pump, the left ventricle, pushes the blood out into the rest of the body, including the brain. The left ventricle also pushes blood through the coronary arteries into the muscle of the heart itself.

The circulatory system is the body's most extensive system. Because it is distributed over such a large area, it is vulnerable to numerous problems. In general, three things can go wrong: (1) the pumping ability of the heart can fail (heart attack, arrhythmia); (2) the arteries carrying blood to the body can fail (hypertension, stroke); and (3) the return mechanism of the veins can fail (edema, varicose veins).

As the blood flows though the body, it accomplishes the major function of the circulatory system—to carry oxygen from the lungs to other organs. Oxygen combines with food to provide energy in the form of movement and body heat. When oxygen is not available, even for as short a period as five minutes, tissues die. For example, if a blood vessel is blocked and oxygen is not supplied to the brain—in my opinion, the body's most important organ—the body is disabled. This condition is called a stroke. When heart tissue dies for similar reasons, it is called a myocardial infarct. Other tissues, such as the kidneys and muscles, also can infarct.

Disorders of the Heart and Circulatory System

In many individuals of advanced age, the cardiovascular system is less able to supply oxygen to the tissue. People to whom this happens must arrange their lives in such a manner as to put less strain on themselves. With less strain, there is less need for energy and, therefore, oxygen. Sometimes less strain will mean less exercise; at other times, it may mean trying to keep emotionally calm. This chapter describes the problems that alterations in the cardiovascular system produce, what to do when they occur, and how to diminish them.

HYPERTENSION (HIGH BLOOD PRESSURE)

(12-2) Blood pressure is a measure of the force generated by the heart as it pumps blood through the body. The pressure actually fluctuates as the heart beats. The highest, or systolic, pressure is due to the contraction of the heart. The lowest, or diastolic, pressure is controlled by the ability of the arteries to expand in relationship to the systolic pressure. Normally, the arteries are highly elastic, enlarging as the heart pushes the blood against the artery walls, and contracting as the force from the heart decreases. When arteries harden they cannot expand, and therefore the diastolic blood pressure rises.

Blood pressure is measured by a sphygmomanometer (a cuff that is wrapped around the arm and attached to a pressure gauge), which gives both the systolic and diastolic pressure. Normal blood pressure increases slightly with age. For example, the normal value for a healthy young adult is 120/80 (read as 120 over 80); at 60 years, 160/95 is considered to be the upper limit of normal.

(12-3) *Symptoms of hypertension.* Hypertension often produces no symptoms until it has caused great damage. For this reason, it is easy to be unaware of hypertension unless it is found during a medical examination. Symptoms that might make a person aware of the disease include morning headaches; shortness of breath while exercising, or while lying down or sleeping (causing sudden awakening); and swelling (edema) of the ankles after sitting or standing for a time.

(12-4) *Damage caused by hypertension.* It is far better to control hypertension when it begins than to wait until it has damaged the body by producing changes in the heart, blood vessels, eyes, and kidneys. The heart becomes larger because it must pump more forcefully. It may outgrow its blood supply, producing angina, heart attack, and possibly heart failure. Arteries become hardened and narrowed so that some areas of the body receive an inadequate blood supply and infarcts (death of muscle or other tissue from lack of oxygen) occur. Severe hypertension can produce changes in vision and occasionly even blindness. The kidneys are affected

After Middle Age

by hypertension in many ways, but they do not fail until the disease has been present for many years or until it accelerates. Accelerated hypertension is known as malignant hypertension.

(12-5) *Diagnosing hypertension.* If you complain of hypertensive symptoms, the physician will want to know more about them—when your headaches occur, what makes your shortness of breath better or worse, and so on. Has anyone in your family had hypertension, heart disease, or diabetes? What about your diet—in particular, how much table salt and animal fat do you eat? The physician will examine with an ophthalmoscope the retina of your eyes—the one place in the body to see blood vessels and determine if they are healthy. The physician will place a hand on your chest, over your heart, and will listen to your heart and lungs with a stethoscope. By feeling and listening to the heart, the physician can estimate its size and how it is beating. Its size and function can also be determined with a chest x-ray and electrocardiogram. (The x-ray will determine whether there is fluid in the lungs, called pulmonary edema, a sign of heart failure.) The urine will be examined for protein and blood. Normal urine should have neither, and their presence may be a sign of kidney damage. The amount of cholesterol in the blood will also be measured.

The level of your blood pressure may be subject to the circumstances under which it is taken. If it is found to be elevated on one occasion, this is not sufficient cause to diagnose high blood pressure. Many people become anxious in the physician's office, and this may increase blood pressure. You may be asked to come back on several occasions to confirm that your blood pressure is not simply elevated by anxiety from the examination. If you have had to run to keep your appointment or have had a very aggravating day, you might ask your physician to take your blood pressure again after you have had a chance to relax for at least fifteen minutes.

If only the systolic pressure is raised—systolic hypertension—it is usually caused by hardening of the arteries (arteriosclerosis, also called atherosclerosis). This condition can also be caused by other diseases such as hyperthyroidism (overactive thyroid gland). Elevation of both systolic and diastolic pressures—diastolic hypertension—affects 15 to 20 percent of the population, and the incidence increases with age. In younger people, it is much more common in men than in women, and in blacks than in whites.

(12-6) *Taking your own blood pressure.* For diagnostic purposes or for frequent monitoring of treatment, some physicians will want you to take your own blood pressure at home. This can be learned easily. You need only two items, a stethoscope and a standard (12.5 by 23 cm) blood

Disorders of the Heart and Circulatory System

pressure cuff. (If you are very heavy, you will need a larger cuff; the pharmacist can help you pick the proper one.) Both items can be purchased at most drugstores.

The cuff has three parts: cuff, pump, and gauge. Wrap the cuff snugly around your upper right arm and fasten it firmly with the arrow pointing to the bend in your arm. Manipulate the rubber pump with your right hand; closing the screw allows you to inflate the cuff, opening it allows you to deflate it. Pump the cuff to 60 points above where you expect the highest pressure reading (systolic). Place the stethoscope in your ears, tapping on the diaphragm at its end to be sure it is working. (You should hear the taps through the stethoscope.) Place the diaphragm in the bend of your right arm at the edge of the cuff and hold it there firmly with your left hand. Now slowly release the air from the cuff as you watch the gauge. When you hear the first beat sound against the diaphragm (this will take some practice), read the gauge. This is the systolic blood pressure. Continue to release air. At the point when you no longer hear the heartbeat through the diaphragm, note the reading on the gauge again. This is the diastolic blood pressure.

The physician will tell you when you are to take your blood pressure and whether it is to be done while you are sitting, lying, or standing.

(12-7) *The electrocardiogram (EKG or ECG).* The heart is controlled by an electrical mechanism (a pacemaker) that keeps it pumping smoothly and regularly. This electrical activity can be detected on the skin and measured with an electrocardiograph. An EKG examination is a routine procedure for any condition affecting the heart. Electrodes designed to pick up the electrical discharge are placed on the chest and connected to the EKG machine. (A salty jelly is placed on the skin to help the electricity pass from the skin to the electrode.) The machine amplifies the signals and records them on a piece of moving paper—the electrocardiogram—from which the physician learns two things: the rhythm of the heartbeat and the electrical voltage, which indicates heart size.

You cannot get a shock during an EKG examination. The electricity can pass only from you to the machine.

(12-8) *Treating hypertension.* A physician who discovers elevated blood pressure in a patient generally carries out a series of tests to find the cause. If the cause is related to another disease (secondary hypertension), it can generally be remedied. More commonly the exact cause is unknown (essential hypertension). In this case, your physician will recommend that you keep your weight at the minimum consistent with good health and appearance, give up smoking, and decrease stress. Adequate drug treatment can greatly decrease the incidence of complications from hypertension.

After Middle Age

(12-9) The most important drugs in the management of hypertension are the *diuretics,* which increase urination and thus decrease the salt and water in the body. This reduces the amount of fluid that must be pushed by the heart. Diuretics also alter the walls of the blood vessels, lowering the resistance the vessels give to blood passing through them.

There are many diuretics, all of them doing much the same work.

The thiazide class of diuretics is very widely used. Although side effects are unusual, there are some warning signs. If you're taking any thiazide, bring to the attention of your physician immediately any of the following: excessive thirst or dryness of the mouth, muscle weakness, pains or cramps, sleepiness or restlessness, nausea and vomiting. If you are a diabetic, taking a thiazide may alter your insulin requirements. (Diabetes is often first diagnosed in patients taking thiazides.)

Cyclothiazide (Anhydron, average dosage 1 to 2 mg once a day) comes in 2-mg pink tablets labeled "U09."

Benzthiazide (Aquatag, average dosage 50 to 200 mg a day) comes in 25-mg tablets and 50-mg tablets. Another benzthiazide (Exna) comes in 50-mg yellow scored tablets with "AHR 5449" imprinted on them.

Methyclothiazide (Aquatensen, average dosage 2.5 to 5 mg a day) comes in 5-mg pink, rectangular-shaped, grooved tablets labeled "Wallace 153."

Chlorothiazide (Diuril, average dosage 0.5 to 1 g twice a day) comes in 250-mg and 500-mg, white, round, scored tablets labeled "MSD214" and "MSD432," respectively.

Methyclothiazide (Enduron, average dosage 2.5 to 10 mg taken once a day) comes in 2.5-mg orange, square tablets and 5-mg salmon, square tablets with "∂" on them.

Hydrochlorothiazide (Esidrix, average dosage 25 to 100 mg a day) comes in 25-mg pink, 50-mg yellow, and 100-mg blue tablets, all scored, with "CIBA" stamped on them. It also comes as HydroDiuril in 25-, 50-, and 100-mg peach, round tablets labeled "MSD42," "MSD105," and "MSD410" respectively, and Oretic, which comes in 25- and 50-mg grooved, white tablets.

Trichlormethiazide (Metahydrin, average dosage 2 to 4 mg tablets a day) comes in 2-mg pink and 4-mg aqua-blue tablets imprinted "Merrell 62" and "Merrell 63," respectively.

Bundroflumethiazide (Naturetin, average dosage 2.5 to 15 mg a day) comes in 2.5-mg green, 5-mg green, and 10-mg orange tablets, imprinted "Squibb 605," "Squibb 606," and "Squibb 618," respectively.

Polythiazide (Renese, average dosage 2 to 4 mg a day) comes in 1-mg white, 2-mg yellow, and 4-mg white tablets, all scored, imprinted "375," "376," and "377," respectively.

Disorders of the Heart and Circulatory System

Hydroflumethiazide (Saluron, average dosage 50 to 100 mg a day) comes in 50-mg white tablets imprinted Bristol.

Diuretics other than the thiazides are often used in combination with a second drug. These may be prescribed as single pills, with the drug proportions and combinations fixed, or as two separate pills, allowing for easier adjustment of the dosages. Three popular nonthiazide diuretics used to treat hypertension are:

Spironolactone (Aldactone, average dosage 50 to 100 mg a day) comes in 25- and 100-mg white scored tablets labeled "Searle 1001" and "Searle 1031," respectively. Spironolactone is used because individuals who take it do not lose potassium. Side effects include the retention of potassium, menstrual irregularity, and painful breast enlargement.

Triamterene (Dyrenium, average dosage 100 mg twice a day after meals) comes in 50- and 100-mg red capsules labeled "HO6" and "HO7," respectively. Since maximum effects occur from two to four hours after ingestion, take the last capsule in the late afternoon to ensure that you are not up all night urinating. Nausea, if it occurs, is prevented by taking Dyrenium after meals.

Furosemide (Lasix, average dosage 40 mg twice a day) comes in 20-, 40-, and 80-mg white tablets, oval, round, and round, respectively, imprinted "Hoechst." Possible side effects are the same as those for the thiazides.

(12-10) *Pills containing potassium* were once widely used with thiazide diuretics, but bowel irritation was frequent and often serious. As a result, most physicians no longer prescribe them. Slow-release tablets (Micro-K, Slow-K, Kaon-Cl, K-Tab, Klotrix, and others) are now widely prescribed, but on rare occasions will produce similar problems. Solutions containing potassium are safer but taste bad, although tomato-flavored Kato powder is better than most. All the solutions can be diluted with water or mixed with juices or milk.

Foods containing sizable amounts of potassium are probably the most pleasant way of ensuring proper potassium intake (3-28). Forty milliequivalents (mEq) per day added to a regular diet is usually recommended. Foods high in potassium include dried apricots (3 oz have 35 mEq), beef (3 oz have 9 mEq), prune or orange juice (8 oz have 14 mEq), milk (8 oz have 9 mEq), raisins (1 cup has 29 mEq), cantaloupe (1 melon has 46 mEq), dates (1 cup has 36 mEq), and bananas (one small banana has 10 mEq).

(12-11) *Nondiuretic antihypertensive drugs* work by decreasing the resistance to blood flow in blood vessels.

Methyldopa (Aldomet, average dosage 250 mg to 2 g a day) comes in 125-, 250-, and 500-mg round yellow tablets labeled "MSD135,"

After Middle Age

"MSD401," and "MSD516," respectively. Methyldopa lowers blood pressure by decreasing the nervous output from the brain to the sympathetic nervous system, which in turn controls heart rate—that is, how hard the heart pumps—and the resistance of blood vessels. Side effects are weakness when getting up from a sitting or lying position, psychological depression, and tiredness.

Reserpine, average dosage 0.1 to 0.25 mg a day, is made by a number of manufacturers and is called Serpasil, Rau-Sed, and Sandril, among others. Reserpine decreases the norepinephrine in the nerves, the chemical that causes the sympathetic nerves to make the blood vessels contract. Because reserpine causes the blood vessels to open, there is less resistance to blood passing through. Side effects include sleepiness and psychological depression. The sleepiness usually disappears after the first few days. The depression disappears too, but only with drug discontinuation, and it can be severe while it lasts. Therefore, reserpine should not be given to persons with a history of depression. Congestion of the nose and flushing of the face also occur with use of reserpine.

Guanethidine (Ismelin, average dosage 10 mg a day) comes in 10-mg pale yellow and 25-mg white tablets imprinted "CIBA." Guanethidine decreases the norepinephrine that the sympathetic nervous system uses to communicate messages to the blood vessels, and decreases the resistance of the vessels to the passage of blood. The most common side effect is weakness and fainting when a person stands up suddenly from a reclining position. Diarrhea and, in men, failure to ejaculate also occur. The antidepressant drugs decrease the function of guanethidine; thus, if you are taking an antidepressant and are given guanethidine, you should tell your physician.

Hydralazine (Apresoline, average dosage 50 mg four times a day) comes in 10-mg pale yellow, 25-mg deep blue, 50-mg light blue, and 100-mg peach tablets imprinted "CIBA." Principal side effects are headaches, feeling your heart beat in your chest, nausea, vomiting, loss of appetite, and diarrhea. These symptoms should be brought to the attention of your physician. Hydralazine may bring on or increase the frequency of angina attacks.

Clonidine (Catapres, average dosage 0.2 to 0.8 mg a day) comes in 0.1-mg tan and 0.2-mg orange tablets stamped "BI 6" and "BI 7," respectively. Clonidine is usually used together with a diuretic to lower blood pressure. Side effects include constipation and occasional failure to ejaculate. Drowsiness and depression may occur too. Since abrupt discontinuation can produce nausea, vomiting, and sharp increases in blood pressure, clonidine must be discontinued slowly. Clonidine works by

Disorders of the Heart and Circulatory System

stimulating small areas of the brain, and these brain areas in turn decrease blood pressure.

Metoprolol (Lopressor, average maintenance dosage 100 mg twice a day) comes in 50-mg light red and 100-mg light blue capsule-shaped tablets. Frequently used with a diuretic, metoprolol works in the body very much like propranolol (12-20), although its action is more clearly directed at the heart. The most common side effects are tiredness, dizziness, psychological depression, and diarrhea.

Nadolol (Corgard, average maintenance dose 80 to 320 mg a day in one dose) comes in 40-, 80-, 120-, and 160-mg blue-scored tablets marked "Squibb 207," "Squibb 241," "Squibb 208," and "Squibb 246," respectively. Nadolol works like metoprolol and propranolol with the advantage that it need only be taken once a day. Its most common side effects include tiredness, dizziness, psychological depression, and diarrhea.

Guanabenz (Wytensin, average maintenance dose 4 to 20 mg twice a day) comes in 4-mg white, round tablets labeled "Wyeth 73," and 8-mg white, round tablets labeled "Wyeth 74." Sedation, dry mouth, and dizziness are frequent side effects. Sexual dysfunction occurs occasionally. To avoid side effects of anxiety, racing heart rate, sweating, and a rebound increase in blood pressure, guanabenz should be discontinued slowly.

Pindolol (Visken, average maintenance dose 15 to 30 mg a day, given in two or three divided doses) comes in 5-mg white tablets labeled "Visken 5," and 10-mg white tablets labeled "Visken 10." The most common side effects are insomnia, dizziness, and fatigue. Nightmares, visual disturbances, swelling of the ankles, sexual dysfunction, and occasional severe lung problems can develop. Pindolol works in the body like propranolol.

Atenolol (Tenormin, average maintenance dose 50 to 100 mg in one dose a day) comes in 50-mg flat, round tablets labeled "Stuart" on one side and "105" on the other, and 10-mg flat, round tablets labeled "Stuart" on one side and "101" on the other. Fatigue and depression are the most common side effects. If possible, atenolol should be avoided by patients with asthma. Atenolol, like guanabenz, should be discontinued slowly.

Timolol (Blocadren, average maintenance dose 20 to 40 mg a day in two divided doses) comes in 20-mg light blue capsule-shaped tablets labeled "Blocadren." Timolol's side effects are similar to those of atenolol. It should be discontinued slowly.

(12-12) *Stress and hypertension.* Researchers have noted that persons (sometimes called type A) whose personalities are characterized by excessive drive, competitiveness, ambition, and impatience have a

After Middle Age

greater frequency of heart attacks. A churning sensation in the stomach and muscle tension in the arms and legs are familiar examples of how many people experience this kind of stress. Persons without these traits (type B) have no chronic sense of urgency and are thus somewhat protected from heart attacks. Ongoing studies are attempting to determine if minimizing some of these drives will lessen personal risk. Treatments of particular interest include behavior modification, biofeedback, relaxation, and transcendental meditation (TM). Until we know which (if any) of these is useful, individuals with type-A tendencies are advised to develop less aggressive habits to prolong their lives. Avoid social and business activities that repeatedly cause a sense of urgency. Leave enough time between appointments so that you are not pressured. If you find that speed reading is unpleasant and causes anxiety, begin to read for pleasure. Learn to laugh.

(12-13) *Diet and hypertension.* There is some controversy over whether diet precipitates hypertension and heart attacks. Because I believe it does (your physician may have other views on the subject), I recommend you consume only moderate amounts of cholesterol and salt in your diet. Your physician will test your blood from time to time to measure blood cholesterol and triglycerides. While the upper limit of normal cholesterol varies depending upon the laboratory making the determination (not all laboratories assay cholesterol in the same way) and upon the age of the individual, levels above 240 to 270 mg are usually considered elevated.

(12-14) *Triglycerides, cholesterol, and heart disease.* Chemically, triglycerides are three molecules of fatty acid attached to one molecule of glycerol. They are the major component of the fat we eat as well as the major form in which our bodies store energy. Cholesterol (3-30) to (3-32) is also a fat, and we need it to form hormones and other substances. But we do not need it in the diet, for we can make all we need from simple fats such as triglycerides.

Both cholesterol and triglycerides play important roles in the development of heart disease. They produce deposits in the arteries called plaque. Plaque grows slowly, eventually narrowing the arteries and preventing the blood from passing through properly. This means that the heart must work harder to pump blood through the narrowed passage—and blood pressure is raised. It is therefore important that a person keep the intake of both cholesterol and fats low. Although there is disagreement, most physicians will not treat a patient unless the triglycerides are above 500 mg/dL.

(12-15) *Avoiding cholesterol.* Foods that are high and low in cholesterol are listed in (3-30). When dietary measures are not successful in lowering very high cholesterol levels, the drug dextrothyroxine (Choloxin) is sometimes prescribed. Persons taking dextrothyroxine may experience the side effect of an increase in angina attacks. These should be brought to the attention of the physician immediately.

(12-16) *The hyperlipidemias* (fatty blood conditions) are hereditary (genetic) conditions in which high concentrations of fats are found in the blood. They are thought to predispose to hypertension and subsequently to heart attacks. Five types (types I–V) of hyperlipidemias are known. Because they are hereditary, they tend to run in families. Therefore, if a family member has had a heart attack at an early age, your blood should be examined for this condition.

Type I. The person in this condition cannot metabolize dietary blood fats in a normal manner. There are frequent abdominal complaints. Greatly reducing intake of fats and alcohol under medical supervision lowers the blood fat levels and controls the symptoms.

Type II. The cholesterol concentration is high, as is the incidence of coronary artery disease. Cholesterol comes from the diet but is also produced in the body. People who have inherited genes that mass-produce cholesterol may end up with high blood cholesterol levels even though they maintain very low cholesterol intake and carefully monitor dietary fats. The medicine cholestyramine has been decreasing coronary artery disease in type II patients.

Type III. This is rare and consists of elevations of both cholesterol and triglycerides. Treatment consists of reducing intake of both and sometimes treatment with the drug clofibrate (Atromid-S). Clofibrate has little effect on cholesterol, but can greatly decrease triglycerides.

Type IV. In this condition, all that is eaten turns into triglycerides. Sufferers tend to be obese and to like sweets and alcohol. Dieting is helpful when it is adhered to. The drug clofibrate (Atromid-S) is useful.

Type V. This is a combination of type I with a generalized increase in blood fat (chylomicrons) and elevated triglycerides. It is rare. Weight reduction is the best treatment.

(12-17) *Salt intake.* At times in the past, physicians recommended that hypertensive patients eliminate all but very small quantities of salt from their diet. Nowadays, rather than placing people on diets that make food unpalatable, physicians prescribe diuretics to reduce the body's salt content. Nevertheless, most physicians agree that moderation in salt intake (to about 5 g a day) is desirable. This restriction usually means using normal amounts of salt in cooking but little or none at the table. For added flavor, you might try using lemon juice. Some medicines, such as sodium salicylate, are very high in salt and should be avoided. Read the packaging label on medicines and foods, looking for the word sodium.

After Middle Age

(12-18) *Some unusual but treatable causes of hypertension* include:

Pheochromocytoma (tumor of the adrenal gland). Among the rarer causes of hypertension is one produced by a tumor of the adrenal gland called pheochromocytoma. The increased blood pressure is usually intermittent and accompanied by a pounding headache, nausea, and perspiration. Tests for this tumor include testing the patient's urine for the tumor's hormone, epinephrine (adrenalin). The tumor, which is usually benign, can be removed by surgery.

Aldosteronism. This rare condition is also caused by a benign tumor of the adrenal gland that produces an excess of the hormone aldosterone, which in turn causes salt retention. There is a moderate increase in blood pressure, muscle weakness, headache, numbness, prickly sensations, excessive urine excretion, and thirst. This tumor can be removed surgically.

Kidney artery hypertension. A narrowing of the artery of the kidney can produce hypertension. It is diagnosed by x-ray techniques and can be corrected by surgery.

ANGINA (ANGINA PECTORIS)

(12-19) *What is angina?* When the coronary arteries—those vessels that supply the heart with blood—are narrowed by atherosclerosis (12-40) or plaque (12-14), the heart muscle does not receive enough blood to furnish needed oxygen during stress. The typical pain that then occurs is known as angina pectoris. Usually described as a heavy or strangling sensation, angina is sometimes more of a discomfort than a pain. It is located mainly beneath the breast bone, but it may extend to the left side of the chest, the left arm, or the lower jaw. In fact, on rare occasions, the pain may extend to almost any part of the body. It usually lasts two to three minutes but can go on up to fifteen minutes. If the pain lasts longer than fifteen minutes, call your physician immediately. The pain frequently occurs during exercise, especially in cold weather, after a meal, or during emotional stress; but in some people it can occur even during sleep. For most persons angina is relieved by quiet rest.

It is important to distinguish angina from other pains occurring in the same area of the body. For instance, some intestinal symptoms are similar to angina, such as the pain of a duodenal ulcer, which can be relieved by antacids. Some people experience pains on the left side of the chest because of "cardiac neurosis"—anxiety about heart disease. These pains usually last only a brief time and are not associated with exercise. They have no medical significance.

Although often painful, angina is not in itself a dangerous condition.

Disorders of the Heart and Circulatory System

But it should be taken as a warning of an increased chance of heart attack. If the angina is not severe, a person can lead a normal life—but under medical surpervision.

(12-20) *Treatment of angina.* The general treatment of angina involves losing weight, eating lighter meals, and avoiding situations that provoke the pain, such as exposure to cold and smoking. Specific treatments include drugs and surgery.

Nitroglycerin dilates the arteries of the heart and slightly lowers the blood pressure. It is given both to relieve pain and to prevent expected pain. In the latter case, it is taken two to three minutes before undertaking exercise or undergoing psychological stress that is known to provoke angina. It is placed under the tongue or is inhaled. Under the tongue, it dissolves in thirty seconds and gives relief in two to three minutes. Extra medicine should be carried at all times. Even when kept in the bottle, nitroglycerin decomposes easily and should be replaced every two to three months. When it loses its burning taste, it has lost its effectiveness. Nitroglycerin, sold under the brand name of Nitrostat, may keep its strength for up to one year when kept in its original bottle, which must be tightly closed after each use.

A number of systems for delivering nitroglycerin through the skin have recently become available (Nitrodisc, Nitro-Dur, Transderm-Nitro). These systems, which look like bandages, have the drug bound to their inner surface. The bandages are applied to relatively hairless parts of the body, but not hands or feet, areas of skin disease, or where there are folds of skin. Nitroglycerin is released over 24 hours and prevents angina attacks from occurring. It takes some experimentation to get the dosage (dependent on site of the bandage and its strength) correct. The most common side effect is headache. The bandages may be irritating to the skin.

Propranolol (Inderal) has a more long-lasting effect than nitroglycerin. It is used to reduce the frequency and severity of angina. But if it doesn't decrease pain or increase exercise tolerance, its use should be ended (withdrawal should be gradual). Propranolol slows the pulse rate and makes the heart less responsive to epinephrine (adrenalin) and thus to the stimulation of excitement. It is also used in the treatment of hypertension. The average dosage is 160 to 240 mg a day in multiple doses. It comes in 10-mg orange, 20-mg blue, 40-mg green, 60-mg pink, and 80-mg yellow tablets labeled with "INDERAL" and the dose. Occasional side effects of propranolol include confusion, forgetting, and severe nightmares.

The following three drugs have recently been introduced for angina. They work by blocking the entry of calcium into heart muscle cells.

Diltiazem (Cardizem, average dose 120 to 240 mg a day given in three or

After Middle Age

four divided doses) comes in 30-mg green tablets labeled "Marion" on one side and "1771" on the other, and 60-mg yellow tablets labeled "Marion" on one side and "1772" on the other side. Adverse effects, which are infrequent, include slowing of the heart rate, dizziness from lowered blood pressure, nausea, headache, and swelling of the feet.

Nifedipine (Procardia, average maintenance dose 10 to 20 mg three times a day) comes in 10-mg orange soft gelatin capsules. In some patients angina increases when nifedipine is first started or when the dosage is increased. It can produce many different side effects including nausea, headache, muscle cramps, and swelling of the ankles, which usually disappear with a reduction in dose.

Verapamil (average maintenance dosage 80 mg three or four times a day) comes as Isoptin in 80-mg yellow and 120-mg white round tablets labeled "Isoptin 80" and "Isoptin 120," respectively. As Calan it comes in 80 mg round, yellow sugar-coated tablets labeled "Calan 80." Common side effects include dizziness, headache, fatigue, swelling of the ankles, nausea, and constipation.

When ordinary medication is not available and you are having severe angina or must prevent it, one ounce of whiskey may help. Obviously, the whiskey treatment should not be used often.

(12-21) *Coronary bypass surgery* is just a few years old, but such operations are now being performed in very large numbers—in particular, when drug therapy has been unsuccessful. When a block in one or more of the coronary arteries makes the passage of blood difficult or impossible, a surgeon can create a detour around the block using a vein taken from the leg. To determine exactly where the blockage is, a cardiologist or a radiologist (x-ray specialist) performs coronary arteriography. In this procedure, the coronary arteries are injected with a radio-opaque dye, which prevents the passage of x-rays, and serial x-ray pictures are taken. If it is decided to proceed with surgery under general anesthesia, the saphenous vein is removed from the leg, the chest is opened, and the vein is grafted around the block in the artery. While some studies indicate very promising results, it is not yet known whether the operation changes the eventual outcome of the disease. But the pain of angina disappears, at least temporarily. Generally, the quality of life greatly improves. As other vessels plug up within three to five years, the angina may reappear, requiring further surgery.

Many people become anxious about various procedures involved in examining the heart. In fact, more patients develop new heart problems in the twenty-four hours before a procedure than in the twenty-four hours after it. I hope the following brief descriptions will take the mystery and the fear out of these procedures which are generally quite safe.

Disorders of the Heart and Circulatory System

(12-22) *Catheterization* of the heart to perform coronary arteriography (also called coronary angiography) is very useful for evaluating the state of these important vessels if surgery is contemplated. A small area on the arm is anesthetized with xylocaine and a tube (catheter) is introduced into an artery and threaded into or near the heart. Measurements of pressure and flow can be made and blood can be withdrawn; or dyes can be injected and monitored by x-ray. In the hands of a well-trained cardiologist or radiologist catheterization is a relatively safe procedure. There is less than one death per thousand, and this number includes very ill patients examined in emergencies.

(12-23) *Thallium scan.* Because there is a very slight risk involved in coronary arteriography, some patients with abnormal EKGs will have a thallium scan to evaluate heart muscle blood flow. While not as informative as arteriography, it is still valuable. After radioactive thallium is injected into an arm vein, the area over the heart is scanned by a radioactivity detector, which then produces a picture of the areas of the heart that the thallium circulates through. Areas where there is poor circulation—cold spots—do not show up on the scan.

(12-24) *Echocardiography* is a relatively new procedure that uses sonar-like techniques to examine the heart in a manner that otherwise would require catheterization or the use of isotopes. It is safe and produces no discomfort, but is very difficult to use and in some patients cannot give the desired information.

(12-25) *The exercise test* is an important way to determine how well your heart is functioning. When you exercise, your heart needs more oxygen. If enough oxygen is not available because the coronary arteries are narrowed, the electrical activity of the heart changes. The change in electrical activity shows up on the EKG. There are many different exercise tests (bicycling, treadmill, walking up and down a step), but basically a person is first wired to an EKG machine and asked to exercise in a standardized manner. Readings from the EKG machine are examined periodically during the exercise. A physician is present throughout the procedure, monitoring the EKG machine as well as noting any symptoms that might develop. Symptoms that might require stopping the test include fatigue, moderate to severe chest pain, low blood pressure, pain in the legs, dizziness, severe shortness of breath, or serious arrhythmias (12-33) on the EKG.

HEART ATTACK

(12-26) The heart is a hollow muscle that contracts sixty to one hundred times per minute, every minute of our lives, pumping blood from the

After Middle Age

veins to the lungs to the heart to the arteries to the body tissues. Like all tissues of the body, the heart requires nourishment, principally oxygen. Oxygen gets to the heart, to a small degree, from the blood inside the heart. This oxygen, however, does not get deep into the muscle wall. For this, the heart has arteries of its own, called coronary arteries.

A heart attack, or myocardial infarction, occurs when that amount of oxygen supplied to an area of heart muscle is so small that the muscle dies. The death of heart tissue produces the pain of heart attack, but more important for survival is the size and location (12-33) of the affected area. If it is small and relatively unimportant, an individual can survive a number of heart attacks—and may even have one without knowing it.

(12-27) *Symptoms of a heart attack.* The principal symptom of a heart attack is pain. It is felt in the center of the chest beneath the breast bone (sternum) and lasts a half hour or more. The pain is frequently felt as a tightening band, as if someone were squeezing or crushing the heart. In some cases the pain extends to the sides of the chest, shoulders, or arms, less commonly to the abdomen, back, jaw, or neck. Shortness of breath and feelings of weakness, nausea, and dizziness may accompany the pain. Vomiting may occur. Unlike angina pectoris (12-19), heart attacks are not brought on by exercise or relieved by rest. The pain does not alter with motion or change of position. Sometimes, especially in an elderly person, the attack is relatively painless. The main complaint may be only the sudden onset of breathlessness or loss of consciousness. Yet there is anxiety, a feeling of imminent death, restlessness, pallor, sweating, and coldness to the touch. Any pain usually begins to subside after twenty-four hours.

The heart is made up of several units. Under normal circumstances, the units work in unison—they beat together with a normal rhythm. A myocardial infarction can cause the system to stop its normal rhythm. An irregular beat (arrhythmia) is the major immediate threat to life following a myocardial infarct (12-33).

It is very important that a heart attack victim receive medical attention quickly. Since you may find yourself in a situation where you must act almost without thinking, it is important that you know what to do ahead of time. For this reason, I urge everyone to take a cardiac pulmonary resuscitation (CPR) course and to update it every two to three years. These courses teach the method and, more important, present a person with the opportunity to practice. The courses are given by rescue squads, fire departments, hospitals, and the American Red Cross. In the next section some of the important emergency procedures are summarized for easy reference.

CPR instructors will tell you to do some things slightly differently from

Disorders of the Heart and Circulatory System

what is presented here; follow the instructor. I believe my method is better only for persons with no experience. The material that follows is to be used in an emergency by people who have not yet taken a CPR course or when help is not immediately available.

(12-28) *If you are or think you are having a heart attack:*
1. Call your physician immediately—do not take nitroglycerin, coffee, or other stimulants.
2. If you cannot reach your physician, you must get to an emergency room.
   a. Do not go by public transportation. Do not drive or have a friend drive you unless no means of emergency travel is immediately available.
   b. Call an emergency vehicle. The phone number of one or more of the following should be listed:
      (1) Ambulance service
      (2) Local rescue squad
      (3) Fire department
      (4) Police department
3. While waiting for help, do not exert yourself—give your heart as much rest as possible. Sit down, loosen your tie and belt. If you are by yourself, open the door so that emergency personnel can get in.

(12-29) *If you are with someone who is or whom you think is having a heart attack,* follow 1, 2, and 3 above. In addition:

4. Keep the person calm. (Don't be anxious yourself.)
5. If the person stops breathing—that is, if there is little or no movement of the chest and abdomen, and you are unable to detect air moving through the mouth or nose—do the following:
   a. Open the airway. Make sure that the connection from the mouth to the lungs is unobstructed.
      (1) With the patient lying on his or her back, tilt head backward.
      (2) Place one hand under the back of the neck and lift, while placing light pressure on the forehead with the other. This lifts the tongue away from the throat, and sometimes breathing will begin again automatically.
   b. If breathing does not begin at once, you must breathe for the patient, using mouth-to-mouth ventilation.
      (1) Tilt the head by placing one hand behind the neck and lifting.
      (2) With the other hand, press your palm lightly on the forehead to open the airway, and pinch the nostrils shut with your fingers.
      (3) Take a deep breath and, with your mouth wide open, fit your mouth over the patient's, making a tight seal.

After Middle Age

   (4) Blow into the patient's mouth, watching the chest move up. The amount of pressure to be used should be enough to make a loud sigh but not enough to blow up a balloon. (Remember, balloons require a good deal of pressure.)
   (5) Remove your mouth. Allow the patient to exhale.
   (6) Repeat every five seconds.
   (7) If the patient vomits, clean out the mouth with your finger. Keep ventilating the patient.
6. How to determine if the heart has stopped:
   a. The breathing stops.
   b. The patient becomes pale, falls to the floor, and is unresponsive.
   c. There is no pulse. To test for the pulse, place four fingers to one side of the Adam's apple and press lightly. Try it on yourself. Do not press both sides at the same time—this will cut the supply of blood to the head.
7. If there is no heartbeat, you must both provide the heartbeat as well as breathe for the patient.
   a. Begin steps 5 and 6. If the patient will not breathe, give him or her two quick breaths.
   b. Quickly remove all clothing and jewelry around the chest.
   c. Perform the precordial thump as follows: With the fleshy bottom of your closed fists, deliver a firm blow to the middle of the sternum—from eight inches away if you are strong, from twelve inches away if you are relatively weak. This will sometimes restart the heart. Feel for the pulse again for a full ten seconds. Count out the time by saying: one thousand, two thousand, three thousand, up to ten thousand.
   d. If the heart does not restart, that is, if there is no pulse, you must repeat the procedure.

(12-30) *How to perform closed heart massage:*

1. The patient must be lying flat on his or her back on a firm surface—the floor or the bed board (not a mattress).

2. Place the heel of your hand over the lower half of the sternum.

3. Place your other hand on top of the first.

4. Get on your knees and place your shoulders over the patient's body.

5. With your arm stiff, press your hand into the patient's chest one and one-half inches vertically downward. Release. Do eighty of these compressions a minute. The motion is a rocking one rather than jablike.

6. After every fifteen compressions, breathe twice for the patient as described in (12-29), step 5b. Return to heart massage.

Disorders of the Heart and Circulatory System

7. If there are two people present, one breathes (every five seconds) while the other pumps, switching when the pumper begins to tire.

Resuscitation is tiring, and even two well-trained people can only maintain it for twenty to thirty minutes. One person can keep it up for only about five minutes.

(12-31) *Treatment at the hospital.* Once a physician or other emergency personnel have arrived, the patient is transported to a hospital, preferably one that has a special coronary care unit (12-32). Treatment includes a pain-relieving drug such as morphine or one of its derivatives and a sedative to help the patient sleep. Many people begin an uneventful recovery on this treatment and are kept in bed on a light diet for the first few weeks. After the first week moderate exercise is allowed for a short time each day. This reduces the risk of blood clotting in the legs. An anticoagulant drug (heparin) also stops blood clots from forming. (Some physicians believe it may prevent a second heart attack.) Oxygen is given in high concentrations to lessen the heart's work.

(12-32) *The coronary care unit (CCU)* provides constant cardiac monitoring by a staff of well-trained nurses who are capable of responding instantly in an emergency. You will not be as comfortable in the CCU as you are in other parts of the hospital because of the continuous monitoring through wires attached to elaborate EKG machines, the intravenous drips, the use of oxygen, and a prohibition of all but a few visitors. The machinery is made fail-safe, but ask the physicians and nurses enough questions to satisfy your concerns—there is a tendency to fear becoming dependent on all that machinery. You will of course be disconnected from the machines when your heart is stabilized and your physician feels it is safe to move you to a conventional room.

It is during the first two days following a heart attack that most complications occur. They include arrhythmias (12-33), heart failure (12-42), and shock (12-47).

(12-33) *What is arrhythmia?* The normal heart beats with great regularity as it pushes blood throughout the body. Internal adjustments compensate for activity and rest, but otherwise there is little alteration in the heart's rhythm. An arrhythmia (or dysrhythmia) occurs when the heart no longer beats regularly. Normally, a group of cells sets the pace for the rest of the heart. These cells may be injured during a heart attack, when it is likely that the heart will stop pumping blood. Arrhythmias may also occur in the absence of a heart attack. These often can be prevented by abstaining from tobacco and caffeine. Colas, coffee, tea, and certain drugs (usually nonprescription) containing caffeine (3-36) should be avoided.

(12-34) *Cardioversion* is used to restore the normal heartbeat in per-

After Middle Age

sons with certain kinds of arrhythmia. (A slight variant of cardioversion, defibrillation, is used when the heart stops altogether.) In this technique, a special electrical current is placed across the chest when a part of the heart that should not be leading becomes the pacemaker. The effect is to return the normal pacemaker as regulator of the heartbeat. As a rule, cardioversion is an elective procedure, done in a hospital. The drug quinidine is given orally every six hours for a day or two prior to cardioversion; this prevents subsequent reversions to the arrhythmia. An anticoagulant is sometimes given for several weeks before cardioversion to prevent the possibility of embolism. Usually, the patient receives a sedative and a tranquilizer just prior to the procedure. There is no feeling of pain or memory of the procedure.

(12-35) *Cardiac pacemakers* are electronic devices that regulate the timing of the heart contraction when the natural pacemaker is not functioning properly. There have been about 200,000 implants done in the United States alone, usually in people over 70. Pacemakers are usually set at seventy beats per minute and temporarily stop their pacing activity when the heart beats faster. Pacemakers start up again when the heart slows or when there is no spontaneous beat. When a pacemaker is necessary, a surgeon places the device just under the clavicle (the collar bone) in the chest wall with thin wires running through a vein to the heart. The operation usually can be done under a local anesthesia with very little discomfort. Electrical current stimulates the heart muscle through the wires.

At one time pacemakers were affected by radar, microwave ovens, and metal detectors (like those used at airports), but these risks have been minimized by new designs. Today's lithium batteries last seven to nine years, although longer-lasting atomic batteries are available. (A lithium battery costs about a third of the cost of an atomic battery.) Thus, periodic follow-up by a physician is mandatory. The battery is designed to fail slowly so that it can be replaced before there is any danger. You can tell when the battery is failing because the pulse rate slows. If the resting pulse is set for seventy, and it declines to about sixty-two, it is usually time for the pacemaker to be changed. Fainting or an irregular or slowed pulse is a sign that the pacemaker may not be working properly.

(12-36) *Measured increases in physical activity* after a myocardial infarction has two goals. The first is to lessen the consequences of being bedridden for a prolonged period. In the coronary care unit and subsequently, patients are asked to do as many things for themselves as possible. These include sitting on the side of the bed, sitting quietly in a chair, and using a bedside commode rather than a bedpan. Patients released from the coronary care unit are encouraged to sit in a chair for longer

Disorders of the Heart and Circulatory System

periods of time and to do rhythmic exercises, such as repeatedly flexing one foot at a time while sitting. (Isometric exercises making one muscle work against another are to be avoided, since they tax the heart.) Finally, the patient walks around the room and down the corridor and, before going home, down a flight of stairs, then up. It is important while still in the hospital to alleviate the natural fear that exercise will bring on angina or another myocardial infarction.

(12-37) *After the hospital—at home.* For a generation, patients were kept on complete bed rest for at least six weeks after a myocardial infarction. Today, there is strong tendency among physicians to discharge their patients from the hospital as soon as possible. It is thought that quick mobilization is healthier than lying in bed, but this usually depends on the ability of those at home to help. If the infarction is not followed by a complication (12-42) to (12-45), and there is someone at home who can be of help, most patients leave the hospital within two to three weeks.

The general requirements for early home care are a cooperative patient with no medical complications, the presence of a responsible family member, the capability of getting to and from doctor's appointments, and the availability of an ambulance for emergencies.

Some patients fear that they will not be able to return to a normal life and will remain invalids, but after three- to four-months' recuperation, most can go back to a normal, if somewhat slower, pace.

At home, light housework and stair climbing (unless the physician advises against it) should begin immediately. The distance walked should be increased gradually. If any symptoms develop, bring them to the attention of the physician. A patient who can walk a mile in twenty minutes is usually able to return to work if the job does not require much physical labor.

(12-38) *Psychological depression after a heart attack,* particularly while at home, is almost universal. There is a realization that life may be shorter, and that it is certainly limited. There is physical weakness (after all, the patient has been in bed for some time) and many patients feel they have not been told the whole truth about the shape they are in. Fortunately, the post-heart attack depression usually dissipates within a few weeks.

(12-39) *Sexual activity after a heart attack.* Sexual intercourse places a moderate amount of stress on the heart: the heart rate increases from 82 to 118 beats per minute. This is no greater stress, however, than climbing up a flight of stairs. It is frequently advisable to return to sex slowly, at about the same rate one returns to work. At first, one might engage only in brief foreplay, then do so for progressively longer periods of time, perhaps employing masturbation, and then engage in intercourse. To prevent an-

After Middle Age

gina, the physician may prescribe a nitroglycerin tablet (12-20) prior to intercourse.

(12-40) *Prevention of heart disease.* An important contributing cause of most heart attacks is a narrowing (atherosclerosis) of the coronary arteries. The prevention of heart attacks, therefore, lies in the prevention of atherosclerosis. Unfortunately, atherosclerosis begins at an early age, and once damage is done it cannot be reversed; however, it can be halted. There are many factors (known as risk factors) in development of atherosclerosis, but no single factor predisposes someone to heart disease. As for hypertension, lowering the consumption of animal fats (cholesterol) and salt, giving up smoking and heavy drinking, and maintaining normal weight significantly lower one's chances of developing coronary artery disease. Unfortunately, even with all these precautions no one is immune.

(12-41) *Can aspirin prevent myocardial infarction?* A number of physicians believe that aspirin taken on a daily basis decreases the coagulation of blood and slightly decreases the incidence of death in individuals prone to myocardial infarctions. Data from studies, however, are far from conclusive: There is far better evidence that aspirin prevents repeated strokes in individuals who have already had strokes. Since the use of aspirin carries with it a small but real risk (7-11)—production of peptic ulcers and bleeding—the decision to take aspirin daily should be left up to the physician.

HEART FAILURE

(12-42) When the heart cannot adequately circulate blood, it is said to be failing. The heart fails because it has an overloaded circulation, because the heart muscle is damaged, or because some disease interferes with the filling of the chambers. Acute heart failure is usually brought on by a heart attack; chronic heart failure usually develops over a long period. At first, the heart compensates by enlarging, but eventually symptoms appear. Either side of the heart can fail first, but if one side fails, and it cannot be corrected, the other eventually follows. The most common cause of right heart failure is left heart failure (also known as congestive cardiac failure), but it may be caused by disease of the heart valves, congenital heart disease, hyperthyroidism (excess activity of the thyroid gland), and severe lung diseases.

(12-43) *The symptoms of right heart failure* are produced by backpressure on the venous system, causing dilation of the veins. The liver may become enlarged and cause pain in the upper right side of the abdomen. If the liver is damaged, there will be slight jaundice (yellowing of the

Disorders of the Heart and Circulatory System

skin). Extra fluid collects in the tissues (edema), causing swelling of the ankles after prolonged standing. When pressure is put on an edematous area it leaves an imprint that takes some time to disappear (pitting edema). Cyanotic (blue) lips, tiredness, and weakness are also common symptoms due to the lowered output of blood by the heart.

(12-44) *The causes of left heart failure* are hypertension, disease of the coronary arteries, and disease of the heart valves. At first, the left ventricle becomes enlarged to compensate for the decreased output of the heart, but eventually it cannot keep the output high enough, and again back-pressure results. In this case, the edema occurs in the lungs (pulmonary edema), and exchange of oxygen between the air and the blood becomes difficult.

(12-45) *Symptoms of left heart failure* can develop gradually or suddenly. If there is a gradual onset, the first complaint is breathlessness (dyspnea) during exercise and the need to sleep propped up on pillows because of restlessness (orthopnea). Later, sleep is interrupted by bouts of coughing, and eventually there is breathlessness at night, known as paroxysmal nocturnal dyspnea, or cardiac asthma, because it resembles an asthmatic attack. When left heart failure begins abruptly, it is usually caused by a heart attack and presents itself as cardiac asthma in an individual with no previous history of breathlessness. A person will awaken after one or two hours of sleep, fighting for breath. After sitting up, the individual will soon cough up large amounts of pink, frothy sputum. The attack passes within an hour. A physician should be called the first time this happens.

(12-46) *Acute heart failure* is treated by sitting upright with the legs hanging over the side of the bed to help the fluid drain away from the lungs. A physician may administer morphine to decrease anxiety, if necessary. The blood volume is lowered by giving a strong diuretic (12-9). In the rare situation where no diuretic is available, blood can be removed from a vein or tourniquets can be put around the limbs to slow the return of blood to the heart. Oxygen is also given, and a course of digitalis, a heart stimulant, is begun. After these emergency measures, the patient will be treated for chronic heart failure. This generally includes rest, drugs such as digitalis, diuretics, and sedatives, and a low-salt diet (3-27) during the early part of the treatment. Resting in an upright position, either in bed or in an armchair, will allow the fluid to drain from the lungs and reduce the work of the heart. At night, patients should have as many pillows as necessary to keep their head raised and to make them comfortable. Bed rest should be continued for about three weeks, when activity should gradually be resumed.

Digitalis, which is a natural extract from the foxglove plant, is the main

After Middle Age

drug used for heart failure. By making the heart work more efficiently, it raises the output, reduces the back-pressure, and thus reduces the edema. Elderly people are very sensitive to digitalis, and the toxic dose is close to the therapeutic dose, so overdosage is common. Signs of mild overdosage are very slow pulse, loss of appetite, nausea, vomiting, diarrhea, and headache. If the overdose is severe, there will be blurred vision, disorientation, a fast pulse, and disturbance of the heart rhythm. Other late signs are yellow or green vision, and white halos or "snow" appearing around objects. When these symptoms occur, a physician should be consulted. The doctor will usually stop the digitalis for a few days and may prescribe potassium salts (12-10) to reverse the effects of digitalis. Diuretics (12-9), drugs which cause water loss, are used with digitalis. Usually, the drug is a thiazide, though it may be a stronger diuretic such as furosemide (Lasix), which gives a faster diuresis.

There are a number of digitalis-derived drugs. Digitalis itself comes in 60- and 100-mg tablets, capsules, and pills; the average dosage is 100 mg a day.

Digitoxin comes in 0.05-, 0.1-, 0.15-, and 0.2-mg tablets; the average dosage is 0.1 to 0.2 mg a day.

Digoxin (Lanoxin) comes in 0.125-, 0.25-, and 0.5-mg tablets; the dosage is calculated by a formula.

Lanatoxide-C (Cedilanid) comes in 0.5-mg tablets; the average dosage is 1 to 1.5 mg a day.

Gitalin (Gitaligin) comes in 0.5-mg tablets; the average dosage is 0.5 mg a day. Acetyldigitoxin (Acylanid) comes in 0.1- and 0.2-mg tablets; the average dosage is 0.1 to 0.2 mg a day.

(12-47) *What is shock?* Shock is the loss of blood flow to such a degree that the body does not get enough oxygen to live. It can come from trauma, surgery, infection, hemorrhage, or heart attack. The shock associated with a heart attack, or myocardial infarction, can take one of two general forms. The heart rate and blood pressure can be relatively normal, but the patient suffers from sweating, nausea, shortness of breath, weakness, and some chest pain. Then, suddenly, the patient may collapse due to arrhythmia. Another form of shock is associated with irregular heart beat and low blood pressure. The patient is pale, cold, short of breath, and has severe chest pain. The treatment for shock that originates from a myocardial infarction is the same as the treatment for the infarction.

CEREBRAL VASCULAR ACCIDENT (CVA, HEMORRHAGE, OR STROKE)

(12-48) The symptoms of a stroke are the sudden loss of function of a part of the body, such as an arm or a leg, or the loss of the ability to speak.

Disorders of the Heart and Circulatory System

The first symptom may be that an arm or a leg begins to feel funny. When you suspect you are having a stroke, call your physician immediately. If you cannot reach your physician, go to the emergency room of the nearest hospital.

A stroke is produced by a disease of an artery within the brain. Specifically, there is either a hemorrhage (blood leak) into the brain or a cerebral thrombosis (block) of the artery. The hemorrhage destroys brain tissue, while the thrombosis prevents oxygen from getting to the brain. A stroke can also occur by cerebral embolism (a clot traveling from another part of the body).

Since each part of the brain serves a different function, the consequences of a stroke depend on which area of the brain has been damaged and to what extent. For many functions, the right side of the brain controls the left side of the body, and vice versa. Most important, the left side of the brain usually controls speech. The most common symptom of a stroke is hemiparesis (weakness of one side of the body), which begins suddenly with or without loss of consciousness. On the affected side, the face droops, the eye closes, and the arm hangs loosely. The affected leg looks normal until movement is attempted; then it looks heavy, as if it were hard to lift. A stroke may also involve areas of the brain controlling sight, in which case peripheral vision (side vision) may be lost. Or it may affect the area of the brain controlling speech and the understanding of language. A person may suffer dysphasia—being able to hear but not to say words—which may be present in varying degrees, from forgetting a few words to being unable to understand or be understood.

A stroke rarely has a severe effect on intellectual functions. If it does, the deterioration usually lasts only a short time. Most sustained difficulties involving poor judgment, memory, reasoning, and knowledge of time, place, or people really result from an inability to communicate. Intelligence does not usually decrease, and mental retardation does not take place. But for reasons unknown, a person may feel tired for many months and sometimes years after a stroke, even after regaining other abilities.

Personality changes may occur after a stroke, but fortunately they usually do not last. There may be depression, crying or laughing for no reason, and quick swings from one mood to another. Often intermittent crying occurs for a period of several weeks. A person who is normally quiet or even passive may become aggressive or violent.

There may be jerking movements (ataxia) following recovery from a stroke. These are caused by damage to areas of the brain (cerebellum or its connections) that act to smooth out rough movements. Some people cannot use their hands or legs because there is a mix-up in the signal from

After Middle Age

the brain to the limb. This is called apraxia, and it usually improves with time. At times, even people with good sight and sensations may not know their limb is there, seeming to forget about it.

As part of recovery, there is a gradual change from flaccidity (limpness) to spasticity (continuous muscle contraction). With spasticity there is resistance to stretching of the muscles and a hunched appearance because it is difficult to straighten the body to its full length.

(12-49) *Small strokes or transient ischemic attacks (TIAs)* are strokes in which the effects last a short time or are hardly noticeable—loss of vision in one eye lasting fifteen minutes followed by complete recovery, inability to speak for a short time, dropping a cup of coffee because the hand suddenly becomes weak, or becoming dizzy for a few minutes. Some TIAs occur when turning the head to one side. There also may be faintness accompanied by nausea or vomiting. These attacks are caused by the pinching or twisting of an already narrowed artery producing temporary loss of blood flow to the brain, or by very small emboli. If symptoms such as these occur, a physician should be consulted immediately because a small percentage of people who experience TIAs will go on to have major strokes.

(12-50) *Treatment of stroke.* Immediate treatment is directed at preventing another stroke, since little can be done right away to reverse the stroke's effects. Blood pressure is monitored and controlled. Sometimes a surgeon removes a narrowed part of a large artery in the chest or neck and replaces it with a graft. The graft can be either a piece of synthetic material or a piece of a person's own vein (usually from the leg).

Total recovery after a stroke is common. Time and a supportive treatment program help many functions return as the area of the brain around the damaged part returns to normal. Some patients recover well, learning to walk and use their hands so they can take care of themselves, but others remain bedridden. A symptom that is extremely disturbing is loss of bowel and bladder control (incontinence). Fortunately, this usually corrects itself.

Successful rehabilitation requires the understanding of simple directions. Walking is the usual goal. Patients who can stand on the uninvolved, or well, leg have the potential to walk. This position causes rigidity (spasticity) in the involved, or stroke-affected, leg at the hip, knee, and foot, which is useful for swinging the leg while walking. Obviously, the uninvolved leg must be strengthened by special exercises since it now has to do the work of two legs. Standing up and sitting down from a progressively higher seat is useful. After several weeks, exercises involving both legs can begin. Going up several steps and then going down (backwards),

Disorders of the Heart and Circulatory System

at first with a brace on the involved leg and then with a cane, works well.

The paralyzed arm should also be exercised, but it must be protected from trauma because the stroke victim doesn't have the ability to get it out of the way when being rolled or moved. The arm can be protected by a sling.

Aphasia is the inability or partial inability to speak. Some patients who have had a stroke simply cannot say what they want. This is called expressive aphasia. Others cannot understand words. This is called receptive aphasia. Depending upon the degree of involvement, however, patients with expressive aphasia may be able to say either yes or no. They may substitute one word for another; or they may repeat words over and over (perseveration), or speak in what sounds like double-talk. A person may talk around a word or subject (circumlocution). Some very fixed automatic idioms may be used such as "I am fine," "Hello," "How are you?" An individual may swear. He or she may be able to sing or count. Those who cannot talk may be able to use hand or eye signals. Books with many pictures help if the patient can point to things. Some of the best books for this purpose are the ones with hundreds of pictures with which young children learn to identify objects. Obviously, if a person can read, write, or draw pictures this is enormously helpful, and a pad and pencil should be attached to the bed rail. Some patients cannot ask for information and should be told what they probably want to know. Remember, many patients will be frightened by what has happened and may not understand it without explanation. A careful explanation from the physician and family is important.

Verbal apraxia is the inability to make the sounds of speech even though the muscles that make speech possible (larynx, tongue, lips) function normally. The speech is slow and labored. Dysarthria occurs when one of the muscles of speech does not function correctly. The speech can be slurred, slow, or halting.

Speech therapy should begin as soon as possible after a stroke. Speech therapists or speech pathologists are certified by the American Speech-Language Hearing Association, 10801 Rockville Pike, Rockville, Maryland 20852. The goals of speech therapy are to get patients to utilize all their undamaged communicative abilities consistently. Most improvement occurs during the first six months of treatment. Some improvement, however, can continue for several years, and an occasional patient will have slow but dramatic improvement after four or five years.

For people who have trouble dialing the phone but are able to use it once the number is dialed, the telephone company can provide a Card Dialer. With this device attached to the phone, numbers are automatically

After Middle Age

dialed when cards bearing identifying names or pictures are inserted. Other kinds of phones with automatic dialing are also available. Ambulance or police numbers can be placed on cards for emergencies.

(12-51) *Rehabilitation medicine.* Physicians specializing in rehabilitation and physical medicine are called physiatrists and are certified as such by the American Academy of Physical Medicine and Rehabilitation, 30 North Michigan Avenue, Chicago, Illinois 60602. Physiatrists work with a team of professionals, including specially trained nurses; physical therapists, who are licensed and specialize in the retraining of the muscles; orthotists, who are trained to make and fit braces and other special devices; and occupational therapists, who use real-life tasks to increase function—helping patients to relearn how to get dressed and accomplish other tasks requiring coordination.

(12-52) *Drugs used to increase cerebral function.* A number of drugs—papaverine (Pavabid, Cerespan), isoxsuprine (Vasodilan), nicotinyl alcohol (Riniacol), and ergot alkaloids (Hydergine)—can be given to increase blood flow to the brain and lessen deterioration. Although there is some encouraging data, particularly for Hydergine, there is, unfortunately, no conclusive evidence that these drugs are effective.

Hydergine comes in 0.5-mg round, white tablets and 1-mg oval tablets labeled "HYDERGINE 0.5" and "HYDERGINE 78-77," respectively. It is taken under the tongue (sublingually) three times a day. Maximal results take up to three to four weeks.

Four-hydroxycoumarin (Dicumarol) dosage is adjusted on the basis of a prothrombin blood test—a measure of the clotting ability of the blood. It comes in 25-mg, 50-mg, and 100-mg tablets. Dicumarol decreases blood coagulation, and for those who have had multiple strokes it may prolong mental function and life. However, excessive dosage can cause bleeding from the gums, into the skin, and into the urine or stool.

13

Disorders of the Digestive System

(13-1) The gastrointestinal (GI) tract, or the digestive system, takes in food through the mouth, metabolizes it (breaks it up so the body can use it), and eliminates what is unnecessary. From cavities to burps to hemorrhoids, the GI system can be counted on to let us know it is there.

Usually when you need a physician's help, you will call your internist or family doctor first. Yet there are times when you will want to go directly to a specialist. For example, if you believe your leg is broken and have confidence in an orthopedist, it saves time to call the orthopedist directly. When the GI system is involved, however, the internist or family practitioner should be the first physician called (except for dental problems). Some internists specialize in diseases of the GI system. They are called gastroenterologists. If you have a known GI problem, you might consider having an internist who is also a gastroenterologist as your regular physician. People are frequently tempted to call a surgeon. Let the internist decide if a surgical consultation is necessary. If there is any doubt, the internist will call on a surgeon for advice.

(13-2) *A word about treating yourself.* Most people will treat themselves with careful diet and medication when nausea, vomiting, or diarrhea occurs. They call it the "flu," particularly if it is associated with a fever and muscle aches all over the body. Flu is in fact a viral GI infection that disappears in one to four days. Severity or persistence of these symptoms, inability to decrease them, or painful or bloody vomitus or stool require cessation of self-treatment and consultation with a physician. If a patient's temperature rises above 102°F (39°C) taken by mouth, a physician should be called.

Another cause of nausea, vomiting, and diarrhea that usually does not involve fever is food poisoning. Symptoms begin a few hours after eating, and can often be terminated by vomiting any food still in the stomach. The nausea and cramps may disappear as soon as the alien substance is eliminated and the patient has recovered from the weakness that follows vomiting. Often the weakness can be helped by eating or drinking something that contains sugar. It is usually better not to eat or drink anything while the vomiting and diarrhea continue. If these symptoms go on longer than twenty-four hours, a physician should be called, because the patient may become dehydrated (loss of fluid) or the food poisoning may require specific treatment (for example, botulism requires an antitoxin).

THE MOUTH

(13-3) *What causes bad breath?* Bad breath (halitosis) is caused by bacteria that produce gaseous odors as they digest food left in the mouth. Bad breath, as the ads tell us, is usually something we do not recognize in ourselves. Aside from the social consequences (which are considerable) bad breath may be associated with a medical problem. If you have bad breath, the first thing to do is pay special attention to mouth hygiene. Careful use of dental floss after each meal and brushing to remove decaying food should be standard practice for everyone. Mouthwashes may make your breath sweeter but they probably do not kill bacteria. Nevertheless, if you have bad breath, using a mouthwash may help. Proper and frequent washing of dental appliances is also a must. If these procedures do not succeed in eliminating bad breath, a visit to the dentist is called for, since tooth decay and gum disease are frequent causes of bad breath. If after this effort the bad breath or a foul taste in the mouth persists, your physician should be consulted.

(13-4) *Canker sores* (recurrent aphthous ulcers) begin as a painful or burning sensation inside the mouth or cheeks, or on the gums or lips. The source of the discomfort is a round or oval white flat sore with a bright red border. The sores are most likely to occur during stress or after a lesion in your mouth, such as biting your lip. The cause is unknown, but some scientists believe the sources are due to an allergy to the bacterium alpha streptococcus, which normally is present in the mouth. While young children and pregnant women cannot use the antibiotic tetracycline because it stains developing teeth, older people can get a prescription for a tetracycline mouthwash. The tetracycline kills the bacteria and probably decreases the length of time a person has a given sore. Local anesthetics (available over the counter) work very poorly because they get washed away by saliva. Nevertheless, if you get canker sores often, these local anesthetics are worth a try, particularly just before eating. You may also try Orabase, which contains a steroid. Orabase is applied directly to the sore, but must be prescribed by a physician.

(13-5) *White spots in the mouth (leukoplakia).* This is a common disorder in which a painless, rough white patch forms on mucous membranes of the mouth, tongue, or lower lip. By itself it is harmless, but it should be watched by a dentist or physician regularly because, on rare occasions, it becomes cancerous. Frequently, leukoplakia is due to irritation from smoking or poor-fitting dentures. The source of irritation should be corrected.

(13-6) *Mouth cancer* is rare, and when it does occur, it is usually treated successfully. The most frequent symptom of mouth cancer is a sore that fails to heal, bleeds easily, and may or may not be painful. Lumps, thickening, whitish patches, pain, difficulty chewing or swallowing, or a chronic sore should also be brought to the attention of a dentist or physician. There may be discomfort on moving the jaw or tongue, or dentures that once fit well may no longer fit. There may also be lumps or swellings around the ear (salivary gland cancer) or neck.

A screening test before biopsy (17-9) is sometimes performed by dentists and physicians. This involves scraping cells from a suspicious area and examining them under a microscope. This test, called an oral cytologic examination, is very helpful in providing an early indication of mouth cancer. A physician who is suspicious about an area will want to take a biopsy and have it examined under a microscope. Surgical removal of the lesion, occasionally also removing the lymph nodes in the neck, is the usual treatment. Radiation is also often used, either to shrink the tumor before surgery or as the major form of treatment.

It has been well demonstrated that smoking and using chewing tobacco greatly increase the likelihood of mouth cancer. Lip cancer occurs very frequently among cigar and pipe smokers.

IMPORTANCE OF TEETH

(13-7) Although teeth are not a necessity of life, their loss often leads to malnutrition and an impaired self-image. Teeth are used primarily to chew food, but they also enhance a person's facial expression and appearance. As individuals lose their teeth, they tend to eat foods that do not have to be chewed, such as bread, potatoes, and liquids. These foods are less nutritious than meat and vegetables, and because food is swallowed rapidly, it loses its taste. When there is a deficiency of vital proteins and vitamins, there is decreased resistance to disease and more tooth decay.

After Middle Age

Loss of teeth also changes the shape of the face; muscles lose their tone, the skin becomes wrinkled, the tongue gets larger to fill in the space, and speech becomes more difficult. For this reason alone, people who lose their teeth may withdraw, walk with their heads down, and become depressed.

With proper education, some money, proper diet, and good genes, teeth can be kept in good condition for a long time, allowing for better physical and psychological health. If teeth have to be removed, artificial teeth should replace them as soon as possible. Although artificial teeth are not as good as natural teeth, they perform most functions and allow a normal diet and social life. Root canal work and other repairs can be done on the elderly as well as on the young.

(13-8) *Taking care of teeth (dental hygiene).* The dentist's office is full of funny smells, stainless steel instruments, whirling and grinding noises, needles to deaden pain, rinsing, picking, etc. For most people dental visits produce anxiety. Fortunately, dentists have been able to do more than physicians in keeping emergency visits to a minimum. Much of dentistry is preventive, and it is becoming more so.

Dental hygiene begins by seeing a dentist twice a year. During your visit, the dentist will examine your teeth, perhaps using x-rays. A specially trained hygienist will remove plaque (mineral deposits that collect on the teeth) and give the teeth a thorough cleaning. The hygienist will also instruct you on proper brushing and flossing of the teeth.

In general, it is advisable to floss and brush your teeth after each meal. Dental floss is used before brushing and must be done very gently in order not to damage the gums. While you were probably taught to brush your teeth in an up-and-down motion, dentists now advise brushing across the teeth. The important thing, however, is that you brush. Finally, use a fluoridated toothpaste.

(13-9) *Loss of teeth* in older adults is usually due to periodontal disease, which affects the gums—the tissues that surround and support the teeth. Periodontists are dentists who treat gum disease. Pyorrhea, caused by loss of bone and gums, is the most common gum condition. Food and bacteria collect around the tooth, irritating and destroying the surrounding tissues by forming calculus, or plaque (mineral deposits). As mentioned, this debris should be removed regularly. Other diseases of the mouth are caused by vitamin deficiencies. The symptoms of vitamin B deficiency (3-13) to (3-17) are a smooth tongue, cracking of the skin at the angles of the mouth, changes in taste, and a burning sensation attributed to loss of taste buds. This may be cured by taking vitamin B and by eating food high in protein. If vitamin C is deficient (3-19), healing takes longer and ulcers occur in the mouth. Teeth are occasionally removed because

Disorders of the Digestive System

they are a source of infection that may affect other organs of the body. There is, however, no chronic disease for which all the teeth must be removed.

(13-10) *False teeth (dentures).* One in every two people over the age of 65 either wears dentures or is in need of them. Often their teeth could have been saved if they had been attended to by a dentist regularly and if the treatment was designed to save teeth rather than extract them. Individuals always feel better psychologically if they have their own teeth rather than artificial ones.

If teeth have to be removed, as few as possible should be taken, and they should be replaced with a partial denture or a fixed bridge. A partial denture is held in place by metal clasps around the natural teeth and can replace as many as fourteen teeth so long as the remaining natural teeth are able to support it. The denture and mouth should be inspected periodically to see that the device is not producing adverse effects on the remaining teeth, gums, or jawbone. A partial denture usually lasts seven to ten years, is simple and inexpensive to repair, can be added to if more teeth must be removed, and takes a relatively short time to construct. Unfortunately, the partial denture is easily broken if dropped. A fixed bridge is permanently attached to the teeth on either side and is used to replace one or two teeth. Since it is permanent, it cannot be lost or broken easily and is cleaned the same way as natural teeth. A fixed bridge is more expensive and takes longer to make than a partial denture, and it cannot be added to if more natural teeth are subsequently lost.

If all the teeth in one or both jaws are lost, full dentures are needed as soon as possible; otherwise, changes in the bone will develop. The upper denture can be retained more easily than the lower as it is held against the palate by suction. The lower denture has less area on which to adhere, and so the muscles of the cheeks, tongue, and lips are used to stabilize it. Dentures take some time to become stabilized; a few visits to the dentist will be needed before they are fully adjusted. The dentist should be seen every six months in order to inspect for irritation or ulceration caused by dentures. It is important that such irritation be eliminated because it can be a cause of mouth cancer.

(13-11) *Care of dentures.* Removable dentures should be taken from the mouth at night and cleaned with a dentifrice. Table salt is as good as any dentifrice, except for those on a low salt diet. The dentures should be removed over a basin filled with water to prevent breakage if they are dropped. The teeth should be brushed away from the gums. Dental floss should be used gently, particularly at first. Where space is tight between the teeth, and the dental floss does not pull out easily, it can be slipped out as if it were a thread being pulled through the eye of a needle. With time,

After Middle Age

the space between the teeth usually becomes greater. An electric toothbrush has no advantage unless you have trouble using your hands. For example, a person with arthritis of the hands might make good use of an electric toothbrush.

(13-12) *Temporomandibular joint pain* is a pain that originates near the ear, between the lower and upper jaw. The pain is aching in nature and is aggravated by chewing. It is sometimes possible to hear a click in the joint. (This differentiates this pain from the pain of angina or a heart attack, which may be felt in the same area.) Arthritis and poor-fitting dentures are common causes of joint pain. If you think the pain may be due to angina or a heart attack, call your physician immediately.

THE ESOPHAGUS AND STOMACH

(13-13) *Common indigestion.* Even people with "cast-iron" stomachs will eat something from time to time that does not agree with them. They usually feel a "gas pain" in the chest or abdomen, start belching or burping, or have nausea and vomiting, often with diarrhea. The discomfort is made worse by anxiety and tension. It is important to discern whether or not this is indigestion or something more serious. Anyone who has a sudden, unfamiliar chest pain should call a physician because of the possibility that it is a heart attack (12-26). Pain in the abdomen that does not disappear within a few hours and frequent pain in the chest require the attention of a physician. If you have eaten something that does not agree with you, you can either vomit it up or live with it for a few hours until your body gets rid of it (13-2). A small amount of antacid usually helps.

(13-14) *Esophagitis (heartburn)* is irritation of the esophagus, the tube that runs from the mouth to the stomach. The major symptom is discomfort under the sternum (breast bone) after a large meal or after eating spicy foods. Frequently the sufferer is overweight. Diagnosis is made by a barium-swallow x-ray (upper GI series). Treatment usually consists of losing weight, raising the head in the bed six to eight inches, administering oxethazaine (Oxaine M), eating more frequent but smaller meals, and avoiding spicy foods.

(13-15) *Gas.* Burping, stomach rumblings, flatulence, stomach bloating, and cramping stomach pains are signs of stomach gas. It is swallowed air and comes from smoking, chewing gum, carbonated beverages, poor-fitting dentures, anxiety, and some drugs. Gas lower down in the abdomen in the large intestines comes from eating foods such as cabbage, broccoli, or beans.

Simethicone (Mylicin, Silain, Ovol, Riopan) by itself or in combinations

Disorders of the Digestive System

(DiGel, Maalox plus Simethicone, Mylanta, Silain-Gel, Riopan Plus) causes gas bubbles to join together, reducing them in total size for easier evacuation. For patients who must watch their sodium intake, Riopan Plus contains the least amount of sodium of the combinations (simethicone plus another agent).

(13-16) *Difficulty swallowing* is an uncommon condition. Victims may be totally unable to swallow or have to swallow repeatedly to get food or liquids down. Liquids may go up into the nose, forcing patients to change head and neck positions in order to swallow successfully. If the condition is present only when a person takes pills, it probably is not important. Usually, difficulty in swallowing is first noted with unground meats and may at first come and go. If the condition comes on suddenly, it most often means something (usually meat) is stuck in the lower part of the esophagus. As a rule, it can be washed down by drinking large amounts of water. Difficulty in swallowing that lasts longer than twenty-four hours or is recurrent should be brought to the attention of a physician.

(13-17) *Hiatal hernia* is usually associated with pain high up in the middle of the abdomen, just below the sternum, or in the back between the shoulder blades. It occurs after meals and is made worse by lying down. These symptoms are similar enough to those of more serious disorders that a physician should be called immediately. The hernia itself is an enlargement of the normal esophageal passageway through the diaphragm, the sheet of muscle that separates the chest from the abdomen. Inadvertently, the stomach pushes through this enlargement and gets caught in the chest. An ulcer forms that may bleed, causing tiredness and black stools. Mild hernias are treated as ulcers. Since pressure on the abdomen produces some of the symptoms, weight reduction is important. Aspirin, alcohol, and fatty foods should be avoided. When medical management fails, which is unusual, surgery is indicated.

The hiatal hernia is different from umbilical and inguinal hernias that develop from weakness in the abdominal wall. In these hernias the gut pushes outward rather than up into the chest, as it does with the hiatal hernia.

(13-18) *Stomach (gastric) ulcer.* The typical symptom of stomach ulcer is a gnawing, burning, or aching feeling just to the left and below the middle of the rib cage. Nausea and vomiting, weight loss, constipation, and fatigue are common, too. The episodes usually occur forty-five minutes to an hour after a meal and are relieved by food.

This complaint should be discussed with a physician, who will want to check the stool for blood, take a sample of venous blood to determine the amount of blood loss that has occurred, and do a barium-swallow (with an opaque dye) x-ray examination. Treatment is the same as that for

After Middle Age

duodenal ulcer, with a response usually within a month. Frequent follow-up examinations are indicated.

(13-19) *Stomach cancer.* The early symptoms of stomach cancer are also common to most digestive disorders—stomach distress that is aggravated by eating, a sudden dislike of normally enjoyed foods, and pain in the area of the stomach. When these symptoms last more than fourteen days, a physician should be consulted. More obvious symptoms such as vomiting, blood in the stools, and rapid weight loss should be attended to immediately.

One of the most useful tests for diagnosing stomach cancer is a barium-swallow x-ray. The barium is swallowed, fills the stomach, and is observed with a fluoroscope and by x-rays taken from several angles. An abnormality or irregularity in the stomach shape produced by cancer or ulcers can be seen by the radiologist. Also, a gastroscope may be passed through the nose down into the stomach, enabling the physician to examine the inner surface of the stomach visually. Cells from the stomach lining can be retrieved by a similar procedure and microscopically examined (this is called exfoliative cytology).

An important distinction must be made between the lesion of a stomach ulcer and that of cancer. The symptoms are very similar, and the x-ray and other tests may be inconclusive. Usually the physician will treat the lesion for several weeks with diet and medication as if it were an ulcer. If the lesion does not clear up on x-ray, a surgeon may perform a diagnostic exploratory operation. Although a duodenal ulcer (in the small intestine) can be treated medically for a long time without fear of cancer, this is not the case with a stomach ulcer. Since stomach cancer has become more readily treatable, this distinction is now even more important.

Traditionally, treatment for stomach cancer has meant surgically removing all or part of the stomach and surrounding tissues, depending on the extent of the cancer. Postoperative digestive difficulties are prevented by a low-carbohydrate, high-fat, and high-protein diet. Many small meals rather than three large ones also help digestion. Recently, treatment with a combination of several drugs along with surgery has proved very promising. (The cure rate is now better than 25 percent.) This type of sophisticated chemotherapy (17-12) is generally administered at a university medical center.

DUODENAL ULCER

(13-20) Ulcers are very common in our society. It has been estimated that one in ten Americans will get an ulcer in the course of a lifetime. An

Disorders of the Digestive System

ulcer is produced when something upsets the delicate balance between the mucous lining of the stomach and intestines and the acid that is needed to digest food. The relative excess of acid literally eats a hole in the mucous lining of the duodenum (small intestine) or stomach and causes a heartburnlike pain described as gnawing, burning, aching, or cramplike. The pain occurs just under the middle of the rib cage forty-five minutes to an hour after meals and is particularly severe between midnight and two A.M. The appetite remains normal and the pain is relieved within thirty minutes of eating food. Vomiting of blood might occur in individuals with known ulcers, but may also be the first sign of ulcer. In either case, a physician should be seen immediately. Blood is not always vomited; the presence of dark stools or a sudden onset of weakness, faintness, dizziness, cold and moist skin, and chills are also symptoms of a bleeding ulcer.

The physician will examine either the vomitus or the stool for blood and then take blood from a vein to help determine how much blood was lost. A barium-swallow x-ray examination enables the physician to see the ulcer (13-19).

Some individuals have symptoms that are early indicators that ulcers could be forming. Warning symptoms include frequent heartburn and burping or upheaval of gastric juices into the mouth, which mix with the saliva to form a sour, bitter taste. These symptoms do not in themselves mean you have or will have an ulcer. They are only warnings and should be brought to the attention of the physician during your routine physical examination.

(13-21) *Treatment of the ulcer.* Anxiety and tension may be the biggest contributors to an ulcer because they increase the flow of acid. People with ulcers should change their lifestyle to avoid stress that produces anxiety and tension. Frequent, short, rest vacations (three-day weekends away from anxiety-provoking situations) and breaks during the day when twenty minutes of quiet rest can be obtained are very helpful. People should not take on more work than they can manage or be under constant pressure to meet deadlines.

Getting enough sleep is important to an ulcer patient's regime because during sleep the body's need to metabolize food (and produce acid) is decreased. When there is less acid, healing can take place. Before bedtime, a snack of milk and crackers taken with an antacid is often recommended. One or more brief naps each day are also helpful, especially after meals.

The diet of an ulcer patient is extremely important. For many years, physicians prescribed large amounts of milk for ulcer patients. Nowadays it is felt that some milk may be useful, but large quantities may lead to increased incidence of heart attacks. In the acute phase of the illness, however, many physicians still recommend milk or milk products in liquid form as well as frequent use of antacids. Gradually, the patient begins to eat regular meals with a high protein content. Coffee, tea, colas, and alcohol, which stimulate gastric secretion, and black pepper and other foods that are found to aggravate symptoms, should be avoided. Liquids should not be drunk when they are very hot or cold. Decaffeinated coffee is a good substitute for regular coffee, though even it should be taken in combination with another food and with cream or milk. Cola drinks should be allowed to become flat if they must be consumed. All food should be thoroughly chewed. The drinking of water should be avoided during meals, although it's fine to drink water at other times. It is important to eat regularly and to maintain high nutritional standards. Salt, which increases the flow of stomach acid, should be avoided.

Pain may require frequent antacid administration between meals and during the night. Side effects, however, include both diarrhea and constipation. The choice of antacid is difficult because there are both advantages and disadvantages to almost every preparation. In general, the liquids are more effective than the tablets, but convenience and taste need to be taken into consideration. Delcid is more concentrated than most other brands, and on a cost-per-dose basis, it is frequently cheaper. Unless the physician recommends otherwise, an antacid containing aluminum hydroxide and magnesium hydroxide (or magnesium trisilicate) such as Maalox, Mylanta, Aludrox, Amphojel, or Gelusil is probably preferable to those containing calcium. If a brand containing calcium is used, the blood calcium should be monitored occasionally. All people in all circumstances must follow the directions on the label or those given by a physician. It is dangerous to overmedicate.

Anticholinergic drugs reduce stomach acidity after eating. These drugs are usually taken at mealtime or immediately afterward. Although somewhat more expensive, propantheline (Pro-Banthine), poldine (Nacton), glycopyrrolate (Robincil), and isopropamide (Darbid) produce fewer side effects, such as dry mouth and blurred vision, than does atropine, or belladonna. The physician should be reminded about the presence of glaucoma and prostatic hypertrophy; anticholinergic drugs tend to make these conditions worse. Occasionally, these drugs also cause the side effects of dizziness, fast heartbeat, or nervousness. Any such reactions should be reported to the physician.

For those ulcer patients who experience frequent tension and worry that cannot be well controlled by other means, it may be useful to occasionally use sedatives or tranquilizers (5-8) under the advice and constant supervision of a physician. Care must be taken not to abuse these drugs.

Disorders of the Digestive System

An important drug in the management of ulcers is cimetidine (Tagamet). Cimetidine suppresses stomach acid secretion and is effective for both treating patients who have symptoms and preventing symptoms from returning in patients with known ulcers. But it is not necessarily a cure for ulcers; that is, the ulcers may return when the drug is discontinued. In older people, cimetidine may cause side effects of diarrhea, muscle pain, mental confusion, slurred speech, and hallucinations. Tagamet comes as pale green 100- and 300-mg tablets labeled with "Tagamet" and the dosage. The usual dosage is one 300-mg tablet taken with meals and at bedtime.

Ranitidine (Zantac, average maintenance dose 150 mg twice a day) comes in white tablets labeled "Zantac 150." Ranitidine works very much like cimetidine. Side effects include headache, rash, and dizziness.

Another useful medication for duodenal ulcer is sucralfate. Sucralfate (Carafate, average maintenance dose 1000 mg or 1 g four times a day) comes in 1-g tablets labled "Marion" on one side and "1712" on the other. While no serious side effects have been reported, dry mouth, constipation, and skin rashes may occur.

Aspirin in moderate or large doses is harmful to the ulcer patient because it decreases the protective mucous lining of the stomach and intestines. When this happens, acid present in the stomach etches the stomach walls. Aspirin substitutes, principally nonsalicylates such as Tylenol, do not have this effect. Other drugs the ulcer patient should be aware of as possibly harmful are: reserpine, used to treat high blood pressure; butazoliden, which is given to reduce pain and fever, often in connection with arthritic conditions; and cortisone or steroids, which are anti-inflammatory drugs. The physician should be informed of any prior prescriptions for these drugs.

THE INTESTINES AND RECTUM

(13-22) *Constipation.* The symptoms of constipation are fullness in the abdomen, gas and pain, and at times fatigue or listlessness. Constipation is caused by firm stools that are difficult to evacuate.

The frequency of bowel movements is highly individualized, and persons who have one movement every few days are normal if they are comfortable. The bowel is very sensitive to emotional changes, travel, and alterations in diet. Constipation is a frequent result, and an occasional mild laxative for this is not unreasonable.

The most common cause of serious constipation is, however, the use of laxatives that were initially taken to remedy either real or imagined con-

After Middle Age

stipation. Continued use of laxatives actually produces worse gas and firmer stools. An escalating cycle develops: more laxative, more constipation. The best way to regularize the bowel is through a low-fat diet consisting of meat, fish, fowl, and a balance of vegetables, fruit, and cereals. A daily breakfast followed by a chance to use the toilet employs a very important reflex, the tendency to empty the bowel shortly after a meal. Coffee, hot tea, and hot chocolate are very useful in triggering this reflex.

There are many laxatives, none of which should be used for any length of time. Perhaps the least expensive and most effective are mineral oil, which is taken by mouth, 1 to 2 tablespoons at bedtime, or milk of magnesia, which is also taken by mouth, 1 to 2 tablespoons at bedtime. Mineral oil reduces the absorption of some vitamins and some anticoagulants, so do not overuse it. Enemas are rarely necessary except during chronic illnesses. It is best to use a nonirritating one such as saline (saltwater) solution, 1 to 2 pints (500 to 1000 mL). The commercially available Fleet Enema contains sodium phosphate and biphosphate. It comes in a disposable bottle with an applicator tip and is usually very effective.

(13-23) *Appendicitis* is generally a young person's disease, but it may occur later in life. The symptoms are either pain over much of the abdomen or the classical pain localized to the lower right part of the abdomen. Nausea, constipation, and diarrhea may also be present. Pressure by a hand on the lower right part of the abdomen usually demonstrates tenderness. These signs should be brought immediately to the attention of your physician. An appendectomy, the operation to remove the appendix, is a relatively simple procedure. About ten days of hospitalization are needed to recover from the surgery. In recent years there has been a tendency to treat appendicitis with antibiotics. This is often done in other countries and works well.

(13-24) *What are hemorrhoids (piles)?* Hemorrhoids are enlarged veins (like varicose veins) that are further enlarged by increased venous blood pressure. External (outside the anus) hemorrhoids rarely produce significant symptoms unless a blood clot (thrombosis) forms in them. The pain occurs fairly suddenly, lasts two to three days, and may recur. Internal hemorrhoids usually announce themselves by bright red bleeding associated with having a bowel movement. The blood may actually drip into the toilet bowl. The blood loss can be severe, although this is unusual. Since rectal bleeding can be produced by a number of conditions, a physician must be alerted and the source of the bleeding verified. Initial hemorrhoid treatment consists of providing conditions in which less strain is needed to have a stool. Stool softeners and laxatives that allow for easy stools are used. If possible, it is also helpful to decrease the amount of time spent standing.

Disorders of the Digestive System

Surgery is reserved for patients with severe symptoms. Surgery for hemorrhoids is painful but very effective. Three to five days of hospitalization are required, followed by a recuperation period that may last several weeks. Some surgeons recommend cryodestruction (freezing), which does not require hospitalization and is relatively painless. Other surgeons simply tie rubber bands around the berrylike hemorrhoids. This procedure produces less pain and requires little or no time off one's feet. The rubber-band procedure usually has to be repeated several times to get complete relief. Photocoagulation produces even fewer side effects than the rubber-band procedure and is just being introduced into outpatient practice.

Self-treatment for hemorrhoids is inadvisable. A physician should make the diagnosis because rectal bleeding may be the first sign of cancer or, less serious but still important, a polyp (13-27).

Preparations that are sold without a prescription may be useful, but they should only be used on the advice of a physician. Those containing anesthetics may cause allergies, and there is no convincing evidence that the widely advertised Preparation H can in any way shrink hemorrhoids or promote healing.

(13-25) *Rectal prolapse* (when the bowel pushes through the anus and hangs out) usually produces symptoms of inability to control the stool and a weighty feeling of a mass protruding from the rectum. The bowel can be pushed back in, but the condition may recur when standing or coughing. It is usually corrected surgically, although nonsurgical techniques are available.

(13-26) *Diverticulosis* is a disease of part of the large bowel (colon) in which the wall of the tubelike colon weakens and pouches form. This condition occurs frequently in older people, but sometimes begins around age 40. It need not cause concern unless these outpouchings become inflamed (diverticulitis). Although the diverticula may show up on an x-ray, the majority of the time they cause no problems. When there are problems, the symptoms may come and go. The symptoms include constipation or straining with defecation. Loss of appetite, distention of the abdomen, and passing of gas are also symptoms. Pain of a cramping nature in the lower left part of the abdomen may occur. Severe pain associated with a fever should be brought to the attention of your physician. It may require hospitalization within several hours. Large amounts of blood in the stool require immediate medical attention. If this happens to you, call your physician, or go directly to an emergency room. Small amounts of blood (a tinged stool) must also be brought to the attention of a physician within twenty-four hours of discovery.

Since it is thought that the outpouching of the colon is caused by pressure from stools, many physicians now recommend trying to soften stools. For this reason bulky, high-fiber diets are in vogue. The fiber attracts water, and this in turn makes the stool looser and easier to pass. Its transient time in the bowel is less, so it exerts less pressure on the colon wall. There is also less strain in defecating. Hard, small foods such as pumpkin seeds or peanuts that are not well-chewed should be avoided. Occasionally serious complications such as rupture or abscesses occur, and these require surgery.

(13-27) *Cancer of the colon and rectum.* The colon, or large bowel, and its connection to the anus at its lower end (the rectum) are common sites of cancer. The symptoms are red blood in the stool, a change in bowel habits, such as either diarrhea or constipation, and lower abdominal discomfort or pain. If traces of blood are found in the stool, or if the other symptoms are present for more than fourteen days, a physician must be consulted. Do not delay: prompt attention is very important.

The discovery of a growth may be made by a digital examination, in which the physician feels the rectum, or by insertion of a proctosigmoidoscope, through which the physician can see well into the large intestine. These procedures are now part of the annual physical for all individuals over age 40. If a growth is found, a piece of it can be removed through the proctosigmoidoscope and examined under a microscope. A newer instrument called a fiberoptic colonoscope is available for examination of the entire large bowel. It is usually used only by specialists called gastroenterologists. X-rays of the large bowel after filling it with a barium solution can be helpful in making a diagnosis.

Occasionally, during a routine examination with a proctosigmoidoscope, a polyp will be found. Polyps are growths into the hollow of the bowel from its mucous membrane. They can be either cancerous or benign. Cancerous polyps are routinely removed, but frequently benign polyps are also removed because they tend to become malignant. Some physicians remove polyps at the time of the initial examination.

Cancer of the colon and rectum is removed surgically. The part of the intestine with cancer is excised, and the end pieces are sewn together. When a great deal of the rectum has to be removed, there may be nothing to sew the upper end to. The colon is then brought through a temporary (or permanent) opening on the wall of the abdomen called a colostomy (13-28).

(13-28) *Colostomy* directs the large bowel (colon) to empty through an opening in the abdominal wall instead of through the rectum. This opening is usually in the upper right or left part of the abdomen. Depending on which part of the colon opens onto the abdomen, the feces will be either formed and odorless or loose. When the feces are loose, great care must

Disorders of the Digestive System

be taken to prevent contact with the skin—these feces still contain digestive enzymes that can irritate the skin. Both the odor and the irritation can be prevented, but this requires considerable care on the part of both patient and physician.

The first few weeks of the colostomy require experimentation with diet. Some foods such as fish and onions and certain medicines are more likely to produce odors than others. Some persons will want to irrigate the opening of the colostomy in the morning, feeling it gives them better control. Others will find this activity has no merit. An oral medication, bismuth subcarbonate, decreases fecal odors. Alternatively, ten drops of Banish placed in the plastic colostomy bag after it is emptied will help prevent odors.

The passing of gas through the colostomy is very common during the first few weeks, but this decreases with time. Skin irritation is eliminated by proper fitting. When irritation does appear, the physician should evaluate it. Karaya gum allows healing and will act as a seal between the opening (stoma) and the bag. Bags thrown into the toilet will clog the plumbing.

It is usual to feel depressed about a colostomy—first because of concern about the cancer, and second because of the social consequences of the colostomy. Of course the operation producing the colostomy greatly reduces the risk of recurrent cancer and increases the individual's comfort, so most people adapt to it in a few weeks. Useful information about colostomies is available from the Colostomy Association, 2001 W. Beverly Boulevard, Los Angeles, California 90057. Most large communities have their own colostomy associations. Physicians, nurses, or social workers will have information about these local groups.

(13-29) *Ultrasonography* is used for examining masses in the abdomen when their nature or size is unclear. It is rapid and safe, and produces no discomfort. A sound wave is passed through the abdomen (like sonar), and its reflections are recorded on a television screen from which an instant picture is made. The picture looks very much like an x-ray but is able to differentiate things x-ray cannot.

THE LIVER

(13-30) *What does it do?* The liver, which is located under the lower ribs on the right side, is one of several organs that clear waste material from the bloodstream. Like any good ecological system, it converts its waste material into something usable, bile, which is then stored in the gall bladder, a fist-sized bag located under the liver. Bile is used by the gastrointestinal system for digestion of fats. Another important liver function is the metabolism of proteins and carbohydrates.

(13-31) *Symptoms of liver disease.* Fatigue, weakness, slight fever, lack of appetite, loss of interest in cigarettes, weight loss, pain in the region of the liver, passing of gas, nausea, and vomiting can all be associated with liver disease. A swollen abdomen and jaundice (yellowing of the skin and whites of the eyes) are common. The changes in consciousness and neurological status seen with advanced liver disease are known as hepatic coma.

(13-32) *Hepatitis.* There are many kinds of liver disease, all requiring expert attention. The most common disease of the liver is hepatitis. This highly communicable disease is caused by a virus that can be transmitted by fecal material that gets into food, from a contaminated needle, or from a blood transfusion. Hepatitis from needles has become rare in recent years because physicians use disposable needles, eliminating the chance of the disease spreading from one person to another through the needle. Hepatitis from transfusion is a real risk, particularly if many units of blood are needed. This type of hepatitis leaves a specific abnormality in the blood that is called Australia or hepatitis B antigen. It can be tested for by taking a small amount of venous blood. Screening for this antigen in potential blood donors has helped eliminate some of the risk of obtaining hepatitis from a blood transfusion.

In hepatitis, the jaundice (yellowness) comes on rapidly, reaching its maximum within about two weeks. Victims are often hospitalized and kept in isolation to prevent spreading the illness to others. The treatment is bed rest or quiet activity until the patient feels able to become more active and the jaundice fades. Foods or drinks high in protein and sugar content are given. Cirrhosis of the liver is discussed in (5-37). Exposed family members are frequently given gamma globulin (antibodies) injections that help prevent them from getting the disease if it is not already incubating. The effect of these shots lasts about four weeks.

THE GALLBLADDER

(13-33) The gallbladder stores digestive juices (bile) made in the liver and delivers them to the small intestine following meals (particularly meals with high fat content). Pain is the primary symptom of gallbladder disease. It usually begins just above the navel, then travels through the body to the area of the spine and up the right side of the back. The pain is a severe, grinding one that persists for about an hour. It is unaffected by movement and leaves soreness for up to several days. It can be associated

Disorders of the Digestive System

with yellowing of the skin (jaundice), first noticed in the whites of the eyes. Fever, chills, nausea, vomiting, belching, bloating of the stomach, gas, and constipation also occur.

A gallstone is the hardening of the bile pigments, cholesterol, or calcium present in the bile that is in the gallbladder. Small stones passed down the bile duct (which leads to the small intestine) cause much of the pain. Large stones get caught in the gallbladder and usually do not cause difficulty unless they block the flow of bile. Gallstones frequently may be seen on a simple x-ray of the abdomen, but physicians usually want to see a cholecystogram, too. In this study, a dye is given by mouth, and many hours later an x-ray is taken showing how much of the dye gets into the gallbladder, thus indicating the extent of the blockage. Sonography may also be done (13-29).

There is no medical cure for gallstones, and most physicians recommend removal of the gallbladder, or at least the gallstones, in people who have repeated attacks and x-ray evidence of gallstones. Surgery for gallstones generally involves a recovery period of several weeks. Recently, several new techniques have been developed that allow for the removal of gallstones without surgery. One is called endoscopic papillotomy and involves the insertion of a long, flexible, hollow tube through the mouth, esophogas, and stomach to the juncture of the bile duct with the small intestine. Because fiberoptic bundles within the tube can throw light into the intestine, the physician can see well enough to pass a thin wire into the bile duct. This wire has a basket at its tip that can snare the stone, or the opening of the bile duct can be enlarged, allowing the stone to pass through. Only light sedation is needed for this procedure and as soon as it is finished, the patient can move about.

For relief of pain, physicians usually prescribe the analgesic meperidine (Demerol) (7-18). A low-fat diet is often ordered. In fact, after the gallbladder has been removed, a low-fat diet is necessary for the rest of one's life. This is because the bile normally helps digestion of fats, and without it, fat is undigested and produces discomfort.

Even though gallstones have been diagnosed, it is a mistake to attribute all digestive symptoms to them. Any severe or lasting GI symptoms should be investigated.

THE PANCREAS

(13-34) The pancreas is an organ in the abdomen that produces both insulin (a hormone excreted into the blood that aids sugar metabolism) and digestive juices—a combination of enzymes (trypsin, amylase, and lipase) and other substances excreted into the small bowel for digestion.

After Middle Age

(13-35) *Acute pancreatitis.* The most prominent symptom is severe pain in the upper-middle abdomen. It begins very suddenly when the pancreas's own digestive juices have turned on itself. Shock (loss of the ability to maintain blood pressure and consciousness) can occur quickly. The pain may diffuse to the back, chest, and lower abdomen. Nausea, vomiting, abdominal bloating, and constipation may also occur. Acute pancreatitis is not only painful but dangerous. Although it is not of the same urgency as a heart attack, the victim should be taken immediately to the hospital. Predisposing conditions are alcoholism, gallstones, ulcers, and abdominal trauma.

(13-36) *The treatment of acute pancreatitis.* Initial treatment for acute pancreatitis occurs in the hospital and involves intravenous feeding, antibiotics, and analgesics to relieve the extreme pain. As improvement occurs, foods are given slowly, beginning with a low-fat, low-calorie diet.

(13-37) *Chronic pancreatitis.* Chronic pancreatitis can begin either with an acute attack, which then recurs, or with a gradual insidious onset. The outstanding symptom is recurring bouts of pain interspersed with periods without symptoms. There is impaired digestion and considerable weight loss. The stool is generally bulky, light in color, and greasy. Proper diet can help, as well as the oral use of pancreatic enzymes (Viokase) after meals.

(13-38) *Pancreatic cancer.* The symptoms of pancreatic cancer are not very specific, but include loss of weight, abdominal pain, and jaundice (yellowing of the skin). Loss of interest in food, nausea, loosening of stools, or constipation also occur.

14

Disorders of the Urinary System

(14-1) The urinary system provides a mechanism for removing toxic materials from the blood and excreting them from the body in urine. The system includes two kidneys to filter the blood, one at either side of the thoracic (chest) cavity in the back, just below rib level; two ureters, which are tubes connecting the kidneys to the bladder; the bladder, which holds urine until urination takes place; and the urethra, a tube leading from the bladder to the exterior through which urine passes during urination. The urethra in women is short; in men, it runs the length of the penis. When the kidneys fail in their job of filtering blood, or when urine cannot get out because the ureter is blocked, the body's toxic products build up. If the bladder or urethra is damaged so that a person cannot control urination, either the bladder fills up, or urination occurs spontaneously.

The diagnostician examines the urine to determine the state not only of the urinary system, but of much of the rest of the body as well. For example, the urine can indicate if a person is diabetic and how well the diabetes is under control. Red blood in the urine, even if observed only once, could be a symptom of a serious problem and should be called to the attention of a physician. Blood in the urine may be produced by an anticoagulant drug taken to decrease blood clotting or by a stone in the kidney, bladder, or ureter. Bladder stones are particularly common with advancing age and following prolonged bed rest. A bladder infection may also be the cause of bleeding and very often is accompanied by pain and discomfort. But of greatest concern is the possibility that the bleeding is produced by a tumor.

There are a number of different kinds of physicians who treat urinary problems. Internists, family practitioners, or primary-care physicians can

After Middle Age

treat most of the urinary problems you are likely to have. They may refer patients to a urologist, a surgeon specializing in disorders of the urinary tract. A gynecologist also may take care of some urinary problems. Nephrologists are internists who specialize in caring for serious urinary tract problems from a medical vantage.

(14-2) *Loss of control of urine.* The major cause of loss of control of urine in older men is prostate trouble; in women, it is stress. Because the female urethra is shorter than the male, some women inadvertently lose urine when they laugh, cough, sneeze, or undergo sudden physical exertion. Typically, there is no warning of the incontinence. Stress incontinence is more annoying than dangerous. Nevertheless, it should be brought to the attention of a urologist or obstetrician-gynecologist. If the condition is mild, exercise of the pelvic muscles can be prescribed, along with the use of a sanitary napkin to prevent spilling onto clothes. A person can learn to use special inflatable balloons that are inserted into the vagina and press against the urethra. The balloon must be deflated every few hours at a convenient time so that urine may pass. Occasionally, a pessary (a ring or cup inserted into the vagina to hold up the uterus) can be helpful. When the problem is severe and cannot be helped by these devices, surgery becomes necessary.

INFECTIONS

(14-3) Urine is normally sterile, and infections of the urinary system occur when bacteria are present anywhere within the system. Usual symptoms are a frequent and urgent need to urinate, a burning sensation or pain when urinating, chills, fever, nausea, and vomiting. You may feel tenderness in your midback region or a dull ache in your lower abdomen. The most usual urinary system infection is cystitis, an inflammation of the bladder. The bacteria usually enter the bladder through the urethra and travel upward. Cystitis occurs more frequently in women than in men, again because of the shorter urethra. Also, frequent intercourse and the use of a diaphragm for birth control tend to predispose women to cystitis—the diaphragm makes it harder for the bladder to empty completely, and intercourse may cause irritation. As women become older, the short urethra gradually becomes less resistant to bacterial invasion.

Kidney infections usually arise from untreated cystitis or follow a series of such infections. There may or may not be any of the above-mentioned symptoms. Yet it's important to diagnose this type of infection because untreated, it can cause permanent kidney damage.

(14-4) *Diagnosis.* The presence of an infection is established by a urine culture. To obtain the urine for a culture, the area around the open-

Disorders of the Urinary System

ing of the urethra is cleansed with sterile soap. (In women, the labia must be spread by hand.) A small amount of urine is allowed to pass into the toilet bowl. Then, halfway through, the urine stream is aimed into the sterile bottle, which is immediately capped and refrigerated. Within six hours the urine should be taken to a laboratory for culturing. The usual criteria for an infection is the presence of more than 100,000 bacteria per cubic milliliter (10^5/mL) of urine. Once the type of bacteria is identified (usually after twenty-four to forty-eight hours), a specific antibiotic is prescribed. This procedure is called culture and sensitivity (C and S).

If the bacteria are sensitive to the antibiotic, symptoms will probably abate within twenty-four hours, and no bacteria should be found in subsequent urine cultures. There is some debate among physicians about how long a patient should stay on antibiotics once the urine becomes free of bacteria. Some physicians recommend a week, but others feel this is not enough. Certainly, longer periods of treatment are recommended after repeated infections. In any case, the patient must follow the physician's instructions carefully. Severe infections may require hospitalization so that antibiotics can be administered intravenously.

(14-5) *Other diagnostic tests.* In addition to culturing for bacteria, the laboratory will examine the urine for blood cells. Normally, there are not more than two white blood cells (WBC) and/or two red blood cells (RBC) seen with the microscope at the same time. More than this raises the suspicion of infection.

An intravenous pyelogram (IVP) is a test in which a dye injected in a vein of the arm collects in the urinary system. Because x-rays normally pass through the tissues but cannot pass through tissues containing the dye, when an x-ray is taken, the dye outlines the inside of the urinary system. This makes it possible for a radiologist or urologist to find any structural abnormalities that might be present. Several x-rays are taken over a few hours, enabling the radiologist to trace the path of the dye (this is also the path of urine) through the kidneys, ureters, and bladder. The IVP usually can be done by a radiologist or urologist in the office or in the outpatient department of a hospital. If you take this test and know you have allergies, particularly to fish, volunteer this information to the radiologist (who of course should ask you). It might be advisable to pretest you for an allergy to the dye.

The retrograde pyelogram is a test in which tubes are placed through the urethra into the bladder and then up into the ureters. As with an IVP, a dye is used and x-rays taken. This procedure allows the urologist to learn more about the bladder and ureters than an IVP, but if you are awake, it is also more uncomfortable. It is usually done under light anesthesia in a hospital's outpatient department.

After Middle Age

(14-6) *Drugs for treating infections of the urinary system.* Sulfa drugs are used for simple acute (those that come on suddenly) infections, unless sensitivity studies demonstrate that another drug should be used. The most widely used sulfa drugs are:

Sulfisoxazole (Gantrisin, average dosage 1 to 2 g four times a day), comes in 0.5-g white, scored tablets labeled "Gantrisin." A common side effect during the first few days is nausea. Rashes usually indicate an allergy.

Sulfamethoxazole (Gantanol, average dosage 1 g twice a day) comes in 0.5-g green tablets labeled "Gantanol." Again, the most common side effect is nausea. Rashes usually indicate an allergy.

Trimethoprim and sulfamethoxazole is a combination of two drugs that are effective in treating urinary infections. The average dosage is one to two tablets every twelve hours. As Bactrim, it comes in green, elongated tablets labeled "Bactrim" and in white, elongated tablets labeled "Bactrim-DS" (DS stands for double strength). As Septra, it comes in pink tablets labeled "Septra Y2B" and in pink, football-shaped tablets labeled "Septra O2C," which are the Septra double strength. Anticonvulsant drugs can interact adversely when taken simultaneously with this drug. Nausea is a common side effect.

A synthetic, penicillin-like drug used for a variety of urinary tract infections is generically known as ampicillin. The average dosage of ampicillin is 500 mg four times a day. It is marketed as Omnipen, in 250- and 500-mg pink and purple capsules labeled "Wyeth 53" and "Wyeth 309," respectively; as Polycillin in 250- and 500-mg gray and red capsules labeled "Bristol 7992" and "Bristol 7993," respectively; as Amcill, in 250- and 500-mg blue and gray capsules labeled "P-D 402" and "P-D 404," respectively; and as Principen, in 250-mg gray and 500-mg light and dark gray capsules labeled "Squibb 971" and "Squibb 974," respectively. The average dosage of ampicillin is 500 mg four times a day. Physicians should ask patients whether or not they are allergic to penicillin, to ampicillin, or to the antibiotics called cephalosporins. If your physician does not ask about allergies, it is important that you volunteer this information. Side effects include nausea, diarrhea, and rashes. Any swelling or difficulty with breathing requires immediate medical attention.

Other drugs for treating urinary tract infections include:

Cephalexin (Keflex, average dosage 250 to 1000 mg four times a day) comes in 250-mg green and white capsules labeled "Dista H69," dark and light green 500-mg capsules labeled "Dista H71," and a light green, elongated 1000-mg tablet labeled "U60." The most frequent side effect is diarrhea. Development of a rash may indicate an allergy to the drug.

Nitrofurantoin (Macrodantin, average dosage 50 to 100 mg four times a

Disorders of the Urinary System

day) comes in 25-mg white capsules labeled "Macrodantin 0007," 50-mg yellow and white capsules labeled "Macrodantin 0008," and 100-mg yellow capsules labeled "Macrodantin 0009." Side effects are loss of appetite and nausea. Rashes usually indicate an allergy to the drug. Occasionally, a reaction consisting of a temperature, chills, cough, and chest pain is produced.

Methenamine (Mandelamine, average dosage 1 g four times a day) comes in 0.5-g brown and 1-g purple football-shaped tablets labeled "PD 166" and "PD 167," respectively. It is usually used for long-term therapy of chronic infections. Many physicians use methenamine with an agent such as methionine. This acidifies the urine and makes methenamine more active. High doses can produce symptoms similar to a urinary system infection, which will require lowering the dosage.

STONES

(14-7) *Stones* (calculi) are produced in the kidneys of some people. Due to the kidneys' filtering function, minerals and organic substances sometimes collect in the kidney, and when conditions are right, they harden into stones. Very small stones are passed out through the ureter, bladder, and urethra without accompanying symptoms. Similarly, very large stones that cannot fit into the narrow ureter do not cause symptoms unless they are so large or numerous that they block the kidney. Intermediate-sized stones, however, produce intermittent excruciating pain in the midback, which moves into the lower abdomen as the stone passes through the ureter. Pain can also be present in the groin or thigh. There may be nausea, chills, fever, and frequent urination. Blood may be seen in the urine.

The physician who suspects that symptoms are caused by stones will x-ray the abdomen. Most stones will show up, but occasionally some will leave no shadow on the film, and the physician will not find them. When the stones block the outflow of urine and do not dislodge themselves, they must be removed surgically.

Essentially, there is no nonsurgical treatment during an acute attack of stones, except to decrease the pain through the use of narcotics. Further management of the problem involves trying to prevent the formation of additional stones. The physician will want to know what caused the problem. So if you excrete a stone, save it, because this helps with the determination. Saving the stone is best done by passing your urine through a food strainer or a cheesecloth. Most stones have no obvious cause, but when a cause is found, it usually is treatable. Stomach antacids that contain calcium, frequent urinary system infections, and gout can cause stones; these can all be treated. It is important for people who have had stones to maintain fluid intake at a high level, especially before going to bed at night. Stones caused by calcium can be helped by switching antacids to one that contains no calcium, and by avoiding milk products and eggs. Stones caused by infections and gout should subside after these conditions are treated.

KIDNEY FAILURE

(14-8) Failure of the kidneys occurs in two forms—acute (short-term) and chronic (long-term). Both are associated with the accumulation in the body of toxic products that are normally excreted by the kidneys. When the kidneys suddenly stop producing urine, a condition called acute kidney failure, the cause is usually a sudden reduction in the kidney's blood supply with subsequent death of kidney cells. The regeneration process takes two to three weeks, during which time the toxic substances accumulate and complications can occur. There are a number of causes of acute kidney failure, including ingestion of toxic agents (such as carbon tetrachloride or arsenic), some drugs, and shock from a severe injury or heart attack.

There are two phases of acute kidney failure. The first, the oliguric phase during which only small amounts of urine are formed, lasts from a few days to three weeks. When the kidneys stop functioning, the accumulated waste products cause a condition known as uremia. The symptoms, which progress over time, are loss of appetite, then nausea and vomiting, muscle twitching, convulsions, sleepiness, and finally coma. The skin commonly itches and is pale and waxy, bruising easily. The cardiovascular system also may be affected, in which case heart failure or hypertension develops. The second, or the diuretic, phase begins as kidney function returns with the production of large volumes of dilute urine, the water that accumulated in the body during the disease.

Treatment takes place in the hospital and is aimed both at the renal failure and at the underlying cause. It also decreases the symptoms considerably. For instance, a restriction of potassium intake prevents abnormal heart rhythms and paralysis of the muscles. During the oliguric phase, physicians try to keep the fluids, salts, and nitrogen in the patient's body in normal balance. Fluids equal to the fluids lost from diarrhea, vomiting, sweating, and urination will be given. The diet will have little or no protein, since protein contains nitrogen compounds that can be excreted only by the kidney. Carbohydrates (fructose or glucose) will be given by mouth or intravenously. The patient will be examined daily for infection, which

Disorders of the Urinary System

is treated immediately with an appropriate antibiotic. If this course of therapy is not successful and the uremia progresses, then dialysis must be used until the uremia subsides.

Dialysis, which is done on an artificial kidney, is a blood-filtering process. Needles are placed in an arm artery and vein, and through them small amounts of blood are withdrawn, put into the machine, and placed back into the body. As the blood moves through the machine, toxic products are removed just as they would be removed by the normal kidney. It can take up to six hours for all the blood to pass through the machine. When used for chronic kidney failure, dialysis can be done as outpatient service at a hospital or at home. When done at home, dialysis usually requires the help of a relative or a friend, but highly trained aides are not necessary. It is truly a marvel of modern technology that in recent years this process has become so mobile and readily available. A person can be kept in good health for years while being dialysized once or twice a week.

When the diuretic phase begins, it is a sign that the kidneys are returning to normal functioning. During this phase, water and salt are replaced so that dehydration does not occur. Protein is still restricted, and examinations for infections are maintained. Complete return to normal kidney function may take many weeks.

Acute kidney failure had a high mortality in the past, but today it usually can be cured. Chronic renal failure results when the kidney has been progressively damaged by chronic nephritis. Chronic nephritis is an inflammation of the kidney that can be produced by drugs, infections, radiation, ingestion of heavy metals, hypertension, or diabetes, and when the kidney is unable to excrete the toxic products as fast as they are formed in the body. This buildup of toxic products produces the symptoms of uremia. At this stage, it is often impossible to determine the underlying cause of the damage because of similarity of symptoms. The urine is always dilute and copious. Chronic kidney failure may also cause hypertension, heart failure, impaired vision, and anemia. Blood transfusions are given for severe anemia, and drugs are given to prevent vomiting or for sedation.

Kidney transplantation is another technique that can be used to treat chronic kidney failure, and with good matching between donor and recipient, there is now less chance of rejection. It is a procedure, however, that is mostly reserved for healthy young adults.

OTHER CONDITIONS

(14-9) *Bladder cancer.* The first sign of bladder cancer is painless, bloody urine. The color of the urine can be smoky, rust, or deep red. In

After Middle Age

some cases this condition may go away only to return much later. Other causes of bloody urine include infections, bladder stones, and benign (not cancerous) tumors. There are several tests that can be used to determine the cause. One of them, cystoscopy, is a simple examination in which a slender tube is inserted through the urethra. The tube functions very much like a periscope on a submarine, enabling the urologist to examine the inside of the bladder visually and, if necessary, to remove a small piece for microscopic examination (biopsy) (17-9).

The most common form of bladder cancer, papillary cancer, usually occurs on the inside surface of the bladder and can be removed easily by surgery. Because it tends to recur, however, the urologist will want to examine the bladder with the cystoscope about every three months for several years after the surgery. If the cancer has invaded the wall of the bladder, part or all of that organ must be removed. Many surgeons recommend treatment with high-energy x-rays for one to four weeks before bladder removal. During surgery, depending upon the amount of bladder tissue removed, the surgeon may route the ureters from the kidneys to a portion of the small intestine, which, in turn, will empty into a plastic pouch (ileostomy) placed on the abdomen.

(14-10) *The nonfunctioning (atonic, neurogenic) bladder* is one that has lost its neural control. Under normal circumstances, nerves from the spinal cord make muscles in the bladder contract to expel urine. There are many neurological disorders that can produce a nonfunctioning bladder, but the most common is an injury to the spinal cord. The injury can come from a penetration wound, such as the one Governor George Wallace received when he was shot, or an automobile accident like the one suffered by baseball star Roy Campanella. The result is the same: the patient is not able to empty the bladder.

There is considerable discussion among urologists about the proper care of this problem. Right now, there is no "best cure." Many urologists employ intermittent catheterization initially; others recommend a continuous catheter. With either method, persons who are able to recover enough to become catheter-free will do so in approximately three months, although occasionally a longer period is required. After three months, bladder training is usually started. Depending upon the location of the spinal cord injury, a person can learn to use a reflex to empty the bladder. A reflex action is an automatic response to a stimulus—like a knee jerk produced by a doctor hitting the tendon at the knee cap with a hammer. Some people who cannot empty their bladders regularly because of a spinal cord injury can learn to do so by touching or stroking an area of skin on their lower abdomen or upper thigh. Thus, these people can control this reflex voluntarily.

Disorders of the Urinary System

For men who are habitually incontinent, there is a special condom appliance that can be attached to the penis. Urine passes from it into tubing that is connected to a bottle or bag. In women with this problem, a catheter must be inserted into the urethra. When there are repeated infections, a diversonary surgical procedure will be performed so that the bladder empties either into a bag placed on the abdominal wall or into the intestine, allowing the urine to pass through the anus.

Urinary catheters can be a great help to persons who, for any reason, cannot pass urine. For problems requiring long-term care, the catheter can be either inserted and removed as needed or left constantly draining. The most important precaution is to ensure that the catheter is inserted into the bladder without also introducing bacteria. The physician or nurse must carefully clean the area. Occasionally, in the treatment of females for whom infections are common, the physician will insert the catheter just above the pubic bone rather than through the urethra. This decreases the chance of infection. Insertion is made while the patient is under local anesthesia. With time, patients can learn to manage their own catheters.

15

Disorders of Sex and the Genitals

(15-1) *Sexual feelings after middle age are normal.* Most men and women in good mental and physical health have sexual interests and capabilities well into their sixties and seventies. Unfortunately, in our society, we have a stereotyped image of sexuality limited to those with youthful beauty. The altered skin and muscle tone, as well as restricted motion that accompanies age, may make sex seem unappealing or cause one to feel no longer sexually attractive. The normal bodily changes that occur with age require adjustments, but usually these changes come gradually and are accepted without difficulty. It is important to keep in mind that despite the physical changes that do occur, sexual feelings remain and are natural. While the passion and urgency of young love may have lessened, the tenderness and understanding of mature love is usually increased.

THE CLIMACTERIC

(15-2) During middle age both men and women go through a critical stage in life known as the climacteric. This is a period of biological and psychological change. The climacteric may last months or even years; it may be virtually painless or extremely traumatic. Dealing with this period of life successfully is related to many factors: physical, social, psychological, and financial.

The most striking characteristics of the climacteric are psychological. The first is a vague feeling of sadness and discontent; it is a sorrow for youth that is gone forever. The second is a feeling of anxiety, worry, and

Disorders of Sex and the Genitals

futility; the future now seems less bright than the past. This combination of sorrow and pessimism may lead to depression and sudden outbursts of anger. It is a period of mourning the loss of one's former self. The anger and sadness often seem irrational and are triggered by trifles. It is important to remember that such expressions of these feelings are produced by the complex psychological issues described above.

During the climacteric, sexual interest may increase, decrease, or both, sometimes in a demanding and confusing manner. A woman at this time may use sex to prove she is still desirable and capable of gaining security through a man's love. A man who associates sexuality and potency with success and power may begin to place an exaggerated importance on sex, particularly if he feels threatened in his business and professional life.

If the woman's rise in sexual interest is not matched by her husband's, marital discord is likely. The husband may be experiencing problems that often occur during the climacteric—declining physical strength, fatigue from overwork, or anxiety about his job and future financial security. If he lacks the energy to engage in frequent sex, this does not imply that he loves his wife less or finds her less sexually appealing. But a woman who already feels insecure because of her own diminished perception of herself—whether because her children have grown up and no longer "need" her or simply because she is afraid of getting old in a youth-oriented society—may interpret her husband's lack of response as a rejection of her and a confirmation of her own feelings.

If a woman is worried or depressed, she may become overly concerned about the physical symptoms she is experiencing. She may have heart palpitations (the feeling of rapid beating in the chest), general weakness, and either increased or decreased appetite. She may develop strong fears—of cancer, of becoming a widow and being left alone, and so forth. A vicious cycle can then be set up that makes the entire household miserable. If this occurs, help from a physician should be sought in order to sort out physical symptoms and put her anxieties in perspective.

The male climacteric is usually less dramatic than that of the female. Generally, men reach their biological sexual peak before females and decline beginning in their twenties. The erect penis becomes slightly less firm with age, and the length of time it takes to produce an erection can vary from a few seconds to many minutes. Irregularity of this nature is normal. The refractory period between ejaculations also increases with age, so that while it once might have taken ten to fifteen minutes to have two ejaculations, it could now take hours. Also, with aging, other physical changes can be expected; for instance, the beard becomes thinner, and the voice becomes higher.

With decline in potency a man may feel the need to look for partners

After Middle Age

outside his marriage to "prove himself." This may work initially, but if the decline in potency stems from physical causes, eventually new partners will not help. He may also look for new partners because the pattern at home has become predictable and has lost its romance. The seeking of new sexual partners by a man in his forties or fifties usually does not mean that the man loves his wife less, although understandably she might interpret his behavior in that way.

When middle-aged or older married people have affairs, it is usually with someone they have known for some time. The man and woman give each other attention and affection without demands. The affair serves both partners as an escape from tensions of home and work and rarely ends in their seeking a divorce.

An excellent chapter, "Sex after Sixty-Five," can be found in William H. Masters and Virginia E. Johnson's *Human Sexual Inadequacy*, Little Brown and Co., 1970. In this chapter, Masters and Johnson recommend the use of estrogen; however, physicians are no longer recommending the liberal use of estrogen in women (15-6).

MENOPAUSE

(15-3) Menopause is the part of the female climacteric that involves the cessation of the menstrual periods and estrogen production. It usually occurs between ages 40 and 50. Age and heredity play a role in determining when menopause occurs (usually a mother and her daughter will go through menopause at the same age). Sometimes the onset is abrupt, particularly if it is caused by surgery, but most often it is gradual, occurring over several months or even years. Most women experience menopause without much difficulty, but for some it is a painful and disturbing time. As the ovaries stop producing estrogen, resulting in hormone imbalances, a woman may become restless, aggressive, anxious, and depressed. The body fat is redistributed, sinking from the breasts into hips, abdomen, and legs. Keeping off unwanted weight may require a special effort. Paradoxically, some women who have trouble putting on weight may have even more difficulty after menopause. The skin begins to dry and wrinkle. The sensation of heat or flushes (hot flashes) can come on suddenly; blood vessels dilate, the face and upper part of the body become red and warm. This may be accompanied by profuse perspiration (unless perspiration accompanies the flush, the flush is not usually noticeable to others). "Sweats" at night can sometimes be drenching, forcing a change of bedclothes. The voice gradually becomes deeper and, after several years, hair may grow on the face. The vagina shrinks in size, and

Disorders of Sex and the Genitals

whereas it used to become moist within thirty seconds of sexual arousal, it may now take minutes or not become lubricated at all. Thus, intercourse may well be rough and painful. Simple lubricants that dissolve in water (not petroleum jellies like Vaseline) such as K-Y jelly are helpful.

Muscle spasms lasting a minute or more may be felt in the vagina and legs. Regular sexual activity helps to overcome these symptoms. Along with some of these difficult changes, there are some advantages to becoming infertile. After menopause, concerns about pregnancy no longer exist. The complete cessation of ovulation and consequent loss of the ability to reproduce may take several months to a year. Therefore, the woman should continue her usual form of contraception for a year after menstruation stops. The mood swings, pain, and fluid gain that may have been part of the menstrual cycle do not exist any longer.

(15-4) *Sex after a hysterectomy.* After a partial hysterectomy (removal of the uterus), it is generally advisable to wait about one month before having sexual intercourse. This gives the surgical wound a chance to heal. While the ability to have sex does not decrease, there is, of course, no longer any chance of becoming pregnant. If in addition to removing the uterus the ovaries are also removed (radical hysterectomy), the vagina will be less well lubricated, and a woman may need to insert a jelly (such as K-Y) before intercourse (15-3). If a woman who has not already gone through menopause has a radical hysterectomy, she will have all the symptoms of menopause (surgical menopause).

(15-5) *Menopausal symptoms requiring medical attention.* The following problems should be brought to your physician's attention: any abnormal vaginal discharge, particularly if it is foul-smelling; spotting between menstrual periods; periods that are excessively long or too frequent; and a feeling of unusual irritation in the genitals. Frequent and regular examinations (every six months) will help the physician to know what is normal and to be aware of any changes that require attention. If any of the above symptoms occurs between examinations, it should be brought to the physician's attention immediately.

(15-6) *The use of postmenopausal estrogen.* A short time ago, the female hormone, estrogen, was prescribed for menopausal women as a replacement for the estrogen they no longer produced. Physicians are more hesitant to prescribe estrogen today, believing it increases the likelihood of breast and uterine cancer. Yet estrogen is still considered useful during menopause, for it prevents flushes. It may be given for a year or so until the flushes dissipate. Estrogen is used for atrophic or "senile" vaginitis, a condition in which the vagina becomes easily irritated from intercourse. The vagina itches, there is a discharge, and bleeding may occur. Small amounts of prescribed estrogen taken orally or in a cream

After Middle Age

(such as Premarin) that is inserted into the vagina help this problem. Estrogen cream is usually used once each night for one week and then twice a week thereafter for two to three months. (Estrogen cream is absorbed into the body and can cause breast tenderness, and on rare occasions uterine bleeding.) Breaking up the itch-scratch cycle is important. Adding cornstarch to the bath water can also help, but the use of creams and soaps should be avoided. There is debate about whether estrogen taken by mouth decreases osteoporosis (loss of bone) or prevents heart attacks. In some women, estrogen taken orally causes spotting, nausea, tenderness of the breasts, and fluid retention. There is fairly strong opinion that neither estrogens nor birth-control pills should be given to a woman with a history of breast or genital cancer, thrombophlebitis (inflammation of the veins), or pulmonary embolism. Male hormones given to women will increase sexual drive, but only in dosages that cause masculinization, including the development of facial hair.

DIFFICULTIES WITH SEX

(15-7) Impotence is the inability of a man to have a complete sexual experience with a woman, even though there is usually continued desire for sexual activity. A number of things may cause impotence. A man may simply be unable to develop an erection or to maintain it in a female partner; the erection collapses inside the vagina or before orgasm. Some men ejaculate consistently either before the penis is inserted into the vagina (premature ejaculation) or very quickly afterward, so that the female has no opportunity for an orgasm. Some cannot ejaculate at all. Fatigue is a common cause of premature ejaculation. While most impotence is the result of psychological factors, medical problems such as uncontrolled diabetes, surgery of the prostate, or any prolonged illness may also be the cause. Particularly in the elderly, inactivity because of an illness or loss of a partner can make it difficult to become sexually active again. Several failures to develop an erection can make a man worry. This anxiety may make it even more difficult for sexual function to return. For the man who is occasionally impotent, a woman's handling of his penis and testicles makes it much easier to get an erection.

When a sexual partner is not available and conditions of health and privacy are suitable, self-stimulation (masturbation) will help breach the period that would otherwise be inactive. For both men and women, masturbation is likely to increase with age as the availability of partners decreases. A sexually frustrated individual may turn to excessive eating, smoking, or drinking as substitutes for sexual activity. A man may also

Disorders of Sex and the Genitals

pretend to have a variety of medical disorders (hypochondriasis) as an excuse to avoid sexual failure. This may not be deliberate, and in fact he may not even be aware of what is occurring. During this time fathers may pressure their sons to have sexual encounters. They see their sons as an extension of themselves. This may add to all-around tension.

If impotence is a problem and a physician has made an examination to exclude medical causes, psychological help should be sought. There are many psychiatrists and other experts trained to deal with sexual dysfunction. Because it is currently a fad for untrained persons to set themselves up as experts, it is particularly important to know the credentials of the professional who provides this help. It is a good idea to ask a physician in whom you have confidence for a referral.

(15-8) *Deviation of an erect penis* to one side with a painful erection is called Peyronie's disease. This condition frequently follows surgical procedures to the penis or prostate. The condition is due to scar tissues, and treatments are not promising.

(15-9) *Frigidity* is the female equivalent of impotence. Although a woman does not need to do much physiologically (no erection or ejaculation) to take part in sexual activity, if she has intercourse without sexual arousal, it is called frigidity (an unfortunately pejorative word meaning frozen and unresponsive to male sexual excitement). A woman thus can take part in intercourse without having an orgasm. Even so, the act may be satisfying in itself, either because she enjoys pleasing her partner or because she likes the intimacy involved.

It is even more true for a woman than a man that prolonged abstinence from intercourse, either from medical reasons or lack of a partner, makes it much harder to begin again. Masturbation during these times is very useful in preserving future sexual function as well as providing sexual satisfaction.

(15-10) *Alcohol and certain drugs* decrease sexual function. Tranquilizers and antidepressants may even prevent orgasm. Many of the drugs used to lower blood pressure can prevent either erection or ejaculation. Taking large quantities of morphine, Demerol, or codeine for pain may result in decreased sexual interest. Once a drug produces initial feelings of sexual inadequacy, there may be a "halo effect" (the effect may continue) that carries over to periods when the drug is not being taken.

(15-11) *There are many potential psychological causes of impotence and frigidity.* These include fatigue, probably the most common cause of impotence and frigidity after age forty-five; and anxiety, which can be related to many causes, such as concern about a job, worry about the future and becoming old, or fears of sexual incapability. For example, as a

After Middle Age

result of changing social and economic conditions, some women are becoming more demanding sexually. This new role can be upsetting to a woman's partner, particularly if he has any doubts about his sexual ability. The man may be afraid of being rejected, of being considered unattractive, or of not being able to fully live up to his partner's real or imagined expectations. Concern about the consequences of intercourse, such as an unwanted pregnancy or venereal disease, may influence the feelings of both men and women.

In sexual matters, sometimes imagination is more important than reality. Some women may actually have orgasms, but have gone through life without knowing it, always looking for something more dramatic. Once the woman learns she is actually having orgasms, she usually starts enjoying them. Anxiety about having orgasms or enjoying them actually prevents them from occurring. Other women need to be stimulated longer, but do not say so. Sex therapists, by providing an atmosphere in which women can talk about their fears and anxieties, can be very helpful. But they do not perform miracles. If an older woman has never liked sex, she probably will not change. Nevertheless, life's circumstances may alter so dramatically for some women that they will want to change, and here, too, sex therapists can help. Finally, sex may be painful. If an older woman has problems with such pain, a gynecologist can usually help.

(15-12) *Aphrodisiacs.* Since ancient times, men and women have searched for ways of enhancing their sexual interest and abilities. Aphrodisiacs are supposed to enhance sexual interest and desire. There are, however, no drugs capable of doing this. "Spanish fly," containing the drug cantharidin, is perhaps the best known aphrodisiac. When taken by mouth, it burns everything as it passes through, including the blood vessels of the penis. The penis becomes enlarged, but rather than intercourse being pleasurable, it is extremely painful; a large dose can be fatal. A small number of patients given the drug L-dopa for parkinsonism have increased sexual desire (7-25). This may be related to the general feeling of well being that comes from a decrease in the major symptoms.

(15-13) *Positions.* There are probably only three positions that are used regularly for intercourse, although many couples try a variety, particularly early in their relationship. The first two, with the male on top of the female or lying beside her, are most common but usually less satisfying than when the woman is on top of the man. The latter has the advantage of allowing the female to be more in control and is the best position for having her clitoris involved in the normal rhythm of intercourse. Spontaneity, however, is the key to successful lovemaking, and whatever manner works between two consenting adults should be pursued.

(15-14) *Sex and medical disorders.* Weight gain is common with age,

Disorders of Sex and the Genitals

making sex less enjoyable for those feeling unattractive to their partners. In addition, obesity makes it physically more difficult to have intercourse. When either partner is very heavy, intercourse can usually be performed best with the woman on top.

Arthritis can make some movements during intercourse painful. Usually, however, a position can be found that minimizes movement of the affected joints.

People who have had a heart attack should have a frank discussion with a physician as to when and how to engage in sexual intercourse. Sometimes it is advisable to wait a period of time before having any sexual activity. Abstinence should not go on indefinitely, however. The exercise is generally beneficial, but even more important is the fact that sex encourages people to take more interest in and care of themselves. Sex is also relaxing and reduces stress. An exercise program for a period of time before having sex may be recommended by the physician. Those who have angina may be advised to place a nitroglycerin tablet under the tongue just prior to intercourse. The side-by-side position places the least strain on the heart.

(15-15) *The love virus.* There are a number of diseases that are communicated through intercourse. The most common and perhaps most difficult to treat in older individuals is herpes. This virus, which affects the genital areas, is a variant of the one that produces fever blisters (9-21). Within two to seven days of contact small red bumps appear on the genitals. These rapidly develop into painful blisters. There may also be fever and pain on urination. It takes ten to fourteen days for healing to occur, but the blisters can recur at any time. There is no known treatment, except prevention—avoiding sexual contact with anyone who has sores in the genital area. Couples who do not have extramarital relations rarely have problems in this area.

THE BREASTS

(15-16) In part because a number of nationally well-known women, such as Betty Ford and Happy Rockefeller, have had breast cancer, many women have developed an almost paralyzing fear of this disease. Even without having breast cancer, these women become its victims, living in an unhealthy state of apprehension. Of course, a small amount of anxiety is helpful in motivating a woman to protect herself, but terror of breast cancer is unwarranted and destructive. The disease affects only about 7 percent of all women, and of these, 85 percent have a localized disease and survive beyond five years (the time usually used to estimate cures).

After Middle Age

Because breast cancer can be treated when caught early, it is important to monitor your breasts closely by self-examination as well as by a physician's palpation.

Occasionally, an examination of the breasts is omitted both by an internist and gynecologist, each believing the other is taking care of it. Make sure both physicians examine you during your regular visits. Don't worry about mild tenderness of the breasts just prior to menstruation; this discomfort is normal. But tenderness that persists after the menstrual period is over should be brought to the attention of your gynecologist or internist. If your physician is unable to find a cause, you might consider purchasing a bra that gives you greater support. Some women, especially those with large, heavy breasts, find that wearing a bra in bed helps.

(15-17) *How to detect breast cancer.* Although breast cancer can occur in younger women, most cancers are found in women after the age of 45, when numerous changes are taking place in the body. (The risk of cancer has not been shown to be increased by injury to the breast or by breast feeding.)

For almost forty years, treatment of breast cancer made little progress. But new methods of detection now allow early diagnosis, reducing both the breast cancer fatality rate and the trauma of its treatment. Finding the lump in the breast, the major symptom, is difficult because these lumps are rarely painful or sensitive. Careful self-examination of the breasts is therefore very important. This is a simple procedure that, if performed at least monthly (following the end of the menstrual period in premenopausal women), could well save your life.

The self-examination should begin with undressing to the waist. Stand in front of a mirror and look for changes in the shape and size of the breast, for dimpling of the skin, or pulling in of the nipples. Do this in different positions: (1) with your arms straight down at your sides, (2) while you are leaning forward, (3) with your arms behind your head, and (4) with your hands on your hips. Also look for any discharge from the nipples or scaling of the skin of the nipples. This procedure of looking should be followed by another of feeling. Lie flat on your back with a pillow under your shoulders and place one arm over your head to stretch the muscles under the breast. Then feel the breast next to the outstretched arm with the opposite hand. Reverse the procedure for the opposite breast. Keeping your hand slightly cupped, feel for lumps or any change in the texture of the breast or skin. Don't compress the breast between the thumb and fingers. This may produce the impression of a lump that is not actually there. Visualizing each breast as a clock, massage at each hourly position on the clock, moving your fingers in a spiral motion. Also examine the area between the breast and armpit as well as the armpit itself.

Disorders of Sex and the Genitals

Any unusual finding—pain, tenderness, nipple discharge, dimpling or skin changes, as well as a lump either in the breast or in the armpit area—should be reported to your physician within two to three days.

In addition to this monthly self-examination, there should also be a manual examination by your physician at least once a year. In women over 50 and those with cysts, lumps, breast thickening, nipple discharges, or a personal or family history of breast cancer, the physician is likely to make a more precise examination using modern techniques such as mammography (x-ray of the breast), thermography (a heat-sensitive device that maps areas of increased skin temperatures, which scientists have observed accompany most breast cancers), and Xerography (a mammography with a machine made by the Xerox Corporation). Both mammography and Xerography expose the patient to small amounts of radiation. The actual radiation risk is unknown, but the normal risk of breast cancer in women over 50 is such that the American Cancer Society recommends screening with palpation and low dose mammography. Mammography is worth the small risk from radiation.

(15-18) *Treating breast cancer.* Most lumps discovered in the breast are benign. Depending on what the mammograph shows, however, a biopsy (17-9) of breast tissue may be performed, usually within a few days of detecting a lump. Although the biopsy can be done with a local anesthetic in the physician's office, it usually is done under a general anesthesia in a hospital operating room. The biopsy material is sent immediately to the pathologist, who determines whether the lump is malignant. If it is not, the surgeon removes only the lesion with a minimum of adjoining breast tissue. This surgery is not disfiguring, and the hospital stay is short.

If the biopsy shows cancer of the breast, there are various types of surgery available for the cancer's removal. Physicians differ on which method is best. Most still advocate a radical mastectomy: removal of the breast with its overlying skin, along with the chest (pectoral) muscles and the lymph nodes in the armpit. This standard method has until recently been considered the safest procedure to prolong life. But many women, particularly in the child-bearing years, do not bear up well under the disfigurement and attendant psychological problems, or the work of rebuilding the muscles to regain full use of the arm.

Another choice is a modified radical mastectomy, wherein the breast and overlying skin as well as the contents (lymph nodes) of the armpit (axilla) are removed. The chest muscles are spared. There is also the simple or total mastectomy, wherein only the breast and overlying skin are removed. (The axillary lymph nodes and chest muscle are left intact.) A subcutaneous (under-the-skin) mastectomy removes the breast tissue but preserves the overlying skin, the nipple, and the muscle of the chest wall. A partial mastectomy removes the cancer and at least an inch of apparently healthy tissue on each side. The overlying skin and underlying membrane that cover the muscle are also removed. The lumpectomy, which is a simple excision of the lump, is regarded by most doctors as leaving too much risk of the disease spreading. But less-than-radical surgery is probably acceptable for the treatment of localized breast cancer.

Patient and physician must make the decision about which of the various options to choose. Many surgeons want their patients to make several decisions before the biopsy is done, involving how the surgery should proceed dependent upon different biopsy results. These early decisions eliminate the need for a second surgical procedure (if the biopsy shows cancer) and lessen the opportunity for a cancer to spread. Increasingly, however, women are asking for a two-step procedure. First they have a biopsy. The results are explained and, if necessary, the second operation is scheduled. The advantage of this is that the woman and her family are much more a part of the decision-making process and are therefore less anxious—they know what will happen each step of the way. Many surgeons feel that the increased risk from two anesthetic procedures and short delays are very small compared with the woman's feeling she has control over her body.

After breast surgery, the physician may suggest use of radiation or chemotherapy or both to prevent further spread of the disease. Also, synthetic hormones developed in the laboratory are often beneficial in treating breast cancer. Cancer recurrence is significantly reduced in premenopausal women treated with L-phenylalanine mustard (L-pam). In postmenopausal women, the rate of recurrence is less markedly reduced. L-pam is given by mouth seven days out of each month for six months. The side effects from this treatment are minimal. Early drug trials indicate that greater protection may be gained by using more than one drug; but this combined drug treatment is more toxic than L-pam. Some premenopausal women respond to removal of the ovaries and adrenals or pituitary. Administration of androgens (male hormones) or estrogens (female hormones) also can induce tumor regression. A laboratory determination (estrogen-receptor assay) of specific cell proteins may be used to predict whether the patient is likely to respond to hormone therapy.

(15-19) *Following a mastectomy* a woman needs a great deal of understanding and reassurance, particularly from her husband and children. Women who are well-adjusted and happy in their family relationships are psychologically better equipped to cope with the removal of a breast. But

Disorders of Sex and the Genitals

all women have many questions to ask, many fears to be allayed, and many myths to be dispelled. They need a period of rehabilitation to work their way through the fear of rejection by those they love. Rehabilitation therapy is offered through the Reach to Recovery program of the American Cancer Society, which helps women who have had breast surgery meet their physical, psychological, and cosmetic needs. A few days after surgery, the patient is visited in the hospital by a volunteer who has adjusted successfully to her own breast surgery. She is well-trained and willing to answer questions. She suggests exercises and offers advice on where to obtain breast prostheses and specially tailored clothing. She will also explain how to care for special problems.

If the lymph nodes in the armpit have been removed, there is frequently a tendency toward swelling of the arm called lymphedema. This usually can be controlled by keeping the arm raised—at night, on a pillow. The surgeon may fit the arm with an elastic sleeve or recommend intermittent treatment with an inflatable sleeve.

Because infections are difficult to treat in the postoperative arm, the National Cancer Institute recommends wearing a glove when using abrasive chemicals, when gardening, or when using strong soaps; using a thimble when sewing; taking special care to avoid burns, including sunburn; avoiding restrictive pressure on the affected hand and arm, including tight gloves, tight clothing, and blood pressure cuffs; having any necessary injections and vaccinations in the unaffected arm; carrying antibiotic ointment (the physician can provide a prescription) and bandages to treat injuries when they occur; and removing hangnails.

Reach to Recovery also sends reading material to husbands and children, guiding them in their understanding of what their wife and mother needs from them at this time. Counseling for them from other husbands can be provided, too. With the aid of modern prostheses and time for adjustment, the esteem a woman has for her own femininity and physical attractiveness will be largely restored.

Finally, for those who feel it is important and who are entirely free of tumor, a plastic surgeon can build a new breast using a silicone implant.

(15-20) *Other kinds of lumps.* Cysts of the breast are very common in middle-aged women. A frequent symptom is premenstrual discomfort or pain in the breast. Lumps are often found in the breast during a routine examination; there may be several in each breast. These lumps move freely within the breast and are usually tender to the touch. If you find such a lump or lumps, have your physician examine it within a few days. It may be advisable to have a mammogram (15-17) or a biopsy (17-9) if there is any possibility that the lumps might be cancerous.

After Middle Age

THE OVARIES

(15-21) The two ovaries are located at the sides of the female's lower abdomen. From puberty until menopause every month they alternate in sending an egg into the fallopian tube to await sperm and to implant in the uterus if fertilized. In addition to their egg-producing capacity, the ovaries make the hormone estrogen, which is no longer produced after menopause.

(15-22) *Cysts of the ovary* are fairly common and occur when there is failure to ovulate—that is, failure to discharge the egg into the fallopian tube. These cysts seldom occur after menopause. The cyst, or sac, fills with fluid but usually remains so small that no treatment is required. Even those that enlarge may disappear spontaneously within a few months.

Most cysts are found during routine pelvic examinations. Symptoms include pain in the lower abdomen (if pain is moderate to severe see your physician at once), painful intercourse, bleeding not associated with the menstrual period, or a lump in the lower abdomen. If you have the latter symptom, bring it to your physician's attention within a few days of discovery.

(15-23) *Noncancerous tumors* of the ovaries occur after menopause in some women. Unless they become large, they will not cause symptoms and are found only on a routine pelvic examination. To be sure that the tumor is not cancerous, a biopsy (17-9) must be performed.

(15-24) *Ovarian cancer* is usually detected by the gynecologist feeling an abnormality in the ovary during a routine pelvic examination. When a tumor is discovered in this manner, and subsequent investigation indicates it hasn't advanced beyond the site of the ovaries, the tumor is removed surgically. The surgeon will also remove the uterus, tubes, and appendix and may instill radioactive phosphorus (P^{32}) into the area vacated by the tumor. Sometimes multiple drug treatment (combination chemotherapy) is then used (17-12). If the tumor has spread beyond the ovary, the surgeon will remove as much as possible, and then an oncologist (17-4) will administer combination chemotherapy.

GROWTHS IN UTERUS AND CERVIX

(15-25) The uterus, or womb, is a small pear-shaped organ in the female pelvis that contains and nourishes the unborn child. It is divided into two parts. The broad top area is called the body or uterus. The narrow or lower portion is called the neck or cervix. Serious disorders of the uterus and particularly of the cervix can be readily prevented when women fully cooperate with their physicians for early detection.

Disorders of Sex and the Genitals

More than thirty years ago, Dr. George Papanicolaou developed an early-detection test for cancer of the uterus and cervix commonly known as the Pap test. This test should be performed as a part of a routine pelvic examination and when there is concern that a malignant disease might be present. It is a quick, simple, painless procedure that involves taking a swab of specimen cells from the vagina and examining them under a microscope to determine if any cells are abnormal. This procedure can be performed in a doctor's office, a clinic, or a hospital. Also, simple kits are available that enable women to obtain their own Pap smears, which are then sent by mail to a laboratory for examination. Although the latter method makes the test available to large numbers of women at low costs, results to date indicate they are not as accurate as smears collected by physicians. Most gynecologists recommend that all women have a Pap test annually starting from the time they first have intercourse or have reached age 25. There is now some thought that women are safe having a Pap test every two years, but I still recommend having them yearly until age 60, and then reducing the frequency to once every two years for women who have had two negative tests.

The Pap test detects not only early, curable cancer, but also may reveal cell changes that indicate cancer is about to develop. If the test reveals abnormal cells, the next step is a simple biopsy—the only sure method of diagnosing cancer (17-9). Biopsy may show that the abnormal cells are not cancerous, indicating the presence of a benign or noncancerous tumor or other abnormal condition. If left untreated, these problems could serve as a contributing cause in the development of cancer.

There are many noncancerous growths of the uterus. Fibromas, also called myomas and fibromyomas, are common growths originating in the muscular wall of the uterus. The major symptoms are excessive menstrual bleeding, bloody discharge between periods, and enlarged abdomen. These tumors can cause the retention of urine in the bladder as well as the frequent need to urinate. They are rarely painful. Fibromas usually develop before menopause and, if present, may diminish in size afterward. Since fibromas are considered by some to be precancerous, and when they are large they cause serious symptoms by their sheer bulk, the physician may recommend a hysterectomy.

Adenomyosis is a condition characterized by growths on the interior wall of the uterus that produce a variety of menstrual irregularities, including failure to menstruate, premenstrual staining, heavy bleeding, and abdominal pain. It occurs most often in women between 40 and 50. It does not lead to cancer.

(15-26) *Endometrial polyps* are fingerlike growths in the lining of the uterus. Their symptoms are recurrent postmenstrual staining. They are treated by a procedure called dilatation and curettage, or D and C, which is done under either spinal or general anesthesia. The narrow entrance to the uterus (cervix) is expanded (dilatation), and the inside scraped out (curettage). Occasionally endometrial polyps turn malignant. These are called adenocarcinomas, grow slowly and have a good prognosis when caught early.

(15-27) *Cervical polyps* are fingerlike structures that protrude from the mouth of the uterus (the cervix). They tend to bleed easily but are not painful. Because cervical polyps can become cancerous, they are frequently biopsied (17-9) in a physician's office.

(15-28) *Cancer of the uterus.* When normal cells somehow become injured, this can bring about the first changes leading to cancer. When cancer spreads to other parts of the body through the blood and lymph systems and sets up new destructive growths, the process is called metastasis. Cancer of the uterus usually begins in the cervix. If the disease is left undetected and untreated, it will develop to the point where metastasis occurs and malignant cells spread directly to the vagina, or through the lymphatic system to lymph nodes (glands) within the pelvis, or through the blood stream to distant organs such as the lungs. Cervical cancer rarely appears before the age of 20 and is most common around age 45. The first visible signs are irregular bleeding or unusual vaginal discharge. Sometimes these symptoms are warning signals for other less urgent conditions, but they should be reported promptly to your physician since the possibility of cancer is too serious a risk to ignore.

Physicians do not always detect early cervical cancer during the pelvic examination because the cervix appears normal. Fortunately, the Pap test (15-25) can detect such cancers, permitting treatment at a time when the odds of a cure are excellent.

Cancer of the body of the uterus usually develops in women during or after menopause. It develops slowly and is not painful unless well established; then a pain may be experienced that is similar to that of menstrual discomfort, indicating the uterus is trying to expel the tumor. Any irregularities in the menstrual cycle should be brought to the attention of your physician, even though irregularities are normal during menopause. Profuse bleeding during periods is another symptom of cancer. Occasionally there may be a watery or blood-stained discharge that is irritating or foul smelling. The Pap test may give a diagnosis, but even if it is negative (indicating cancer is not present), a biopsy should be taken.

Uterine cancer is treated by surgery or radiation or a combination of the two. Treatment varies for each individual. Surgery is performed to remove all cancerous tissue, and in many cases is highly successful.

If radiation therapy is necessary, the objective is to use a dose powerful

Disorders of Sex and the Genitals

enough to destroy the cancerous growth, but not so powerful as to seriously damage normal cells. Radiation can be beamed to the cancerous tissue from an outside source such as a cobalt therapy machine or a linear accelerator. Radium can also be enclosed in a capsule and inserted through the vagina directly into the cancerous growth. Drugs, particularly synthetic hormones, also are used in treating advanced uterine cancer.

(15-29) *Prolapse of the uterus* is a slipping down of the uterus into the vagina from its normal vertical position. Frequently there are no symptoms, but victims may feel a weight dragging down, a lump in the lower abdomen or vagina, loss of urine when straining (stress incontinence), pain with intercourse, and a backache that is eased by lying down. Treatment depends upon the amount of discomfort and the patient's general health. There is no danger from the prolapse. Initially, a pessary (an instrument inserted into the vagina to support the uterus) can be helpful if tolerated. Eventually, in women who are otherwise healthy, the uterus is surgically removed and the vagina left in place. This allows for continuation of intercourse. When poor health makes it inadvisable to remove the uterus, a surgical procedure is done to support the uterus. This usually makes normal intercourse impossible.

(15-30) A *hysterectomy* is an operation to remove the uterus. A total hysterectomy removes both the body of the uterus and its cervix. In a radical hysterectomy, there is additional removal of lymph nodes and ligaments near the uterus. The ovaries and fallopian tubes may also be removed. There are many reasons why the uterus may have to be removed—chronic infection, uncontrollable bleeding, fibroids, prolapse, adenomyosis (the inside grows out of control, but is not malignant), and cancer. The hysterectomy is an old and relatively safe type of surgery, with the major complication being injury to the bladder or urethra. When the hysterectomy is performed through the vagina, recovery is usually more rapid than when it is done through an incision in the lower abdominal wall. The latter also leaves a scar, but may be necessary for some conditions, particularly if the ovaries are to be removed or if cancer is suspected. Most women are able to leave the hospital within a week, gradually returning to full activity in six to eight weeks. A hysterectomy should cause no change in a postmenopausal woman's life.

THE PROSTATE

(15-31) The prostate is a walnut-sized gland in men that manufactures a lubricating fluid that is ejected during ejaculation. Because it surrounds the outlet of the bladder, any alteration in the prostate makes it difficult to

After Middle Age

pass urine. About a third of all middle-aged men will at some point have a form of prostatic difficulty.

(15-32) *Benign enlargement* (hypertrophy, hyperplasia) is very common and is what is usually meant by prostate trouble. It is simply an enlargement—not a cancer—and will not spread. It does, however, press on the urethra, making urination a little more difficult. As the bladder compensates by developing more muscle, its capacity becomes smaller—it can hold less urine. Urination thus becomes more frequent, which is particularly irritating at night. In time, the bladder muscle becomes tired and fails to empty fully. The result of this is more frequent urination. After a prolonged period, pouches called diverticulae develop in the wall of the bladder. They retain urine. Eventually, the kidneys become enlarged and filled with water (hydronephrosis). Infection may also develop.

Any significant reduction in the force of urinary stream is a warning and is not just part of growing older. Dribbling, inability to get a full stream started, and frequency of urination are all signs of prostate trouble. As this condition develops, men seek out restrooms in restaurants and at parties more often. Subsequently, there may be an enormous need to get to a bathroom quickly. Blood in the urine and a cloudy or foul-smelling urine are other warning signs.

Complete shutoff of urination can occur when out in the cold or after drinking alcohol. This is painful and must be treated by passing a catheter into the bladder to empty it. Under no circumstances should this be done by anyone but a physician.

A thorough physical examination requires the physician to feel the prostate by doing a digital examination through the rectum. With this procedure the physician can check both for benign enlargement and prostatic cancer. Rectal examinations are somewhat uncomfortable but, fortunately, brief.

(15-33) *Treatment for benign enlargement.* There is no medical treatment for benign prostatic enlargement. If it is going to happen, there is no way to prevent it. The enlargement is slow growing. Antibiotics can be used to clear up a urinary tract infection if it occurs, but eventually a decision has to be made about surgery. Usually operations for benign prostatic enlargement are elective and depend on how much inconvenience you have. For some it can wait until it threatens to alter function irreversibly. Of course, the smaller the enlargement the less danger of it becoming malignant. On the other hand, there is less risk with surgery at a younger age.

There are a number of approaches to prostate surgery, and a urologist can best determine which one will give the best results. After surgery, a catheter (plastic tube) threaded into the penis allows bladder drainage.

Disorders of Sex and the Genitals

Initially there is pain, and narcotic analgesics (7-16) are used for several days. (Patients should not hesitate to ask for them.) The catheter comes out generally within a week, and normal urination can begin, though it may take a little while to reestablish itself. As in most other operations, it is important for the patient to get out of bed and start walking. Blood is usually present in the urine for a few days after the operation, then on and off for up to six weeks. Dribbling may occur for some time, and a couple of pieces of tissue can be used to prevent wetting the clothes. Depending upon the type of operation, sexual activity is occasionally affected by prostate operations. A frequent postoperative change is retrograde ejaculation, called the "dry runs." Because the surgery removes a one-way valve, the orgasms are normal except that the sperm flows up into the bladder instead of out the penis. The man can no longer impregnate a woman, but sex is still satisfying—he is not impotent.

(15-34) *Prostatitis* is an inflammation of the prostate gland that is caused by infection. The symptoms are acute fatigue after intercourse and painful ejaculations. It is not serious but should be treated with antibiotics, local heat, rest, and a bland diet under a physician's care.

(15-35) *Primary testicular failure* occurs when the testes stop functioning earlier in a man's life than would be normally anticipated. It is a medical illness and can happen at any age. The physical symptoms that occur are at times similar to those a woman experiences during the menopause. There are no direct emotional effects, although a man may feel the loss.

(15-36) *Prostatic cancer.* Cancer of the prostate occurs when the cells grow, most often slowly, beyond their normal boundaries. Because this growth occurs close to the rectal surface, it can be easily felt during the physician's digital examination. Symptoms rarely occur before the cancer can be felt in this way; that is why the digital examination through the rectum is so important. The first symptoms may be shooting pains in the pelvis, lower back, or upper thighs, or the symptoms may be the same as for benign prostatic enlargement. These include weak flow or dribbling of urine, particularly at night; difficulty starting urination; blood in the urine; and pain and burning on urination. The diagnosis is ultimately made by a biopsy. Also, an x-ray taken after dye has been injected into a vein (intravenous pyelogram) determines how much the urinary tract is blocked. An x-ray of the bones following injection of a radioactive dye is also taken (bone scan) to determine if there is tumor in the bone (10-8).

When the cancer is localized only in the prostate, it can be removed surgically. Although a new technique often preserves potency, most operations for prostatic cancer result in the inability to have or to sustain an erection. More extensive disease is treated by removal of the prostate and

After Middle Age

the pelvic lymph nodes and by administration of estrogen, given by mouth on a daily basis. The female hormone, estrogen, reduces male sexual activity in many but not all persons.

Recent advances in radiation therapy have produced cures that are very encouraging. Very high energy x-ray therapy is itself painless; however, there are usually some side effects, including diarrhea, from radiation that hits the bowel.

HERNIAS

(15-37) *Enlargements of the scrotum* are not uncommon. They are usually produced by a hernia, although they may be due to a tumor or infection. A hernia is a protrusion of the intestine through the abdominal wall. When the intestine protrudes into the scrotum, it is an inguinal hernia. When these develop late in life, it is sometimes related to increased pressure in the abdomen pushing the intestine out. Frequent coughing or chest disease can increase abdominal pressure and produce a hernia.

Usual symptoms of a hernia are enlargement in the groin or scrotum. A scrotal enlargement should be brought to the attention of a physician when it is first noticed. Any pain in or near the scrotum needs the immediate attention of a physician.

16

The Endocrine Glands

(16-1) The body has a number of mechanisms by which it communicates among its various parts. The brain talks to itself as well as to the rest of the body through long, narrow cells called neurons. When many neurons going to and from the same place are packaged together, they are called nerves. These nerves or "wires" serve us by transmitting messages quickly. Sometimes we are aware of what these messages say, as when we command our arm and hand to open a locked door. At other times, we are totally unaware that our nerves are sending messages. For example, we usually are not conscious of a message that tells our heart to speed up or slow down. The only way we know this is happening is when we feel our heart pounding in our chest or when we take our pulse. The actual transmission of the signal is done unconsciously.

Within both the brain and the rest of the body there are glands that exert control over other parts of the body by sending their messages through the bloodstream. Called endocrine glands, they send their messages via hormones, and they respond to needs much more slowly than do the nerves. While the nerves respond within a fraction of a second, the endocrine glands may take several minutes. There is another difference. The brain can provide the nerves with messages of great specificity, enabling an individual to have the dexterity to be a violinist. The hormones usually direct their message to a single target, too, but through the bloodstream. Because they circulate, these hormones may affect many targets and, at times, provide a general effect. One generalized effect is the adrenaline response produced by excitement or fear.

THYROID

(16-2) *Thyroid,* which is Greek for "shield"—the shape of the bone under the thyroid gland—is the name of a gland in the neck, just under the Adam's apple, that produces two thyroid hormones—thyroxine (T_4) and triiodothyronine (T_3). The function of thyroid hormone is to regulate and stimulate the rate at which the body uses energy. Without this thyroid hormone, the metabolic rate is at a very low level and the body vegetates. The amount of thyroid hormone made and secreted by the thyroid gland is controlled by hormones made in the pituitary gland in the brain. Excessive (hyperthyroid) or deficient (hypothyroid) thyroid hormone makes the body work at either a rapid or slow rate. When the thyroid enlarges and presses on the neck—and is not a cancer—it is called a goiter.

(16-3) *Goiter* is due to lack of iodine, which is needed to make thyroid hormone. In an attempt to overcome the iodine insufficiency, the gland grows. The thyroid enlargement is caused by another hormone, the thyroid stimulating hormone (TSH), produced by the pituitary gland, which is located a few inches behind the bridge of the nose. The only symptoms of goiter are an enlargement in the neck and whatever results from the enlarged gland pressing on the neck. The later symptoms include wheezing and difficulty breathing and swallowing. Normally, the intake of one gram of iodized table salt (the amount in heavily salted food) each day is sufficient to prevent goiter. The usual treatment of goiter, once it has developed, is either thryoid hormone, levothroxine, or drops of iodine solution taken by mouth. If the gland size cannot be reduced by medical treatment, the gland may have to be removed surgically.

(16-4) *Hypothyroidism* can be due to a disorder of the gland itself or to abnormalities in TSH (16-3). The signs of hypothyroidism are muscle weakness and tiredness, increased sensitivity to cold (feeling cold when others are comfortable), dry skin, nervousness, constipation, and abnormal menstruation. If hypothyroidism progresses, there is swelling of the legs (edema), pain in the chest, yellowing of the skin, and slowed heart or pulse rate. Laboratory findings indicate a decrease in blood T_4 (usually under 3.5 µg/100 mL). Blood cholesterol may be high. TSH will be elevated if the disease is located in the thyroid gland and low if it is located in the pituitary gland. A physician probably will recommend two additional tests. The first of these is a radioiodine uptake test to see the results when a patient swallows radioactive iodine. Since the thyroid gland traps iodine (it needs iodine to make thyroid hormone), the amount of iodine that is taken into the thyroid in twenty-four hours is a measure of thyroid function. The second test is a thyroid scan; another radioactive substance is injected into a vein and eventually collects in the thyroid gland. In this

The Endocrine Glands

case, instead of just counting the amount of radioactivity in the gland, the presence of radioactivity allows a picture (scintigram) to be taken. This picture outlines the thyroid and pinpoints abnormal areas.

Adult hypothyroidism that originates in the thyroid gland is treated with replacement of thyroid hormone. The object is to restore the normal metabolic condition. Thyroid hormone, which comes in many different preparations, is usually taken once a day. If one day is inadvertently missed, little harm is done. This is because thyroid hormone takes a week or more to build up in the body and a week or more to disappear. Although the physician will carefully monitor the blood thyroid hormone level, how the patient feels is the best index of successful treatment. The first indication of improvement is increased frequency of urination and decreased puffiness of the skin. An increase in the pulse and appetite and loss of constipation should follow. A possible undesirable effect of one of the drug preparations, liothyronine (T_3) is an increase in angina. This should be brought to the physician's attention. (Liothyronine, however, is used only in emergencies.)

(16-5) *Hyperthyroidism (thyrotoxicosis)* is the overproduction of thyroid hormone, causing symptoms of nervousness, irritability, tiredness, loss of weight (sometimes with a large appetite), excessive sweating, trembling of the hands, unusual discomfort due to heat, feeling of one's heartbeat (palpitation) in the chest, and rapid pulse. There also may be blurred vision, the appearance of the eyes bulging from their sockets (exophthalmos) and staring. The blood T_4 or T_3 will be elevated. The uptake of radioactive iodine into the thyroid gland is increased. The TSH will probably be low. When the abnormality is spread throughout the gland, which is usual, it is called Graves' disease or diffuse toxic goiter. When the abnormality is located in one part of the thyroid gland, a rarer occurrence, it is called nodular toxic goiter or adenoma.

Treatment is directed at bringing the secretion of thyroid hormone within the normal boundaries. Surgical removal of the thyroid gland was the principal treatment for many years. Treatment with drugs, however, is now usually attempted first. Hospitalization is not usually necessary unless the symptoms are very severe. Propylthiouracil and methimazole (Tapazole) decrease thyroid hormone by preventing iodine from being converted into its hormonal form.

Propylthiouracil, average dosage 100 to 200 mg every eight hours, is taken until the symptoms abate and the blood tests return to normal. It comes in 50-mg tablets. Methimazole comes in 5- and 10-mg scored tablets and is given in 10- to 15-mg doses every eight hours until the blood tests return to normal. Both drugs are continued after thyroid function tests return to normal, but at a markedly reduced dosage. After one to two years of drug administration, the disease disappears in about half the cases, making the drugs no longer necessary. Occasional side effects of both drugs include skin rashes and a decrease in the blood elements. For the latter reason, the physician may want blood taken at frequent intervals. A common side effect is hypothyroidism, which can be alleviated by decreasing the drug dosage.

Radioactive iodine (^{131}I) is excellent treatment for hyperthyroidism. It collects in the thyroid gland in high concentrations and, because it is radioactive, destroys the surrounding tissue. The dosage is much higher than that used for diagnostic tests. A major problem is that too much iodine may produce irreversible hypothyroidism. Another problem is the dosage of radiation may be carcinogenic and thus produce subsequent thyroid cancer.

After initial drug treatment, surgery is sometimes performed. Removal of part of the thyroid gland (subtotal thyroidectomy) produces a permanent cure of hyperthyroidism. In this operation, a part of the thyroid gland is removed through a necklacelike incision. The incision is made in this manner so that the scarring is in the normal folds of the neck and can be covered with jewelry or high-collared clothes. The surgeon tries to remove just enough of the gland so that normal function is left. When too much of the gland is removed, patients may become hypothyroid, which means having to take thyroid hormones for the rest of their lives. The major risk, however, is simultaneous removal of the parathyroid glands, which are buried in the thyroid gland and control calcium metabolism. If they are removed, parathyroid hormonelike drugs (dihydrotachysterol or calciferol) will have to be taken on a daily basis.

After the hyperthyroidism is under control, the patient's large appetite may continue. Even for those who had been losing weight while they were hyperthyroid, this large appetite may subsequently produce excessive weight gain. It is therefore wise to watch caloric intake for a while after recovery.

(16-6) *Adenoma and cancer.* The thyroid gland can have benign and malignant tumors. The benign tumor, or adenoma, produces thyroid hormone and is usually treated in the same way as hyperthyroidism. The malignant tumors usually do not alter the function of thyroid hormone. Thyroid cancer tends to grow and metastasize to local tissues slowly. The first symptom is usually the awareness of a mass in the front of the neck. Treatment of thyroid cancer is to remove the gland and lymph nodes it might have spread to. The parathyroid glands also are usually removed. After surgery, thyroid hormone and parathyroid hormone-like drugs must be taken daily.

The Endocrine Glands

DIABETES MELLITUS (SUGAR DIABETES)

(16-7) Diabetes is actually a group of diseases, all of which have as principal difficulty a disordered sugar metabolism (hyperglycemia). This is due either to an insulin deficiency or an inability for the insulin that is present to function properly. To understand diabetes, it is important to know something about the physiology of sugar and insulin. Sugar is converted within the cells of the body to energy, which is in turn used for a number of functions. It is converted to heat, it makes the muscles work, and it converts the light that falls on our eyes into messages that can be sent to the brain. Insulin is necessary for sugar to get from the blood into the cells where it can be used. If there is an insulin deficiency, sugar does not get into the cells, but stays in the blood, eventually being filtered into the urine by the kidneys.

Two kinds of diabetes occur from insulin deficiency—a severe form, which begins in juveniles in whom virtually no insulin is present, and a mild to moderate form, which affects nonobese adults. In the latter, some insulin is present, but it is insufficient to fill all the body's needs. These two kinds are called insulin-dependent diabetes (type I). Another, more common form of diabetes occurs in adults who are usually overweight—enough insulin is made and is present in the blood, but the cells that need it are unable to use it. There is something in the blood or on the surface of the cells that prevents the cells from using insulin. This form of diabetes is due to a relative insulin deficiency and is sometimes called maturity-onset diabetes, or non-insulin-dependent diabetes (type II).

(16-8) *The symptoms* of diabetes are thirst accompanied by the production of a large amount of urine, blurred vision, numbness and tingling of the fingers and toes, and fatigue. Frequent infections are common, a symptom of which, in women, might be itching around the vagina. Weight loss is common in the insulin-dependent form. People are usually overweight to begin with and have a great deal of difficulty reducing. In non-insulin-dependent diabetes, there are usually no recognizable symptoms, and the diabetes is first found by laboratory tests. With the passage of time—in severe cases of insulin-dependent diabetes—there usually are a number of symptoms, of which probably none are due to lack of insulin. Their cause is unknown. These include cataracts, bleeding into the back of the eye (retina), and retinal detachment. There may be difficulty getting blood to the legs and feet, with the feet feeling cool to the touch. The toes and feet may be prone to infection. Ultimately, there may be gangrene of the toes. Neurological symptoms also develop; with loss of feeling in the toes, there is a decrease in perception of pain, temperature, and vibration.

After Middle Age

Later, difficulty emptying the bladder and, in males, impotence (15-7) may develop. Skin spots—painless, round, brownish lesions—may occur on the shins of adult diabetics.

(16-9) *Diagnosis.* In the laboratory, the urine is examined for sugar (glucose) and ketones. The latter, which smell like nail polish remover, are abnormal products of sugar metabolism and are not generally present in the urine. Also, blood may be measured for sugar content. This last test is normally performed after a night's fast. Depending upon the biochemical method of analysis and the patient's age, a value greater than 105 to 120 mg/dL (read "milligrams per deciliter") is generally considered abnormal. High values require further evaluation, and a diagnosis is usually not made until repeat fasting values are greater than 140 mg/dL.

Further evaluation will also include a glucose-tolerance test. Prior to this test, the patient should participate in normal activity, be free from acute illness such as a cold or the flu, eat 150 to 200 g of carbohydrate each day for three days, then fast overnight before the test, and in the morning drink a glucose-containing syrup. Blood will then be drawn at timed intervals in order that blood glucose and, in some cases blood insulin, can be measured. If the body cannot process the glucose rapidly, the glucose concentration will be high at one and at two hours, the intervals generally used to make the diagnosis. In normal individuals, the value increases with age; thus, what is abnormal in a 30-year-old may well be normal in a 70-year-old. The insulin level indicates what kind of diabetes the patient has.

(16-10) *Treatment of diabetes* varies according to the form of diabetes. Also, there is a great deal of controversy as to what serves as the best treatment. Yet there are some clear rules. Absolute insulin insufficiency, for instance, requires the administration of insulin. Regular, measured exercise is usually recommended for all groups of diabetics. Exercise helps to control diet and weight and to maintain vigor. If the exercise is regular and constant, the amount of insulin or drug dose can also remain more constant. During times of heavy exercise or stress of any kind, extra medication—or, frequently for the elderly, a snack to avoid becoming hypoglycemic—may be required.

(16-11) *Diet* control is the most important aspect of treating diabetes. For maturity-onset diabetes, in fact, it may be the only treatment that is necessary because the problem is due to the tissues' insensitivity to insulin rather than the lack of insulin. Thus, by reducing the amount of tissue (fat) the insulin must act on, the insulin the body does produce goes a longer way. Although it is very difficult for non-insulin-dependent diabetics to reduce weight, once the proper weight is achieved, most are able to eat a normal diet. Overall weight, or fat, is the most important factor,

The Endocrine Glands

whereas for individuals with insulin-dependent diabetes, it is usually most important to keep to a strict schedule of meals as well as a carefully planned diet. Adequate amounts of starch or carbohydrates are emphasized. Refined and simple sugar should be avoided, but bread, potatoes, and rice do not pose a problem so long as total calories are limited. Adequate proteins are recommended, too, along with reduced consumption of fats, particularly animal fat, which speeds up hardening of the arteries.

(16-12) *Drugs.* If non-insulin-dependent diabetics require medication for their diabetes, it will usually be in the form of an oral hypoglycemic drug rather than insulin. These drugs act by releasing insulin into the blood from its source in the pancreas. The only groups of oral hypoglycemic drugs in use in the United States are the sulfonylureas. Another class represented by phenformin (DBI or Mettrol) was taken off the U.S. market in 1977 because patients taking them had a higher-than-average incidence of heart attacks.

Tolbutamine (Orinase, average dosage up to 2000 mg (2 g) a day, usually taken before each meal and at bedtime) comes in 250- and 500-mg white tablets with "Upjohn 701" and "Upjohn 100" imprinted on them. Some patients may require only one or two tablets a day.

Chlorpropamide (Diabinase, average dosage 200 to 500 mg once a day) comes in 100- and 250-mg blue, D-shaped tablets labeled "393" and "394," respectively.

Acetohexamide (Dymelor, average dosage 250 to 1500 mg once a day) comes in 250-mg white and 500-mg yellow, oblong tablets labeled "Lilly U03" and "Lilly U07," respectively.

Tolazamide (Tolinase, average dosage 300 mg once a day) comes in 100-, 250-, and 500-mg white tablets labeled "Upjohn 70," "Upjohn 114," and "Upjohn 477," respectively.

One side effect of oral antidiabetic drugs is a low blood sugar level, similar to that of patients taking insulin. This hypoglycemia may last hours or even days, requiring fairly continuous feeding of glucose. This problem is most common in the elderly and in patients taking dicumarol, phenylbutazone, or sulfonamide. Any rashes that appear should be brought to a physician's attention. A very peculiar side effect sometimes occurs in individuals who take oral antidiabetic drugs after drinking alcohol. They become flushed, nauseated, short of breath, and feel their heart beating (palpitate). This may be prevented by taking a small dose (25 mg) of an antihistamine such as diphenhydramine (Benadryl) one hour before drinking alcohol. Diabetics should consult a physician about this.

(16-13) *Insulin.* When the body does not make enough insulin, it must be supplied from the outside. There are several kinds of insulin replacement:

After Middle Age

1. Regular, or crystalline, insulin is a clear solution having an effect within one-half to one hour, peaking at two to three hours, with a maximum duration of five to eight hours.

2. Protamine-zinc insulin (PZI) is a milky-looking fluid that first takes effect between six and eight hours, reaches its peak between twelve and eighteen hours, and fades after twenty-four hours. Because PZI does not fully work for twelve to eighteen hours, it is given in the morning; it may produce nighttime insulin reactions.

3. NPH insulin is a balanced mixture of regular and PZI insulin. Its onset is between two and four hours, its peak is between seven and eleven hours, and its effect diminishes after eighteen to twenty-four hours.

4. Lente insulin comes in three forms: Semilente is similar to regular, Lente is similar to NPH, and Ultralente is similar to PZI. The three forms of Lente insulin may be mixed to meet individual patient needs.

5. Globin insulin (GI) is intermediate between regular and NPH insulin.

(16-14) *The use of insulin.* For many years, insulin was administered in concentrations of 40 and 80 units per milliliter (1 mL equals 1 cc). These multiple concentrations and the odd numbers (40 and 80 units) are confusing, and so it is probable that all insulin will soon come in 100 units (U-100) concentration. This will also be true of the syringes used. The syringes are now 1 mL (0.5 mL syringes are used for small dosages). While it was not possible to mix insulin in the same syringe a few years ago, today regular, Lente, or NPH insulin can be mixed in the same syringe.

To mix insulins, first fill the syringe with an amount of air equivalent to the amount of insulin needed. Inject the air into the bottle. Turn the bottle upside down and withdraw the proper amount of insulin. Repeat with the second bottle. Give the injection immediately after loading the syringe, and do not try to mix up the insulin once it is in the syringe. Most of the insulin in this country is manufactured by Eli Lilly and Co. under the trade name Iletin, and comes from pork. Lilly is now marketing a newer, more purified form, Iletin II. There should be very few allergic-type reactions (redness, itching at site of injection or rash over all of the body) to Iletin II because pork and human insulin are very similar. Iletin II is used in the same dosages as Iletin.

The visually handicapped may be able to use the specially designed Cornwall syringe or the Inject-Aid, which permits accurate withdrawal of predetermined insulin doses. Or since insulin remains active when kept in the refrigerator in disposable syringes for up to two months, a relative or visiting nurse can preload several weeks' supply of disposable syringes. These must be kept sterile.

The Endocrine Glands

(16-15) *The site of injection* may be any part of the body where the skin is loose, such as the thigh, abdomen, upper part of the arm, or upper part of the buttocks. Insulin should be injected into the fat just beneath the skin. The needle should be 1/2 to 5/8 inches long (the shorter needle used for thin persons) and 26 or 27 gauge (27 gauge is smaller in diameter). Avoid bending the needle, particularly when withdrawing insulin from the bottle; a bent needle can break off during injection. After wiping the area with alcohol, plunge the needle straight in, perpendicular to the skin. Change the site of injection so that no area is used more than once every four weeks; this avoids scarring. Injecting insulin into areas where there has been scarring or thickening of the tissue under the skin produces uneven insulin absorption, making it difficult to tell when it will be maximally effective. Hives occurring in the area of injection during the first few weeks of insulin administration usually disappear with time, but they should be brought to the physician's attention. For convenience, most people prefer to use disposable plastic syringes rather than glass syringes, which require constant sterilization. Both needles and syringes made by different manufacturers vary in sharpness and comfort as well as ease of use. Most people use several brands before they find one they like.

(16-16) *Regulating the amount of insulin* taken is a process that varies greatly among diabetic patients as well as physicians. The amount of insulin needed depends on the state of the patient's general health, how closely the prescribed diet has been followed, and the results of urine or blood tests that are done at least every morning (in some patients, more often). Patients with increased food intake, pregnancy, decreased exercise, weight gain, and infections, and those who are taking thyroid medication or some diuretics usually require more insulin. Decreased food intake, increased exercise, and weight reduction usually call for a decreased insulin requirement.

(16-17) *Too much insulin (insulin reaction)* produces hypoglycemia, or low blood sugar, which can also result from failure to eat at proper intervals and unusual physical activity. The symptoms, particularly in older individuals, can take the form of confusion, bizarre behavior, and finally coma. In most people, there is first hunger, nausea, heart palpitation, sweating, and tremulousness. These symptoms can be relieved quickly by giving glucose in the form of table sugar, hard candy, or orange juice. Individuals who are unable to take glucose by mouth should be given glucagon (16-19). If glucagon is not available, they should be taken to a hospital immediately. In a real crisis, when no help is available, a rectal suppository containing any kind of sugar water will work.

(16-18) *Diabetic coma, or ketacidosis,* usually begins with heavy fluid intake and urine output. The urine has a fruity odor (like nail polish

After Middle Age

remover) that can also be smelled on the breath, and that remains in the urine for several days. Fatigue sets in with subsequent nausea and vomiting. The face becomes flushed, and finally there is unconsciousness. This condition occurs when there is not enough insulin, or too much food, stress, infection, or injury. Experienced diabetics can usually make the diagnosis themselves and can learn to relieve their mild symptoms. Since coma develops over a period of two to twenty-four hours, there is ample time to adjust the insulin. If the symptoms do not abate, a physician should be seen immediately. If these symptoms occur in a person who is not known to be diabetic, immediate medical attention is necessary.

(16-19) *What a diabetic should carry.* Most diabetics learn to recognize when their diabetes is not under sufficient control and to take appropriate corrective action. Diabetics should always carry some form of sugar and an identification card, bracelet, or necklace. This is an important precaution so that strangers can provide the correct treatment in an emergency. Many people wear a Medic Alert bracelet or medallion and carry a wallet identification card describing their medical problem. On the card is the Medic Alert around-the-clock emergency telephone number. The person answering the Medic Alert phone can give important medical information if a family member or private physician is not available. The address is Medic Alert, P.O. Box 1009, Turlock, California 95381-1009.

Diabetics should also carry a glucagon kit. The glucagon comes in two vials, the contents of which must be mixed by drawing the clear fluid into a sterile syringe and injecting it into the vial containing the powder. After this solution has been shaken, it is withdrawn into the syringe and injected just like insulin. Any unused insulin syringe will do the job (be sure it is unused to avoid contamination with insulin). Maximum effects can be expected in ten to fifteen minutes. After the patient is alert, glucose should be given by mouth. Glucagon is given as an emergency measure, and its effects are only temporary.

(16-20) *Foot care.* Diabetics can have great difficulty with their feet because of poor circulation and changes in the nerves serving the legs and feet. Therefore, extra foot precautions must be taken. Socks or stockings should be thick and well-fitting to prevent friction between the foot and shoe and to keep the feet warm. High-heeled, open-toed, or fad shoes should not be worn. New shoes can be worn around the house until they are broken in. It is dangerous to go barefooted because loss of feeling in the feet can cause diabetics to be unaware that they are stepping on sharp objects. The feet must be kept clean by washing daily in warm water (never hot water, which can burn diabetics without their being aware of it), and patting dry—including between the toes. It is a mistake to soak the feet. They can be kept soft with a small amount of powder, which

The Endocrine Glands

should not be allowed to cake. Alternatively, a small amount of vegetable oil can be used. The feet should be rubbed upward away from the toes toward the body to increase circulation. Garters, tight stockings, or anything that might decrease circulation should never be worn. When sitting, feet remain flat on the floor. Crossing the legs decreases circulation. Toenails should be kept the length of the toes, but not shorter, cut straight across, without trimming the corners. Minor injuries must be treated immediately—any reddening, blistering, pain, or swelling should be seen by a physician. Any corns or calluses should be cut by a podiatrist (foot doctor), who can do any minor surgery that is necessary. Because corns and calluses come from improperly fitting shoes, people whose feet begin to thicken should make sure their shoes fit properly. Individuals with diabetes may lose feeling in their toes and must check them for sores daily.

17

Cancer

(17-1) *What is cancer?* The basic building blocks of the human body are microscopic clumps of cells that join together to form skin, heart, bones, liver, and other organs. In many parts of the body the cells reproduce themselves at regular intervals by cell division (a cell forms its exact likeness, then splits into two separate cells). In young people, cell division makes growth possible, while in mature individuals it is simply part of a process of regular replacement of worn-out tissue. When this normal process controlling cell division is lost (exactly how this happens is one of the mysteries of cancer), one of two things may occur: (1) masses of cells grow in a single location and produce an enlargement, a benign tumor that can be removed by a surgeon and will never return or (2) masses of cells can grow and then invade adjacent organs and spread to other parts of the body. These cells are abnormal, out of control, and form a malignant tumor, or cancer, requiring highly specialized treatment.

Among the malignant tumors, distinction is made between carcinomas that originate in the active part or covering tissues of an organ and sarcomas that originate in supportive (bone), connective (muscle), and fatty tissues. Lymphomas are malignancies of the lymphatic system; leukemias are malignancies of the white blood cells.

(17-2) *Preventing cancer.* While the causes of most cancers are unknown, people can do a lot to protect themselves. Several statistics emphasize this point. Cancer in Utah among Mormons causes about 103 deaths per 100,000 people, while in the population-at-large in Massachusetts it causes 201 per 100,000. Similarly, Seventh Day Adventists have a comparatively low incidence of cancer deaths. Members of these two religious groups drink little if any alcohol, are careful about their diets,

Cancer

and do not smoke. There is little doubt that personal habits play an important role in cancer prevention, and given the current state of knowledge about cancer, exercising care in your nutrition (3-1), drinking alcohol only in moderation, and abstaining from smoking (11-26) are the most important things you can do.

(17-3) *What to look for.* The seven signs of possible cancer (slightly altered from those publicized by the American Cancer Society) are as follows:

1. Any unusual bleeding or discharge from a sore or opening into or out of the body—these include the nose, ear, mouth, nipple, penis, urethra, vagina, and rectum.

2. A lump or thickening in or beneath the skin on the breast or elsewhere.

3. A change in a wart or a mole, including changes in color, enlargement, itching, or bleeding.

4. A sore that does not heal.

5. A change in bladder or bowel habits.

6. Hoarseness or cough.

7. Indigestion or difficulty in swallowing.

If 1 through 3 occur at all, or if 4 through 7 last more than two weeks, the symptoms should immediately be brought to the attention of a physician. Early recognition and treatment of cancer greatly increase the likelihood of full recovery.

DIAGNOSIS AND TREATMENT

(17-4) *Whom to go to.* If you believe you have any symptom of cancer, the first thing you should do is see your family physician. If the symptoms warrant, you will be referred to a surgeon who may remove a small part of the suspected area for examination under a microscope (biopsy). (Occasionally it is preferable to remove all of the suspected area immediately, as with most skin cancer.) If the suspected cancer can be removed surgically (like a breast cancer), the surgeon may wait in the operating room while the tissue from the biopsy site is examined. If cancer is present and it is one for which surgery is indicated, many experts recommend that it be removed at the time of biopsy. In recent years, there has been a tendency to remove the cancer in a second operation so that the patient can be more involved in making this important decision. Other tumors such as lymphomas, which are spread over a large area or

After Middle Age

are in organs that do not lend themselves to surgical removal (such as the liver), are rarely treated with surgery. Those who have cancer, whether or not it is removed surgically, should only remain in the care of a surgeon for the surgical recovery period. After surgery, there is a follow-up for possible postoperative complications, but few surgeons have the specialized training to provide the further treatment that may be needed. Patients should be placed under the care of an oncologist (a physician who specializes in the treatment of cancer with drugs) or a radiotherapist (a physician who uses x-rays for treatment). At times, both oncologist and radiotherapist will cooperate. In my experience, it is not easy to pick an oncologist. The goal is to find the kind of physician who is *at war* with the cancer and will judiciously use everything in the medical armamentarium to destroy it. Patients who are in such a physician's hands have the best chance for survival.

Unfortunately, being at war with the cancer also means being at war with the victim's body. Radiation or drug treatments make most people sick in some way. Good treatment combines minimizing the toxic effect of high doses of radiation or drugs while maximizing their chance of killing the cancer. A physician who wants to keep the patient comfortable may make the mistake of keeping toxic effects so slight that no benefit is received from the treatments. Putting up with burns or loss of hair from radiation or nausea and vomiting from drugs can eventually bring the benefits of good health to the patient. Tragically, all the misery and pain can go for nought, too.

(17-5) *Quacks and charlatans.* Quackery implies that a treatment is unproved, or worse, that no attempts are being made to prove its utility; or where attempts to prove it were tried, they failed. Increasingly, as treatments for cancers improve—and they are improving at a very rapid rate—the gap between the alleged success of someone's home-brewed vitamin extract or secret electric box and the proven success of treatments available from traditional medicine is becoming wider. In the past, there was no reason to believe that quack treatments ever cured anyone, while surgery and radiation, particularly when a cancer was found early, cured many. As we are coming to understand how to use more powerful radiation, and as our knowledge of drugs vastly increases, the cure rate of traditional medicine is continuing to improve. Quack treatments, fad diets, large doses of vitamins, and black boxes simply have not worked for most people. And with cancer it is extremely important not to go to a quack.

How do you determine quackery? Ask some of the following questions: (1) Is the "doctor" a licensed M.D. or D.O. (osteopath)? Anyone without such accreditation has no business practicing medicine. (2) Does the M.D.

or D.O. have admitting privileges in a hospital approved by the American Hospital Association? Since at some time in the treatment for cancer a patient may have to go into a hospital, having a physician with admitting privileges is an absolute necessity. (3) Is the drug or other form of treatment available only from the doctor? If so, this is cause for concern. An investigational or experimental drug may be available from a small number of physician investigators, but if it is investigational, it will not be sold. Such physicians will probably charge only for their time. There will be no mysteries about the drug or other form of treatment, however, and any drug used will be approved for research purposes by the Food and Drug Administration (FDA). (4) Is the doctor claiming to be persecuted or that the cure is being sabotaged by the medical profession? If so, be concerned. While occasionally scientists making major breakthroughs in medicine have had to fight tradition for acceptance, most breakthroughs have come from within traditional medicine. Most doctors have been happy to learn about valuable new treatments for use in their practices. They have no financial or other reason for preventing their patients from receiving such treatment, providing it will help the patient. Most experienced physicians are overworked; they don't need to keep anyone sick to be busy or to make a living. Of course, there are exceptions. If your doctor refuses or discourages consultations with other doctors, be concerned. Good physicians can learn as much as you can from a consultation.

(17-6) *Laetrile: A drug that does not work.* Laetrile, also called Bee-Seventeen and Aprikern, comes from ground apricot pits. For over twenty years it has been claimed that Laetrile is a cancer cure. Over and over again, cancer experts have found no reliable scientific evidence that Laetrile is effective. Nevertheless, a large body of laypeople and some physicians maintain that it is. For cancer specialists to consider a drug useful, they first want documented evidence that the patient receiving the drug actually had cancer; and second, they want documented evidence that the patient was cured. The proponents of Laetrile have never satisfactorily backed up their claims of success with the necessary evidence that the disorder treated by Laetrile was in fact cancer and that it did in fact show a remission.

One might ask despite the scientific failings of the Laetrile data, why don't oncologists try it experimentally on their own patients? There are a number of reasons why these cancer specialists don't use Laetrile. In the first place, animals with cancer that respond to drugs that are useful in treating human cancer do not respond to Laetrile. One could argue that humans might not always respond in the same way as animals. This may be true for some forms of cancer, but since most human and animal cancers are very similar, Laetrile's failure to help animals cannot be ignored. There is no reason why cancer specialists would drop the use of radiation, surgery, drugs, and other treatments that have proven successful, in favor of Laetrile, a drug they think is inactive. Why deprive patients of active, proven drugs?

Many people propose giving Laetrile in addition to more traditional treatments. Yet this might not be without financial and human costs. In combination with potent drugs, Laetrile could be toxic. Also, there are several hundred less well publicized drugs with no demonstrated effectiveness that could be prescribed just as well as Laetrile. Making a judgment about which of these to choose would be hopeless and pretty much determined by the advocate who screamed the loudest. Taking any drugs of unproven value can only result in distracting from a well-planned treatment program.

What about the psychological effects on patients who think they are getting an active drug with few or no side effects? Nobody wants to restrict this pleasing "placebo effect," but inevitably the inactive drug also would be given to patients who would benefit from active drugs (17-12). Precious time would be lost and lives that might otherwise be saved would be wasted. Unfortunately, to my mind, the National Cancer Institute embarked on a clinical trial of Laetrile in spite of the evidence. Laetrile was not found useful.

(17-7) *Reasons not to go to a physician at all.* The reasons people can find not to visit a physician are limitless. One can be "too busy—particularly right now!" One can have an urge to let nature take its course: "If my time is up, my time is up." "Getting transportation to the office is difficult." "I can't afford it." "Every time I go, it takes four hours to get in and out." "I usually can't get an appointment for weeks." "What do doctors know?" "If he is such a good one, why doesn't he look healthier himself?" "She may tell me I have cancer, or that I have to lose weight, or to stop smoking." "It's so embarrassing." "I hate to bother him." Some of these reasons have some legitimacy; for example, under normal circumstances it might take several weeks to get an appointment with a physician. But if you have symptoms that indicate cancer or any other serious problems, let your physician know this and get an appointment quickly. Some physicians run their offices so that there is always a long wait. If this is a consistent pattern, and if you are as put off by a long wait as I am, find a physician whose practice is more punctual.

(17-8) *What to do if told you have cancer.* First, stop everything and catch your breath. You may be very frightened. There are two areas of concern that generate this natural fear. The first is obvious and gives rise to questions like: *What will happen to me? Will I die? Will I be in pain?*

More subtle questions every bit as frightening are: *What should I do? How do I begin?*

The doctor will want to begin treatment quickly. This may involve surgery, drugs, radiation, or some combination of these. More important than speed is the proper choice of treatment. In the last ten years, enormous advances have been made and a sizable number of people have been cured. Few physicians in private practice, even those specializing in cancer, see a large number of the rarer forms of cancer. Since specific experience in treating each disorder is vital, and since better methods are constantly evolving, the best treatment is nearly always found at a large medical center specializing in cancer therapy. Frequently, going to such a center will mean a sacrifice in terms of time and perhaps increased living expenses, but the inconvenience can be worthwhile. It's important, first, to give careful thought before making any decisions, perhaps talking to people who have had similar problems, and then to get moving.

(17-9) *Diagnostic procedures.* The following procedures are designed to determine the size and extent of metastasis (spread) and the kind of tumor that may be present. Not all tests will be performed for any given tumor, and if a test such as the biopsy indicates the tumor is benign, the need for further tests is usually diminished.

In a biopsy the surgeon will remove a piece of the suspected tumor for examination under a microscope by a pathologist. If there is an enlarged lymph node in the neck, under the arm, or in some other convenient location, it will be removed. Occasionally this can be done with a local anesthetic—a procedure that can take place in a doctor's office in an hour or so. Xylocaine, the same drug dentists use for a local anesthetic, prevents discomfort. Usually, however, general anesthesia is needed, which may require that the patient stay in the hospital at least overnight.

It may also be necessary to determine if there is cancer in the bone marrow. There will be a thorough examination of the blood taken from a vein, and perhaps a bone marrow biopsy, a procedure in which a needle is put into the hip bone (after a xylocaine injection) to withdraw bone marrow. The bone marrow normally produces red blood cells, but when there is cancer present, it is much less able to do so.

The liver and spleen are evaluated by an x-ray procedure after a dye has been administered through a vein. This is called a liver scan. The dye allows the liver and spleen to be seen on an x-ray film, revealing any tumor that might be there. Blood tests are also performed to see if the liver is functioning normally. A biopsy of the liver, through the skin with a needle, may be done after anesthetizing the area with xylocaine. Alternatively, the surgeon may decide to operate and look directly at the liver and spleen with the patient under general anesthesia. The spleen may be taken

After Middle Age

out at the same time, because removal of the spleen makes treatment of some tumors easier. The spleen, which is located just below the ribs in the left side of the back, normally destroys old platelets in the blood. Platelets are made continuously and prevent bleeding. Since many cancer treatments themselves destroy platelets, removing the spleen helps keep up the platelets level during treatment.

X-rays of the chest and abdomen are taken before and after a dye has been placed into the abdomen and chest. This lymphangiogram allows the radiologist to look at the lymph nodes that might be filled with tumor. The procedure requires several hours of lying quietly on one's back, and usually does not hurt. A blue dye remains visibly present in the feet and legs for a few weeks.

Another x-ray procedure is a bone scan, which involves looking at the bone for tumor, again after injecting a dye into a vein.

An intravenous pyelogram is an x-ray examination of the kidneys after a dye has been injected into a vein. The dye concentrates in the kidneys and then is passed into the bladder.

X-rays of the chest and abdomen may be taken.

In an upper and lower gastrointestinal (GI) x-ray series using barium swallow and barium enema, the barium fills a part of the GI tract. Since x-rays cannot pass through the barium, the part is silhouetted on the film.

A local anesthetic, xylocaine, is commonly used to prevent pain in some of these procedures. Individuals differ in how quickly they respond to the anesthetic effects of xylocaine. For most people, xylocaine produces numbness within a few minutes, but there are exceptions. The physician should plan the biopsy so that it is done when the xylocaine has had its maximum effect.

THE THEORY BEHIND THE TREATMENT OF CANCER

(17-10) *Surgery.* The aim of treatment is to destroy or remove from the body all malignant cells. From the turn of the century until about 1960, the only effective treatment was for surgeons to attempt to remove the organ in which the tumor was located. If the organ could be removed without also killing the patient, and if the cancer had not spread beyond the organ (metastasized), the treatment was generally successful. Since then, even with the advances in drugs, surgery is still the most effective treatment for most localized cancers. Surgery is also used to remove parts of cancers that produce symptoms by virtue of their position—when the tumor is blocking a vital function or producing pain. What surgery cannot do is to remove cancer cells that have spread out into the body.

(17-11) *Radiation therapy.* Some forms of cancer are especially sensitive to radiation, but since radiation can be used only over limited areas of the body, it is frequently given in conjunction with either surgery or drugs or both. In special situations, however, such as localized Hodgkin's disease (a cancer of the lymph nodes), radiation may be the only treatment used. It is not known how radiation treatment kills cancer cells, but it probably disrupts the cell's reproductive capacity. It is given in moderate dosages over several weeks, which allows patients to tolerate much more radiation than they could if it were given all at one time. An important distinction to make with radiation therapy is whether it is given to cure the disease or to decrease symptoms (the latter is called palliative therapy). The cost in terms of money, time, and discomfort may be well worthwhile if a cure is hoped for, but may be less so if it is only a temporizing treatment. Patient and physician need to discuss this fully.

(17-12) *Chemotherapy.* Early attempts to treat cancer with drugs did poorly, extending the lives of patients for only a short time. The drugs also tended to be toxic. In recent years, however, drug treatment has had increasing success. Experts have gained much experience in determining which drugs to use, how much to use, and how often to give them. Most important has been the development of combination drug therapy. By giving three or four drugs at the same time, each of which has a slightly different biochemical action, a great deal of power can be gained against the cancer cell.

MANAGING TREATMENT

(17-13) Drug treatment and radiation treatment not only destroy cancer cells, they badly injure normal cells as well. Patients can expect a certain amount of discomfort from this injury. How well they cope is very much dependent upon their individual psychological state. Maintaining a positive state of mind in the presence of cancer is not easy. The rough treatment they have to undergo wears down many people. It is important to maintain normal activity as much as possible. Those who are working should try to continue. Best off are those fortunate enough to have a job with flexible hours or work that can be done, when necessary, at home. Those patients whose work involves a fairly rigid schedule, or is physically taxing, or both, may want to consider stopping work until they have recovered.

Treatment consists of ups and downs, some of which are predictable, some of which are not. Interests or hobbies should be kept up. It's also important not to let treatment interfere with regular social engagements.

After Middle Age

People who have to give up some activities should start new ones. For instance, a person who must temporarily give up tennis or golf might take up photography, or painting, or some equally interesting activity that is not physically taxing.

Psychologically, the most helpful adaptive mechanism for dealing with cancer is denial. Few people can successfully be in constant emotional contact with the full realization of a life-threatening disease as well as the disfiguring and painful treatment. Success usually means using denial—having less apparent awareness of or concern for the realities of the situation. Denial decreases the inner stress and makes it possible to cope. Too much denial, however, is also ruinous; it may mean forgetting important treatments, not taking care of oneself, or not reporting new symptoms. I have coined the term "rational-denial," meaning a healthy denial, a denial that is not so great as to preclude proper dealing with reality. Sometimes for rational-denial to work it must be shared by two or more people—a patient and a spouse, for example. The spouse takes care of everything that the patient ignores.

A particularly unpleasant coping mechanism that most people with cancer employ at one time or another is projection—blaming someone for something for which that person is not responsible. It is not uncommon for a cancer patient to blame the one who prepared the meal, saying, "It tastes awful" when in fact the food may be well prepared, but tastes bad to the patient with cancer. Usually this hostility passes within a few months, but if it becomes a constant part of a patient's life, professional help is needed.

(17-14) *Toxic effects of treatment.* The personal appearance of many people changes under treatment. Some may lose hair and weight. Radical surgery may cause a scar or even loss of function in one part of the body. The use of a prosthesis (an artificial replacement of part of the body), such as a wig, or a padded bra after breast surgery, can help one's appearance, as can plastic surgery and physical therapy. These devices need not be either hidden or advertised. The objective is to appear normal, moving easily in society, not drawing attention to oneself.

(17-15) *"Can treatment cause death?"* On rare occasions surgery, radiation, or drug treatment for cancer is fatal or produces complications that end in death. The risk is greatly reduced when the procedures are done by a thoroughly experienced physician. Such physicians tell their patients what risks are involved. Of course, with new treatments, the risks may not be thoroughly known.

(17-16) *"Does radiation cause burns?"* To some degree, yes, but with modern x-ray machines the incidence of severe skin burns is markedly reduced. The force of the radiation produced by these machines is usually so great that the beam passes right through the skin. Any skin burns that do develop should be kept dry and, when possible, exposed to air. Baby powder lessens itching. If the burn oozes fluid, a cream containing vitamins A and D is helpful. For severe burns a steroid cream may be prescribed (9-2). Hair will be lost in the area of skin burns, but it will regrow in time.

In addition to skin burns, there are also burns of the mouth, stomach, intestines, and respiratory tract. The most common problem from radiation to the mouth and throat is difficulty in swallowing. This condition is made worse by smoking or being in smoke-filled rooms, eating hot or spicy foods, and drinking alcoholic beverages. Chewing an aspirin-containing gum, using a combination of aspirin and glycerin (aspirin mucilage), or using viscous xylocaine for local anesthesia before eating may help.

Burns to the stomach produce nausea and vomiting. Patients with these problems may find relief in a dark, quiet place, away from the smells of food. Most nausea and vomiting occur in waves. When constant or severe, medications will probably be needed.

Prescription drugs such as prochlorperazine (Compazine) can be given. Prochlorperazine comes in 5-, 10-, and 25-mg yellow sugar-coated tablets labeled "SKF C 66," "SKF C 67," and "SKF C 69," respectively. It also comes in anal suppositories wrapped in colored foil.

Trimethobenzamide (Tigan) comes in 100-mg blue and white and 250-mg blue capsules labeled "Tigan 100" and "Tigan 250," respectively. It also comes in suppositories wrapped in foil. The suppositories should be kept in the refrigerator.

These drugs may make the patient sleepy and produce a strange, uncomfortable feeling in the head. If they produce these side effects, meclizine may be useful. It can be purchased without a prescription and is also useful against motion sickness. While meclizine works against radiation nausea, it works poorly against drug-induced nausea.

A number of investigators have found that the active ingredient of marijuana, delta-9-tetra-hydrocannabinol (THC), decreases nausea. Currently in most states, only those involved in an approved research study can obtain marijuana legally. It appears that in the near future many cancer patients will be able to use it with a physician's prescription. Patients who do not know how to inhale cigarettes probably will not be able to use marijuana, and many patients who have not used marijuana previously will not like the strange feelings it produces.

Diarrhea also can be produced by radiation. The diarrhea usually responds to drugs such as Kaopectate, which can be purchased without a prescription. The opiate diphenoxylate (Lomotil), which is not absorbed into the body and therefore does not produce a psychological high, may also be used, but it requires a prescription. It comes in white tablets labeled "Searle" on one side and "61" on the other. Constipation sometimes follows its use.

Patients undergoing radiation treatment will see the radiotherapist regularly, as well as the highly trained technicians who administer the treatment. Any problems that occur during treatment should be brought to their attention immediately.

(17-17) *"Will radiation to the mouth cause any teeth to fall out?"* Radiation to the mouth markedly reduces secretion of saliva, which is important because it dilutes and removes mouth acids that may etch the teeth. In addition, it cleans the teeth of plaque, which causes decay. Thus, when saliva secretions are reduced by radiation, other means must be found to accomplish the tasks it usually performs.

Proper and frequent brushing and flossing of the teeth will prevent the development of cavities. Teeth should be brushed after snacks and meals. Plaque should be removed at least once every six months by a dentist, who may also recommend applying fluoride at home. A number of mouth washes are available for this purpose, but they require a prescription. It is a good idea to use a fluoridated toothpaste.

(17-18) *"Will the treatment cause me to bleed more easily?"* Both widespread radiation and aggressive drug treatments may cause loss of blood platelets—small components of the blood that are important in preventing bleeding. Usually, careful monitoring of the platelets allows the physician to adjust treatment to prevent their number from falling so low as to cause bleeding. In some severe cases, however, platelets may be decreased to a point that will require a platelet transfusion. These usually are outpatient procedures taking only a few hours.

(17-19) *"What about infections?"* Occasionally radiation, but much more frequently drug treatment, decreases the number of white cells in the blood. These are the cells that normally fight infection. The dosages of the drugs generally can be adjusted to prevent the white cells from being suppressed to the point of infection. If this does happen, however, the patient may receive white cell transfusions.

(17-20) *"What are the chances of becoming sterile or impotent?"* Radiation that is aimed directly at a patient's testicles or ovaries will make that individual sterile. But such radiation is not at all necessary unless there is a tumor in these organs. The area can often be screened off during radiation therapy to prevent damage. For women who have gone through menopause, this is of little concern. Unfortunately, many drug treatments produce sterility. The capacity to have children, however, may return with time. During the time of radiation or drug treatment, there may be a loss of the ability to have an erection or an orgasm, but this does not last unless the individual has to go through many treatments.

(17-21) *"What about weight loss and diet?"* Weight loss with cancer is extremely common, and treatment sometimes causes even more weight loss. Some patients who were overweight to begin with take a perverse pleasure in watching themselves lose weight—perhaps for the first time in their lives—without effort. A considerable amount of the weight loss is due to the lack of desire to eat (anorexia), and for most people this is a source of concern. The physician, usually in conjunction with a dietitian, will seek to increase the patient's caloric intake. Most often, however, weight control cannot be accomplished until the cancer is controlled. At the same time, cancer responds best to treatment in well-nourished patients, so it is important to do everything possible to maintain proper weight. Those who find themselves full after eating very small quantities should then eat many small meals. It is essential to keep regular mealtimes with others as well as eating between meals and before bed. Peculiar tastes in food become the rule, with strong dislikes for once well-liked foods.

(17-22) *Discomfort and pain* are usual occurrences at some time during the course of cancer and its treatment. Each of us has his or her own pain threshold. To complicate matters further, two people who perceive discomfort at the same level may react differently. Thus, some people can tolerate pain, while others cannot. The reasons for these differences, which are sometimes considerable, are not fully understood. They are probably due to a combination of genetic makeup and social background.

Perhaps the most important component is fear of what lies ahead. Will the pain go on and on, and of even more concern, will it become worse? Patients crave answers to these questions, but as a rule, the answers are hard to come by. Close relationships with the physician and nurses, as well as with other patients who have had similar cancers and treatments, will provide some knowledge of what to expect. Some hospitals sponsor discussion groups for cancer patients, where one may learn a lot from the other patients about what to expect. For most people, the known is much easier to deal with than the unknown.

For patients who have a reasonable chance of surviving the cancer, the discomfort and pain associated with the disease and its treatment are tolerable. If discomfort is caused by treatment that has a good chance of affecting improvement, it may even be looked forward to as one of a series of necessary landmarks on the road to health. If return to a reasonably normal life is unlikely, however, pain caused by cancer becomes less tolerable. While drugs that produce analgesia can be used both in the curable and the incurable, physicians are much freer to use them in high doses in the latter case. Many of these drugs not only relieve pain but bring about a feeling of well-being or euphoria. With time many patients develop tolerance—that is, they need more of a drug or a stronger drug to get the same effect. The dose of pain killers can be made as high as necessary to make the patient comfortable. This should be discussed in some detail with the physician. Before taking any drug, even aspirin, patients being treated for cancer must clear it with the physician to make sure that it will not interfere with the treatment program.

Other techniques are also available for alleviating pain. For example, drugs can be injected into nerves to destroy or block the pain-carrying fibers from a variety of areas of the body.

(17-23) *Further cancer information* may be obtained by calling a special cancer information service available in most communities. Look up Cancer Information Services in the white pages of the telephone book.

18

What to Do in Emergencies

(18-1) Throughout this book, various emergencies have been described—how to recognize them, what to expect to find when they occur, and what to do about them. This chapter describes emergencies not covered elsewhere as well as some general principles of first aid. If you do not find what you need here, use the index in the back of the book.

When you face an emergency, often you also face your own fear, which may make you scream or even freeze. A moment of either is almost inevitable. Nevertheless, do your best to stay calm. You will have to use first aid only rarely, but when you do need it, you will want to do the right thing in the right order, so take a first-aid course and update it regularly. These courses are given by the Red Cross, many church and school groups, fire departments, rescue squads, and hospitals.

You already know more than you think you do about coping with an emergency, but if a physician, policeman, fireman, or rescue squad can be summoned quickly, or if you can transport yourself or the victim to professional help, do so. When in a serious emergency and there are two or more of you, one should always seek help by telephone or in person. If a victim is immobile and you cannot determine what is wrong, it is almost always best to let a professional move the victim. But if an object is pinning the person down and is preventing proper breathing, or if there is a threat of an object falling on a victim, move one or the other quickly! Similarly, if any victims are in a gas-filled room or exposed to fire or other immediate danger, they must be removed. Loosen ties and belts and let the person lie on a flat surface, chin up, Do not allow the victim to drink or eat.

After Middle Age

WHAT GOES IN A FIRST-AID KIT

(18-2) You should determine your first-aid needs, now, before they are needed. Clear a portion of your medicine chest or a bathroom closet for this purpose. Do not place first-aid materials in a separate place because there is a good chance that when you or someone else needs them, they will be hard to find. Medicines and the first-aid kit should be conveniently located so that you can get them without disturbing others in the house who may be asleep. This is especially important when you want to get something in the middle of the night.

A first-aid kit should include:

A bottle of aspirin

A box of activated charcoal to absorb swallowed poison

A small bottle of ipecac (to produce vomiting) and a tablespoon

A large box of assorted adhesive bandages

Sterile, separately wrapped 4-inch square gauze pads

A 1-inch wide roll of adhesive tape

Scissors for cutting adhesive tape or gauze

A box of cotton swabs

Two elastic bandages (Ace bandage)

Ampule of spirits of ammonia

A tube of petroleum jelly

A bottle of calamine lotion to stop itching

Fine tweezers with a point capable of holding onto a hair to use for removing splinters and ingrown hairs

An eye cup to wash out foreign bodies in the eyes

Sharp pocket knife

Two safety pins

Cake of mild soap such as Ivory or Dial

Box of matches

Pencil and pad

Flashlight, with long-lasting batteries

Alcohol pads in sterile containers

Two oral thermometers

Electric heating pad

Several large plastic sandwich bags with ties.

What To Do in Emergencies

The plastic sandwich bags are used to hold ice, which should be applied to an injury for the first twenty-four hours after trauma to decrease swelling. (Use two plastic bags, one inside the other, for the ice.) Following this period, mild heat should be applied with the electric heating pad to promote circulation. (The same pad can be used for mild muscle aches.)

Only oral thermometers are included in the first-aid kit because there is little reason to use rectal thermometers for adults. The thermometer is placed under the tongue with the mouth closed for three minutes. We are used to thinking of temperature in degrees Fahrenheit (F), with 98.6 representing normal for the human body. Hospital (and some home) thermometers use degrees centigrade (C), with 37 representing normal. The following table gives conversions from one system to another.

Fahrenheit	Centigrade (Celsius)
97.7	36.5
98.6 (normal)	37.0
99.5	37.5
100.4	38
101.3	38.5
102.2	39
103.1	39.5
104	40

BREATHING AND CHOKING

(18-3) *What to do when breathing has stopped—clearing an airway.* To determine whether a person has stopped breathing, listen for breathing, look for chest movements, and look for moisture by holding a mirror in front of the nose.

If the person is choking, look into the mouth and throat and remove any liquid or food with your finger. If there is a pulse (12-29), begin mouth-to-mouth respiration (12-29). Any victim who is in a gas- or smoke-filled room should be removed to fresh air and placed on his or her back. Lift the neck, pushing the forehead back. Move the chin, stretching the neck so that it points upward, toward the ceiling. Pinch the nostrils. Place your mouth firmly over the victim's mouth and blow into it until the chest rises. Remove your mouth, and let the victim exhale. Repeat once every five seconds. Stop only when the victim begins to breathe. Call a doctor or ambulance at the first opportunity.

(18-4) *What to do when choking on food.* When an individual who is

After Middle Age

eating suddenly cannot speak, has his mouth wide open, appears to be gagging, and brings his hands up to his neck as if he is trying to rip something out, it is very likely that a piece of food is lodged in the windpipe. Choking on food is a common problem, particularly among people who are somewhat debilitated. Since death occurs within several minutes if this condition is not remedied, you must act quickly. Use the Heimlich maneuver to knock the wind out of the victim and thus force the lodged food out of the windpipe. Stand behind the choking victim and place your arms around the victim's chest, clasping your hands three or four inches below the ribs. This places your arms just beneath the diaphragm and your hands act just like a knot in a rope. With a sudden, jerking motion, hug the victim forcefully—pushing the diaphragm up. This compresses the lungs and the air inside them. In turn, matter is expelled from the windpipe. If the Heimlich maneuver does not work, a sharp blow to the middle of the upper back is worth a try.

If you are alone and start to choke on food, you can dislodge the food in much the same manner. Drape your abdomen over the back of a chair or porch rail. Suddenly put your full weight on the chair back, forcing the air from your lungs and the food from your windpipe. The force should come slightly above your navel. Alternatively, but more difficult, make a fist slightly above your navel. With your other hand press in and up as vigorously as you can, repeating in a pumping fashion until the particle of food is dislodged.

BLEEDING AND WOUNDS

(18-5) When a limb or other part of the body is cut and the bleeding is severe, the heart will no longer be able to pump blood, and brain damage will result. On the other hand, small amounts of bleeding from a scratch or cut are useful because the bleeding pushes bacteria and debris out of the wound. Therefore, small cuts should be allowed to bleed a few minutes before being washed. If a wound is clean, it need simply be kept clean thereafter with the aid of some form of covering bandage.

(18-6) *Bleeding that either flows or spurts* continuously for more than a few minutes is potentially dangerous. Heavy bleeding from the body, neck, or head must be stopped by applying firm pressure over the bleeding area with the cleanest object available. Pressure must be applied firmly for at least ten minutes for a clot to form. Because most people tend to overestimate time, it's best to time yourself with a watch or clock. Resist the temptation to look to see if the blood has clotted fully before the ten minutes are up; breaks in pressure make it impossible for a clot to form.

What To Do in Emergencies

For a bleeding limb, first apply direct pressure to the bleeding area. This usually will work, but if it doesn't, apply pressure above and below the bleeding area while at the same time elevating the limb. Massive arm or leg bleeding that cannot be stemmed by applying pressure above and below can be stopped by applying pressure to the artery (pressure points) supplying the limb. But, unless you have had experience finding pressure points for arteries, you probably should use a tourniquet. Before doing so, read section (18-8) carefully. A victim with severe bleeding should be taken to an emergency room immediately.

(18-7) *Finding pressure points for a severely bleeding limb.* Properly done, this emergency procedure is preferable to using a tourniquet. Pressure points are areas where the major artery that supplies blood to the limb crosses a bone. The artery can be shut off by forcing it against the bone, thus cutting off circulation to the entire limb. Therefore, the technique should not be used unless necessary, and then only until the bleeding stops or professional help arrives.

The pressure point for the arm is found on the inside, midway between the armpit and the elbow, in a groove between the two muscles that run the length of the arm. With your thumb on the outside, grasp the middle of the victim's upper arm. The flat part of your fingers (which are on the inside) should press toward the thumb. The bone and brachial artery will be caught between.

The pressure point for the leg is just below the middle of the crease of the groin—where the leg joins the front of the body. With the victim on his or her back, keep your arm straight, lean forward, and place the heal of your hand over the pressure point. This forces the femoral artery up against the pelvic bone.

(18-8) *Use of a tourniquet.* A tourniquet should only be used as a last resort when there is severe bleeding. It will control bleeding from a limb but will also stop all circulation below its placement. If left on too long, a tourniquet will kill the area below it; on the other hand, if it is not tight enough, it will increase bleeding because the venous return is cut off while blood continues to run through the artery. Finally, releasing the tourniquet may produce shock as well as resumption of bleeding. With caution in mind, when bleeding is severe and you cannot stop bleeding in any other way, apply a tourniquet. It is far better to risk losing a part of a limb than a life.

A tourniquet can be placed just above, but not actually touching, the wound. It can be made of a wide band of cloth, a belt, a tie, or other material, but avoid narrow bands such as wire or rope. The tourniquet is wrapped twice around the limb and then tied like the first stage of a shoelace knot—under and over. Place a stick, pen, or other sturdy object on the knot, and tie it down securely with more knots. Twist the stick so that the band tightens around the limb. When the bleeding stops, tie the end of the stick to the upper part of the limb so that it will not loosen. Write down the time the tourniquet was placed on the limb. Attach the note to the victim's forehead or a visible piece of clothing. Do not cover or loosen the tourniquet; this may produce shock. Get the victim to an emergency room as fast as possible.

(18-9) *Abrasions and scratches.* Unless a person has an unusual susceptibility to infection or poor healing of wounds, the treatment of shallow cuts and other small breaks in the skin is simple. Hold the wound under cold running water, getting all the dirt out with a little mild soap. Let the wound bleed a bit, which pushes out particles and bacteria. Make sure there are no particles left in the wound. If necessary, lift them out with tweezers or a flick of a fine needle dipped in alcohol (whiskey will do). Cover the wound with a sterile bandage or gauze. Antiseptics such as alcohol are usually not needed, and the use of iodine, Mercurochrome, Bactine, or Zephiran is no longer recommended. If after a few days pus forms (yellow or whitish material), soak the wound in warm (not hot) water three or four times a day for twenty minutes each. The pus will usually work its way out. If the pus increases and redness around the wound enlarges, see a physician.

(18-10) *When to call the doctor.* If red streaking begins to run up the arm or leg from a wound, there may be an infection, and this should be seen by a physician. Slitlike wounds greater than an inch in length also should be treated by a physician. They usually require a stitch or two. The suturing should be done within twelve hours of the cut. Shorter-length wounds in areas with little tension on them should be brought together by pieces of tape that both bridge and pull the skin together; these are called butterfly bandages. Wounds that are not in areas where an eventual scar is of concern can be treated at home. Puncture wounds, those that have a small entrance but are deep, such as those resulting from a nail, should be seen by a physician within an hour or so because of the possibility of a bacterial infection and tetanus. The physician will give a tetanus booster shot to those who have not had one recently. Prior to being examined by a physician, the wound should be cleaned in the manner described above.

BURNS

(18-11) Clothing that is on fire should immediately be smothered by wrapping up and rolling on the floor in a blanket, coat, or rug. Then the burned area should be immersed quickly in cold (not ice) water. If the burn covers a sizable portion of the body, keep the victim lying down. Cut

What To Do in Emergencies

away the clothing except where it is stuck to the burn and get the victim to an emergency room. Do not clean the area or apply medication.

(18-12) *Degree of skin burns and treatment.* Skin burns are classified by their depth as well as by the amount of area they cover. Determining the degree of a burn may be very difficult, even for the expert, until some time has elapsed. Any burn larger than a postage stamp that you are not sure about should be seen by a physician, especially if it is on the face, hands, feet, or genitals.

First-degree burns, like most sunburns, are those caused by brief exposure to heat or chemicals. They are red, slightly swollen, and painful. The pain lasts forty-eight hours, and then the skin peels. There is no scarring, but there is a temporary darkening of the skin. To treat a first-degree burn, apply cold (not ice) water until the pain begins to subside. Then apply a thin layer of unsalted butter or a petroleum jelly such as Vaseline. If the burned area needs to be protected from rubbing or exposure, place a bandage or light dressing over it.

Second-degree burns produce destruction extending into the deeper layers of the skin. They are very painful—moreso even than third-degree burns because with the latter, the nerve endings are destroyed. There are patches of red and white as well as blisters. These burns are wet and within a few hours become swollen. Second-degree burns come from exposure to severe sunshine, heat, flame, and chemicals. To treat, apply large amounts of cold (not ice) water immediately—this dissipates the heat and may prevent damage to deeper skin layers. Do not break the blisters or attempt to prevent the wound from oozing. Do not apply grease, oil, or any other home remedies. Cover the burn for protection only while moving with a sterile, light piece of gauze. Remember, the burn itself has cleansed the area of bacteria. You do not want to introduce new bacteria by exposing the area to an unsterile cloth or towel.

Third-degree burns completely destroy the skin, so there is no chance for it to regenerate. These burns eventually require skin grafting. The burn is not blistered, but is white and charred. There is little pain. Initial treatment is the same as with any burn—immediately immerse the burned area in cold (not ice) water. Then get the victim to an emergency room quickly. Do not try to remove particles that are stuck to the skin or attempt any other treatment. The care of severe burns that cover large parts of the body is a difficult, rapidly developing science, and so it is important that severe burns be treated only by physicians who make burn care a specialty. Many major metropolitan areas have designated a special hospital unit as a burn center. After first aid has been administered in the local emergency room, find out if there is a burn specialist or burn center in your area.

POISONS

(18-13) *Swallowed poisons or drug overdose.* When anyone has ingested a poison or taken a drug overdose, it is most important to identify the poison and the approximate amount ingested. Try to get the container or any other remnant of the poison. This will expedite treatment and save precious time by avoiding unnecessary chemical analysis of stomach materials prior to treatment. If the person is unconscious, nothing should be done except to arrange transportation to a hospital or medical office as quickly as possible. If the victim is conscious and an antidote is recommended on the container, follow those instructions. Otherwise call the poison control center. This service is free and available in most communities. Get the number from the phone book or through the operator. If a poison control center cannot be reached, call a physician. If no help is available immediately, do the following: If the ingested substance is an acid (such as sulfuric, carbolic, phosphoric, nitric, hydrochloride, or acetic), or an alkali (such as ammonia, detergent, sodium, and potassium hydroxide or lye), or a petroleum product (such as gasoline, kerosene, toluene, benzine, or cleaning fluid) *do not* induce vomiting. Dilute and absorb the poison by giving three or four glasses of milk or a half cup of flour, starch, or dried potatoes. If nothing else is available, try water. If activated charcoal is available, give 1 tablespoon.

If the poison is not caustic or a petroleum product as described above, vomiting should be induced immediately. The victim should drink two glasses of water to facilitate vomiting, then one tablespoon of syrup of ipecac, followed by another glass of water. If vomiting is not induced, the ipecac can be taken again in thirty minutes. If ipecac is not available, try one teaspoon of mustard powder in a glass of water. This and other household materials, however, rarely are able to induce vomiting. Sometimes vomiting can be induced by putting a finger down the victim's throat.

In all cases of poisoning, a physician should be called.

(18-14) *Gas poisoning*—whether from heating, oven gas, or the exhaust of an automobile (carbon monoxide)—always produces the same symptoms. Dizziness, headache, and weakness are early signs; drowsiness, rapid breathing, blue lips, and coma are late signs. Carbon monoxide, however, can kill without warning because it is colorless and odorless. It can come from a faulty exhaust system, running a car in the garage, or running a car with the windows closed—particularly when stationary—or from a faulty oil burner in a poorly ventilated room. If you discover someone who has been exposed to this type of poisoning, first turn off the gas or otherwise eliminate the source of the problem. Then, if you are inside, open the windows—break them with your shoe if you have to—to allow fresh air into the area. Move the victim to fresh air. Keep the victim quiet, warm, lying down. Loosen the clothes, and give the victim nothing to drink. If breathing has stopped, provide artificial mouth-to-mouth respiration (18-3). If the heart has stopped, give cardiopulmonary resuscitation (12-30). Get help so that the victim can be taken to the hospital.

(18-15) *Stings from wasps, bees, yellow jackets, and hornets* hurt a bit, but for the most part are harmless. The stinger should be removed by gentle scraping rather than pulling. An ice pack applied to the afflicted area will help alleviate the pain.

For people who are sensitive or allergic, stings can be serious. A gentle tourniquet can be applied immediately above the sting area to slow absorption of the poison. The tourniquet should not be so tight as to occlude the pulse or to produce throbbing. Ideally, your index finger should fit between it and your arm. Under no circumstances should this tourniquet be left on for more than thirty minutes.

Persons who are allergic (11-7) develop large swellings at the site. They should go immediately to an emergency room since breathing may become difficult within twenty to thirty minutes. If you know you are highly allergic, you should carry a kit containing epinephrine, which can be injected to provide relief. Your physician will write a prescription for the kit, and generally the physician's nurse will show you how to use it.

(18-16) *Snakebites.* It is very unusual for hikers, gardeners, backpackers, or anyone except those who regularly handle snakes to be bitten. When bites do occur, they are commonly on the arms or legs. In the entire United States, less than twenty snakebite deaths occur during a year. The pit vipers, which include the rattlesnakes, copperheads, and water moccasins (cottonmouths), account for almost all of the deaths. Coral snakes account for one or two. Pit vipers have a facial pit midway between eye and nostril on the side of the head. They cannot strike at a distance of more than half their length, and about 20 percent of the time they do not discharge venom with a bite. The bite may be with either one or both fangs. After a bite from a pit viper, there is immediate burning and local swelling of the area. Coral snakes are banded with red, yellow, or white and black. Their venom usually takes three to four hours to work, at which time there may be slurred speech, salivation, difficulty swallowing, and numbness at the site of the bite.

If you are bitten by a snake, and you suspect the snake is poisonous, treat it as if it was poisonous. The purpose of first aid is to prevent the venom from traveling into the body. As soon as possible, a constrictive bandage (the broader the better) made from a belt, rope, or scarf should be tied gently just above the bite—that is, between the bite and the body—if the bite is on the arm or leg. It should be tight enough to make the veins bulge but not tight enough to occlude the pulse or to produce throbbing pain. The constrictive bandage should be loosened for ninety seconds every fifteen minutes. Then, immobilize the limb in a splint. Do not make the traditional cross-cut or other incisions; they heal very poorly. If possible, kill, or at least be able to identify the snake so the proper antivenom can be given. Proceed quickly to an emergency room, keeping the victim quiet until you get there.

FAINTING AND HEAT STROKE

(18-17) *Fainting.* A person who faints suddenly loses blood from the head. Vision constricts so that everything appears as if it is being seen through a tunnel. Breathing is weak; pulse is feeble but present. The face becomes pale or even white, and beads of sweat form. Fainting occurs in warm, poorly ventilated rooms and in situations that generate sudden emotions. It also can arise from hunger, loss of blood, pregnancy, and even standing up quickly. It rarely occurs while resting or during physical exercise.

Fainting results from pooling of the blood in the feet and legs, which drains it away from the head. Treatment is aimed at reversing this blood flow by gravity. A person who feels faint should sit or lie down. The head should be placed lower than the rest of the body. This is best done by having the person lie with head down and legs raised, breathing easily. Loosen belts, ties, and other tight clothing. If available, a breath of spirits of ammonia is helpful. When a faint lasts more than two to three minutes, the person should be kept warm and taken immediately to a physician.

(18-18) *Repeated fainting* may be common as people get older, especially when they rise from a bed or chair. The blood vessels that normally allow for quick postural changes no longer can do so. If you feel faint frequently, the condition should be evaluated by your physician. If it happens as you sit or stand up, move slowly. When rising from bed, sit up first, then slowly place your legs over the side of the bed and stand up slowly from this position.

A great number of drugs can produce feelings of faintness, again, particularly when a person stands up quickly. Almost any drug used to treat the heart or blood pressure (12-9), as well as tranquilizers and antidepressants (5-15), can produce fainting. The drug L-dopa used to treat parkinsonism also can produce fainting (7-25).

(18-19) *Heatstroke* is a major disturbance of the body's heat-regulating

What To Do in Emergencies

mechanism, caused by prolonged exposure to high temperatures. Contributing to heatstroke are strenuous exercise, intense sun (sunstroke), and poor ventilation. It usually occurs during a heat wave in people who are debilitated by other illnesses or who fail to drink enough fluids.

Victims usually have a headache and are weak, dizzy, irritable, and nauseated. Sweating stops; the skin is hot, dry, and flushed. Cramps occur. The pulse becomes rapid, and the temperature may rise to 105°F (40.6°C) or even 106°F (41.1°C). The person may become unconscious.

Get the person out of the heat—under shade, if outside—remove heavy clothing, pour cool water over the body, place the victim in a cold bathtub, wrap the head and body in cold, wet towels or sheets. Massage the arms and legs upward toward the heart. Check the temperature every ten minutes until it comes down to 101°F (38.3°C). Do not let it drop rapidly below that level because a sharp fall in temperature may produce shock. Ice cold water or soda will cool the inside of the body. Get the person to an emergency room. Convalescence from heatstroke may take several weeks.

If heatstroke is mild, characterized by tiredness, headache, and cold skin, place the person in the shade or a cool room. Over a period of one hour, give three glasses of cold water, each containing a half teaspoon of salt.

BROKEN BONES, BACK, AND NECK

(18-20) *Broken bones.* The signs of a broken bone are pain at the site, such as tenderness to pressure, and sometimes bleeding into the skin that produces discoloration and swelling. There is frequently a deformity and loss of normal movement, though bones can be broken with the only sign being pain. Diagnosis and treatment require a physician's attention. Even if the bone is protruding from the skin, make no attempt to clean the area. If there is severe bleeding, however, stop it (18-5) to (18-10). Do not allow the victim to stand on a broken leg. When moving the victim, allow as little motion as possible and no pressure; make a splint to keep the bones from moving. The splint can be made from boards, broomsticks, rolls of paper, or magazines. The splint should be padded with a towel to prevent skin abrasions from rough material rubbing against the skin. It should be long enough to reach the joint above and below the break. Tie the splint to either side of the limb snugly, but not so tight as to prevent circulation. Make sure you can feel the pulse below the splint. If necessary, an unbroken leg can serve as a splint for a broken one.

(18-21) *Dislocated joints.* The signs of a dislocated joint are not much different from those of a broken bone except that the dislocation always occurs at a joint. When a joint is dislocated, do not try to move or set it. Move the two bones of the dislocation as a unit, or call an ambulance to get the victim to an emergency room. Apply an ice bag to relieve the pain and swelling.

(18-22) *Broken neck or back.* If an individual who has been in an accident is conscious, has tingling or numbness around the shoulders, or cannot move fingers, toes, or feet, the neck or back may be broken. Pain in the neck or back is also a sign of a possible break. Do not move the victim and do not allow the victim to move. Movement could further stretch or tear the spinal cord. Loosen the clothing around the neck and waist, and call for professional help. Anyone, conscious or unconscious, who might have a broken neck or back should be moved only by experienced medical personnel.

At the hospital, steroids may be given to lessen swelling of the spinal cord, which can cut off circulation to the cord. Traction is used if the vertebrae (the bones of the spine) have been dislocated. Later, physical therapy is very important to keep the limbs and joints in good condition. In persons with spinal cord injury, rehabilitation is best carried out in centers specializing in such care.

STILL OTHER EMERGENCIES

(18-23) *Hiccups* are probably more difficult to stop in the aged than in younger individuals. Taking a level teaspoon of granulated sugar is an old cure, excellent though not understood. The sugar should be swallowed with as little chewing and melting in the mouth as possible, and with no water. Another teaspoon of sugar can be swallowed in a minute or two. Sleep sometimes relieves hiccups, but if they continue for more than a few hours, a physician should be called, since protracted hiccupping is very fatiguing.

(18-24) *Muscle cramps.* The most common form of cramps occurs in the calves or bottoms of the feet while sleeping. These cramps are usually caused by poor circulation to the most distant part of the body. Most people find help by wearing warm, loose-fitting socks or sleeping under an electric blanket. The way to release a cramp is to pull against it. If the cramp is in the calf or bottom of the foot, pull the foot forcefully and smoothly—not jerkily—up toward the knee until the cramp releases. Pulling in this fashion is painful but usually works.

Cramping can occur in the same muscles during walking or exercise. This is frequently due to arteriosclerosis (hardening of the arteries). If cramps occur in the calf when walking (intermittent claudication), disappear with rest, and return again with walking, there is probably decreased blood supply to the muscles of the leg. If there is also pain at rest, the degree of blockage in the artery to the muscle is greater. Occasionally, pacing can help because it forces the heart to pump harder. In general, however, walk slowly, take small short steps, avoid stairs, and make brief stops to avoid pain. Smoking is an important contributor to intermittent claudication. A number of tests can be done to determine where the artery is blocked as well as the extent of the blockage. These include arteriography—x-rays taken after injecting dye into a leg artery—and the Doppler ultrasonic blood velocity indicator, which painlessly determines blood flow. Depending on the seriousness of the problem and on other factors, the surgeon can either replace the blocked artery with a graft or ream the blockage out.

(18-25) *Emergency cold leg* is the sudden onset of a painful, cold, white paralyzed limb that has lost its circulation. The first symptoms are paleness, tingling, numbness, and loss of sensation beginning in the toes and in ten to twenty minutes working its way up the leg. This condition requires immediate medical attention.

19

Hospitals

CHOOSING A HOSPITAL

(19-1) *How to choose a hospital.* Usually which hospital you go to will depend upon where your physician has admitting privileges. Therefore, one of the factors to be considered in choosing a physician is whether he or she has privileges at a hospital acceptable to you.

If a hospital is accredited, it has at least met minimum requirements set by a national examining commission. When a hospital loses accreditation, it is usually front-page news in the local papers. If there is any question about whether or not the hospital is accredited, check with the administrator's office. If there is any choice, avoid being admitted to a hospital that is not accredited.

(19-2) *Different kinds of hospitals.* Most hospitals are not in business to make a profit but are run by a university, church, community, or other service organization. University and other hospitals heavily involved in teaching have both advantages and disadvantages. A major advantage is that the quality of medicine you finally receive is usually high since everyone is always looking over everyone else's shoulder. A disadvantage is that there are inexperienced people poking at you. These include medical students, nursing students, interns (just out of medical school), and residents (physicians taking training in a specialty). Procedures that a more experienced person might be able to do easily sometimes take longer or have to be repeated when done by less experienced people. Histories and physical examinations are repeated by physicians at each level of training. The repetition is tedious, and some of the financial cost is passed on to the patient. Occasionally, however, a medical student, intern, or resident finds something that the primary physician overlooked. Probably the tradeoff is better medical care in return for more annoyance and expense. Patients with complicated problems are often better off in a teaching hospital. For uncomplicated problems patients may be more comfortable in a small local or community hospital. It will certainly be less expensive.

Some hospitals are run for profit and because of this, these hospitals are often run very efficiently (profitably). While the first thought that comes to mind is that the efficiency and profit come from dangerously cutting corners, this usually is not the case, and in many communities the best hospitals are profit-making.

To form an idea about how a hospital functions, try to talk with former patients to gather their impressions. Even better, talk with any of the hospital's employees that you know. Do this before you need to use the hospital.

Another important source of information comes from brochures and annual reports published by the hospital. Are the department heads full-time, or is this important function performed by a physician who is also trying to run an office in some other part of the community? Check the phone book to determine if the heads of the medical and surgical departments have outside offices. Also, how many of the physicians have board certification in their specialty? That is, have they had special training, passed an examination, and been recognized by other physicians as being specialists in their field?

EMERGENCIES

(19-3) *Getting to the hospital fast.* Many communities have a special phone number to be used in an emergency. The number most often used is 911, but to be sure, find the number on the first page of the phone book. You can also call the operator (dial 0). Volunteer rescue squads, fire and police departments, and private ambulances (depending on the community) provide both rescue—including first aid—and ambulance service. Unless you ask for a specific hospital, most services will take you to the nearest emergency room.

INPATIENT CARE

(19-4) *What to take to the hospital.* In a real emergency all you need to take to the hospital is yourself. A relative or friend can bring your things later on. Short of an emergency, use the following checklist: An inexpensive electric clock that you can read in the dark; at least two pairs of simple pajamas (nightshirts are particularly handy); a bathrobe; two sets of underwear, including socks or stockings; a pair of shower clogs which can double as slippers; a toothbrush; toothpaste; shaving equipment; hair grooming equipment including shampoo; paper, pencil, and pen; and something to read. Most hospital rooms have a TV set, but if you have an inexpensive portable radio with an earphone, bring it along. You will need, also, your Blue Cross or other insurance identification and your telephone-address book. Do not take anything of value except a check to pay your way out.

(19-5) *What happens in the hospital?* In an emergency, go to the emergency room directly through the outside entrance. Many hospitals, unless the emergency is a matter of life and death, do not begin treatment until you present evidence that you can pay, so bring your Blue Cross card or other proof that you have insurance. Medicare and Medicaid cards also are useful.

If you are admitted in a normal, nonemergency way, you will go to an admission desk at an assigned time. You will be asked some simple questions. A plastic bracelet will be placed around your wrist with identifying information, and then an aide will take you to your ward. This procedure can take from fifteen minutes to two hours, depending on how busy the hospital is. After arriving at the ward, you will be shown to your bed, introduced to your roommate if you are in a double room, and asked to get into your pajamas. A nurse should come by to ask about allergies to drugs and foods.

If you are in a teaching hospital, the house interns and residents and perhaps a medical student (they will probably all look too young) will spend a good deal of time taking your history and doing their own examination. If you are slated to have surgery, the anesthesiologist will stop in to listen to your heart and lungs and ask you about any previous surgery. If you have had a difficult time in the past with anesthesia, or if anyone in your family has had anesthesia difficulty, or if a drug such as Demerol makes you nauseated, be sure to tell the anesthesiologist.

20

Nursing Homes and Outside Care

WHEN IS A NURSING HOME NECESSARY OR DESIRABLE?

(20-1) The need for nursing home care may occur suddenly at any time. For example, many victims of disabling stroke need professional care. Or, while it may not be absolutely necessary, it may be desirable when the care of an aging parent at home becomes too stressful to family life. It is time to start thinking about some kind of outside care when:

1. An individual is either socially or physically isolated and is uncomfortable or worried about it.

2. An individual has a loss of motor control serious enough to cause accidents.

3. The required medical supervision can no longer be given at home.

4. An individual is no longer able to maintain an independent lifestyle, and family and friends are not able to meet his or her needs properly.

As a rule of thumb, *nursing home care* is needed when a person requires more than eight hours of supervision a day. *Outside care* is indicated when personal grooming and dressing, meal preparation and eating, and bathroom routines can no longer be performed without help.

(20-2) *Defining the needs requiring outside care.* Before deciding what type of outside care is required, it is a good idea to define as specifically as possible the current level of the individual's function. The following are six aspects of an individual's functioning. Problems in any of these areas might suggest a need for outside care, but the type of help required depends on the degree of difficulty encountered.

After Middle Age

1. *Moving about independently.* The range of difficulty extends from needing a cane, a crutch, or a walker to being completely bedridden.

2. *Maintaining personal hygiene.* Here the problems may be relatively minor, such as being unable to reach a zipper, or buttons; or serious, such as being unable to attend to grooming, dressing, and especially to bathroom needs.

3. *Self-feeding and the need for special diets.* The problems can range from difficulty in preparing simple meals to maintaining a special diet, monitoring fluid intake, or requiring intravenous or tube feeding.

4. *Making good judgments and sound decisions.* This may be a difficult area to evaluate. Problems may be in the form of forgetfulness (failing to turn off the stove), in paying attention to details, or in very severe forms of confusion with unrealistic expectations and plans. Some elderly people may be vague as to whether it is Thursday or Friday but be well aware of the month and year; others may be so mentally disabled that they cannot recognize their own children.

5. *Showing an appropriate emotional response and adjusting to new situations.* Does the person find it difficult to meet new people in a familiar setting? Do small alterations in the daily routine cause severe upset? It's not uncommon for a person to become irritated at children for being silly or making noise. In more severe instances, there may be uncontrollable laughing or crying. Some older people can be set in their ways, and mild objections to change are to be expected, even if they may be annoying to others.

6. *Recent medical events and special therapy needs.* Has the person had a series of medical problems within the last year requiring immediate care? Have there been multiple heart attacks or strokes? Is the difficulty a gradual decline, where one can anticipate the changes that will occur? Is costly apparatus necessary, or are frequent visits to a physical therapist required?

DIFFERENT LEVELS OF OUTSIDE CARE

(20-3) *Supportive care* is designed to help the individual to live a near-normal life. The simplest level of outside care for an aging individual is provided in one of three settings: the individual's own home, the home of a family member, or in a community day-care center. Supportive care provides a variety of services designed to meet individual needs: telephone reassurance, meals-on-wheels (2-23), transportation and escort services, visiting nurses, homemaker service, and outpatient medical care.

Nursing Homes and Outside Care

Some communities have senior citizen residences. These are apartment complexes for older people who can manage independently but may need limited daily help. A resident manager supervises the building and grounds and maintains special services such as group shopping. There is often a nurse to help give medications, change dressings, and monitor treatment progress.

Retirement centers are becoming very popular. These are large complexes of houses, apartments, dining facilities, stores, clubs, and medical offices that usually are close to a hospital. Although living in a retirement center may be costly and has the disadvantage of segregating the older person from other age groups, it can provide a full range of activities and services with safety and protection.

Elderly people who own their homes might consider providing a room to a younger person in exchange for services such as mowing lawns, shoveling snow, and light maintenance. This kind of exchange may also provide a source of companionship. Sharing an apartment with another older person has its advantages. Unless the two people are on intimate terms, however, be sure that privacy can be maintained. Community centers or senior citizen organizations in the community can put people in touch with others who desire this type of arrangement.

Many communities have centers where older people may spend much of the day, engage in various activities, and meet other people with common interests. Some of these centers are sponsored by religious groups, others by local health and welfare organizations. Some nursing homes also have daily programs that nonresidents may attend for a nominal fee. Information about senior centers in the community can be obtained from the department of social services at a local hospital or Social Security office, senior citizen group, nearby church, or retirement home.

(20-4) *Intermediate-care facilities.* The next level of care is custodial supervision at a home for the aged or a nursing home. Intermediate-care facilities are used by individuals who need nursing supervision but not continuous care. They provide attractive rooms with housekeeping services and linens; well-prepared meals and assistance with eating if necessary; help with personal care and hygiene, such as bathing or washing hair; a well-designed program of activities during the day; an attentive and well-trained, though not necessarily professional, staff; and a clear plan for attending to medical emergencies. Residents are generally under the care of their own physicians. A good intermediate-care facility will have recreational and rehabilitation therapy programs. A well-run facility will attract many volunteers to help run the programs. A resident whose main difficulty is confusion, inappropriate behavior, or lack of motivation can usually be cared for adequately in an intermediate-care facility.

After Middle Age

(20-5) *A skilled-nursing facility* (convalescent or extended-care center) gives the highest level of care and should be chosen when comprehensive around-the-clock services are needed. These facilities have a full-time medical director and physicians on call at all times. They also make regular visits to familiarize themselves with the patients and their needs. These institutions are usually private (for profit), but a few may be nonprofit, operated by a religious or government agency. Skilled-nursing facilities are generally used by individuals in failing health who have had acute episodes of illness and have been hospitalized. It is often the alternative to continuous hospitalization. Residents require frequent therapeutic intervention and often special equipment.

HOW TO FIND THE KIND OF FACILITY NEEDED

(20-6) After you have determined the kind of nursing home or outside-care institution that meets your needs, it is time to begin the search for the specific place. The first thing to do is make a list of all the nursing homes in your area. The local medical society, health department, or hospital department of social services can provide names of licensed facilities. You can also ask the Social Security or nearest social welfare office. Some communities have nursing home associations. The Yellow Pages of the telephone book contain a listing under the heading "Nursing Homes." You should also ask people such as clergymen and physicians about the reputations of nursing homes with which they are familiar. It is likely that no single source will be able to provide you with information about all the available services in your community. It is a good idea to pursue several of the above routes, then to cross-check the names that appear frequently.

It's not necessary to visit every place on your list. Use the telephone to find out the following things: Does the facility provide the type of service you are looking for? Are they licensed (20-7), and by whom? Are they eligible for Medicare and Medicaid payment? If the answers to these questions are favorable, find out when it would be possible for you to visit. Plan to spend an hour or more, preferably around a mealtime. Ask if they have any informational brochures that can be sent in advance of your visit. These may answer some of your questions and also provide you with some of your own to ask. You can also see if the institution lives up to its advertising.

THINGS TO LOOK FOR DURING A NURSING HOME VISIT

(20-7) *Licenses of nursing home facilities.* Somewhere in every nursing home, generally in the office of the administrator, are the certificates of licensing. It may not be enough for someone to tell you the institution is licensed. If there is any question, ask to see the certificates yourself. Any reputable administrator will be happy to show them.

The most important license is that required by the state, and every state requires nursing homes to have a license. If a home qualifies for Medicare and Medicaid, it must also meet federal requirements. The minimal requirements for a license are far from ideal and should be viewed as just that—the minimum required of a home. All states except Arizona require a license for nursing home administrators. The Joint Commission on Accreditation of Hospitals is a nongovernment association that evaluates hospitals and nursing homes. This commission issues a certificate, which is a favorable sign, but is not an absolute assurance of top quality. Check if the facility is a member of the American Nursing Home Association or the American Association of Homes for Aging.

State health departments maintain records available to the public about whether a home promptly corrected any deficiencies cited during past inspections. Finally, a nursing home with high standards requires a physical examination of a patient before entrance.

(20-8) *Convenience.* One of the most important considerations in choosing a nursing home is location. It should be conveniently located for the resident, visitors, and the patient's regular physician. A pleasant, safe neighborhood, served by a good public transportation system, is the ideal. Is the nursing home close to shops and services that the residents can use if they are able to leave the home? Can the sidewalks and intersections be easily crossed? Is convenient parking available for visitors? Can the residents of the nursing home come and go as they see fit, and as medically indicated? Finally, are visiting hours liberal enough so families and friends can see the residents?

(20-9) *The buildings and grounds.* Nursing homes are best located in quiet, attractive surroundings. In the heart of the city, there should be ample soundproofing. The grounds should provide the opportunity for the residents to be outside in the fresh air. At the very least, there should be a patio or a garden spot for use during pleasant weather. Some excellent nursing homes even provide gardening beds for the residents to cultivate. Many nursing homes are in older buildings that were built for other purposes. In these cases, examine how well the conversion was done. Note if the heat and air conditioning can be controlled for each room; if the doors to the outside areas have screens; if the windows open for fresh air.

Begin your assessment of a nursing home immediately when you enter. Is there a lobby area with a reception desk for visitors and deliveries? Are the lobby and hallways clean, attractive, and well-lit? Are there plants and recent magazines as well as comfortable chairs for waiting? A sure sign of neglect are wilting or artificial plants and two-year-old magazines. Is there a bulletin board that posts activities, menus, and other announcements? Is the person who greets you welcoming and helpful?

Notice the hallways. Are they wide enough so that two wheelchairs can easily pass? Are ramps and stair railings provided? Are the halls clean and free of small objects that might be tripped over? Is there an unpleasant odor in the halls? It is very difficult to completely erase the odor of urine, but if it is strong or masked by strong perfume, it is a sign of poor housekeeping.

Aside from the lobby and patients' rooms, there also should be a social room with chairs, couches, and a color television set; a small library; rooms for physical therapy; and a place for quiet pursuits such as reading, letter writing, or games. A canteen where gifts and small items can be purchased is a nice plus.

Are there adequate toilet facilities and drinking fountains throughout the building? Can they accommodate wheelchairs? Are there public telephones at wheelchair height? Many good nursing homes provide special rooms for those who are critically ill. This kind of intensive-care situation gives the patient extra supervision and also serves to separate those who are very ill from other residents upon whom this might have an upsetting effect. Another helpful arrangement is a special room and bathroom for isolating a patient who develops a contagious disease. Ask to see all these areas, not just the lobby, administrator's office, and a typical room. If you are put off, be firm about wanting to see everything. Your visit will probably take at least an hour—maybe more.

(20-10) *Safety.* Of paramount importance is how safe the home is. Since many of the residents have a difficult time getting from one place to another, a fire escape plan is absolutely necessary. Beyond this, a nursing home must be made of fire-resistant materials and have fire exits clearly marked and readily available to all residents. It is preferable that room windows be of the kind that can be opened rather than those that are fixed closed, which are so common in modern buildings. You might ask to see a report of the home's last fire safety inspection.

All good nursing homes will have call buttons in each room, but they do not all work in the same way. The button should trigger a buzzer as well as a light, and the signal should be turned off only at the site of the call button. A light might not be noticed by a nurse who is occupied with something else and is not facing the light board. The call button should also be within reach of a person lying on the floor in case of a fall.

(20-11) *Personnel.* A nursing home is only as good as its personnel. A perfect physical plant with either an uncaring or an overworked staff is still a miserable place to live. The number of staff members and their

Nursing Homes and Outside Care

degree of training is very important, but so are their attitudes and personalities. The nursing home is no place for the militant, the depressed, or the angry. The staff members should be calm, cheerful, optimistic, and happy working with the elderly. They should be ready to provide the continued encouragement that residents may need. Their approach must be positive, yet realistic. Each staff person should be committed to the understanding that no matter how disabled some patients might be, they still must be recognized as unique and important individuals.

If any kind of medical care is needed, two kinds of nurses should be available on a twenty-four-hour basis. The first is the graduate, or registered, nurse (R.N.) who has the most extensive training of the nursing staff—at least two years of specialized schooling, and probably more. The licensed practical nurse (L.P.N.) has had at least one year of specialized training. An R.N. generally supervises the work of the L.P.N. The ratio of R.N.s to patients in a nursing home should be high enough to ensure that they can spend time with the patients personally and not be forever occupied with supervisory duties. There also should be nurses' aides who have participated in a training program for several weeks and whose performance is regularly evaluated.

In addition to the nursing personnel, there should be a medical director with an associate medical staff on call at all times. While it is desirable for all patients to have their own physicians, someone should be available to see a resident in an emergency.

Many nursing homes have a full- or part-time social worker on the staff. This individual should have an M.S.W. degree (Master of Social Work) and perhaps be a member of the Association of Certified Social Workers (ACSW), which indicates further training. In addition, most states require a license for social workers. A social worker can be invaluable as a liaison with community resources and can also do individual and group counseling with the residents. A social worker also is very helpful in working with family members, enlisting their cooperation in meeting the nursing home's goals for the resident. Often family members have feelings of guilt, and worry about their loved one moving into the home. The social worker can help them deal with these feelings and become more comfortable. When the resident is admitted, the social worker will talk to family members and write up a social history that will be part of the patient's medical record.

Most good nursing homes have arrangements with specialists such as dentists, podiatrists, ophthalmologists, psychiatrists, and physical therapists. Be certain to find out how these services are arranged.

Volunteers from the community can also provide many services, such as reading, help with grooming, or just visiting regularly and providing companionship and interest. Some nursing homes also arrange for barbers and beauticians to come to the home regularly. It should be the policy of every nursing home that tipping is absolutely forbidden.

(20-12) *Medical considerations.* Medical care of the residents is a vital concern in well-run homes. First, the patient's private physician should be allowed to visit as often as necessary. According to federal regulations, an attending physician must visit at least once a month. The medical director of the home should be familiar with all its residents and take an active interest in their medical well-being. A physician should always be on call for emergencies. The home ought to have arrangements with a nearby hospital for efficient emergency admissions. Naturally, the attending physician should have hospital privileges there.

A medical plan should be established for each patient, and detailed records must be kept, both for staff use and to ensure proper remuneration from insurance plans. Ask to see an example of how the records are kept. Inquire if patients who are able to participate in decisions are directly consulted about their own treatment plans. Are the closest relatives consulted? Are patients told what medications they are receiving and the reasons for them? Are they told about possible side effects and given ample opportunity to bring complaints to the attention of a physician?

(20-13) *The rooms.* Most people prefer to be in a private or a semiprivate room rather than a dormitory where many share the same facilities. A private bathroom adds dignity to one's life and is usually cleaner than a community bathroom. Each bedroom should have a direct door to the corridor and its own window, both of which can be kept either open or shut. If there is more than one bed in the room, there should be hanging curtains arranged for privacy. Each room should have a nurse call bell, (20-10) and a place for a drinking glass by the bed. Individual residents should have their own closet and chest of drawers. Reading lights of at least 100 watts by the bed and chairs as well as an overhead room light should be provided. Each room should have an easy chair, too. Daily maid service keeps the rooms neat and clean. Towels and sheets should be changed often and should be of good quality.

Residents should be permitted to decorate their own rooms with personal belongings and wear their own clothing if they desire. Private telephones should be permitted (this may be at an additional charge). Although most nursing homes do not provide a television set in each room, residents should be able to bring their own. Check to see if the rooms have an outlet for an outside antenna, which may be necessary for good reception. There should be outlets for an electric clock and a radio.

Pay special attention to the toilet facilities. Can they accommodate wheelchair patients, and is there a call button and a grasp bar near each

Nursing Homes and Outside Care

toilet? Are there nonslip floors and grasp rails in the tubs and showers? Is there a cabinet for personal hygiene supplies?

If private rooms are not available, ask about the roommate policy. Is an effort made to find a compatible room partner? Is some choice available, with an opportunity to change if it is desired?

(20-14) *Food.* There is no reason why nursing home food should not be both appealing and nutritious. Special diets must be available for those who need them. It is desirable to have snacks provided between meals and before bedtime. The menus should be planned by a licensed dietitian, and a certain amount of choice should be available. Menus, posted in advance, should avoid the monotony of chicken every Sunday, veal every Monday, and so on through the week. Fresh fruits and vegetables should be served frequently and varied according to what is available and fresh with the seasons.

Meals should be served at times close to normal: breakfast around eight, lunch at noon, and dinner at six. A nursing home that serves dinner at four-thirty is more concerned about its own schedule than that of the residents.

If the dining room is not cheerful and attractive, furnished with comfortable chairs, something is wrong. Also, ask if the residents can choose where they sit or if there is an assigned place. Are wheelchairs easily managed in the dining room? If possible, eat a meal with the residents to see if the food is well-prepared and if what is served matches the posted menu. Do the patients who need help in eating or cutting their food receive it promptly and courteously? Ask if visitors are allowed to bring food and if there are refrigeration facilities. (Medications should never be kept in the same refrigerator with food; one could possibly be mistaken for the other.)

Ask to visit the kitchen, and see if it is clean and if dishwashing and garbage-elimination facilities are adequate. Can you see food left standing about that should be refrigerated? Is equipment reasonably modern and up to date? Did the kitchen pass its last inspection by local health inspectors?

(20-15) *Activities.* The nursing home is not a resort, but it is a home where people spend twenty-four-hour days for a considerable length of time. Because of this, the home must provide planned activities for those who can and want to participate. These include movies and television, games, social hours, exercise, and craft activities. It is important that there be times the residents can meet each other so that they do not become isolated. Recreation programs should be available on weekends and in the evenings as well as on weekdays.

Each patient should have an activity schedule that is geared to his or her own interests and abilities. While severely disabled patients may not be able to participate in some of the physical activities, music and art can be a great source of pleasure.

For those who are capable of traveling outside the nursing home, activities should include visits to parks, theaters, and museums. Library facilities either at the home or as part of a community program should be available. People of all ages from the community should be encouraged to visit and volunteer. It is a good sign if there is an active residents council that meets regularly.

All good nursing homes provide the residents with an opportunity to worship in the manner they please, although whether or not one pursues religious activities should always be a matter of choice. Visits by individual clergy are often a source of comfort for residents. If the church formerly attended can include the resident in church-sponsored activities, this should be permitted and encouraged by the nursing home.

COSTS AND CONTRACTS

(20-16) *Fees and what is included.* Nursing home care is always expensive. The cost is dependent upon the location, the range of services provided, and whether or not the facility is public or private. Public facilities, as well as those owned by churches or run by nonprofit community groups, often have a sliding scale of fees geared to what a person can afford.

Most nursing homes bill in advance, either weekly or monthly. Generally, advance payments will be refunded if the resident leaves the home early, but the home's policy on this issue should be clarified before any payments are made. It also should be made clear what services are included in the basic price and what services cost extra. Examine a copy of the nursing home's contract, which should detail all of this information.

Generally speaking, routine nursing care, food preparation and service, maid and linen service, and room rent are included in the basic price of a nursing home. Social and recreational activities are usually included, too. Delivery of mail and newspapers should be part of the basic cost, as is the use of exercise facilities. If there are specific medical needs that must be met, it should be determined whether these services can be provided in the nursing home and at what cost.

Other services may be available but for an additional fee. Use of wheelchairs and walkers may or may not be included. Frequently, dental care and podiatry services are available at an extra cost. Beauty and barber shops are usually available in nursing homes, but their services also are at additional cost.

A contract also states the legal issues involved in care. Importantly, sometimes this describes circumstances that would *require* the resident to be transferred away from the nursing home.

Some facilities require giving over one's assets to the facility and in return the residents have a lifelong guarantee that they will not be required to pay extra. This can be either good or bad, depending on individual circumstances. On one hand, it deprives the heirs of anything the resident may have wanted to leave them. On the other hand, it is a good insurance policy that one will be cared for throughout one's lifetime. At the very least, the assets of the nursing home should be evaluated to be sure that it is not likely to go out of business. A lawyer is helpful in dealing with these issues.

PSYCHOLOGICAL ISSUES

(20-17) Occasionally, older people who recognize that the demands of their care are too great for the family to handle will choose to enter a nursing home. These people prefer maintaining a level of independence in a nursing home to being completely dependent on family members at home. More often, however, it is the painful task of a family member to explain to the elderly relative that the needs of the family to function normally cannot be met due to the physical or psychological care that must be extended. This event can precipitate an emotional crisis for all concerned. If the crisis is handled effectively, it can resolve many problems; if it is not, great unhappiness and bitterness may result.

The most common psychological problems that older persons experience when nursing home care becomes necessary are the fear of abandonment and rejection. For their part the other family members often must deal with feelings of guilt and anger. The guilt arises out of an unrealistic expectation of assuming complete responsibility for the patient's care and well-being, the anger comes from the unfairness of not being able to do so because the burdens are too heavy. Family members can feel some comfort in knowing that a nursing home setting is often the only logical solution to the problems caused by the patient's increased physical or mental disability. In fact, relationships among family members often improve considerably when the stresses and tensions of home care are removed.

It is best by far to deal openly and honestly with the issues of moving to a nursing home. Patients feel more positive about such a move if they are afforded the respect of being included fully in all decisions and their own preferences taken into consideration.

Nursing home residents do not cease to be important members of a family just because they are no longer living at home. They can be helped to understand that they will be visited as often as possible and will be lovingly aided by the family in their adjustment to the new setting. Some older people have great fears of moving to a nursing home because they do not know how good a modern, well-run nursing home can be. It may be possible to reassure future residents by correcting any misconceptions they may have about what life in a nursing home is like. If it can be arranged, a preadmission visit by a prospective resident to the nursing home can be very helpful.

During all discussions about the nursing home, family members should be perfectly candid. If it is realistic to hope for future recovery and return to a noninstitutional setting, this should be brought up. On the other hand, if this is to be a final home, it's best to be open about this and to allow the patients to express their personal feelings. In many situations the approach is to say that the future is uncertain and must be dealt with one week or one month at a time.

On the day of admission and during the first weeks of residence in the nursing home, it is wise for the family to visit as often as possible to help provide support and services. New residents should be allowed plenty of time to adjust and to get their own picture of the way things work. In the beginning, they should participate in nursing home activities only to the degree that they feel comfortable.

21

Paying for Physicians, Hospitals, and Nursing Homes

Methods for payments to physicians, hospitals, and nursing homes are changing so rapidly that I can offer only general guidelines of what to expect. Examples given are based on late 1984 figures. For information on specific costs and payment schedules you should contact your local social service agency or insurance agent. Generally, medical bills for hospital and nursing home stays and outpatient and medically required home care are at least partially paid for by one of a variety of insurance policies. The most common form of medical insurance for the elderly is Medicare. Medicaid, federally supported health care insurance administered at the state level, is also widely used. Some elderly individuals may use private, supplemental health insurance policies or belong to health maintenance organizations (HMOs). Because Medicare is so frequently used, I will discuss it first.

MEDICARE

(21-1) *Medicare* is a hospital and medical insurance program run by the Social Security Administration for those 65 and older and for some disabled individuals under 65. Like most programs that are large, Medicare is complicated. One needs to be patient, and more important, persistent in order to obtain proper benefits. In many communities, Social Security offices provide advisors to help people through the maze of regulations. Once you find someone who understands the system, try to return to that person each time you have a problem.

To be eligible for Medicare one must be over 65 years old. It is also available to younger people who have been receiving Social Security

After Middle Age

disability benefits for at least two years. You should apply for Medicare benefits three months before your sixty-fifth birthday.

(21-2) *Hospital services.* Medicare provides for three kinds of care: (1) Inpatient hospital care; (2) inpatient nursing home care; and (3) outpatient or home health care. The amount of service is limited by the benefit period which begins when the patient enters the hospital or other approved facility for the first time after being covered, and it lasts for 90 days in a hospital and 100 days in a nursing home. A new benefit period starts after the patient has been out of the hospital or other facility for 60 consecutive days. The number of benefit periods is unlimited. In participating hospitals, the bill goes directly to Medicare. If you are admitted to a nonparticipating hospital or a hospital outside the United States, you are going to need help—sometimes provided by the hospital, but more likely from an advisor at the Social Security Administration. You have a total of 60 "reserve" days which can be used after a benefit period has elapsed at any time during your lifetime. During this reserve period, you are responsible for the first $152 charged for each day.

(21-3) *Conditions.* A doctor must prescribe hospital care, the hospital must participate in Medicare, and the hospital's Utilization Review Committee must not disapprove the hospitalization. Medicare will pay all covered expenses, except for the first $356 in each benefit period, for up to sixty days. From the sixty-first to the ninetieth day, you must pay the first $89 per day.

Medicare pays for (1) a semiprivate room (two to four beds in a room) or its equivalent, unless you need a private room for medical reasons; (2) all meals including special diets; (3) regular but not private-duty nurses; (4) intensive-care units; (5) drugs; (6) lab tests; (7) x-rays including radiation therapy; (8) medical supplies; (9) wheelchairs and walkers; (10) operating and recovery rooms; (11) rehabilitation services such as occupational or physical therapy. Medicare does not cover costs that are not directly billed by the hospital such as those for television, radio, or telephone, or for the first three pints of blood used in a benefit period.

(21-4) *Psychiatric care.* Medicare will pay for 190 days of psychiatric hospitalization per lifetime. But those who have been in a psychiatric unit during the 150 days immediately prior to the time their Medicare coverage starts must subtract the number of hospitalized days from the total benefit.

(21-5) *Outpatient services at the hospital.* Medicare will pay for 80 percent (you pay the first $75) of reasonable outpatient charges at a participating hospital. These include services provided at an emergency room or clinic, blood transfusions, and laboratory services billed by the hospital, including x-rays and medical supplies such as casts and drugs that

Paying for Physicians, Hospitals, and Nursing Homes

cannot be self-administered. Medicare does not cover routine examinations, even though given at a hospital, nor does it pay for eye and ear examinations, for glasses or hearing aids, for immunizations (unless they are given as part of emergency care), or for routine foot care.

(21-6) *Outpatient services outside the hospital.* Medicare will pay for 80 percent (after $75 a year deductible) of speech or physical therapy costs included as part of the doctor's bill. Medicare will pay no more than $400 a year in benefits (after the $75 deductible) if a physical therapist bills you directly, and then only if the therapy is prescribed by a doctor. Medicare will pay for x-ray and diagnostic tests done at an approved independent laboratory when prescribed by a doctor, and it will pay for ambulance service if it is approved and if any other form of transportation would be dangerous to your health. But Medicare will only pay for the ambulance service to a local facility or, if necessary, to the nearest facility outside the local area.

Medicare will pay for heart pacemakers, lenses needed after a cataract operation, colostomy and ileostomy bags, artificial limbs, braces, and orthopedic shoes if they are part of the braces. It does not pay for dental plates.

Medicare will pay for oxygen equipment, wheelchairs, and dialysis equipment when prescribed by a doctor. Since Medicare will only make a monthly payment, it frequently is better to rent equipment than to buy it. Furthermore, if you no longer need a piece of equipment and have bought it, Medicare will stop payments on it.

(21-7) *Home care.* Medicare will help when approved medical care is given at home. The following is covered: part-time nursing care; physical, speech, and occupational therapy; and social service part-time home health aides. Medicare will not pay for full-time nursing care; drugs and biologicals; meals delivered to the home; and homemaker services. Medicare hospital insurance pays for home care if (1) you were in a participating hospital three days in a row; (2) the care is for the treatment of a condition treated in the hospital or nursing home; (3) care includes part-time nursing care or physical or speech therapy; (4) you are confined to home; (5) a physician sets up the plan; and (6) the agency participates in Medicare. A visit is each time a professional comes to the house. It includes services by physicians; licensed nurses; and physical, occupational, and speech therapists. The medical insurance will pay for up to 100 visits each calendar year if (1) a physician determines you need part-time nursing care or speech or physical therapy; (2) you are confined to home; or (3) the agency providing service is approved by Medicare. You must pay the first $75 per year.

(21-8) *Nursing home care.* Medicare covers part of the cost of nursing home facilities under certain circumstances. The first requirement is that the nursing home be approved to participate in the Medicare program. Second, the patient must be placed in the nursing home by a physician. A federally funded Utilization Review Committee, which is made up of at least two physicians, must agree that inpatient care is both reasonable and necessary. Another group, the Professional Standards Review Organization (PSRO), may also review the care prescribed.

Medicare does not provide coverage when the care is mainly custodial, even if care is given in a skilled nursing facility. Custodial care means meeting personal needs that could be provided by nonprofessional personnel, for example, helping an individual get in and out of bed, walk, bathe, dress, eat, and take medications by mouth.

The following four requirements must be met prior to receiving Medicare help to pay for a nursing home facility: (1) There must have been at least three days of continuous hospitalization (not counting the day of discharge) prior to transfer to the nursing home facility, or the patient must have been a resident in a home within the past fourteen days. (2) The transfer to the nursing home must be made to provide further care for the condition that was treated in the hospital. (3) The admission to a nursing home must be within thirty days of leaving the hospital. (4) A physician must certify and confirm that the patient needs (and will receive) skilled nursing or rehabilitation services on a daily basis. Skilled nursing is that which is given directly or under the supervision of a licensed nurse. Skilled rehabilitation services include physical therapy or that which is given under the supervision of a professional therapist. In addition, the Utilization Review Committee must not disapprove the stay.

Medicare pays for all covered services during the first twenty days of a patient's residence in a nursing home. During days 21 to 100 there is a deductible of $44.50 a day, which the patient must pay. There are no Medicare benefits after the hundredth day (21-2).

The following nursing home services are covered by Medicare.

1. A semiprivate room consisting of two to four beds
2. Meals, including special diets
3. Regular nursing services
4. Rehabilitation services such as physical, occupational, and speech therapy
5. Drugs furnished by the facility
6. Medical supplies such as splints and casts
7. Use of appliances such as a wheelchair or walker

The following services are among those not covered by Medicare.

Paying for Physicians, Hospitals, and Nursing Homes

1. Entertainment items such as a radio, telephone, or television in the room
2. Private duty nurses
3. Charges for a private room unless specifically for medical purposes
4. The first three pints of blood received in a benefit period

In most states, supplemental Blue Cross, usually called Blue Cross 65, covers the $44.50 deductible during days 21 to 100 (21-10).

MEDICAID

(21-9) *Medicaid* is an assistance program offered by individual states for people of relatively low income. Each patient's physician must affirm the need for skilled nursing care. Any skilled nursing facility that qualifies for Medicare will also qualify for Medicaid.

Some state programs are more generous than others. Eligibility requirements also vary from state to state. Some states limit Medicaid benefits to those persons who are dependent upon welfare funds. Others give funds to those who would be crippled financially by the increased need for medical care. Applications for Medicaid can be made through local social service or welfare offices which also have information about requirements and benefits.

When a patient has Social Security benefits, a pension, or another source of income, all of these funds must go to cover the cost of nursing home care. A person who has money in the bank may not apply to Medicare until these funds have been exhausted or have fallen below a fixed amount set by the state. The children and siblings of an adult needing nursing home care are not required to meet the costs, no matter how wealthy they may be. Also, if a spouse or parent lives with the recipient, they are not required to pay.

A patient in a nursing home who is receiving Medicaid benefits and has no other source of income is also granted a personal monthly allowance.

Medicaid can cover the complete cost of a semiprivate or private room (a private room has to be medically prescribed), including meals, nurses, recreation, rehabilitation, and other aspects of the home program.

In different states, Medicaid provides coverage for a variety of other services such as physicians' fees, drugs, and medical equipment. Under Medicaid, unlike Medicare, the patient is not required to be hospitalized before entering the nursing home. Medicaid does not include payments for patients who are mentally ill or who have tuberculosis.

There is no time limit on services as long as a patient qualifies. A

After Middle Age

Medicaid review committee meets at least annually to see if a patient requires aid. A physician, a registered nurse, and a social worker constitute the review committee.

If a patient is eligible to receive both Medicare and Medicaid, Part A of Medicare pays for the first twenty days in a skilled nursing home. After that, in most states, Medicaid will pay the deductible to those eligible. After the Medicare benefit period is over, Medicaid will pay full costs for as long as the patient qualifies. Both Medicaid and Medicare can be terminated under various circumstances: if the patient no longer requires the same level of care, if a less costly institution can meet the needs, or if the patient's finances improve. Patients who are removed from Medicare generally receive only three days' notice. A longer period of time is given for arrangements to be made by Medicaid.

This, at least, is the case as of the present time. The federal regulations for Medicaid, however, are going through a period of transition. The new federal regulations give the states greater flexibility in determining eligibility and what services will be covered. Cuts in federal funds to the states have been made, and how or to what degree the individual states will make up the difference is not clear. Your local Social Services Administration office will have information about any changes in your area.

PRIVATE INSURANCE

(21-10) *Private insurance.* Although they are expensive, private health care policies can be helpful. If you have not previously carried private insurance, many private insurance companies have specific periods during which you can apply for coverage. For example, Blue Cross allows individuals to apply from one month before an individual is 65 to one month after the individual turns 65, or in July or any year. Many companies require a physical examination before granting coverage for the first time.

If, however, you have been carrying private insurance consecutively for at least one to two years prior to turning 65, you are then eligible for what is generally called "over 65 complementary coverage." These private policies provide benefits supplementary to those paid by Medicare. For example, Medicare Part A has a $356 deductible for the first 60 days of hospital inpatient care. The supplementary Blue Cross policy pays this deductible fee. Medicare pays 80 percent of approved doctor's fees. The supplementary Blue Cross policy pays the remaining 20 percent of the Medicare approved costs. The tables in sections (21-12) and (21-13) outline the coverages of Medicare and Blue Cross.

Paying for Physicians, Hospitals, and Nursing Homes

To find out the terms of various private insurance plans, call the insurance plans in your area. Their phone numbers will be listed in the Yellow Pages under "Insurance."

HEALTH MAINTENANCE ORGANIZATION (HMO)

(21.11) *Health maintenance organizations,* or HMOs, are a relatively new alternative to conventional private health insurance. HMOs are prepaid health care plans to which an individual makes a commitment of membership on a yearly basis. For a fee, which is paid monthly and is usually slightly higher than the monthly payments to conventional private insurance companies, almost all medical expenses are covered. A few plans require a $1 to $2 fee for office visits and prescriptions to discourage overuse, but otherwise all costs are covered by the prepaid monthly membership fee.

Not every area has an HMO. To find out if there is one in your area, write for information to the Group Health Association of America, 624 Ninth Street NW, Suite 700, Washington, D.C. 20001. If there is an HMO in your area, shop wisely. (1) Find out where the HMO's health care or physicians' offices are located and what hospitals the HMO uses. Talk to HMO staff and members. (2) Find out if the HMO is federally qualified and which professional organizations the HMO has joined (such as the American Group Practice Association and the Joint Commission on Accreditation of Hospitals). (3) Find out if the HMO's membership is growing and what percentage of the members dropped out in the past year. (4) Find out how long you have to wait for routine examinations, and the medical specialists included among the staff physicians.

If you have been an HMO member before your sixty-fifth birthday, no change will occur in your membership status. If you have not been a member, there are set times of entry. The entry and health requirements for your local HMO should be obtained from their office.

After Middle Age

(21-12)   **Hospitalization and Nursing Care Costs**

Medicare Hospital Insurance		Blue Cross (over 65)
Pays	Does not pay	Usually pays*
In an approved hospital:		
Covered services for 60 days per period	First $356 in each benefit period	First $356 in each benefit period
Part of covered services from day 61 through day 90 of period	First $89 a day	First $89 a day
Part of covered service for total of 60 reserve days per life	First $152 a day	First $152 a day from day 91 through day 820
In an approved nursing home:		
Covered services for first 20 days per period		
Part of covered services from day 21 through day 100 of 100-day period	First $44.50 a day	$44.50 a day from day 21 through day 100
	Care outside U.S. except in special situations	Hospitalization outside U.S. for first 120 days; after day 120, there is a break period of 90 days

*Varies from state to state.

Paying for Physicians, Hospitals, and Nursing Homes

(21-13)   **Physician Services**

Medicare Medical Insurance		Blue Shield (over 65)
Pays	*Does Not Pay*	*Pays*
Medical and surgical services	First $75 in a calendar year	
X-rays, drugs, and biologicals that cannot be self-administered	20% of additional charge	20% of charges
Medical supplies	Routine physical exam	
Physical and speech therapy included in doctor's bill	Routine foot care	
	Exams for prescription glasses or hearing aids	
	Immunizations unless as part of emergency treatment	
	Cosmetic surgery unless to repair the result of an injury or to improve a malformed part of the body	

22

Death

ATTITUDES TOWARD DEATH

(22-1) Few people think about death without some fear. The most basic fears arise from unknowns: What will be the time and cause of death; who will be present during the last moments; and how will death be faced? A "good death" has a different meaning for everyone, but most people in Western cultures do not want to die, do not like to think about dying, and become depressed or disturbed when they do think about it.

No one has answers to all the questions about death, but when thoughts of death or dying inhibit one from living fully, it is a tragedy greater than death itself. Sometimes fears about death are really fears about life and how to live. Such fears can become an excuse for not plunging in, taking worthwhile risks, and living fully.

When people can look at fears and worries about death in a rational way, they can get a great deal of relief. Those who lament, "When I die, I will be all alone," might reflect that they have always been alone in exactly the same sense: in birth, in pain, and in their thoughts. Aloneness is a natural and basic part of the human experience.

Practically everyone has the regret, "After I am dead I will miss what is going on." Yes, but everyone has already missed a lot—the golden age of Greece, the Renaissance, knowing our ancestors. The richness and experience of present-day life offers a great deal to those who participate. It is far more useful to relate to what is going on today than to dwell on the imponderables of the future.

The same holds true for people in their later years who worry, "I didn't accomplish enough." Few people ever do what they feel is enough. The great gift, however, is to use wisely all the time that is left. Even from a hospital bed, one can exalt in a symphony, ponder the meaning of poetry, and dream at the stars. Part of what makes living so precious is its finiteness. Death can be viewed as a point in a journey down an endless road full of travelers who have gone before and who will follow. During the journey all leave their own unique mark along the way, enriching those they have encountered and accompanied.

One of the most painful anxieties about death concerns the family that is left to carry on. It is indeed sad to think about how much one is needed and will be missed. Yet each person must cope with, and grow from, the experience of grief and loss. No one can do this for another. People must deal with their own feelings and sort out their own thoughts. One trial families can be spared is the sometimes difficult decisions about funeral plans and financial matters. Everyone—young or old—who is responsible should have an up-to-date will and maintain all household and business affairs in order. Those who are unable to do this for themselves should be helped by a close friend or family member. If a sizable estate is involved, advice from a lawyer is a necessity. There is comfort in knowing one has eased the way for those who will be left behind. Once this is done, attention can be turned to enjoyment of family and friends. The problems caused by failure to do this are discussed later in this chapter (22-7).

DYING

(22-2) *Where to die.* People who know they are about to die often express a preference to die at home, in a hospital, or in a nursing home. Some individuals and family members prefer a hospital setting so that everything possible can be done to postpone the moment of death. Others wish to be in a familiar and loving setting—to die on one's own bed. There are times when choosing to die in a hospital can be an act of kindness to the family, particularly if impressionable children are in the home. (Another view is that death is a natural part of life and early exposure can lead to a wholesome acceptance of death.) This is an extremely personal decision, and whenever possible it should be left up to the dying individual. If the choice is to remain at home, the family members can discuss with the physician how to make the dying person as comfortable as possible—a private nurse may be advisable.

When death occurs at home, the patient's physician should be called. He or she may visit the home immediately or suggest that an ambulance transfer the body to a hospital.

(22-3) *Hospice* is a European term meaning a sheltered place for weary travelers. In recent years hospices have been established for those who are expected to die, to help them over the attendant and emotional trauma and to help them maintain their maximal quality of life. Hospices are physician-directed services primarily for outpatient but also for inpatient care. The hospice, when needed, provides psychological, social, and religious assistance as well as sufficient analgesics to diminish pain. The word "holistic," which emphasizes the importance of treating all the parts as a unit, is sometimes used to describe the hospice. Family members are invited to participate as much as they can and at any time. The hospice is made available on the basis of a patient's need, and the cost is usually considerably less than for a hospital. One important aspect of the hospice is to allow the patient or family members to self-administer pain-relieving medications (usually by mouth) to prevent severe pain from developing—severe pain is easier to prevent than to treat once it has developed. Since hospices are relatively new, they are for the most part available only in major urban areas. Medicare pays a set rate, depending on the intensity of use, for hospice care.

(22-4) *Feelings of distance.* Often family members and friends feel a gap opening between themselves and the dying person. Frequently this distance is perceived by the dying person as well. These feelings are appropriate and need not be disturbing. Dying people need to be alone for a last introspection and self-integration. But "alone" need not mean lonely—dying people need love, companionship, and kindness. Most of all, they need the acknowledgment that they are still full human beings and a part of the lives of their loved ones.

Although feelings may be deep, the expression of emotion may have a cooling rather than an intensifying quality. This may lessen the pain of the situation for all concerned. Visits should be friendly, casual, and positive. The nearness of death can be acknowledged or not—cues must be taken from the dying person.

(22-5) *Denial of death.* Because death is painful to face, some people deny its presence, both to themselves and others. In most of these cases, it would be cruel to break through the protective shield. But it is neither necessary nor desirable to offer false hope for the future. The best course is to avoid the topic, not to lie about it. When people ask if they are going to die, they usually want an honest answer—and they deserve one. This is a difficult question for physicians, who generally avoid predicting when a person will die. In most instances, they do not know, and they have learned through experience that their estimates are often incorrect.

Sometimes people say in advance of an exploratory operation, "If it's bad, don't tell me." That, too, should be honored. Sometimes, as death nears, an initial denial of the impending end gives way to a desire to talk about it, so no rigid stand of "never tell them the truth" should be taken.

A flexible, human approach is necessary. People change their minds as to how they feel about dying just as they change attitudes about other things.

(22-6) *Religion* may or may not be a comfort to a dying individual. Sometimes the faith of a lifetime sustains in shining certainty. At other times, beliefs that have been held throughout life seem empty and devoid of meaning. When this happens, it can be very disturbing to both the patient and the family. For some people, nearness to death encourages new faith where none has been before. Whatever the specific circumstances, members of the clergy have had much experience in giving comfort and solace to the very ill and dying, and their visits can be a source of consolation, relief, and strength for all concerned.

(22-7) *Getting affairs in order.* All too frequently people are irresponsible about their wills. Even heads of families do not leave their affairs in proper order. What can the family do when no will has been written, no provisions made for spouse or children, and no disposition of possessions? If a person is dying but is denying it, the family faces a difficult problem. A close friend or relative may be able to broach the subject in a round-about, general way. Great tact is necessary, and it may take several visits to get any results.

The following are some examples of how this might be done. (As any prepared speech, they would be stilted and forced if followed verbatim; they should be thought of only as general outlines for approaching a very difficult subject.)

One might say to a dying person, "I read in the paper when John Smith died he left three wills and a mess of papers. The family will be squabbling over it for years. What a pity John didn't routinely keep up his papers!"

Or, a young and healthy person could remark, "I've just come from the lawyer. A friend of mine had a serious accident and that made me realize it could happen to any of us at any time. I made out a will and got my papers organized. I sure feel good about it, although it was hard to do."

If the hospitalization is a long one, a trusted friend may offer to help with finances, bookkeeping, etc.; if it appears that some things need attention, the friend should bring this up in a routine manner.

Another approach might be to say, "Mom, we have every reason to hope you are going to fully recover, but your illness reminds us that we don't know very much about your finances. Perhaps now is a good time to familiarize us with them, if it's all right with you."

When financial affairs and the disposition of the will are discussed, there may be results that the family had not anticipated, such as bad investments or an unequal distribution to family members. These matters must be handled with tact and respect. It is important to remember that it is the wishes of the dying person that must receive primary consideration, not those of the family members.

FUNERALS

(22-8) *Selection of burial property.* Anyone who wants to be buried in a cemetery should purchase a plot prior to death. This can save a great deal of anguish for those who survive. It is burdensome to find a plot at the right price in the few days between death and burial. People who buy a plot for themselves before death should consider the following: Who will you want to be buried with? Is there room? Is there any chance that you will move and change your mind about where you want to be buried? (Cemetery plots can be very difficult to sell.) If you buy the plot on credit, make sure you understand the interest charges. Does the purchase price include perpetual care? Is the plot in an established area of the cemetery? If it is not, and you should die before the plot becomes usable, is there a charge for transfer to a usable area? Is a burial vault required, and if so, what will it cost? What costs are there for opening and closing the grave? Is there a restriction of the style of grave markers? Must it be bought from the cemetery? At what cost?

(22-9) *The service.* Once a cemetery plot has been acquired, very little else has to be done ahead of time. Nevertheless, many people have found it useful to discuss with a friend, relative, member of the clergy, or funeral director the style of service desired, degree of elaborateness, choice of who will lead the service, and resources available to pay for everything. A funeral director can be chosen from previous experience, that of friends, or on the advice of the clergy. It is wise to check with the local Better Business Bureau. A funeral director can prove especially helpful in handling such aspects of death as transfer of the body from one location to another. Some funeral homes offer prearranged funeral services. Recently passed legislation requires funeral homes to disclose prices and what is required by law, and to make this information available in writing upon request.

(22-10) *Finances.* In metropolitan areas, complete but modest funerals—not including the plot—can cost several thousand dollars. Alternative methods of handling funeral payments are discussed below. Funeral expenses up to $250 are covered by Social Security for those who are eligible; these benefits are not automatic and must be applied for. Under certain circumstances the Veterans Administration will pay up to $400 to families of qualified veterans. Furthermore, a family member of a person already buried in a federal cemetery may also be eligible to be buried there.

(22-11) *Alternative dispositions.* While most people choose to be buried in a cemetery lot with an appropriate marker or monument, there are other alternatives. For instance, a mausoleum is a building above ground especially designed to house the dead. Except in regions where flooding is common, mausoleums offer no advantage except to those who have emotional reasons for not wanting to be in the ground.

Cremation reduces the body to ash by intense heat—accelerating the natural decomposition process. The ash is placed in an urn which then may be buried, placed in a columbarium (an above-ground building), or, in states that allow it, spread over an area such as a lake or mountain. Cremation is the procedure preferred by most members of funeral societies, which were formed to simplify things and decrease expenses. Those who join these volunteer or church societies for a modest fee, may have their preference in funeral arrangements placed on file, thus relieving survivors of the need to make such arrangements at short notice. Also, most societies have worked out a reduced schedule of charges with one or more reliable funeral directors.

The Continental Association of Funeral and Memorial Societies, 2001 S Street NW, Suite 530, Washington, D.C. 20009, publishes a brochure with lists of names, addresses, and phone numbers of local societies.

(22-12) *A list of things to do following a death.*

1. Call a physician if one has not pronounced the person dead.

2. Call relatives and close friends.

3. Call a funeral director, who will get the proper permits and death certificate and follow your directions in making funeral plans.

4. Arrange for a funeral notice in local newspapers.

5. Ask friends to be casket bearers.

6. Talk to a clergyman, if you choose to use one.

7. Notify the attorney you wish to handle the estate.

8. File insurance claims.

23

A Note to Children and Grandchildren

RELATIONSHIPS BETWEEN THE GENERATIONS: THE FOUR-GENERATION FAMILY

(23-1) *The extended family.* Until very recently, there were traditionally three generations: the child, the parent, and the grandparent. The child was viewed as young, the parent as middle-aged, and the grandparents as old. Today, because we live longer, a family frequently has four generations: child, parent, grandparent, and great-grandparent. The relationships among the members of a four-generation family are more complicated—needs that may have been filled in the three-generation family often go unmet in the four-generation family, and furthermore, new problems and demands occur.

(23-2) *Roles and conflicts.* Accepting all the roles of being a member of a four-generation family often requires much insight and patience. Some examples of the types of conflicts that may arise in this situation are the following.

A 26-year-old working mother has two children, 4 and 2 years old. Her mother is an active, vibrant 52-year-old who is too busy with her own life to perform the traditional grandmotherly role. The younger woman is also the grandchild of a 74-year-old widow who lives in a nursing home and is remembered as the old-fashioned, wonderful grandma of her childhood. This young mother may feel resentful that she is not getting the help that her own mother got from her mother, and may also feel guilty that she is not doing more to make her grandmother's last years more fulfilling. But she feels that her responsibilities are to her husband and children and to her own career.

A Note to Children and Grandchildren

The 52-year-old grandmother feels that she, too, is in a bind. She loves to spend time with her grandchildren, but there are five of them in all (from her own three children), and there is so much else to do. There are social demands from her and her husband's business lives, along with community responsibilities that she has built up over the years. She also has recently assumed primary responsibility for her own mother, who has come to depend upon her since she is the only child who lives in the same town and can have regular contact with her.

Then there is the 74-year-old great-grandmother. She now feels useless, as if life has passed her by. She was active for several years after her husband died, but has become increasingly disabled by arthritis and other physical ailments. She did not want to impose upon her daughter and so chose to move to a nursing home. There she receives good care, but sorely misses being part of a family in the same sense she has always known. She keeps pictures of her family—children, grandchildren, and great-grandchildren—around the room and awaits their visits with great anticipation, then relives them for days afterwards. The visits provide her special joys, even though she is not in touch with the family as much as she would like.

And what is the effect on the young children? Their lives are filled with a progression of teenage baby-sitters, and they attend nursery school at ages 2 and 4 to permit their parents and grandparents the freedom to manage their own lives. These children may sometimes feel they are not getting enough time with their parents and grandparents, even though there is opportunity for enrichment from other sources.

THE NEED FOR CLOSENESS

(23-3) *We need contact with all age groups.* Everyone needs to feel close to others. Family members and dear friends can offer love, strength, warmth, and intimacy. Other social contacts provide enrichment and stimulation. Association among all ages gives the satisfaction of "passing the baton" from one generation to another. Dialogue with each other gives both the elderly and the young the richness of other perspectives. No matter what the ages of those involved, in all mature relationships there is an acceptance that life begins, develops, and wanes. There is continuity both with those who have come before and those who will continue afterward. From this continuum of life comes our individual feeling of belonging. All pieces in the human structure have their own integrity, dignity, and importance.

This perspective, which many of the elderly possess, often takes a lifetime to acquire. Younger people are often caught up in the immediacy of their own ambitions and their more active, aggressive, complex lives. This is part of what people have come to call the generation gap. If an effort to bridge this gap is not made, the effect may be to deprive the elderly, the middle-aged, and the young of the benefits of closeness with people of different ages. Many older people find it difficult to initiate and sustain this kind of contact because of their own lack of mobility, the loss of loved ones and friends, poor health, and society's stereotypes about the elderly. Often it must be the younger person who takes the initiative to create the time, place, and atmosphere for a close relationship to develop.

(23-4) *Keeping up with family news.* As we get older, interest may wane in the wars, woes, and even the advances of the outer world. Yet there is often increased interest and emotional investment in the family and its activities. Thus it is important to involve the elderly by keeping them in touch with children's and grandchildren's work, school, athletic teams, and hobbies. When the young begin to achieve beyond their parents and grandparents, this brings great joy to the mature person. Parents and grandparents enjoy the harvest that comes from the seeds they have sown. It is a kindness when talking about family news to stress relationship and continuity—how a grandson is a "chip off the old block who can put anything together with his hands" or how a granddaughter has her grandfather's green thumb.

(23-5) *Exploring the past.* Often, after news of the family has been exchanged, there seems to be little left to say. Many elderly people do not have much in the way of active participatory news to contribute, and trying to talk about foreign affairs or the rising cost of living may seem forced and unrewarding. Although the present lives of some elderly people may seem passive, a great deal can be learned from their past. The sharing of these experiences, the richness of an elderly person's childhood memories, can give younger people a valuable picture of life in another time and place. Life in this or other countries can be brought into a new focus by personal experience. Find out how other family members fit into the picture and chronology. Learn why Aunt Mary settled in Chicago while her brother stayed in Boston. Explore the family tree to discover what occupations, problems, and lifestyles were popular among previous generations. Younger children are especially fascinated by the minutiae of life—what did a family do before the advent of television and frozen dinners?

One of the most rewarding aspects of this type of exploration is that by knowing about the older person's youthful, achieving years, we grow to understand and feel real kinship with the total person. It is very important to remember and acknowledge who the elderly person once was and still thinks of himself or herself as being. This invisible inner self is very real to the elderly person, and perhaps provides the key to really knowing the grandparent who may seem distant and impenetrable.

(23-6) *Acknowledging achievements and the fulfillment of goals.* The achievements of the past and present, no matter how insignificant, enhance the sense of worth and self-appreciation. Continuing contributions to the family and community can be encouraged and reinforced. The human interactions resulting from these efforts help to prevent isolation and withdrawal. Furthermore, when one person does something for another, it becomes an investment in that person, and that is part of what relationships are about.

(23-7) *Talking about feelings.* But it is not enough merely to recognize the past life and achievements of elderly persons; their present thoughts and feelings need to be acknowledged as well. Elderly persons want to know that you care what they are thinking and feeling and can sense this care by the way you look at them and relate to what is going on. If they seem tired or sad, comment on it and wait for a response. Give them ample opportunity to repeat many times, if necessary, their frustration over, say, the limitations of arthritic hands. Encourage better medical attention if that is appropriate, and if nothing further can be done for the discomfort, sympathy and empathy will help. If it is difficult for your grandmother or grandfather to express their feelings, you can say, "I know how hard it is for you not to be embroidering or gardening any more," or "It must be very annoying to have that blurred vision." Simply acknowledging the state of being can be very comforting. Try not to see the expression of bodily feelings as complaints that you would rather shut out, but rather as a picture of what the other person is experiencing and trying to tell you about. To encourage communication, use reflective listening techniques—repeating what has been said in a relaxed way. For example, you might rephrase what someone has just said, saying, "So you weren't able to get out because of your sore leg."

VISITING

(23-8) *Plan ahead for a successful visit.* There are several things that can make a visit to an elderly person an event that's rewarding for all concerned. Thinking ahead and making some simple preparations are the way to accomplish this.

(23-9) *Bring an interesting snack.* The pride of older people is often hurt because they feel that they can no longer entertain graciously. Turn this concern around by appearing with something fun to eat: an instant pudding to make, a pint of ice cream of an unusual flavor. Sometimes it's

After Middle Age

nice to bring a new product from the market that might either be unfamiliar or outside a limited budget: mint tea bags, instant café-au-lait. Does the older person know about powdered lemonade or instant oatmeal? How about bringing an unusual pastry as a treat, or an ethnic food? This can stimulate discussion and outside interests as well as demonstrating that you care enough to be thinking ahead and looking forward to your visit.

(23-10) *Perform a service.* During a visit, offer to shampoo or cut hair, or to help care for both finger- and toenails. You might bring one of the new inexpensive and easy-to-hold hair dryers and leave it as a gift. How about replacing dim lightbulbs with strong ones, and putting in a night light near the bed or in a hall or bath? Would a remote control switch on the television make bed viewing easier? Toss some things in the laundry that might otherwise not be attended to, like throw rugs or bath mats.

Look around and take note of things that could make life more pleasant and comfortable. How about a new set of colorful sheets that don't need to be ironed or a washable comforter or an extra-big bath towel? Would a push-button telephone with an adjustable ring or a light-up dial be easier to use? Are there nonslip treads in the bath tub or shower? Is a bath caddy needed to make supplies handier? Would blackout window shades in the bedroom make sleeping easier? Is a large, prop-up pillow needed for bed or sofa? Is there a bed tray handy? Would an older man enjoy a long flannel nightshirt? Are slippers soft and comfortable? The list could go on and on. The idea is to put yourself into the setting and think about what you would do to make *yourself* more comfortable. Chances are that it would be a welcome focal point for your next visit.

(23-11) *Bring a gift.* Everyone likes presents, especially when there is no special occasion. Bring a gift—the kindness benefits the giver and receiver. A plant, large-print books from the library, a lighted digital clock, or a heating pad are often needed and appreciated. A toaster-oven could make it possible to prepare a wider variety of food simply and easily. Photographs of the family are wonderful and cherished. Ask to see old pictures, learn the stories behind them, and put them together into a new lovely album for hours of pleasure.

(23-12) *Visiting with children.* Young children will enjoy visits more with their older relatives if some simple preparations are made. Keep a box of toys right there if visits are frequent. Blocks, stacking toys, small dolls, cars, and trains are ideal for toddlers. For older children, keep a supply of crayons and paper and scissors and Scotch tape. Picture books, a child's record player, and some records are good for a variety of ages. Some cans of apple juice and a few boxes of crackers and cookies should be stocked. Disposable diapers and perhaps a potty chair are helpful. This

A Note to Children and Grandchildren

way, the child can play and not be a nuisance while the grandparent or great-grandparent can better enjoy seeing and watching the child.

WHEN YOU CANNOT BE THERE

(23-13) The arrival of the mail is a daily event to anticipate. Make it special by sending magazine subscriptions and postcards. Most communities have picture cards of local sights in the drugstores. Sending something as mundane as a picture of a shopping center and a "thinking of you" can greatly help to brighten a day and make the receiver feel cared for. Long distance calls at nonbusiness hours that can be inexpensive are most welcome. It's a wonderful way to surprise an elderly person and the pleasure of the call can last for hours.

Index

Index entries are referenced to section numbers rather than page numbers.

Abrasions, how to treat, **18-9**
Accident prevention, **2-4**
   automobile and, **2-13**
   falls, **2-10**
   fires, **2-11**
      smoke detectors and, **2-12**
   with medicines, **2-9**
   preparation for emergencies and, **2-15**
   protection from cold and, **2-14**
Ace bandages for varicose veins, **9-25**
Acetaminophen (Tylenol, Tempra, Valadol, Febrolin), **7-13**
Acetazolamide (Diamox), **8-20**
Acetohexamide (Dymelor), **16-12**
Acetyldigitoxin (Acylanid), **12-46**
Acid, swallowed, **18-13**

Action Agency, **2-25**
Activities:
   cancer patients and, **17-13**
   diet and, **3-45**
   insomnia and, **5-26**
   in nursing homes, **20-15**
Acylanid (Acetyldigitoxin), **12-46**
Adam's apple, **11-1**
Adapin (Doxepin), **5-15**
Addiction:
   to antianxiety drugs, **5-8**
   to pain-relieving drugs, **7-16**, **7-18**
Adenocarcinomas, **15-26**
Adenoma of thyroid gland, **16-5**, **16-6**
Adenomyosis, **15-25**
Administration on Aging, **2-25**

Index

Admissions at reduced price, **2-20**
Admitting privileges of physician, **17-5, 19-1**
Adrenal gland tumor, **12-18**
Adult Physical Fitness, **1-6**
Aero-otitis media, **4-3**
Aging, **1-1**
Air filter, **11-7**
Air travel:
  ear pain and, **4-3**
  motion sickness and, **4-4**
  ozone and, **4-6**
  sleep and rhythms and, **4-5**
  swelling of ankles and, **4-2**
Airway, clearing, **18-3**
Akineton (Biperiden), **7-25**
Al-Anon, **5-40**
Alcohol:
  antidiabetic drugs and, **16-12**
  effects on body, **5-37**
  insomnia and, **5-27, 5-29**
  interactions with drugs, **5-38**
  minimizing effects of, **5-36**
  sexual function and, **15-10**
  use to relieve pain, **8-19**
Alcoholic hallucinosis, **5-37**
Alcoholics Anonymous (AA), **5-40**
Alcoholism, **5-35** to **5-40**
  misconceptions about, **5-39**
  treatment of, **5-40**
Aldactone (Spironolactone), **12-9**
Aldomet (Methyldopa), **12-11**
Aldosteronism, **12-18**
Alkali, swallowed, **18-13**
Allergy(ies):
  alveolitis, **11-23**
  to antibiotics, **14-6**
  conjunctivitis and, **8-12**
  to drugs [*see* Drug(s), allergies to]
  to dust, **11-7**
  to insect stings, **18-15**
  intravenous pyelogram and, **14-5**
  rashes and, **9-5** to **9-6**
  rectal itching and, **9-3**
  rhinitis, **11-7**
Allergy shots, **11-7**
Allopurinol (Zyloprim), **10-7**
Alopecia, **9-38**
Alopecia areata, **9-39**
Alpha-one-antitrypsin, **11-17**
Alprazolam (Xanax), **5-8**

Aludrox, **13-21**
Alveoli in emphysema, **11-17**
Alveolitis, allergic, **11-23**
Alzheimer's disease, **6-1, 6-2**
Alzheimer's Disease and Related Disorders Association, **6-3**
Amantadine (Symmetrel), **7-25, 11-13**
Ambivalence, psychotherapy and, **5-43**
Ambulance, how to call, **19-3**
Amcill (Ampicillin), **14-6**
American Academy of Physical Medicine and Rehabilitation, **12-51**
American Association of Homes for Aging, **20-7**
American Association of Retired Persons, **2-25**
American Cancer Society, **15-19**
American Express, list of physicians provided by, **4-17**
American Medical Association, **10-3**
American Narcolepsy Association, **5-33**
American Nursing Home Association, **20-7**
American Speech-Language Hearing Association, **12-50**
Amino acids, **3-3**
Aminophylline (Somophyllin), **11-16**
Amitriptyline (Elavil), **5-15**
Amoxapine (Asendin), **5-15**
Amphetamine, **3-50**
Amphojel, **13-21**
Ampicillin (Omnipen, Polycillin, Amcill, Principen), **14-6**
Anacin, **7-3**
Anal fissures, **9-3**
Analgesics, **7-10** to **7-20**
  in cancer treatment, **17-22**
  with colds, **11-5**
  (*See also* Aspirin; *specific drugs*)
Anemia, pernicious, **3-17**
Anesthesiologist, **19-5**
Angina, **12-19, 16-4**
  treatment of: diagnosis and, **12-22** to **12-25**
  drugs in, **12-20**
  surgical, **12-21**
Anhydron (Cyclothiazide), **12-9**
Ankle:
  replacement of, **10-5**
  swelling of: air travel and, **4-2**
  hypertension and, **12-3**
Anorexia, cancer therapy and, **17-21**

Index

Antabuse (Disulfiram), **5-40**
Antacids, duodenal ulcer and, **13-21**
Antianxiety drugs, **5-8**
Antibiotics:
  with colds, **11-3**
  with flu, **11-11**
  with pneumonia, **11-18**
  for urinary system infections, **14-4**
  with viral pneumonia, **11-20**
Antibody, **4-7**
Anticholinergics:
  with duodenal ulcers, **13-21**
  in Parkinson's disease, **7-25**
Anticoagulants:
  foreign travel and, **4-19**
  with heart attack, **12-31**
  with lung embolism, **11-24**
Anticonvulsants, **7-40**
  interaction with Septra, **14-6**
Antidepressants, **5-10, 5-15**
  interaction with guanethidine, **12-11**
  sexual function and, **15-10**
Antidiabetics, **16-12**
Antidiarrhea drugs, **4-14** to **4-16**
Antidust program, **11-7**
Antiemetics, **8-29**
Antihistamines, **8-29**
  with colds, **11-5**
  for itching, **9-2**
  in Parkinson's disease, **7-25**
  side effects of, **11-7**
Antimalarial agents, **4-7**
Antiseptics for abrasions and scratches, **18-9**
Anturane (Sulfinpyrazone), **10-7**
Anxiety, **5-4, 5-23, 5-27, 5-29**
  blood pressure and, **12-5**
  causes of, **5-5**
  pain perception and, **7-2**
  senility and, **6-4**
  symptoms of, **5-6**
  treatment of, **5-7**
  drugs in, **5-8, 5-22**
APC (Aspirin compound), **7-12**
Aphasia following stroke, **12-50**
Aphrodisiacs, **15-12**
Apnea, sleep, **5-32**
Appearance:
  cancer and, **17-14**
  importance of, **1-3**
  teeth and, **13-7**

Appendectomy, **13-23**
Appendicitis, **13-23**
Appetite:
  cancer therapy and, **17-21**
  digitalis and, **3-50, 12-46**
Appointments with doctor, **1-4**
Apraxia, stroke and, **12-48**
Apresoline (Hydralazine), **12-11**
Aprikern (Laetrile), **17-6**
Aquatag (Benzthiazide), **12-9**
Aquatensen (Methyclothiazide), **12-9**
Arcus senilis, **8-2**
Arm, pressure point for, **18-7**
Arrhythmia, **12-27, 12-32, 12-33**
Artane (Trihexyphenidyl), **7-25**
Arteries, **12-1**
  blood pressure and, **12-2, 12-4, 12-14**
Arteriography, **18-24**
  coronary, **12-21** to **12-22**
Arteriosclerosis:
  cholesterol and, **3-29**
  hypertension and, **12-5**
  LDL and HDL and, **3-32**
  muscle cramps and, **18-24**
  prevention of, **12-40**
  senility and, **6-1**
Arthritis, **10-2** to **10-7**
  osteo-, **10-4, 10-10**
  rheumatoid, **10-3**
  sexual activity and, **15-14**
Arthritis Foundation, **10-3**
Artificial mouth-to-mouth resuscitation:
  for carbon monoxide poisoning, **18-14**
  with heart attack, **12-29**
Artificial sweeteners, **3-37**
Ascorbic acid (*see* Vitamin C)
Asendin (Amoxapine), **5-15**
Asian flu, **11-13**
Aspartame, **3-37**
Aspirin, **7-11**
  with arthritis, **10-3**
  for backache, **10-10**
  buffered, **7-11**
  with colds, **11-5**
  with duodenal ulcers, **13-21**
  enteric-coated, **7-11**
  for headaches, **7-3**
    migraine, **7-4**
  heart attack and, **12-41**
  with lung embolism, **11-24**
  with sore throat, **11-8**

317

Index

Aspirin compound (APC, Empirin, Fiorinal), **7-12**
Aspirin substitutes, **13-21**
Assertiveness, importance of, **1-4**
Asthma, **11-23**
   cardiac, **12-45**
Astigmatism, **8-5**
Ataxia, stroke and, **12-48**
Atenolol (Tenormin), **12-11**
Atherosclerosis (*see* Arteriosclerosis)
Athlete's foot, **9-24**
Ativan (Lorazepam), **5-8**
Atromid-S (Clofibrate), **12-16**
Atropine, **13-21**
Audiologist, **8-23**
Aura, seizures and, **7-39**
Autoimmunity, arthritis and, **10-3**
Automatic behaviors, **5-33**
Automobile, preventing accidents in, **2-13**
Autophony, **4-3**
Aventyl (Nortriptyline), **5-15**

Back, broken, emergency treatment of, **18-22**
Backache, **10-8, 10-10** to **10-11**
   how to avoid, **10-11**
   kidney stones and, **14-7**
Bactine for abrasions and scratches, **18-9**
Bactrim, **14-6**
Bactrim-DS, **14-6**
Bad breath, **13-3**
Balance, **8-27**
Baldness, **9-38**
Balloon for incontinence, **14-2**
Barbiturates, interactions with alcohol, **5-38**
Bariatrician, **3-50**
Barium x-ray (*see* X-ray, barium)
Basal cell epithelioma, **9-30**
Bathroom scale, **3-52**
Bathtubs, preventing falls in, **2-10**
Batteries for pacemakers, **12-35**
Beauty marks, **9-31**
Beclomethasone (Vanceril), **11-17**
Bed sores, **9-27**
Bee-Seventeen (Laetrile), **17-6**
Behavior modification therapy, **5-43**
Belladonna, **13-21**
Bell's seventh nerve palsy, **7-28**
Benadryl (Diphenhydramine), **5-34, 7-25, 8-29**

Bence-Jones protein, **10-8**
Bendopa (L-dopa), **7-25**
Benemid (Probenecid), **10-7**
Benzocaine with sore throat, **11-8**
Benzthiazide (Aquatag, Exna), **12-9**
Benztropine (Cogentin), **7-25**
Beriberi, **3-13**
Bifocals, **8-8**
Biopsy, **15-25, 17-4, 17-9**
   of bone marrow, **17-9**
   of breast, **15-18**
   of liver, **17-9**
   of lung, **11-25**
Biperiden (Akineton), **7-25**
Bismuth subcarbonate, **13-28**
Blackheads, **9-20**
Blackout spells, alcohol and, **5-37**
Bladder, **14-1**
   cancer of, **14-9**
   infection of, **14-1**
   inflammation of, **14-3**
   nonfunctioning, **14-10**
Bladder stones, **14-1**
Bleeding, **17-3, 18-5** to **18-10**
   from abrasions and scratches, what to do for, **18-9**
   finding pressure points to stop, **18-7**
   flowing or spurting, how to stop, **18-6**
   rectal, **9-3, 13-24**
   as sign of cancer, **17-3**
   use of tourniquet for, **18-8**
   from vagina, **15-22, 15-25** to **15-27**
   when to call doctor for, **18-10**
   (*See also* Blood)
Blindness caused by oxygen, **3-7**
Blinking, **7-23**
Blood:
   coughing up, **11-1**
   in stools, **13-24, 13-26, 13-27**
   in urine, **14-1, 14-7, 14-9**
   vomiting, **13-20**
Blood clot (lung embolism), **11-24**
Blood pressure:
   diastolic and systolic, **12-2, 12-5, 12-6**
   how to take, **12-6**
   (*See also* Hypertension)
Board certification, **2-6**
Body temperature, maintaining, **2-14**
Bone(s):
   age-related loss of, **10-12**
   broken, emergency treatment of, **18-20**

Index

Bone(s) (*Cont.*)
   calcium and, **3-22**
   magnesium and, **3-24**
   of middle ear, **8-25**
   phosphorus and, **3-23**
   tumors of, **10-8**
Bone marrow biopsy, **17-9**
Bone scan, **10-8**, **15-36**
Bonine (Meclizine), **4-4**, **17-16**
Brain:
   abscesses of, **7-35**
   CT scan of, **6-2**, **7-38**
   stroke and, **12-48**
   tumors, **7-37**
      CT scans and, **7-38**
Breast:
   cysts of, **15-20**
   examination of, **2-4**, **15-16**, **15-17**
Breast cancer, **15-16**
   detection of, **15-17**
   treating, **15-18** to **15-19**
Breath, bad, **13-3**
Breathing:
   clearing airway and, **18-3**
   shortness of breath and, **11-1**, **11-7**, **11-23**, **11-24**, **12-3**, **12-27**
   emphysema and, **11-17**
   heart failure and, **5-28**, **12-45**
   at night, **5-28**, **12-45**
   shock and, **12-47**
   sleep apnea and, **5-32**
Bromocriptine (Parlodel), **7-25**
Bronchitis, **11-14**
   diagnosis of, **11-15**
   with emphysema, **11-17**
   treatment of, **11-16**
Bronchoscopy, **11-15**, **11-25**
Bronkometer (Isoetharine), **11-16**
Bufferin, **7-11**
Bundroflumethiazide (Naturetin), **12-9**
Bunion, **10-14**
Burial property, selection of, **22-8**
Burn(s), **18-12**
   cancer treatment and, **17-16**
Burn centers, **18-12**
Bursitis, **10-15**
Butazolidin (Phenylbutazone), **10-3**, **10-7**, **13-21**

Cafergot, **7-4**, **7-5**

Caffeine:
   in APC, **7-12**
   arrhythmia and, **12-33**
   controlling intake of, **3-36**
   effects of, **3-36**
   with ergotamine, **7-4**, **7-5**
   insomnia and, **5-27**
   migraine headaches and, **7-4**
Calamine lotion:
   for itching, **9-2**
   for poison ivy, **9-7**
   for shingles, **9-23**
Calan (Verapamil), **12-20**
Calciferol (Vitamin D), **3-10**
Calcitonin (Calcimar), **10-9**
Calcium:
   antacids containing, with duodenal ulcer, **13-21**
   in diet, **3-22**
   nails and, **9-33**
Calcium deposits with bursitis, **10-15**
Calculus (*see* Plaque)
Calendar for medications, **2-9**
Call buttons in nursing home rooms, **20-10**
Calories, **3-2**
   monitoring intake of, **3-52**
   variation in need for, **3-45**
Calories Don't Count, **3-47**
Cambridge Diet, **3-48**
Cancer, **17-1**
   artificial sweeteners and, **3-37**
   biopsy and (*see* Biopsy)
   of bladder, **14-9**
   of bones, **10-8**
   of breast, **15-16**
      detection of, **15-17**
      treating, **15-18** to **15-19**
   brown spots on skin and, **9-14**
   of cervix, **15-28**
   of colon, **13-27**
   denial and, **17-13**
   diagnosis and treatment of: diagnostic procedures and, **17-9**
      laetrile and, **17-6**
      quacks and charlatans and, **17-5**
      reasons not to go to a physician and, **17-7**
      what to do if cancer is diagnosed, **17-8**
      whom to go to, **17-4**
   laryngeal, **11-10**
   of lip, **13-6**

Index

Cancer (*Cont.*)
  loss of hair and, **17-14**
  of lung, **11-25**
    smoking and, **11-26**
  managing treatment of, **17-13**
    blood and, **17-18**
    burns and, **17-16**
    diet and, **17-21**
    infections and, **17-19**
    pain and, **17-22**
    radiation to mouth and, **17-17**
    risk of fatality and, **17-15**
    sterility and impotence and, **17-20**
    toxic effects and, **17-14**
  of mouth, **13-6**
  nitrosamines and, **3-38**
  of ovaries, **15-24**
  of pancreas, **13-38**
  phenacetin and, **7-12**
  prevention of, **17-2** to **17-3**
    role of fiber in, **3-34**
    vitamin A and, **3-9**
  projection and, **17-13**
  prostatic, **15-36**
  rectal, **13-27**
  of salivary gland, **13-6**
  seven signs of, **17-3**
  of skin (*see* Skin, cancer of)
  of stomach (*see* Stomach, cancer of)
  theory behind treatment of: chemotherapy and, **17-4**, **17-12**
    radiation therapy and, **17-11**
    surgery and, **17-10**
  of thyroid gland, **16-6**
  of uterus (*see* Uterus, cancer of)
  weight loss and, **17-14**, **17-21**
Candidiasis, **9-3**
Canker sores, **13-4**
Cantharidin, **15-12**
Capillaries, **12-1**
Carafate (Sucralfate), **13-21**
Carbamazepine (Tegretol), **7-8**
Carbidopa, L-dopa and, **7-25**
Carbo-Calorie Diet, The, **3-47**
Carbohydrates, **3-4**
  controlling intake of, **3-47**
Carbon monoxide poisoning, **18-14**
Carbonic anhydrase inhibitors with glaucoma, **8-20**
Carcinomas, **17-1**
Card Dialer, **12-50**

Cardase (Ethoxzolamine), **8-20**
Cardiac asthma, **12-45**
Cardiac catheterization, **12-22**
"Cardiac neurosis," **12-19**
Cardiac pacemakers, **12-35**
Cardiac problems:
  ozone and, **4-6**
  (*See also* Arteriosclerosis; Heart failure)
Cardiopulmonary resuscitation (CPR), **12-27**
  for carbon monoxide poisoning, **18-14**
Cardioversion, **12-34**
Cardizem (Diltiazem), **12-20**
Carotene, **3-9**
Carpal-tunnel syndrome, **7-31**
Carpet, folds in, and falls, **2-10**
CAT scan (*see* Computed tomography scan)
Cataplexy, **5-33**
Catapres (Clonidine), **7-6**, **12-11**
Cataract, **8-9**, **8-15**, **8-20**
  diabetes and, **16-8**
Catheterization:
  cardiac, **12-22**
  urinary, with neurogenic bladder, **14-10**
Cedilanid (Lanatoxide-C), **12-46**
Centrax (Prazepam), **5-8**
Cephalexin (Keflex), **14-6**
Cerebellum, **7-1**
Cerebral cortex, **7-1**
Cerebral thrombosis, stroke and, **12-48**
Cerebral vascular accident (CVA) (*see* Stroke)
Cerespan (Papaverine), **12-52**
Cervix, **15-25**
  cancer of, **15-28**
  polyps of, **15-27**
Change, adaptation to, anxiety and, **5-5**
Charlatans, **17-5**
Cheese, monoamine oxidase inhibitors and, cautions regarding, **5-15**
Cheilitis, **9-18**
Chemotherapy, **17-4**, **17-12**
Cherry angiomas, **9-8**
Chest pain, **11-18**, **12-19**, **12-27**, **12-47**
Chest x-ray (*see* X-ray, of chest)
Children:
  preventing drug accidents to, **2-9**
  visits from, **23-12**
Chiropractor, **10-18**

Index

Chloral hydrate (Noctec, Kessodrate, Felsules), **5-34**
   interaction with Lasix, **5-34**
Chlordiazepoxide (Librium), **5-8**
Chloroquine, **4-7**
Chlorothiazide (Diuril), **12-9**
Chlorpheniramine (Chlor-Trimeton), **11-5, 11-7**
Chlorpropamide (Diabinase), **16-12**
Choking, what to do in case of, **18-4**
Cholecystogram, **13-33**
Cholera, vaccination against, **4-7, 4-8**
Cholesterol, **3-29**
   food content of, **3-29, 3-30, 3-31**
   heart disease and, **12-13** to **12-16**
   LDL and HDL and, **3-32**
Cholestyramine, **12-16**
Choloxin (Dextrothyroxine), **12-15**
Chrysotherapy, **10-3**
Chylomicrons, **12-16**
Chymopapain (Chymodiactin), **10-10**
Cigarettes (*see* Smoking)
Cimetidine (Tigamet), **13-21**
Circulatory system, **12-1**
Circumlocution following stroke, **12-50**
Cirrhosis, **5-37**
Classes, free, **2-20**
Claudication, **18-24**
Clergyman, **5-45**
   suicide prevention and, **5-13**
Climacteric, **15-2**
Clinoril (Sulindac), **10-3**
Clioquinol (Iodochlorhydroxyquin), **4-15**
Clock, internal, **4-5**
Clofibrate (Atromid-S), **12-16**
Clonidine (Catapres), **7-6, 12-11**
Closed heart massage, how to perform, **12-30**
Clothing:
   burning: how to extinguish, **18-11**
      preventing, **2-11**
   during cold weather, **2-14**
   tight-fitting, **4-2**
      rectal itching and, **9-3**
Codeine, **7-19, 9-23**
   for headaches, migraine, **7-4**
   sexual function and, **15-10**
Coffee (*see* Caffeine)
Cogentin (Benztropine), **7-25**
Cola (*see* Caffeine)
Colchicine, **10-7**

Cold, **11-2**
   antibiotics with, **11-3**
   cough medicines with, **11-4**
   nonprescription remedies for, **11-5**
   protection from, **2-14**
   vitamin C and, **11-6**
Cold cream for itching, **9-2**
Cold sensitivity, **16-4**
Cold sores, **9-21**
Colloid milium, **9-17**
Colon, cancer of, **13-27**
Colonoscope, fiberoptic, **13-27**
Coloring of skin, sudden loss of, **9-19**
Colostomy, **13-27, 13-28**
Colostomy Association, **13-28**
Columbarium, **22-11**
Coma, diabetic, **16-18**
Comedones, **9-20**
Community resources, **2-16** to **2-25**
Compazine (Prochlorperazine), **17-16**
Compensation strategies, **5-3**
Complete Scarsdale Medical Diet, The, **3-48**
Complete Slimmer, The, **3-47**
Computed tomography (CT or CAT) scan, **6-2, 7-38, 10-10**
Concussion, **7-32**
Confabulation, alcoholism and, **5-37**
Confusion, **5-29, 5-32, 5-34, 6-1, 7-25, 13-21**
Congestive cardiac failure (*see* Heart failure, left)
Conjunctivitis (pink eye), **8-11, 8-12**
Conservatism, compensation strategies and, **5-3**
Constipation, **13-22**
   diverticulosis and, **9-26**
   fiber and, **3-34**
Consultations:
   doctors discouraging, **17-5**
   when and how to seek, **2-7**
Contact lenses, **8-9**
   with cataracts, **8-15**
Continental Association of Funeral and Memorial Societies, **22-11**
Convalescent center, **20-5**
Convulsions, **7-39**
   delirium tremens and, **5-37**
   electrically produced, **5-16**
   emergency treatment of, **7-40**
   (*See also* Epilepsy)
Cooking oil for moisturizing, **9-2**

Index

Copper, 3-26
Corgard (Nadolol), 12-11
Corn(s), 9-28
Cornea, 8-9, 8-16
Corneal transplantation, 8-16
Coronary arteriography, 12-21 to 12-22
Coronary bypass surgery, 12-21
Coronary care unit (CCU), 12-32
Cortisone, 13-21
    cautions concerning, 10-3
Cost:
    of custodial care, 6-4
    of hearing aid, 8-23
    of institutional care, 6-4, 6-7
    of nursing homes, 20-16
        insurance coverage for, 21-8, 21-12
    of psychotherapy, 5-46
    (*See also* Insurance)
Cough, 11-1, 17-3
    on airplanes, 4-6
    cancer and, 11-25, 17-23
    smoker's (*see* Bronchitis)
    with tuberculosis, 11-22
    with viral pneumonia, 11-20
Cough medicines with colds, 11-4
Couples psychotherapy, 5-43
CPR (*see* Cardiopulmonary resuscitation)
Cramps:
    nocturnal, 5-28
    treatment of, 18-24
Creativity, importance of, 5-3
Cremation, 22-11
Cretinol (Vitamin A), 3-9
Cromolyn (Nasalcrom), 11-7
Cryodestruction for hemorrhoids, 13-24
CT scan (*see* Computed tomography scan)
Cuticle, 9-33
CVA (cerebral vascular accident) (*see* Stroke)
Cyanocobalamin (Vitamin B_{12}), 3-17
Cyclamate, 3-37
Cyclothiazide (Anhydron), 12-9
Cylert (Pemoline), 5-33
Cyst(s):
    of breast, 15-20
    of ovaries, 15-22
Cystitis, 14-3
Cystoscopy, 14-9

D and C (dilation and curettage), 15-26

Dalmane (Flurazepam), 5-34
    interactions with alcohol, 5-38
Dandruff, 9-42
Dandruff shampoo, 9-42
Daranide (Dichlorphenamide), 8-20
Darbid (Isopropamide), 13-21
Darvon (Propoxyphene), 7-14
DBI (Phenformin), 16-12
Deafness (*see* Hearing loss)
Death:
    attitudes toward, 5-5, 22-1
    choosing place for, 22-2
        hospice as, 22-3
    denial of, 22-5
    feelings of distance and, 22-4
    preparing affairs before, 22-7
    religion and, 22-6
    what to do following, 22-12
    (*See also* Funeral; Suicide)
Decongestants with colds, 11-5
Decubitus ulcers, 9-27
Defibrillation, 12-34
Degenerative joint disease, 10-4
Deja vu, seizures and, 7-39
Delcid, 13-21
Delirium tremens (DTs), 5-37
Dementia, 6-1
    presenile, 6-2
    vascular, 6-1
    (*See also* Senility)
Demerol (Meperidine), 7-18, 13-33
    sexual function and, 15-10
Denial:
    cancer and, 17-13
    of death, 22-5
Dental hygiene, 2-4, 13-8
    bad breath and, 13-3
    floss and, 13-7, 13-8, 13-11
Dentifrice, 13-11
Dentists, 13-9
Dentures (*see* Teeth, false)
Dependence on antianxiety drugs, 5-8
Depilatory creams, 9-40
Depression, 5-6, 6-1, 7-25
    causes of, 5-1, 5-9
    climacteric and, 15-2, 15-3
    endogenous, 5-9
    following heart attack, 12-38
    insomnia and, 5-24, 5-28
    reactive, 5-9
    with reserpine, 12-11

Index

Depression (*Cont.*)
  senility and, **6-2, 6-4**
  suicide and, **5-12**
    preventing, **5-13** to **5-14**
    treatment of, **5-10** to **5-11**
      drugs in, **5-15**
      electroconvulsive therapy in, **5-16**
    when to see physician about, **5-11**
Desensitization, **5-43**
  to poison ivy, **9-7**
Desipramine (Norpramine, Pertofrane), **5-15**
Desyrel (Trazadone), **5-15**
Dextroamphetamine (Dexadrine), **5-33**
Dextromethorphan, **11-4**
Dextrothyroxine (Choloxin), **12-15**
Diabetes mellitus, **16-7**
  coma and, **16-18**
  diagnosis of, **16-9**
  emergency supplies to carry for, **16-19**
  foot care and, **16-20**
    corns and, **9-28**
    warts and, **9-29**
  symptoms of, **16-8, 8-18**
  treatment of, **16-10**
    diet in, **16-11**
    drugs in, **16-12**
    insulin in, **16-13** to **16-17**
Diabetes Travel Services, Inc., **4-17**
Diabinase (Chlorpropamide), **16-12**
Dialysis, **14-8**
Diamox (Acetazolamide), **8-20**
Diapers, **6-4**
Diarrhea:
  causes of, **13-2**
  with digitalis, **12-46**
  foreign travel and, **4-14**
  radiation therapy and, **17-16**
  treatment of, **4-14** to **4-16**
Diazepam (Valium), **5-8, 5-34, 8-29, 10-10**
Dichlorphenamide (Daranide, Oratrol), **8-20**
Dicoumarol (Four-hydroxycoumarin), **12-52**
  with lung embolism, **11-24**
Diet, **3-2, 3-47** to **3-55**
  activity and, **3-45**
  cancer therapy and, **17-21**
  carbohydrates in, **3-4, 3-47**
  cholesterol in, **3-29** to **3-31, 12-15** to **12-16**

Diet (*Cont.*)
  coffee, tea, and cola in, **3-36**
  dandruff and, **9-42**
  diabetes and, **16-11**
  drugs and, **3-51**
  duodenal ulcer and, **13-21**
  fad, **3-46**
  fats in, **3-5**
  fiber in, **3-34, 13-26**
  with gallbladder disease, **13-33**
  gout and, **10-6**
  hypertension and, **12-13** to **12-17**
  with kidney failure, **14-8**
  minerals in, **3-21**
    calcium, **3-22**
    iron, **3-25**
    magnesium, **3-24**
    phosphorus, **3-23**
    potassium, **3-28, 12-10**
    sodium, **3-27, 12-17**
    trace metals, **3-26**
  nitrates and nitrites in, **3-38**
  osteoporosis and, **10-12**
  proteins in, **3-3, 3-48**
  sugar in, **3-33**
  surgery and, **3-52**
  synthetic sweeteners in, **3-37**
  teeth and, **13-7**
  vegetarian, **3-35**
  vitamins in, **3-6**
    folic acid, **3-18**
    megavitamins and, **3-7**
    naming of, **3-8**
    recommendations regarding, **3-20**
    vitamin A, **3-9**
    vitamin B_1, **3-13**
    vitamin B_2, **3-14**
    vitamin B_3, **3-15, 8-29**
    vitamin B_6, **3-16, 7-25**
    vitamin B_{12}, **3-17**
    vitamin C, **3-6, 3-7, 3-19, 3-20, 11-6**
    vitamin D, **3-10**
    vitamin E, **3-12**
    vitamin K, **3-11**
  weight and, **3-40** to **3-44**
  (*See also* Food; Nutrition)
Diet clubs, **3-49**
Diet for Living, A, **3-54**
Diflunisal (Dolobid), **10-3**
DiGel, **13-15**

Index

Digestive system (see Gastrointestinal tract)
Digitalis, **12-46**
  appetite and, **3-50, 12-46**
  foreign travel and, **4-19**
  toxic dose of, **12-46**
Digitoxin, **12-46**
Digoxin (Lanoxin), **12-46**
Dilantin (Phenytoin), **7-8, 7-40**
Dilation and curettage (D and C), **15-26**
Diltiazem (Cardizem), **12-20**
Diphenhydramine (Benadryl), **5-34, 7-25, 8-29, 16-12**
Diphenoxylate (Lomotil), **4-16, 17-16**
Dipyrone, cautions regarding, **4-18**
Disc, low back pain and, **10-10**
Discharge:
  as sign of cancer, **17-3**
  vaginal, **15-5, 15-6**
Discomfort, insomnia and, **5-25**
Disipal (Orphenadrine), **7-25**
Disorientation, senility and, **6-1**
Disulfiram (Antabuse), **5-40**
Diuretics, **8-29, 12-9, 12-46**
  dieting and, **3-50**
Diuril (Chlorothiazide), **12-9**
Diverticulitis, **13-26**
Diverticulosis, **13-26**
Dizziness (vertigo), **8-28**
  in Ménière's syndrome, **8-29**
Doctor [see Physician(s)]
Dr. Atkin's Diet Revolution: The High Calorie Way to Stay Thin Forever, **3-47**
Doctor's Quick Weight Loss Diet, The, **3-48**
Dolobid (Diflunisal), **10-3**
L-Dopa (Bendopa, Dopar, Larodopa):
  carbidopa and, **7-25, 15-12**
  interaction with pyridoxine, **7-25**
Dopamine (Intropin) with lung embolism, **11-24**
Dopar (L-dopa), **7-25**
Doppler ultrasonic blood velocity indicator, **18-24**
Doriden (Glutethimide), **5-34**
Doxepin (Adapin, Sinequan), **5-15**
Doxycycline (Doxy-II, Vibramycin), **4-14**
"DPT" (diphtheria, pertussis, tetanus) shot, **4-12**
Dramamine, **4-4**

Dreams:
  bad, **5-22**
  narcolepsy and, **5-33**
Drinking habits, **3-1**
  (*See also* Diet; Water when traveling)
Drinking Man's Diet, The, **3-47**
Driving:
  at night, **2-13**
  in storm conditions, **2-15**
Drowsiness:
  with antihistamines, **11-5, 11-7**
  with reserpine, **12-11**
  (*See also* Sleep)
Drug(s):
  allergies to: conjunctivitis and, **8-12**
    flu shots, **11-11**
    rashes and, **9-5**
  with angina, **12-20**
  antianxiety, **5-8**
  anticonvulsant (*see* Anticonvulsants)
  antidepressant (*see* Antidepressants)
  antiemetic, **8-29**
  bad dreams caused by, **5-22**
  with bursitis, **10-15**
  caffeine in, **3-36**
  in cancer treatment, **17-22**
    ovarian, **15-24**
    stomach, **13-9**
  to decrease pain: habit-forming, **7-16 to 7-20**
    nonhabit-forming, **7-10 to 7-15**
  for diabetes, **16-12**
  for diarrhea, **4-14 to 4-16**
  with duodenal ulcers, **13-21**
  experimental, **17-5**
  fainting produced by, **18-18**
  generic and brand-name, **2-8**
  for glaucoma, **8-20**
  for gout, **10-7**
  to increase cerebral function, **12-52**
  insomnia caused by, **5-27**
  interactions with alcohol, **5-38**
  in management of hypertension: diuretic, **12-9**
    nondiuretic, **12-11**
    potassium and, **12-10**
  with osteoporosis, **10-12**
  overdose of, **18-13**
  and pain (*see* Pain, drugs used to decrease)
  with Parkinson's disease, **7-25**

Index

Drugs (*Cont.*)
 preventing accidents with, **2-9**
 price of, **2-8**
 as reducing aid, **3-50**
 for rheumatoid arthritis, **10-3**
 senility and, **6-8**
 sexual function and, **15-10**
 side effects of, **2-9**
 sleeping, **5-34**
 sodium in, **12-17**
 tremors and, **7-22**
 with urinary system infections, **14-6**
 when traveling, **4-19**
 withdrawal from, **5-27**
 (*See also* Chemotherapy; *specific drugs; specific types of drugs*)
Dry cleaning fluid, danger of fire with, **2-11**
"Dry runs," **15-33**
Duofilm, **9-29**
Dust, allergy to, **11-7**
Dymelor (Acetohexamide), **16-12**
Dyrenium (Triamterene), **12-9**
Dysarthria following stroke, **12-50**
Dyskinesias, **7-23**
Dysphasia, **12-48**
Dyspnea (*see* Breathing)
Dysrhythmia (*see* Arrhythmia)

Ears:
 balance and, **8-27**
 discharge from, **8-26**
 dizziness and, **8-28**
 fluid in, **8-22**
 hearing loss and, **8-22**
  hearing aid and, **8-23**
  talking to person with, **8-24**
 infections of, **8-26**
 otosclerosis and, **8-25**
 pain in, **8-26**
  air travel and, **4-3**
  causes of, **7-3**
  Ménière's syndrome and, **8-29**
 physicians treating, **8-32**
 reconstruction of, **8-26**
 ringing in, **8-29**
 wax in, **8-22**
Eating habits, **3-1, 3-53**
 (*See also* Appetite; Diet; Food; Nutrition)

ECG (*see* Electrocardiogram)
Echocardiography, **12-24**
Ecotrin (Aspirin), **7-11**
Ectropion, **8-10**
Edema (*see* Swelling of feet and legs)
Ejaculation(s):
 premature, **15-7**
 refractory period between, **15-2**
 retrograde, **15-33**
EKG (*see* Electrocardiogram)
Elastic bandages and stockings for varicose veins, **9-25**
Elavil (Amitriptyline), **5-15**
Electric adapters, **4-19**
Electric toothbrush, **13-11**
Electrical cords, cautions regarding, **2-11**
Electrical power failure, preparation for, **2-15**
Electrocardiogram (EKG, ECG), **12-5, 12-7, 12-25**
Electroconvulsive therapy (ECT), **5-10, 5-16**
Electroencephalogram (EEG), all-night, **5-30**
Electrostatic air filter, **11-7**
Electrosurgery for hair removal, **9-40**
Embolectomy, **11-24**
Embolism in lung, **11-24**
Emergencies, **18-1**
 bleeding, **18-5** to **18-10**
 broken bones, **18-20**
 broken neck or back, **18-22**
 burns, **18-11** to **18-12**
 choking, **18-3, 18-4**
 dislocated joint, **18-21**
 exits for, **2-11**
 fainting, **18-17, 18-18**
 fallen objects, **18-1**
 first aid kit for, **18-2**
 gas, **18-1, 18-3, 18-14**
 heat stroke, **18-19**
 Heimlich maneuver and, **18-4**
 hiccups, **18-23**
 muscle cramps, **18-24**
 poisoning, **18-13** to **18-16**
 puncture wounds, **18-10**
 snakebites, **18-16**
 stings, **18-15**
 sunstroke, **18-19**
 preparation for, **2-15**
Emergency cold leg, **18-25**

325

Index

Emergency phone number, **19-3**
Emphysema, **11-17**
Empirin (Aspirin compound), **7-12**
Encephalitis, **7-36**
Endocrine glands, **16-1** to **16-21**
Endometrial polyps, **15-26**
Endoscopic papillotomy, **13-33**
Enduron (Methyclothiazide), **12-9**
Enemas, **13-22**
Entero-Vioform (Iodochlorhydroxyquin), **4-15**
Entropion, **8-10**
Epilepsy, **7-39**
   emergency treatment of, **7-40**
   grand mal, **7-39**
   partial, **7-39**
   (*See also* Convulsions)
Epilepsy Foundation of America, **7-40**
Epinephrine with insect strings, **18-15**
Equal (sweetener), **3-37**
Equanil (Meprobamate), **5-8**
   interactions with alcohol, **5-38**
Erection:
   cancer therapy and, **17-20**
   climacteric and, **15-2**
   painful, **15-8**
Ergomar (Ergotamine), **7-4**, **7-5**
Ergot alkaloids (Hydergine), **12-52**
Ergotamine (Ergomar, Gynergen), **7-4**, **7-5**
   with caffeine, **7-4**, **7-5**
Erythromycin (Erythrocin), **11-19**
Esidrix (Hydrochlorothiazide), **12-9**
Esophageal speech, **11-10**
Esophagitis, **13-14**
Esophagus, **13-13** to **13-17**
Estrogen:
   breast cancer and, **15-18**
   postmenopausal, **15-6**
   prostatic cancer and, **15-36**
Estrogen-receptor assay, **15-18**
Ethamide (Ethoxzolamine), **8-20**
Ethchlorvynol (Placidyl), **5-34**
Ethoxzolamine (Cardase, Ethamide), **8-20**
Eustacian tube, **4-3**, **8-26**
Exercise, **1-5**, **1-6**
   diabetes and, **16-10**
   following heart attack, **12-36**
   isometric, **4-2**, **12-36**
   with lung embolism, **11-24**
   senility and, **6-4**
   sleep and, **5-18**

Exercise (*Cont.*)
   following stroke, **12-50**
Exercise test, **12-25**
Exfoliative cytology, **13-19**
Exits for emergency, **2-11**
Exna (Benzthiazide), **12-9**
Exophthalmos, **16-5**
Extended-care center, **20-5**
Extrapyramidal system, **7-1**
Eye(s), **8-2**
   ache in, **8-19**
   cataracts and, **8-15**
   conjunctivitis and, **8-12**
   contact lenses and, **8-9**
   corneal transplantation and, **8-16**
   examination of, **8-8**
   floating spots in, **8-17**
   foreign bodies in, **8-14**
   glaucoma and, **8-19**
      drugs used to treat, **8-20**
   hyperopia and, **8-7**
   myopia and, **8-5**
   physicians treating, **8-3**
   presbyopia and, **8-8**
   reading light and, **8-6**
   red, **8-12**
   retinal detachment and, **8-17**
   senile macular degeneration and, **8-4**
   tearing of, **8-11**
   transient loss of vision and, **8-21**
   vitrectomy and, **8-18**
   watering, **8-8**
   (*See also* Vision)
Eye drops, **8-14**
Eye strain, **8-7**
Eye washes, **8-13**
Eyelid, drooping, **8-10**
   after surgery, **8-15**

Facial pain, **7-8**
Facial palsy, **7-28**
Fad(s), avoidance of, **3-1**
Fad diets, **3-46**
Fainting, treatment of, **18-17** to **18-18**
Falls, preventing, **2-10**
False teeth (*see* Teeth, false)
Family:
   caretaking member of, **6-5**
   decisions regarding care and, **6-3**
   of dying patient, **22-3**

Index

Family (*Cont.*)
  extended, **23-1**
  need for closeness with, **23-3**
  psychological response of, to nursing home, **20-17**
  roles and conflicts in, **23-2**
  sharing experiences with, **23-5** to **23-6**
  sharing news of, **23-4**
  suicide prevention and, **5-13**
  talking about feelings with, **23-7**
  visiting by: children and, **23-12**
    gifts and, **23-11**
    importance of, **20-17**
    performing services during, **23-10**
    snacks and, **23-9**
Family practitioner, **13-1, 14-1**
Family psychotherapy, **5-43**
Farsightedness (hyperopia), **8-7**
Fat(s), **3-5**
  gallbladder disease and, **13-33**
  polyunsaturated, **3-5**
  saturated, **3-5**
    controlling intake of, **3-29**
  unsaturated, **3-5**
Fatigue:
  in diabetes, **16-8**
  hyperthyroidism and, **16-4, 16-5**
Fatty blood conditions, **12-16**
Fear(s), **5-4**
  of abandonment, **20-17**
  of cancer, **17-7** to **17-8, 17-22**
  of death, **22-1**
  following heart attack, **12-37**
  of sleep, **5-21**
Febrolin (Acetaminophen), **7-13**
Feelings, importance of talking about, **23-7**
Feet:
  asleep, **4-2**
  athlete's foot and, **9-24**
  care of, diabetes and, **16-20**
  corns on, **9-28**
  warts on, **9-29**
Feldene (Piroxicam), **10-3**
Fellow of organization, **2-6**
Felsules (Chloral hydrate), **5-34**
Fenfluramine (Pondimin), **3-50**
Fenoprofen (Nalfon), **10-3**
Fever:
  with cold, **11-2**
  with encephalitis, **7-36**
  with flu, **11-11**

Fever (*Cont.*)
  with occupational lung disorders, **11-23**
  with pneumonia, **11-18, 11-20**
Fever blisters, **9-21**
Fiber in diet, **3-34, 13-26**
Fibromas, **15-25**
Fibromyomas, **15-25**
Financial aspects of care (*see* Cost)
Financial planning, **2-2**
  free information on, **2-3**
Fingernails [*see* Nail(s)]
Fiorinal (Aspirin compound), **7-12**
Fire prevention, **2-11**
Fire safety, nursing homes and, **20-10**
First aid:
  course in, **18-1**
  kit, contents of, **18-2**
  (*See also* Emergencies)
Fish, fat in, **3-29**
Fissures:
  anal, **9-3**
  of mouth corners, **9-18**
Floors, care of, for safety, **22-10**
Flu, **11-11, 13-2**
  Guillain-Barré syndrome and, **11-12**
Flu shot, **11-11**
  alternatives to, **11-13**
Fluorescent light for herpes infections, **9-21**
Flurazepam (Dalmane), **5-34**
Flushes, hot, **15-3**
Folic acid (pteroylglutamic acid), **3-18**
Follicular keratosis, **3-9**
Food:
  cost of, **3-39**
  headaches caused by, **7-3**
  monoamine oxidase inhibitors and, cautions regarding, **5-15**
  in nursing homes, **20-14**
  sense of taste and, **8-30**
  when traveling, **4-14**
  (*See also* Appetite; Diet; Nutrition)
Food poisoning, **13-2**
For Older People, Eating Right for Less, **3-39**
Foreign body in eye, **8-14**
Foreign travel (*see* Travel)
Forgetfulness (*see* Memory loss)
Four-hydroxycoumarin (Dicoumarol), **12-52**
Freckles, **9-14**

327

Index

Freezing for hemorrhoids, **13-24**
Friend(s):
   of dying patient, **22-3**
   suicide prevention and, **5-13**
Friendly visiting, **2-22**
Frigidity, **15-9** to **15-12**
   psychological causes of, **15-11**
Frog in throat, **11-10**
Fulvicin-U/F (Griseofulvin), **9-36**
Funeral:
   alternatives for, **22-11**
   cost of, **22-10**
   selection of burial property and, **22-8**
   service for, **22-9**
Funeral societies, **22-11**
Furosemide (Lasix), **12-9, 12-46**
   interaction with chloral hydrate, **5-34**

Gallbladder, **13-33**
Gallstone, **13-33**
Gantanol (Sulfamethoxazole), **14-6**
Gantrisin (Sulfisoxazole), **14-6**
Gargles, **11-8**
Gas:
   in chest, **13-13**
   danger of fire with, **2-11**
   inability to smell, **8-30**
   intestinal, **13-15**
   poisoning by, **18-1, 18-3, 18-14**
Gastric ulcer, **13-18**
Gastritis, alcoholic, **5-37**
Gastroenterologists, **13-1, 13-27**
Gastrointestinal (GI) tract, **13-1**
   disorders of, self-treatment of, **13-2**
   intestinal gas, **13-15**
Gastroscope, **13-19**
Gelatin, nails and, **9-33**
Gelusil, **13-21**
Generation gap, **23-3**
Generativity, importance of, **5-3**
Gifts during visits, **23-11**
Gitaligin (Gitalin), **12-46**
Glasses:
   bifocal, **8-8**
   with cataracts, **8-15**
   contact lenses, **8-9**
   for farsightedness, **8-7**
   for nearsightedness, **8-5**
   for presbyopia, **8-8**
   prescription for, when traveling, **4-19**

Glaucoma, **8-9, 8-15, 8-19**
   caution regarding use of Dalmane with, **5-34**
   drugs used for, **8-20**
Gliomas, **7-37**
Glossopharyngeal neuralgia, **7-9**
Gloves to prevent burns, **2-11**
Glucagon, **16-17**
Glucagon kit, **16-19**
Glucose-tolerance test, **16-9**
Glutethimide (Doriden), **5-34**
Glycerol, **8-19**
Glyceryl guaiacolate, **11-4**
Glycopyrrolate (Robincil), **13-21**
Goiter, **16-3**
   diffuse and nodular toxic, **16-5**
Gold salts, **10-3**
Golden age pass, **2-20**
Gonadotropin, chorionic, **3-50**
Gout, **10-6**
   drugs in treatment of, **10-7**
Grab bars, **2-10**
Grand mal attack, **7-39**
   emergency treatment of, **7-40**
Graves' disease, **16-5**
Gray Panthers, **2-25**
Grease fires, **2-11**
Grief reaction, **5-9**
Griseofulvin (Grifulvin V, Fulvicin-U/F), **9-36**
Grossan Nasal Irrigator Tip, **11-7**
Group Health Association of America, **21-11**
Group psychotherapy, **5-43**
Group tours, planned for the elderly, **4-1**
Guanabenz (Wytensin), **12-11**
Guanethidine (Ismelin), **12-11**
Guillain-Barré syndrome, **11-12**
Gums:
   bleeding, **3-19, 12-52**
   disease of, **13-9**
Gynecologists, **14-1**
Gynergen (Ergotamine), **7-4, 7-5**

Hair, **9-37**
   dandruff and, **9-42**
   excessive growth of, **9-40**
   graying of, **9-37, 9-41**
   loss of, **9-38**
   sudden and patchy, **9-39**

Index

Halazepam (Paxipam), **5-8**
Halcion (Triazolam), **5-34**
Halitosis, **13-3**
Hallucinations:
  delirium tremens and, **5-37**
  hypnagogic, **5-33**
  seizures and, **7-39**
  sleep apnea and, **5-32**
Hallways, preventing falls in, **2-10**
Hand(s), redness of palms of, **9-13**
Handrails, **2-10**
Hangover:
  alcohol and, **5-37**
  with sleeping pills, **5-29, 5-34**
Hay fever [*see* Allergy(ies)]
HDL (high-density lipoproteins), **3-32**
Head injuries, **7-32**
Headache, **7-3**
  with brain tumor, **7-37**
  cluster, **7-7**
  with cold, **11-2**
  with flu, **11-11**
  with head injury, **7-32**
  histamine (*see* cluster, *above*)
  hypertension and, **12-3**
  with meningitis, **7-34**
  migraine (*see* Migraines)
  with monoamine oxidase inhibitors, **5-15**
  presbyopia and, **8-8**
  following spinal tap, **7-34**
  tension, **7-3**
Heaf Test, **11-22**
Health department, nursing home standards and, **20-7**
Health maintenance organizations (HMOs), **21-11**
Hearing aid, **8-23**
  otosclerosis and, **8-25**
Hearing loss, **8-22**
  in Ménière's disease, **8-29**
  sudden, **8-25**
Heart, **12-1**
  effect of hypertension on, **12-4**
Heart attack, **12-1, 12-26**
  arrhythmia and, **12-33**
  aspirin and, **12-41**
  cardioversion and, **12-34**
  depression following, **12-38**
  emergency procedures for, **12-28** to **12-30**
  estrogen and, **15-6**

Heart attack (*Cont.*)
  hospital treatment of, **12-31** to **12-32**
  morphine and, **12-31**
  pacemakers and, **12-35**
  physical activity and, **12-36**
  recovery period following, **12-37**
  sexual activity following, **12-39, 15-14**
  symptoms of, **7-3, 12-27**
Heart disease, prevention of, **12-40, 12-41**
Heart failure, **12-42**
  acute, treatment of, **12-46**
  left: causes of, **12-44**
    symptoms of, **12-45**
  right, symptoms of, **12-43**
Heart massage, how to perform, **12-30**
Heartbeat, feeling, **3-17**
Heartburn, **13-13, 13-14**
Heat, how to use, **18-2**
Heatstroke, treatment of, **18-19**
Heimlich maneuver, **18-4**
Hemiparesis, stroke and, **12-48**
Hemorrhage:
  with head injury, **7-32**
  (*See also* Stroke)
Hemorrhoids, **9-3, 13-24**
  fiber and, **3-34**
Heparin:
  with heart attack, **12-31**
  with lung embolism, **11-24**
Hepatitis, **13-32**
  coma and, **13-31**
  prevention of, **4-7**
  reused needles as source of, **4-18**
Hernia:
  hiatal, **13-17**
  umbilical and inguinal, **13-17, 15-37**
Heroin, **7-20**
Herpes, genital, **15-15**
Herpes simplex, **9-21**
Herpes zoster, **9-23**
Hiccups, treatment of, **18-23**
High blood pressure (*see* Hypertension)
High-density lipoproteins (HDL), **3-32**
High-protein diets, **3-48**
Hip joint, replacement of, **10-5**
Hives, **9-5**
  insulin injections and, **16-15**
Hoarseness, **11-9**
  with cancer, **11-10, 11-25, 17-3**
Hodgkin's disease, **17-11**
Home care, Medicare coverage for, **21-7**

Index

Home maintenance workers, 2-24
Homemaker service, 2-24
Hopelessness, 5-9
Hormones, 16-1
   with arthritis, 10-3
   breast cancer and, 15-18
   prostate cancer and, 15-36
   thyroid (*see* Thyroid hormone)
   (*See also* Steroids)
Hospice, 22-3
Hospital:
   admission to, 19-5
   cost of, insurance coverage for, 21-12
      Medicare coverage for, 21-2
   getting to, in emergency, 19-3
   how to choose, 19-1
   types of, 19-2
   what to take to, 19-4
   (*See also* Visiting)
Hospitalization for depression, 5-10
Hot flushes, 15-3
Human Sexual Inadequacy, 15-2
Human Sleep and Its Disorders, 5-33
Hydergine (Ergot alkaloids), 12-52
Hydralazine (Apresoline), 12-11
Hydro Med Inc., 11-7
Hydrochlorothiazide (Esidrix, Hydrodiuril), 12-9
Hydrocortisone acetate ointment for itching, 9-2
HydroDiuril (Hydrochlorothiazide), 12-9
Hydroflumethiazide (Saluron), 12-9
Hyperglycemia, 16-7
Hyperlipidemias, 12-16
Hyperopia (farsightedness), 8-7
Hypertension, 5-32, 12-2
   causes of, 12-18
   damage caused by, 12-4
   diagnosing, 12-5
   diastolic, 12-5
   diet and, 12-13 to 12-17
   essential, 12-8
   malignant, 12-4
   secondary, 12-8
   stress and, 12-12
   symptoms of, 12-3
   systolic, 12-5
   treating, 12-8
      drugs and, 12-9 to 12-11
Hypertensive crisis with monoamine oxidase inhibitors, 5-15

Hyperthyroidism, **16-4, 16-5**
Hypnotics, **5-34**
Hypoglycemia:
   antidiabetic drugs and, **16-12**
   as insulin reaction, **16-17**
Hypoglycemic drugs, **16-12**
Hyposensitization, **11-7**
Hypothermia, **2-14**
Hypothyroidism, **16-4**
Hysterectomy, **15-30**
   sexual activity after, **15-4**

Ibuprofen (Motrin), **10-3**
Ice, how to use, **18-2**
Idoxuridine (Stoxil), **8-12, 9-23**
Ileostomy, **14-9**
Iletin, **16-14**
Iletin II, **16-14**
Imipramine (Tofranil), **5-15**
Immune globulin, hepatitis and, **4-7**
Immunization, **4-7**
   for cholera, **4-8**
   for pneumonia, **11-18**
   for polio, **4-11**
   for smallpox, **4-10**
   for tetanus, **4-12**
   for typhoid, **4-13**
   for typhus, **4-9**
Immunization certificates, **4-19**
Impotence, **15-2, 15-7**
   cancer therapy and, **17-20**
   psychological causes of, **15-11**
Incontinence, stress, **14-2, 15-29**
Independence Factory, The, **10-3**
Inderal (Propranolol), **7-6, 12-20**
Indigestion, **13-13, 17-3**
Individual psychotherapy, **5-43**
Indomethacin (Indocin), **10-3, 10-7, 10-9**
Infarct, **12-4**
Infection(s):
   of brain, **7-35**
   cancer therapy and, **17-19**
   of ear, **8-26**
   frequent, diabetes and, **16-8**
   following mastectomy, **15-19**
   of nails, **9-34, 9-36**
   rectal itching and, **9-3**
   red streaking and, **18-10**
Influenza (*see* Flu)
Information, free sources of, **2-25**

Index

Ingrown nails, **9-35**
INH (Isoniazid), **11-22**
Injections, cautions regarding, in foreign countries, **4-18**
Insect stings, treatment of, **18-15**
Insomnia, **5-17, 5-33, 7-25**
  causes of, **5-18** to **5-28**
  treatment of, **5-29** to **5-31**
  drugs in, **5-34**
"Instant tan" centers, **9-32**
Institutional care, **6-5**
  compulsory admission and, **6-6**
  (*See also* Nursing home)
Insulin, **16-13**
  overdose of, **16-17**
  regulating amount of, **16-16**
  site of injection for, **16-15**
  use of, **16-14**
Insulin reaction, **16-17**
Insurance, **21-10**
  chiropractic care under, **10-18**
  proof of, **19-5**
  psychotherapy under, **5-44, 5-46**
  (*See also* Medicaid; Medicare)
Intercourse (*see* Sexual activity)
Intermediate-care facilities, **20-4**
Intermedic, **4-17**
Intern, **19-2**
Internal clock, **4-5**
International Association of Laryngectomees, **11-10**
International unit (IU), **3-9**
Internist, **13-1, 14-1**
Internship, **2-6**
Intravenous pyelogram (IVP), **14-5, 15-36, 17-9**
Intrinsic factor, **3-17**
Intropin (Dopamine), **11-24**
Iodine:
  for abrasions and scratches, **18-9**
  goiter and, **16-3**
  radioactive, **16-5**
Iodochlorhydroxyquin (Entero-Vioform, Mexaform, Clioquinol), **4-15**
Ipecac to induce vomiting, **18-13**
Iridectomy, **8-19**
Iris, **8-16**
Iron in diet, **3-25**
Irritability, **16-5**
Ismelin (Guanethidine), **12-11**
Isocarboxazid (Marplan), **5-15**

Isoetharine (Bronkometer), **11-16**
Isolation, psychological problems and, **5-1**
Isoniazid (INH), **11-22**
Isopropamide (Darbid), **13-21**
Isoptin (Verapamil), **12-20**
Isoxsuprine (Vasodilan), **12-52**
Itching:
  of feet, **9-23**
  of poison ivy, **9-7**
  rectal, **9-3**
  significance of, **9-2**
  treatment of, **9-2**

Jane Brody's Nutrition Book, **3-54**
Jaundice, **13-32**
  alcohol and, **5-37**
Jaw pain, **7-3**
Jejuno-ileal bypass, **3-51**
Joint(s):
  diseases of (*see* Musculoskeletal disorders)
  dislocated, emergency treatment of, **18-21**
  pain in, **10-2**
  stiffness of, **10-3, 10-4**
Joint Commission on Accreditation of Hospitals, **20-7**
Joint replacement, **10-5**

K-Tab, **12-10**
Kaon-Cl, **12-10**
Kaopectate, **17-16**
Karaya gum, **13-28**
Kato powder, **12-10**
Keflex (Cephalexin), **14-6**
Kemadrin (Procyclidine hydrochloride), **7-25**
Keralyt, **9-28**
Kessodrate (Chloral hydrate), **5-34**
Ketacidosis, **16-18**
Ketosis, dieting and, **3-47**
Kidney(s), **14-1**
  effect of hypertension on, **12-4**
  failure of, **14-8**
  infections of, **14-3**
  intravenous pyelogram and, **17-9**
  sleeping pills and, **5-34**
  stones in, **14-7**
  transplantation of, **14-8**

Index

Kidney artery hypertension, **12-18**
Klotrix, **12-10**
Knee, replacement of, **10-5**
Korsakoff syndrome, **5-37**
Kyphosis, **11-17**

Lacto-ovo-vegetarians, **3-35**
Lacto-vegetarians, **3-35**
Ladder:
  for emergency escape, **2-11**
  safe use of, **2-10**
Laetrile (Bee-Seventeen, Aprikern), **17-6**
Lanatoxide-C (Cedilanid), **12-46**
Lanoxin (Digoxin), **12-46**
Larodopa (L-dopa), **7-25**
Laryngitis, **11-9**
Laryngoscope, **11-10**
Larynx, **11-1**
Lasix (Furosemide), **12-9, 12-46**
  interaction with chloral hydrate, **5-34**
Last Chance Diet, The, **3-48**
Laxatives, **13-22, 13-24**
  dieting and, **3-50**
LDL (low-density lipoproteins), **3-32**
Learning as compensation strategy, **5-3**
Leg(s):
  cold, emergency, **18-25**
  cramps in, nocturnal, **5-28**
  crossing, **4-2**
  pressure point for, **18-7**
  ulcers of, **9-26**
Legionnaires' disease, **11-19**
Leukemias, **17-1**
Leukoplakia, **13-5**
Levodopa (Bendopa, Dopar, Larodopa), **7-25**
Levothroxine, **16-3**
Librium (Chlordiazepoxide), **5-8**
  interactions with alcohol, **5-38**
License:
  medical, **2-6**
  of nursing home, **20-7**
Licensed practical nurse (L.P.N.), **20-11**
Licensing for psychotherapists, **5-46**
Lifting with back pain, **10-10**
Light(s):
  fluorescent, for herpes infections, **9-21**
  headaches and, **7-3**
  nightlight, **6-4**
  for reading, **8-6**

Light(s) (*Cont.*)
  on stairs, **2-10**
Lightning, precautions regarding, **2-15**
Liothyronine (T3), **16-4**
Lip, cancer of, **13-6**
Liquids with cold, **11-2**
Lithium batteries for pacemakers, **12-35**
"Live flesh," **7-23**
Liver:
  biopsy of, **17-9**
  disease of: alcohol and, **5-37**
    hepatitis (*see* Hepatitis)
    symptoms of, **13-31**
  functions of, **13-30**
  sleeping pills and, **5-34**
Liver palms, **9-13**
Liver scan, **17-9**
Living Bank International, The, **8-16**
Local anesthetics with canker sores, **13-4**
Lomotil (Diphenoxylate), **4-16, 17-16**
Lopressor (Metoprolol), **12-11**
Lorazepam (Ativan), **5-8**
Low back pain, **10-10**
Low-density lipoproteins (LDL), **3-32**
Ludiomil (Maprotiline), **5-15**
Lump, diagnosis of, **17-3**
Lumpectomy, **15-18**
Lung:
  biopsy of, **11-25**
  cancer of (*see* Cancer, of lung)
  occupational disorders of, **11-23**
  sleeping pills and, **5-34**
Lung embolism (blood clot), **11-24**
Lung scan, **11-24**
Lymphangiogram, **17-9**
Lymphedema, **15-19**
Lymphomas, **17-1**
Lysine, **9-21**

Maalox, **13-15, 13-21**
Macrodantin (Nitrofurantoin), **14-6**
Magnesium in diet, **3-24**
Mail, importance to patient, **23-13**
Malaria, protection against, **4-7**
Male hormones:
  breast cancer and, **15-18**
  following menopause, **15-6**
Malignancy, **9-31, 17-1**
  (*See also* Cancer)
Mammography, **15-17**

Index

Mandelamine (Methenamide), **14-6**
Mannitol, **8-19**
Maprotiline (Ludiomil), **5-15**
Marijuana in cancer treatment, **17-16**
Marplan (Isocarboxazid), **5-15**
Martinis and Whipped Cream, **3-47**
Mastectomy, **15-18**
   adjustment to, **15-19**
Masturbation, **15-7, 15-9, 5-20**
Mausoleum, **22-11**
Meals-on-wheels, **2-23**
Measurements, weight equivalencies and, **3-55**
Meats, saturated fats in, **3-29**
Meclizine (Bonine), **4-4, 17-16**
Medic Alert, **16-19**
Medicaid, **21-9**
   coordination with Medicare, **21-9**
   nursing home qualification for, **20-7**
   proof of, **19-5**
Medical appointment, making, **1-4**
Medical doctor (M.D.), **2-6**
Medicare, **21-1**
   conditions of, **21-3**
   coordination with Medicaid, **21-9**
   coverage for chiropractic care under, **10-18**
   custodial care and, **6-4**
   home care covered by, **21-7**
   hospital services covered by, **21-2**
   nursing home care covered by, **21-8**
   nursing home qualification for, **20-7**
   outpatient services covered by, **21-5** to **21-6**
   proof of, **19-5**
   psychiatric care and, **21-4**
Medications [*see* Drug(s)]
Medicine as art and science, **2-6**
"Medicine's Back to Work Plan," **10-3**
Megavitamins, **3-7, 3-20**
Melanomas, **9-14, 9-31**
Memory loss, **5-5, 5-37, 6-1** to **6-3**
Ménière's syndrome, **8-29**
Meningiomas, **7-37**
Meningitis, **7-34**
Menopause, **15-3**
   surgical, **15-4**
   symptoms requiring medical attention, **15-5**
   use of estrogen following, **15-6**
Menstrual irregularities, **15-5, 15-25, 15-28**

Mental health professional for anxiety, **5-7**
Mental reserve, **5-2, 5-5**
Meperidine (Demerol), **7-18, 13-33**
Meprobamate (Equanil, Meprospan, Miltown), **5-8**
   interactions with alcohol, **5-38**
Mercurochrome for abrasions and scratches, **18-9**
Metahydrin (Trichlormethiazide), **12-9**
Metastasis, **15-28**
Methazolamide (Neptazane), **8-20**
Methenamide (Mandelamine), **14-6**
Methimazole (Tapazole), **16-5**
Methionine, **14-6**
Methyclothiazide (Aquatensen, Enduron), **12-9**
Methyldopa (Aldomet), **12-11**
Methylphenidate (Ritalin), **5-33**
Methyprylon (Nodular), **5-34**
Methysergide (Sansert), **7-6**
Metoprolol (Lopressor), **12-11**
Metric conversion tables, **3-56**
Mettrol (Phenformin), **16-12**
Mexaform (Iodochlorhydroxyquin), **4-15**
Micro-K, **12-10**
Migraines, **7-3, 7-4**
   loss of vision and, **8-21**
   prevention of, **7-6**
   treatment of, **7-5**
Milk, duodenal ulcer and, **13-21**
Milk of magnesia, **13-22**
Miltown (Meprobamate), **5-8**
   interactions with alcohol, **5-38**
Mineral(s), **3-21**
   calcium, **3-22**
   iron, **3-25**
   magnesium, **3-24**
   phosphorus, **3-23**
   potassium, **3-28**
   sodium, **3-27**
   trace metals, **3-26**
Mineral oil:
   as laxative, **13-22**
   for moisturizing, **9-2**
Moisturizers, **9-2**
Molds, allergy to, **11-7**
Mole, change in, **9-31, 17-3**
Moniliasis, rectal, **9-3**
Monoamine oxidase inhibitors, cautions regarding, **5-15**
Monosodium glutamate, **3-27**

Index

Mood changes, senility and, **6-1**
Morphine sulfate, **7-17, 12-31**
Motion sickness, **4-4**
Motrin (Ibuprofen), **10-3**
Mouth:
  bad breath and, **13-3**
  cancer of, **13-6**
  cracking of skin at angles of, **13-9**
  fissures in skin around, **9-18**
  radiation therapy and, **17-16**
  sores in, **3-14, 13-4, 13-6**
  white spots in, **13-5**
Mouth-to-mouth ventilation:
  for carbon monoxide poisoning, **18-14**
  with heart attack, **12-29**
Mouthwash, **13-3**
Movement disorders:
  abnormal involuntary movements, **7-23**
  Parkinson's disease, **7-22, 7-24**
    drug treatment of, **7-25**
  stroke and, **12-48**
  tremors, **7-22**
Multiple vitamins, **3-20, 3-22, 3-25, 3-26**
Murine, **8-13**
Muscle cramps:
  nocturnal, **5-28**
  treatment of, **18-24**
Muscle weakness:
  carpal-tunnel syndrome, **7-31**
  facial palsy, **7-28**
  of one side, **12-48**
  radial nerve palsy, **7-30**
  ulnar nerve palsy, **7-29**
  (*See also* Paralysis)
Musculoskeletal disorders, **10-1**
  bone tumors, **10-8**
  bunion, **10-14**
  bursitis, **10-15**
  joint diseases: arthritis (*see* Arthritis)
    gout, **10-6, 10-7**
    total joint replacement and, **10-5**
  low back pain, **10-10 to 10-11**
  osteoporosis, **10-12**
  Paget's disease, **10-9**
  physicians specializing in, **10-16 to 10-18**
  tennis elbow, **10-13**
Mustard powder to induce vomiting, **18-13**
Myasthenia gravis, **8-10**
Mycoplasma (primary atypical pneumonia), **11-21**
Mycostatin (Nystatin), **9-3**

Myelogram, **10-10**
Myeloma, multiple, **10-8**
Mylanta, **13-15, 13-21**
Mylicin (Simethicone), **13-15**
Myocardial infarction (*see* Heart attack)
Myomas, **15-25**
Myopia (nearsightedness), **8-5**

Nacton (Poldine), **13-21**
Nadolol (Corgard), **12-11**
Nail(s):
  care of, **9-33**
  infection of, **9-34**
    fungal, **9-36**
  ingrown, **9-35**
  splitting of, **9-23**
  thickening of, **9-36**
Nail polish, **9-33**
Nalfon (Fenoprofen), **10-3**
Napping, insomnia and, **5-18**
Naproxen (Naprosyn), **10-3**
Narcolepsy, **5-33**
Narcotics, **7-16**
Nardil (Phenelzine), **5-15**
Nasal irrigation, **11-7, 11-8**
Nasalcrom (Cromolyn), **11-7**
National Association for Hearing and Speech Action, **8-23**
National Cancer Institute, **11-27, 15-19**
  test of Laetrile by, **17-6**
National Council on the Aging, **2-25**
National Gray Panthers, **2-25**
National Office on Smoking and Health, **11-27**
National Park Service, **2-20**
Naturetin (Bundroflumethiazide), **12-9**
Nausea:
  causes of, **13-2**
  digitalis and, **12-46**
  flu and, **13-2**
  food poisoning and, **13-2**
Nearsightedness (myopia), **8-5**
Nebulizer, **11-16**
Neck:
  broken, emergency treatment of, **18-22**
  stiff, **7-32**
  thickening of skin of, **9-16**
Neck injuries, **7-33**
Nembutal (Pentobarbital), **5-34**
Neo-Synephrine (Phenylephrine), **8-10**

Index

Nephritis, **14-8**
Nephrologist, **14-1**
Neptazane (Methazolamide), **8-20**
Nerve(s), **16-1**
Nerve deafness, **8-22**
Nervous system, **7-1**
  infections of: brain abscesses, **7-35**
    encephalitis, **7-36**
    meningitis, **7-34**
Nervousness, **5-4**
  (*See also* Anxiety)
Neurologist, **7-41**
  senility and, **6-2**
Neurons, **16-1**
Neurosurgeon, **7-41**
Neutrogena, **9-2**
Nevi, **9-31**
New Voice Clubs, **11-10**
News of family members, importance of sharing, **23-4**
Niacin (Vitamin B_3), **3-15, 8-29**
Nickel, contact dermatitis and, **9-3**
Nicotinamide (Vitamin B_3), **3-15**
Nicotinic acid (Vitamin B_3), **8-29**
Nicotinyl alcohol (Riniacol), **12-52**
Nifedipine (Procardia), **12-20**
Night blindness, **3-9**
Night fears, **6-4**
Night sweats, **9-4, 11-22, 15-3**
Nightlight, **6-4**
Nightmares, **5-22**
Nitrates and nitrites in diet, **3-38**
Nitrofurantoin (Macrodantin), **14-6**
Nitroglycerine (Nitrostat, Nitrodisc, Nitro-Dur, Transderm-Nitro), **12-20**
Nitrosamines, **3-38**
Noctec (Chloral hydrate), **5-34**
Noludar (Methyprylon), **5-34**
Norpramine (Desipramine), **5-15**
Nortriptyline (Aventyl, Pamelor), **5-15**
Nose:
  physicians treating, **8-32**
  smell and taste and, **8-30**
Nosebleeds, **8-31**
Numbness, **7-26**
  in hands and feet, **3-17**
  in leg, **18-25**
Nurses in nursing homes, **20-11**
Nursing, skilled, **21-8**
Nursing home:
  choosing: activities and, **20-15**

Nursing home, choosing (*Cont.*)
  buildings and grounds and, **20-9**
  convenience and, **20-8**
  food and, **20-14**
  licensing and, **20-7**
  medical considerations and, **20-12**
  personnel and, **20-11**
  rooms and, **20-13**
  safety and, **20-10**
  cost of, **20-16**
  insurance coverage for, **21-8, 21-12**
  need for, **20-1**
  psychological issues and, **20-17**
  (*See also* Outside care; Visiting)
NutraSweet, **3-37**
Nutrition:
  senility and, **6-4**
  (*See also* Appetite; Diet; Food)
Nystatin (Mycostatin), **9-3**

Obesity, sexual activity and, **15-14**
Occupational lung disorders, **11-23**
Occupational therapists, **12-51**
Oculist (ophthalmologist), **8-3**
Ocusert Pilo-20, **8-20**
Ocusert Pilo-40, **8-20**
Odor:
  colostomy and, **13-28**
  of urine: diabetes and, **16-9, 16-18**
  in nursing homes, **20-9**
Oliguria, **14-8**
Omnipen (Ampicillin), **14-6**
Oncologist, **15-24, 17-4**
One-Step-At-A-Time filter system (Water Pik), **11-29**
Onychomycosis, **9-36**
Ophthalmologist (oculist), **8-3**
Optician, **8-3**
Optometrist, **8-3**
Orabase, **13-4**
Oral cytologic examination, **13-6**
Oral hygiene (*see* Dental hygiene)
Oratrol (Dichlorphenamide), **8-20**
Orgasm (*see* Sexual arousal)
Orinase (Tolbutamine), **16-12**
Orphenadrine (Disipal), **7-25**
Orthomolecular medicine, **3-7**
Orthopedist, **10-14, 10-16**
Orthopnea, **12-45**
Orthotist, **12-51**

335

Index

Osteoarthritis, **10-4**
  low back pain caused by, **10-10**
Osteopath (D.O.), **2-6, 10-17**
Osteoporosis, **10-12**
  estrogen and, **15-6**
Otitis, external, **8-26**
Otitis media, **8-26**
Otolaryngologist, **8-32**
Otosclerosis, **8-25**
Outpatient services, Medicare coverage for, **21-5** to **21-6**
Outside care:
  finding kind of facility needed, **284**
  levels of: intermediate-care facilities, **20-4**
    skilled-nursing facilities, **20-5**
    supportive care, **20-3**
  need for, **20-1** to **20-2**
  (*See also* Nursing home)
Ovaries, **15-21**
  cancer of, **15-24**
  cysts of, **15-22**
  noncancerous tumors of, **15-23**
Overstimulation, insomnia and, **5-27**
Ovol (Simethicone), **13-15**
Oxazepam (Tranxene), **5-8**
Oxethazaine (Oxaine M), **13-14**
Oxygen:
  circulatory system and, **12-1**
  retrolental fibroplasia and, **3-7**
Oxyphenbutazone (Tandearil), **10-3**
Ozone, air travel and, cardiac and respiratory problems and, **4-6**

Pacemakers, **12-35**
Paget's disease, **10-9**
Pain:
  abdominal, **13-35**
    appendicitis and, **13-23**
    cancer and, **13-27**
    gallbladder and, **13-33**
    hiatal hernia and, **13-17**
    ovaries and, **15-20** to **15-24**
  of angina, **12-19**
  in arthritis, **10-2**
  in back (*see* Backache)
  in bone, **10-8**
  in breast, **15-20**
  bunion and, **10-14**
  cancer and, **17-22**
    prostatic, **15-36**

Pain, cancer and (*Cont.*)
    of stomach, **13-19**
  in chest, **11-18, 12-19, 12-27, 12-47**
  with diverticulitis, **13-26**
  drugs used to decrease, **7-10** to **7-20**
    in dying patient, **22-3**
    habit-forming, **7-16** to **7-20**
    nonhabit-forming, **7-10** to **7-15**
  with duodenal ulcer, **13-20**
  in ear (*see* Ears, pain in)
  near ear, **13-12**
  with erection, **15-8**
  facial, **7-8**
  with gallbladder disease, **13-33**
  with genital herpes, **15-5**
  with glaucoma, **8-19**
  in gout, **10-6, 10-7**
  with heart attack, **12-27**
  with hemorrhoids, **13-24**
  intercourse and, in females, **15-34**
  in jaw, **12-19, 12-27**
  in joints, **10-2**
  in left arm, **12-19, 12-27**
  in leg, **9-24**
  in osteoarthritis, **10-4**
  with osteoporosis, **10-12**
  in Paget's disease, **10-9**
  with pancreatitis, **13-35, 13-37**
  rectal, **13-24**
  referred, **10-10**
  in rheumatoid arthritis, **10-3**
  sensitivity to, **7-2**
  with shingles, **9-23**
  in stomach, **13-15**
    cancer and, **13-19**
    ulcers and, **13-18, 13-20**
  with stones, **14-7**
  temporomandibular joint and, **13-12**
  in throat, **7-9, 11-8**
Pain clinics, **7-21**
Pain of Obesity, The, **3-54**
Palliative therapy, **17-11**
Palms, redness of, **9-13**
Palpitation, **3-17, 5-6**
Pamelor (Nortriptyline), **5-15**
Pancreas, **13-34**
  acute pancreatitis and, **13-35**
    treatment of, **13-36**
  cancer of, **13-38**
  chronic pancreatitis and, **13-37**
Pap test, **15-25, 15-28**

Index

Papaverine (Pavabid, Cerespan), **12-52**
Papillary cancer, **14-9**
Para-aminobenzoic acid (PABA), **9-32**
Paragoric, **10-7**
Paralysis, **7-27** to **7-31**
  of one side of face, **7-28**
  sleep, **5-33**
  spinal cord injury and, **7-33, 14-10**
Paranoia, **6-1**
Parathyroid glands, **16-5**
Parkinsonism, **7-24**
Parkinson's disease, **7-22, 7-24**
  drug treatment of, **7-25**
Parkinson's Disease: A Guide for Patient and Family, **7-24**
Parlodel (Bromocriptine), **7-25**
Parnate (Tranylcypromamine), **5-15**
Paronychia, **9-34**
Paroxysmal nocturnal dyspnea, **12-45**
Pavabid (Papaverine), **12-52**
Paxipam (Halazepam), **5-8**
Pellagra, **3-15**
Pemoline (Cylert), **5-33**
Penis, deviation of, **15-8**
  (*See also* Erection)
Pentazocine (Talwin), **7-15**
Pentobarbital (Nembutal), **5-34**
Pepto-Bismol, **4-14**
Periodontal disease, **13-9**
Periodontist, **13-9**
Perleche, **9-18**
Pernicious anemia, **3-17**
Perseveration following stroke, **12-50**
Personality:
  stroke and, **12-48**
  type A, **12-12**
  type B, **12-12**
Pertofrane (Desipramine), **5-15**
Pessary, **14-2, 15-29**
Petroleum jelly:
  for moisturizing, **9-2**
  for rectal itching, **9-3**
Petroleum product, swallowed, **18-13**
Peyronie's disease, **15-8**
Phenacetin, **7-12**
Phenelzine (Nardil), **5-15**
Phenergan (Promethazine), **8-29, 9-2**
Phenformin (DBI, Mettrol), **16-12**
Pheniramine, **11-5**
Phenobarbital, **5-8, 7-40, 8-29**
Phenol, injection into trigeminal nerve, **7-8**

L-Phenylalanine mustard (L-pam), **15-18**
Phenylbutazone (Butazolidin), **10-3, 10-7**
Phenylephrine (Neo-Synephrine), **8-10**
Phenylpropanolamine, **11-5**
Phenyltoloxamine, **11-5**
Phenytoin (Dilantin), **7-8, 7-40**
Pheochromocytoma, **12-18**
Phlegm (*see* Sputum)
Phosphorus in diet, **3-23**
Photocoagulation for hemorrhoids, **13-24**
Physiatrist, **12-51**
Physical examinations, importance of, **2-5**
Physical therapist, **12-51**
Physical therapy, **10-10**
Physician(s):
  admitting privileges of, **17-5, 19-1**
  assertiveness with, **1-4**
  attending, in nursing home, **20-12**
  board certification of, **19-2**
  choosing, **2-6**
  for diagnosis of cancer, **17-4**
  discussing psychological problems with, **5-46**
  education of, **2-6**
  for gastrointestinal tract disorders, **13-1**
  insurance coverage for fees of, **21-13**
  licensing of, **2-6**
  locating, in foreign country, **4-17**
  medical doctor, **2-6**
  on nursing home staff, **20-11**
  reasons to consult for insomnia, **5-27**
  relationship to, **2-6**
  removal of foreign body from eye by, **8-14**
  specialists, **2-6**
    in bone disorders, **10-16** to **10-18**
    in ear, nose, and throat, **8-32**
    in nervous system, **7-41**
    osteopath, **2-6, 10-17**
    referral to, **2-7**
    in rehabilitation medicine, **12-51**
    in urinary problems, **14-1**
    in weight reduction, **3-50**
    (*See also specific specialists*)
  suicide prevention and, **5-13**
  when to call, **18-10**
  when to see about depression, **5-11**
Pick's disease, **6-2**
Piles, **13-24**
Pilocarpine, **8-19, 8-20**
Pindolol (Visken), **12-11**

Index

Pink eye, **8-11, 8-12**
Piroxicam (Feldene), **10-3**
Pituitary gland tumors, **7-37**
Placebo effect, **1-5**
    Laetrile and, **17-6**
Placidyl (Ethchlorvynol), **5-34**
Plantar warts, **9-28, 9-29**
Plaque:
    in arteries, **12-14**
    on teeth, **13-8**
        gum disease and, **13-9**
Plasma cell myeloma, **10-8**
Platelets, cancer and, **17-9, 17-18**
Plegine, **3-50**
Pleural effusion, **11-21**
Pleurisy, **11-18**
Pneumoconioses, **11-23**
Pneumonia:
    bacterial, **11-18**
        with flu, **11-13**
    primary atypical, **11-21**
    viral, **11-20**
Pneumovax, **11-18**
Pnu-Imune 23, **11-18**
Podiatrist, **10-14**
Poison(s):
    gas, **18-1, 18-3, 18-14**
    insect stings, **18-15**
    snakebites, **18-16**
    swallowed, **19-13**
Poison control center, **18-13**
Poison ivy, oak, or sumac, **9-7**
Poldine (Nacton), **13-21**
Police, suicide prevention and, **5-13, 5-14**
Polio immunization, **4-11**
Pollen, **11-7**
Pollution, bronchitis and, **11-14**
Polycillin (Ampicillin), **14-6**
Polyps:
    cervical, **15-27**
    in colon, **13-27**
    endometrial, **15-26**
Polysomnographers, **5-30**
Polythiazide (Renese), **12-9**
Pondimin (Fenfluramine), **3-50**
Post Card Clubs, **11-10**
Postnasal drip, **11-2**
Potassium:
    in diet, **3-28**
    with hypertension, **12-10**

Potency, **15-7**
    cancer therapy and, **17-20**
    decline in, **15-2**
    prostatic cancer and, **15-36**
    psychological aspects of, **15-11**
Potholders to prevent burns, **2-11**
Poultry, fat in, **3-29**
Power of attorney, **6-7**
Prazepam (Centrax), **5-8**
Precordial thump, **12-29**
Prednisolone, **10-3**
Prednisone, **10-3**
    with bronchitis, **11-16**
Preludin, **3-50**
Premarin, **15-6**
Preparation H, **13-24**
Pre-Sate Syndrox, **3-50**
Presbycusis, **8-22**
Presbyopia, **8-8**
Prescriptions:
    when traveling, **4-19**
    [*See also* Drug(s)]
Pressure points, how to find, **18-7**
Pressure sores, **9-27**
Preventive medicine, **2-4**
    annual physical examination and, **2-5**
Primary-care physician (*see* Family practitioner)
Primary neuronal degeneration, **6-1**
Principen (Ampicillin), **14-6**
Pro-Banthine (Propantheline), **13-21**
Probenecid (Benemid), **10-7**
Procardia (Nifedipine), **12-20**
Prochlorperazine (Compazine), **17-16**
Proctosigmoidoscope, **13-27**
Procyclidine hydrochloride (Kemadrin), **7-25**
Professional associations, **2-6**
Professional Standards Review Organization (PSRO), **21-8**
Projection, cancer and, **17-13**
Promethazine (Phenergan), **8-29, 9-2**
Propantheline (Pro-Banthine), **13-21**
Propoxyphene (Darvon), **7-14**
Propranolol (Inderal), **7-6, 7-22, 12-20**
Propylthiouracil, **16-5**
Prostate, **15-31**
    benign enlargement of, **15-32**
        treatment for, **15-33**
    cancer of, **15-36**
    enlarged, nighttime urination and, **5-28**

Index

Prostate (*Cont.*)
  primary testicular failure and, **15-35**
  prostatitis and, **15-34**
Prostatitis, **15-34**
Protein(s), **3-3**
  cost of, **3-39**
  dieting and, **3-48**
  sources of, **3-3**
Protein-sparing diets, **3-48**
Prothrombin time (PT), **11-24, 12-52**
Pruritis (*see* Itching)
Pruritis ani, **9-3**
Pseudoephedrine, **11-5**
Pseudo-scars, **9-12**
Psychiatric care, Medicare coverage for, **21-4**
Psychiatric nurse, **5-45**
Psychiatric problems (*see* Psychological problems)
Psychiatrist, **5-45 to 5-47**
  for anxiety, **5-7**
  myths and facts about, **5-48**
Psychoanalysis, **5-43**
Psychoanalyst, **5-45**
Psychological problems, **5-1**
  alcoholism (*see* Alcoholism)
  anxiety (*see* Anxiety)
  compensation strategies and, **5-3**
  depression (*see* Depression)
  insomnia (*see* Insomnia)
  mental reserve and, **5-2, 5-5**
  narcolepsy, **5-33**
  nervousness, **5-4**
    (*See also* Anxiety)
  nursing home and, **20-17**
  psychotherapy and (*see* Psychotherapy)
  rigidity, **5-3, 5-5**
  sleep apnea, **5-32**
  suicide (*see* Suicide)
Psychological testing, **5-45, 5-46**
Psychologist, **5-45**
Psychosis, suicide and, **5-12**
Psychotherapist(s):
  choosing, **5-46 to 5-47**
  myths and facts about, **5-48**
Psychotherapy, **5-41**
  aims of, **5-42**
  choosing a therapist and, **5-46**
  for depression, **5-10 to 5-11**
  family support and, **6-4**

Psychotherapy (*Cont.*)
  myths and facts about psychiatrists and psychotherapists and, **5-48**
  practitioners of, **5-45**
  psychoanalytically oriented, **5-43**
  types of, **5-43**
  when to seek, **5-44**
Pteroylglutamic acid (Folic acid), **3-18**
Ptosis, **8-10**
Pulmonary edema, **12-5, 12-44**
Pulmonary embolism, **11-24**
Pulse:
  rapid, **5-6**
  test for, **12-29**
Pupil, **8-16**
Purines in foods, **10-6**
Pus in middle ear, **8-26**
Pyelogram:
  intravenous, **14-5, 15-36, 17-9**
  retrograde, **14-5**
Pyorrhea, **13-9**
Pyridoxine (Vitamin B_6), **3-16**
  interaction with L-dopa, **7-25**
Pyrilamine, **11-5**

Quackery, **17-5**
Quinidine, **12-34**

Radial nerve palsy, **7-30**
Radiation therapy, **17-4, 17-11**
  bleeding and, **17-18**
  burns and, **17-16**
  for laryngeal cancer, **11-10**
  for prostatic cancer, **15-36**
  teeth and, **17-17**
  for uterine cancer, **15-28**
Radioiodine uptake test, **16-4**
Radiotherapist, **17-4**
Ragweed, **11-7**
Range (stove), cautions regarding, **2-11**
Ranitidine (Zantac), **13-21**
Rapid eye movement (REM) sleep, narcolepsy and, **5-33**
Rash, **9-3, 9-5 to 9-6**
  allergic contact, **9-6**
  poison ivy, oak, and sumac and, **9-7**
  on face, **3-14**
  as reaction to drug, **9-5**
Rating the Diets, **3-54**
Rau-Sed (Reserpine), **12-11, 13-21**

Index

Reach to Recovery, **15-19**
Reading, difficulty with, **8-2, 8-4**
Receptors, **7-1**
Rectum:
  cancer of, **13-27**
  prolapse of, **13-25**
Registered nurse (R.N.), **20-11**
Rehabilitation:
  skilled, **21-8**
  following stroke, **12-50**
Rehabilitation medicine, **12-51**
Relatives (*see* Family)
Religion, death and, **22-6**
Religious activities in nursing homes, **20-15**
Renal failure, **14-8**
Renese (Polythiazide), **12-9**
Representative, assertiveness in, **1-4**
Reserpine (Serpasil, Rau-Sed, Sandril), **12-11, 13-21**
Residency, **2-6**
Resident, **19-2**
Respiratory problems, ozone and, **4-6**
Respiratory reserve, **11-1**
Respirometer, **11-17**
Retina, **8-4, 8-17**
  detachment of, **8-17, 16-8**
Retirement, financial planning for, **2-2**
Retirement centers, **20-3**
Retrograde pyelogram, **14-5**
Retrolental fibroplasia, oxygen and, **3-7**
Retroperitoneal fibrosis, **7-6**
Rheumatic nodules, **10-3**
Rhinitis, **11-7**
Rhythms, air travel and, **4-5**
Riboflavin (Vitamin B$_2$), **3-14**
Rifampin (Rifadin), **11-22**
Rigidity, **5-3**
  anxiety and, **5-5**
Ringworm of the feet, **9-24**
Riniacol (Nicotinyl alcohol), **12-52**
Riopan (Simethicone), **13-15**
Riopan Plus, **13-15**
Risk factors for atherosclerosis, **12-40**
Risk-taking behavior, importance of maintaining, **5-3**
Ritalin (Methylphenidate), **5-33**
Robincil (Glycopyrrolate), **13-21**
Rodent ulcer, **9-30**
Roommate policy of nursing homes, **20-13**
Routine, insomnia and, **5-26**
Rumination, insomnia and, **5-19**

Saccharine, **3-37**
Sadness (*see* Depression)
Safety of nursing homes, **20-10**
Salivary gland cancer, **13-6**
Salt:
  as dentifrice, **11-8, 13-11**
  heart disease and, **12-17**
  (*See also* Sodium)
Saluron (Hydroflumethiazide), **12-9**
Sandril (Reserpine), **12-11, 13-21**
Sansert (Methysergide), **7-6**
Sarcoma, **17-1**
Scale, bathroom, **3-52**
Schedule for medications, **2-9**
Sciatica, **10-8, 10-10**
Scintigram, **16-4**
Sclera, **8-9**
Scopalamine, **5-34**
Scratches, how to treat, **18-9**
Scrotum, enlargement of, **15-37**
Scurvy, **3-6, 3-19**
Seat belts, **2-13**
Seborrhea, **9-42**
Secobarbital (Seconal), **5-34**
Second opinion:
  doctors discouraging, **17-5**
  when and how to seek, **2-7**
Second sight, **8-15**
Sedatives:
  with duodenal ulcers, **13-21**
  insomnia caused by, **5-27**
  (*See also* Sleeping pills)
Seizures (*see* Convulsions; Epilepsy)
Selsun Blue shampoo, **9-42**
Semicircular canals, **8-29**
Senile macular degeneration, **8-4**
Senile pruritis, **9-2**
Senile purpura, **9-12**
Senile tremor, **7-22**
Senility, **5-5, 6-1**
  before age 65, **6-2**
  decisions regarding care and, **6-3**
    compulsory admission and, **6-6**
    financial affairs and, **6-7**
    home care and, **6-4**
    institutional care and, **6-5**
    use of drugs and, **6-8**
Senior centers, **2-19, 20-3**
Senior citizen residences, **20-3**
Septra, **14-6**
Serax (Oxazepam), **5-8**

Index

Serpasil (Reserpine), **12-11**
Services, opportunity to share, **2-18**
Sex therapists, **15-7, 15-11**
Sexual activity:
  alcohol and drugs and, **15-10**
  benign prostatic enlargement and, **15-33**
  following heart attack, **12-39**
  medical disorders and, **15-14**
  following menopause, **15-3**
    surgical, **15-4**
  positions for intercourse, **15-13**
Sexual arousal:
  cancer therapy and, **17-20**
  climacteric and, **15-2**
  insomnia and, **5-20**
Sexual disorders, **15-7** to **15-15**
Shampoo for dandruff, **9-42**
Shingles, **9-23**
Shock, **12-47**
  release of tourniquet and, **18-8**
Shock treatment (*see* Electroconvulsive therapy)
Shoes, corns and, **9-28**
Shortness of breath (*see* Breathing)
Shoulder, bursitis in, **10-15**
Shower stall, preventing falls in, **2-10**
Silain (Simethicone), **13-15**
Silain-Gel, **13-15**
Simethicone (Mylicin, Silain, Ovol, Riopan), **13-15**
Sinemet (L-dopa and carbidopa), **7-25**
Sinequan (Doxepin), **5-15**
Sinuses, **11-2**
  pain and, **7-3**
Sitting with back pain, **10-10**
Skilled nursing, **21-8**
Skilled-nursing facility, **20-5**
Skilled rehabilitation services, **21-8**
Skin:
  aging of, **9-1**
  athlete's foot and, **9-24**
  blackheads and, **9-20**
  cancer of, **9-30**
    moles and melanoma and, **9-31**
    sunburn and, **9-32**
    treatment of, **17-16**
  cold sores and, **9-21**
  drug rashes and, **9-5**
  dry, **9-2, 16-4**
  freckles and brown spots on, **9-14**
  itching of (*see* Itching)

Skin (*Cont.*)
  other lesions of, **9-8** to **9-12, 9-15, 9-17, 9-18**
  rash (*see* Rash)
  redness of palms and, **9-13**
  shingles and, **9-23**
  sores on, dementia and, **6-4**
  sudden loss of coloring in, **9-19**
  thickening on neck, **9-16**
  vascular problems of: leg ulcers, **9-26**
    pressure sores, **9-27**
    varicose veins, **9-25**
  warts and, **9-22**
Skin grafting, **18-12**
Skin tests:
  for allergies, **11-7**
  for tuberculosis, **11-22**
Sleep:
  air travel and, **4-5**
  amount required, **5-17**
  with back pain, **10-10**
  duodenal ulcer and, **13-21**
  fear of, **5-21**
Sleep disorder(s):
  anxiety and, **5-6**
  apnea, **5-32**
  insomnia (*see* Insomnia)
  narcolepsy, **5-33**
Sleep disorder clinics, **5-30** to **5-31**
Sleep paralysis, **5-33**
Sleeping pills, **5-29, 5-32, 5-34**
  insomnia caused by, **5-27**
  travel and, **4-5**
Slow-K, **12-10**
Smallpox vaccination, **4-10**
Smell, **8-30**
  sense of, **8-30**
  (*See also* Odor)
Smoke detectors, **2-12**
Smokenders, **11-29**
Smoker's cough (*see* Bronchitis)
Smoking, **2-11**
  how to stop, **11-17** to **11-29**
  lung cancer and, **11-26**
  muscle cramps and, **18-24**
  need to quit: bronchitis and, **11-16**
    with emphysema, **11-17**
Snacks during visits, **23-9**
Snakebites, treatment of, **18-16**
Snoring, **5-32**
Snow, shoveling, **2-15**

Index

Soap, 9-2
Social Security, 2-2, 2-3
    funeral expense coverage under, 22-10
Social workers, 5-45
    on nursing home staff, 20-11
Sodium:
    controlling intake of, 3-27
    (*See also* Salt)
Solar lentigines, 9-14
Somophyllin (Aminophylline), 11-16
Sonography, 13-29, 18-24
Sore throat, 7-9, 11-8
Sores as sign of cancer, 17-3
"Spanish fly," 15-12
Spasticity, stroke and, 12-48
Specialists [*see* Physician(s), specialists]
Specialty boards, 2-6
Speech:
    esophageal, 11-10
    stroke and, 12-48, 12-50
Sphygmomanometer, 12-2
Spinal cord, 7-1
Spinal cord injury, 7-33
    neurogenic bladder and, 14-10
    prevention of, 18-22
Spinal shock, 7-33
Spinal tap, 7-34
Spironolactone (Aldactone), 12-9
Spleen, removal of, 17-9
    bacterial pneumonia and, 11-18
Splurge eating, 3-53
Spores, allergy to, 11-7
Sputum, 11-1
    in bronchitis, 11-14, 11-16
    with heart failure, 12-45
    with tuberculosis, 11-22
    with viral pneumonia, 11-20
Squamous cell carcinoma, 9-30
Stairs:
    climbing, 2-15
    preventing falls on, 2-10
Standing with back pain, 10-11
Stapedectomy, 8-25
Start hesitation, 7-25
Status epilepticus, 7-40
Steam, burns caused by, 2-11
Sterility, cancer therapy and, 17-20
Steroids, 13-21
    with arthritis, 10-3
    creams, 9-2
        for allergic rash, 9-6

Steroids, creams (*Cont.*)
        for fissures around mouth, 9-18
        for poison ivy, 9-7
    with emphysema, 11-17
    (*See also* Hormones)
Stiff neck, 7-32
Stiffness of joints, 10-3
Stimulants:
    narcolepsy and, 5-33
    as reducing aids, 3-50
Stings, 18-15
Stockings, elastic, for varicose veins, 9-25
Stomach, 13-15 to 13-19
    cancer of, 13-19 to 13-21
        radiation therapy and, 17-16
    cancer of colon and rectum, 13-27
    ulcer and, 13-18, 13-20
    (*See also* Diarrhea; Gastrointestinal tract; Pain, abdominal; Vomiting)
Stones:
    bladder, 14-1
    gall-, 13-33
    kidney, 14-7
Stool(s), 13-22
    blood in, 13-24, 13-26, 13-27
    dark, 13-20
Stool softeners, 13-24
Storms, preparation for, 2-15
Stove, cautions regarding, 2-11
Stoxil (Idoxuridine), 9-23
Streaking, red, 18-10
Strep throat, 11-8
Streptokinase with lung embolism, 11-24
Streptomycin, 8-29
Stress:
    duodenal ulcer and, 13-21
    hypertension and, 12-12
    incontinence and, 14-2, 15-29
Stroke, 12-1
    causes of, 12-48
    hearing loss and, 8-25
    small, 12-49
    speech and, 12-48, 12-50
    symptoms of, 12-48
    treatment of, 12-50
        drugs and, 12-52
        rehabilitation medicine and, 12-51
Stucco keratosis, 9-15
Sucralfate (Carafate), 13-21
Sugar, 3-33
Sugar diabetes (*see* Diabetes mellitus)

Index

Suicide, **5-9, 5-12, 5-27**
  preventing: in others, **5-14**
    in yourself, **5-13**
Suicide prevention centers, **5-13, 5-14**
Sulfa drugs with urinary system infections, **14-6**
Sulfamethoxazole (Gantanol), **14-6**
Sulfinpyrazone (Anturane), **10-7**
Sulfisoxazole (Gantrisin), **14-6**
Sulfonylureas, **16-12**
Sulindac (Clinoril), **10-3**
Sun, brown spots on skin and, **9-14**
Sun protection factor (SPF), **9-32**
Sunburn, **9-2**
  cancer and, **9-32**
  doxycycline and, **4-14**
Sunscreens, **9-32**
Sunshades, **9-32**
Sunstroke, **18-19**
Superstitions as basis for treatments, **1-5**
Supportive care, **20-3**
Surgery:
  with appendicitis, **13-23**
  for benign prostatic enlargement, **15-33**
  with bunions, **10-14**
  for cancer, **17-4, 17-10**
    of bladder, **14-9**
    of breast, **15-18**
    of colon or rectum, **13-27**
    prostatic, **15-36**
    of stomach, **13-19**
    uterine, **15-28**
  with cataracts, **8-15**
  coronary bypass, **12-21**
  electrosurgery, for hair removal, **9-40**
  for gallstones, **13-33**
  with glaucoma, **8-19**
  for hemorrhoids, **13-24**
  in hyperthyroidism, **16-5**
  with lung embolism, **11-24**
  in Ménière's syndrome, **8-29**
  otosclerosis and, **8-25**
  to reconstruct ears, **8-26**
  to remove warts, **9-22**
  retinal detachment and, **8-17**
  with stroke, **12-50**
  for varicose veins, **9-25**
  vitrectomy, **8-18**
  for weight reduction, **3-51**
Swallowing:
  difficulty in, **13-16, 17-3**

Swallowing (*Cont.*)
  radiation therapy and, **17-16**
Sweating, **5-6**
  nocturnal, **9-4, 11-22, 15-3**
Swelling of feet and legs, **4-2, 9-25, 12-3**
Swine flu vaccine, **11-12**
Symmetrel (Amantadine), **7-25, 11-13**

Tabatran (Tybamate), **5-8**
Tagamet (Cimetidine), **13-21**
Talking about feelings, **23-7**
Talwin (Pentazocine), **7-15**
Tandearil (Oxyphenbutazone), **10-3**
Tanning, **9-2**
  lotions and pills for, **9-32**
Tapazole (Methimazole), **16-5**
Taste:
  sense of, **8-30**
  sour, **13-20**
Tea (*see* Caffeine)
Tears, overproduction of, **8-11**
Teeth:
  care of (*see* Dental hygiene)
  false, **13-10**
    care of, **13-11**
  importance of, **13-7**
  loss of, **13-9**
  radiation therapy and, **17-17**
  (*See also* Gums)
Tegretol (Carbamazepine), **7-8**
Telangiectasis, **9-11**
Telephone, dialing, following stroke, **12-50**
Telephone reassurance programs, **2-21**
Temporomandibular joint pain, **13-12**
Tempra (Acetaminophen), **7-13**
Tennis elbow, **10-13**
Tenormin (Atenolol), **12-11**
Tenuate, **3-50**
Tepanil, **3-50**
Testes, failure to function, **15-35**
Tetanus:
  danger of, **18-10**
  vaccination against, **4-12**
Tetracycline with canker sores, **13-4**
Thallium scan, **12-23**
THC, cancer therapy and, **17-16**
Thermography of breast, **15-17**
Thermometer, how to use, **18-2**
Thiamine (Vitamin B_1), **3-13**
Thiazides, **12-9, 12-46**

Index

Thirst, **16-8**
36-Hour Day: A Family Guide to Caring for Persons with Alzheimer's Disease, Related Dementing Illnesses, and Memory Loss in Later Life, **6-3**
Throat:
  clearing, **11-10**
  physicians treating, **8-32**
  radiation therapy and, **17-16**
  sore, **7-9, 11-8**
Throat lozenges, **11-8**
Thrombosis, **12-48**
Thyroid gland, **16-2**
  adenoma of, **16-6**
  cancer of, **16-6**
  goiter and, **16-3**
  hyperthyroidism and, **16-5**
  hypothyroidism and, **16-4**
Thyroid hormone, **16-4**
  diet and, **3-50**
Thyroid scan, **16-4**
Thyroid stimulating hormone (TSH), **16-3**
Thyrotoxicosis, **16-5**
Thyroxine (T_4), **16-2**
TIAs (transient ischemic attacks), **12-49**
Tic douloureux, **7-8**
Tigan (Trimethobenzamide), **17-16**
Timolol (Blocadren), **12-11**
Tinactin (Tolnaftate), **9-24**
Tine Test, **11-22**
Tingling, **7-26**
Tocopherol (Vitamin E), **3-12**
Toe, pain in, in gout, **10-6**
Toenails (*see* Nails)
Tofranil (Imipramine), **5-15**
Toilet facilities in nursing homes, **20-13**
Tolazamide (Tolinase), **16-12**
Tolbutamine (Orinase), **16-12**
Tolmetin (Tolectin), **10-3**
Tolnaftate (Tinactin), **9-24**
Tongue:
  smooth, **13-9**
  sore, **3-17**
Tonometry, **8-19**
Toothache, **7-3**
Toothbrush, electric, **13-11**
Tophi, **10-6**
TOPS (Take Off Pounds Sensibly), **3-49**
"Tourista," **4-14** to **4-16**
Tourniquet:
  with insect stings, **18-15**

Tourniquet (*Cont.*)
  use of, **18-8**
Trace metals, **3-26**
Trachea, **11-1**
Tracheostomy, sleep apnea and, **5-32**
Tranquilizers, **54**
  with duodenal ulcers, **13-21**
  interactions with alcohol, **5-38**
  sexual function and, **15-10**
  [*See also* Drug(s)]
Transderm-Nitro (Nitroglycerine), **12-20**
Transference in psychotherapy, **5-43**
Transient ischemic attacks (TIAs), **12-49**
Transportation, community resources for, **2-17**
Tranxene (Chlorazepate), **5-8**
Tranylcypropamine (Parnate), **5-15**
Travel, **4-1**
  by air (*see* Air travel)
  diarrhea and, **4-14**
    medications for, **4-15** to **4-16**
  immunizations and (*see* Immunization)
  locating medical care and, **4-17** to **4-18**
  what to pack for, **4-19**
Travel agent, **4-1**
Trazadone (Desyrel), **5-15**
Treatment plans in nursing homes, **20-12**
Trembling, **5-6**
Tremors, **7-22**
  action, **7-22**
  intention, **7-22**
  Parkinsonian, **7-22**
  in Parkinson's disease, **7-24, 7-25**
  senile, **7-22**
Triamterene (Dyrenium), **12-9**
Triazolam (Halcion), **5-34**
Trichlormethiazide (Metahydrin), **12-9**
Trigeminal neuralgia, **7-8**
Trigger zone:
  for glossopharyngeal neuralgia, **7-9**
  for tic douloureux, **7-8**
Triglycerides, hypertension and, **12-14**
Trihexyphenidyl (Artane), **7-25**
Triiodothyronine (T_3), **16-2**
Trimethobenzamide (Tigan), **17-16**
Trimethoprim, **14-6**
TSH (thyroid stimulating hormone), **16-3**
Tuberculosis, **11-22**
Tumor:
  of adrenal gland, **12-18**
  benign, **17-1**

Index

Tumor (*Cont.*)
  of brain, **7-37**
    computed tomography scans and, **7-38**
  of ovaries, noncancerous, **15-23**
  (*See also* Cancer)
Twitching, **7-23**
Tybamate (Tabatran), **5-8**
Tylenol (Acetaminophen), **7-13, 13-21**
Type A (Asian) flu, **11-13**
Type A personality, **12-12**
Type B personality, **12-12**
Typhoid immunization, **4-13**
Typhus immunization, **4-9**

Ulcer(s):
  alcohol-related, **5-37**
  aphthous, **13-4**
  decubitus, **9-27**
  duodenal, **13-20**
    treatment of, **13-21**
  hiatal hernia and, **13-17**
  of leg, **9-26**
  rodent, **9-30**
  stomach, **13-18, 13-20**
Ulnar nerve palsy, **7-29**
Ultrasonography, **13-29, 18-24**
Underwear, nylon, rectal itching and, **9-3**
U.S. Consulate, locating physician abroad and, **4-17**
U.S. Embassy, locating physician abroad and, **4-17**
U.S. Public Health Service, **4-7**
Upper respiratory infection (URI) (*see* Cold)
Urea, **8-19**
Uremia, **14-8**
Ureters, **14-1**
Urethra, **14-1**
Uric acid in gout, **10-6**
Urinalysis, **14-1**
  diabetes and, **16-9**
  hypertension and, **12-5**
Urinary system, **14-1**
  disorders of: bladder cancer, **14-9**
    infections, **14-3 to 14-6**
    kidney failure, **14-8**
    loss of control of urine, **14-2**
    nonfunctioning bladder, **14-10**
    stones, **14-7**

Urination:
  in female: frequent, **15-25**
    loss with straining, **14-2, 15-29**
  in male: prostatic cancer and, **15-36**
    prostatic enlargement and, **15-32**
  nocturnal, **5-28**
Urine:
  blood in, **14-1, 14-7, 14-9**
  burning, **14-3**
  large amounts of, in diabetes, **16-8**
  loss of control of, **14-2**
  odor of:
    diabetes and, **16-9, 16-18**
    in nursing homes, **20-9**
    prostatic enlargement and, **15-32**
Urine culture, **14-4**
Urokinase with lung embolism, **11-24**
Urologist, **14-1**
Uterus, **15-25**
  cancer of, **15-28**
    adenocarcinoma, **15-26**
  endometrial polyps and, **15-26**
  prolapse of, **15-29**
  removal of, **15-30**
Utilization Review Committee, **21-8**

Vaccination (*see* Immunization)
Vagina:
  bleeding from, **15-22, 15-25 to 15-27**
  discharge from, **15-5, 15-6**
  feeling of weight in, **15-29**
  itching and, **15-6, 16-8**
Vaginitis, atrophic, **15-6**
Valadol (Acetaminophen), **7-13**
Valium (Diazepam), **5-8, 5-34, 8-29, 10-10**
  interactions with alcohol, **5-38**
Vanceril (Beclomethasone), **11-17**
Vaporizer, **8-26**
  with colds, **11-3**
Varicose veins, **9-25**
Vaseline (*see* Petroleum jelly)
Vasodilan (Isoxsuprine), **12-52**
Vegans, **3-35**
Vegetarians, **3-35**
Veins, **12-1**
Vena caval interruption, **11-24**
Venous lakes, **9-10**
Venous stars, **9-9**
Verapamil (Isoptin, Calan), **12-20**
Verbal apraxia following stroke, **12-50**

Index

Verruca, 9-22
Vertigo (dizziness), 8-28
  in Ménière's syndrome, 8-29
Veterans Administration, funeral expense coverage under, 22-10
Vibramycin (Doxycycline), 4-14
Viokase, 13-37
Visine, 8-13
Vision:
  blurred or double, 8-15, 12-46
  effect of hypertension on, 12-4
  halos and, 8-19
  migraine headaches and, 7-4
  night, driving and, 2-13
  stroke and, 12-48
  transient loss of, 8-21
  [See also Eye(s)]
Visiting:
  by children, 23-12
  gifts and, 23-11
  importance of, 20-17
  performing services during, 23-10
  snacks and, 23-9
Visiting Nurses Association, 2-24
Vitamin(s), 3-6
  fat-soluble, 3-8
  gum disease and, 13-9
  mega-, 3-7
  minimum daily requirement for, 3-7
  nails and, 9-33
  naming, 3-8
  water-soluble, 3-8
Vitamin A (Cretinol), 3-9
Vitamin B_1 (Thiamine), 3-13
Vitamin B_2 (Riboflavin), 3-14
Vitamin B_3 (Nicotinamide, Niacin), 3-15
Vitamin B_6 (Pyridoxine), 3-16
Vitamin B_{12} (Cyanocobalamin), 3-17
Vitamin C (Ascorbic acid), 3-7, 3-19, 3-20
  with colds, 11-6
  gums and, 13-9
  scurvy and, 3-6
Vitamin D (Calciferol), 3-10
Vitamin deficiencies, senility and, 6-4
Vitamin E (Tocopherol), 3-12
Vitamin K, 3-11
Vitiligo, 9-19
Vitrectomy, 8-18
Vitreous, the, 8-18
Voice, change in, 11-10

Vomiting, 7-4
  of blood, 13-20
  causes of, 13-2
  inducing, poisoning and, 18-13
  in Ménière's syndrome, 8-29
  radiation therapy and, 17-16

Walking:
  following stroke, 12-50
  painful, bunion and, 10-14
Warfarin with lung embolism, 11-24
Warming up, 1-6
Wart(s), 9-22
  change in, 17-3
  on feet, 9-29
Water when traveling, 4-14
Water Pik, 11-7, 11-29
Water pills (see Diuretics)
Wax in ear, 8-22
Weight:
  diet and, 3-40 to 3-44
  normal, 3-40 to 3-43
  thyroid disorders and, 16-5
Weight loss, 3-46 to 3-55
  aids to, 3-53
  books on, 3-54
  cancer therapy and, 17-21
  diet clubs and, 3-49
  drugs and, 3-50
  fad diets and, 3-46
  high-protein and protein-sparing diets and, 3-48
  low-carbohydrate diets and, 3-47
  metric conversion tables and, 3-56
  rules for, 3-52
  surgery for, 3-51
  weights and measurement equivalencies for, 3-55
Weight Watchers, 3-49
Weights and measures, 3-55
Wheezing, 11-16
  with asthma, 11-23
  with emphysema, 11-17
Whiplash, 7-33
Will, importance of, 22-1, 22-7
Windows, how to clean, 2-10
Womb (see Uterus)
Work:
  cancer patients and, 17-13
  importance of, 1-2

Index

Worry, insomnia and, **5-23**
Wounds:
  puncture, **18-10**
  slitlike, **18-10**
Wytensin (Guanabenz), **12-11**

X-ray:
  barium: barium-swallow, **13-18** to **13-20**, **17-9**
  lower-GI, **13-27, 17-9**
  of chest, **11-22**
    cancer and, **17-9**
    hypertension and, **12-5**
    with lung cancer, **11-25**
Xanax (Alprazolam), **5-8**

Xanthines, **3-36**
Xerography of breast, **15-17**
Xerophthalmia, **3-9**
Xerosis, **9-2**
Xylitol, **3-37**
Xylocaine, **17-9**

Yeast infections, rectal, **9-3**
Yellow fever inoculation, **4-7**

Zantac (Ranitidine), **13-21**
Zephiran for abrasions and scratches, **18-9**
Zinc, **3-26**
Zyloprim (Allopurinol), **10-7**

About the Author

Richard Jed Wyatt, M.D., is a psychiatrist and psychopharmacologist. Chief of the Adult Psychiatry Branch at the National Institute of Mental Health, Dr. Wyatt has studied extensively the health and illnesses of adults, especially in the areas of depression, alcoholism, drugs of abuse, diet, and health services. Currently, he and his colleagues are exploring a new scientific frontier, the transplanting of living tissues in the brain.